The Greatest Ballpark Ever

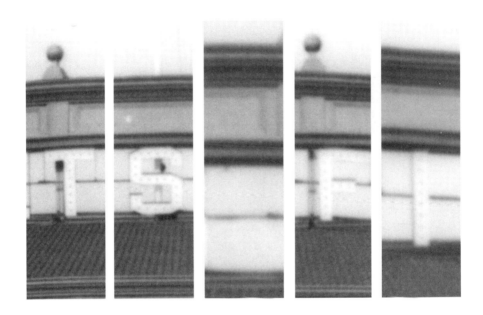

Ebbets Field
and the Story of
The Brooklyn Dodgers

The Greatest Ballpark Ever

Bob McGee

Rivergate Books
An imprint of Rutgers University Press
New Brunswick, New Jersey, and London

Library of Congress Cataloging-in-Publication Data

McGee, Bob, 1952–
The greatest ballpark ever: Ebbets Field and the story
of the Brooklyn Dodgers/Bob McGee.
p. cm.
Includes bibliographical references and index.
ISBN 0–8135–3600–6 (hardcover)
1. Ebbets Field (New York, N.Y.)—History. 2. Brooklyn
Dodgers (Baseball team)—History. I. Title.
GV416.N48M36 2005
796.357′068747′23—dc22

A British Cataloging-in-Publication record for this book is
available from the British Library.

Manufactured in the United States of America

For my parents,
Raymond R. McGee
(1915–2002)
and
Agatha McGee,
and also
for Frank Fennell
(1922–1992),
our dear family friend,
and

IN MEMORIAM FOR SONS OF BROOKLYN ALL

Mark Carducci
Bill Carney
Bruno Caputo
Candolero Donato
Chip Jaccarino
Joe Lauro
Charlie Lomando
Joseph Rosse
Raymond Sinnott

Contents

Preface

On a cold, icy night in December 1972, fresh from reading Roger Kahn's *Boys of Summer*, I kick-started a red Honda 350 for a fifteen-minute pilgrimage up Bedford Avenue from Brooklyn College, off to see a place that was part of my birthright, yet impossible to find. I was off to a place far away, requiring travel back in time, but I knew that simply by taking measure of the geography, I might somehow grasp a sense of what once had been. The frigid blackness was slick, crystalline, and the streets whipping by were lonely. In search of a memory, so was I.

Inspiration for the sojourn came in part from the wistfulness of those peopling my youth, speaking of something they found difficult to put into words. These were articulate people, and yes, they were from Brooklyn. The problem: speaking the truth. What is so impossible to convey turns out to be nothing less than a sense of who you really are, what you really care about. When distilled, it turned out to be this: the Brooklyn Dodgers were a religion. For those who bought into the faith, Ebbets Field was a holy place.

The understanding came from varying quarters, communicated to me mostly by Frank Fennell and Bill Carney. They didn't put their sentiments into exactly those words, but it was easy enough to decipher what they meant. How they loved every aspect and intricacy of the game! Frank, whose blue eyes would light up at the mere mention of the Bums, never felt the same way about baseball after the day in 1957 the announcement was made that his Dodgers were gone, a way of life changed forever. A passion that burned deep within him was extinguished. And so it was in tale after tale in every corner of Brooklyn and beyond.

The reader should know that I grew up in Brooklyn, in Bay Ridge, on the corner of 97th Street and Third Avenue, during the years when some of the Dodgers, the Duke and Pee Wee and Oisk, were still around: Pee Wee up the block on Barwell Terrace, the Duke down on Marine Avenue, corner of 97th, Oisk on 94th, down Lafayette Walk. At the time, I had cartoon heroes and was oblivious to their presence. I imagine that Bev Snider and Dottie Reese bought their aspirin at Mr. Arida's drugstore or got the kids toys at Bon-ni-Land, each on opposite corners on Third and 97th. My father, who was occasionally mistaken for the Duke in the local Key Food—"You're him, aren't you, you're him!?" "Who him?" he'd answer—preferred his sports as a participant rather than as a fan; we never went to Ebbets Field. Instead, he pitched to me down the Shore, and on days I didn't care to hit and preferred to watch the Three Stooges or Popeye, he said it would matter to me some day, that I would value the time we spent, and he was right.

By the time I'd reached the age of reason, the Dodgers and Giants were history, the Mets not even in the birthing. When Uncle John and Mr. Rosse took me out to Yankee Stadium for Old Timer's Day in 1961—too rainy for the old timers to play, but Zack Wheat . . . *Zack Wheat* . . . was there—Jackie Brandt and Yogi hit homers, the Yanks won 5–4, and I was hooked.

That is how this started.

Loving the game is easy. Not just a Brooklyn thing; an American thing. It helped that Dad pitched, that Pat Maloney hit pop flies to his son Brian and me, that Patrick Rega took his boys Peter and Tommy and the rest of us out to Yankee Stadium or to Jones Beach. It was only later, after Maris and Mantle, the M&M Boys, had their great season, or after the Mets were born and we'd had a chance to see a game at the Polo Grounds, after Kennedy was shot and after slowly, inexorably, the world changed, after every American institution's credibility had fallen into question, that this quest began. What was so wonderful about the way it used to be? Why was it so? What was it like? When did it change? Why did it happen?

I rode around Montgomery and Sullivan and McKeever and Bedford that cold night. Rode around four or five times. I tried to see the building. Tried to imagine what it was like. I have returned many other times since, endeavoring to find out more—and have enlisted the assistance of many people. In my quest for memories, I found out how well an older generation of Americans can write, receiving wonderful letters from all corners of this land. I also have had countless conversations, read crumbling newspapers, spooled innumerable reels of microfilm, reopened cherished books and have found other books to love, and in between, gradually put these pages together. There was a time, truth be known, that Fenway Park and Wrigley Field were thought passé by individuals instrumental in the operation of those franchises; times when it was rumored that they too would disappear. Other generations have grown to love and experience those places since, many parents taking their children thousands of miles for the summer chance of doing precisely that. It is good that this is so.

Onetime voice of the Dodgers Red Barber never went back to Ebbets Field after he finished working for the team; said as far as he was concerned, it was always still there. We who would have loved to see it, but never had the chance, are left only to imagine what Ebbets Field was really like.

Bob McGee
July 29, 2004

Acknowledgments

Between the beginning and end of this effort, many who have helped have died, and if I have any regret, it's that I'm not able to share this book with them. I would want them all to know that I am most grateful.

I owe much to my lovely wife, Maureen, who has permitted my indulgence in a magnificent obsession; were there a market for a volume on "The Best Wife Ever," I might be able to fill its pages for the number of allowances or dispensations she's provided for trips to the ballpark, to Monte's on MacDougal in the Village, for hours buried in books, or for the regular late night appointments in front of the solid-state opiate, watching Fred Hickman on the postgame show. So too, the sentiments for my as-well lovely daughter Raena, off in her own life now, doing something good for society with the youthful enthusiasm that I now vaguely recall with a fond glimmer.

I owe more than I can say to my parents, Raymond and Agatha, for their encouragement and support; I would have, of course, loved it if Dad had been able to see this project finished, given his respect for perseverance and seeing things through. My mother's goodness, which has prompted any number of those in her acquaintance, close or not, to testify, "When her time comes, she's going straight up, no waiting," has been a sustenance. And I know my brother, Ray, has always been rooting for me.

I am also thankful for Joseph White, a great friend, always there with excellent counsel; similarly, and lucky I am in this regard, Brian Naylor, Ray Ferrari, Dr. George Nassoor, Joe Petta, and Svein Arber, whose extraordinary book *Seasons Past* should be reissued and allowed to find the new audience it deserves; I am grateful to Leonard Koppett and Harold Rosenthal, who were both instrumental in helping me locate Svein.

And thanks also to Mike and Betty Brassington, great friends who have both celebrated and provided shelter from the storms, including a few we rode out together; Bill Birenbaum, a mentor, for believing; Bill Heyman, who put me in touch with Marty Appel, who in turn provided the bridge to agent Rob Wilson; senior editor and acquiring editor Kristi Long at Rutgers, along with others there: Marilyn Campbell, Adi Hovav, Anne Hegeman, Kenya Henderson, Jessica Pellien, and my copyeditor, Elizabeth Gilbert, who did more than plenty to make this a better book.

I need to thank a few very special librarians: Tom Bourke, now retired from the New York Public Library, was an immense help in my efforts, especially in setting me up with the Ebbets file in the *New York Sun* morgue; so were Judith Walsh and Susan Aprill at the Brooklyn Public Library's Brooklyn Collection, Gail Whittenmore at the Pace University Law Library, and Maja Keech at the Library of Congress. I also wish to thank the San Francisco Public Library, the White Plains Library, the North Salem Free Library, and the Yale University Law Library for assistance provided.

I thank Paul Hirsch and Dick Cohn, who read the manuscript in California; Arthur Pincus and Jeff Graubard, who read it in New York, Mike Moffitt, who read it with crisp knowledge of most of the characters; extraordinary photographer Ted Beck, who helped with pictures, assisted by Scott Cohen; Dave Pine, legal guru of the new economy and a pragmatic idealist whose talents deserve to be well harnessed in California's public realm, was on board with this from the beginning; New Hampshire historian Chuck Brereton, who is that and more; Greg and Susan Herman, who have shared ballpark expeditions; Brooklyn baseball historian Tom Knight, as well as Dodgerdom enthusiasts Marty Adler and Norman Kurland, who shared both memories and expertise; SABR ballparks expert Bob Bluthardt; Rory Costello; photo historian Ray Medeiros; national treasure Arthur Richman, whom President Bush promised to appoint as a goodwill ambassador to someplace, another political promise as yet unfulfilled. Good friend Joe Ferraro, and his uncle, Tommy Holmes, who lived it. And to others who wrote about it: Dave Anderson, who remembers it firsthand; Richard Goldstein for *Superstars and Screwballs*; Philip Lowry for *Green Cathedrals*; Frank Graham, for his informal history; Robert Creamer, for his wonderful biographies. To Martha Skinner, Charley's great-granddaughter, for her incredible insight into the Ebbets family, and too, for the same reason, Edward Steele, the Ebbets family genealogist; to Doug Van Buskirk, for sharing about his father, Bertram, and his grandfather, Clarence, the ballpark's architect.

In addition to Leonard Koppett, who died in 2003, there are other stellar individuals whom I miss and who I think of just about every day: Tim Fazzinga, Clark Gesner, Jack Mann, Norman Rosten, Dr. Leon Epstein, John Kamps, and Charlie Lomando.

Further thanks to Andy Jurinko, for all he has portrayed. For their help, friendship, or for sharing information: Kay Gunther, Penny Marwede, Tom Edwards, Nat Kapel, W. G. Costello, Neil Lanctot, Seymour Siwoff, Al Stern, Bruce Stern, Billy DeLury, Mel Feiner, Elliott Abramson, Burton Appleton, Stanley Barkin, Paul Bresnick, Larry Block, Lois Bermont, Donald Crosby, Brad Curtis, Babe Dahlgren, Jerry Denmark, Murray Rubin, Lou Dallojacono, Victoria Bordagary, Ann Dermansky, Richard Elman, Edgar Feldman, Joyce Giardano, Arthur Harrow, Joe Harth, Martha Hunt, Max Israelite, Richard Karlin, Arthur Kellman, Charlie Knapp, Len Krasner, Mike Koretski, Joe Laurice, Richard Leeds, James Loughran, S.J., Buddy Hassett, Hank Lieberman, Vincent Lipinski, Steve Lipinski, Edie McCaslin, Bob Moss, John Nichols, Paul Pepe, Larry Bersin, Joe Pollack, Frank Prendergast, Jack Lang, Alfred Rubin, Sal Saporata, Ann and Dick Lee, Gloria Fennell, Bryan and Cathy Fennell, Marvin Schacter, Edward Watts, Sy Siegel, Rebecca Silverstein, Linda Gebroe, Diane Fraser, Joni Herron, Frank Spiro, Roberta Spector, Milt Strassberg, Karen Hammonds, Eli Barker, Lawrence Stetler, John Sineno, Neil Sullivan, Kris Twining, Jules Trachten, Joseph Dorinson, Vinnie Russo, E. J. Maynard, Bob Kesterbaum, Richard Leeds, Jerry Hirsch, Joe Pignatano, Bobby Bragan, Dr. John Rutherford, Carl Erskine, John Olguin, Peter Quinn, John Hayes, John Nichols, Howard Koppelman, Helen Granetelli, Dorothy Kushner, Stan Zicklin, Barbara Naylor, Stephanie Ferraro, Fran Ferrari, Barry Landesman, Herman Franks, Bobby Morgan, Dennis Szabega, Bob and Marilyn Messreni, Matthew Green and Joyce Sellers, Matt and Emily Jaros, Dr. Michael Palumbo, Dr. Abraham Chachoua, Larry Calieri, Dr. Paul Benzer and Rita Benzer, Ralph and Melinda Mendelson, David and Ellen Samel, Ron Lent, Mark Larsen, Byron Rhett, Everett Shockley, James Orellana, Bill Maynard, Phil Moore, Anthony Kirby, Les Larsen, and Tim Boylan. Also Howard Smith, Stan Isaacs, Jim McCormack, Dave Jordan, Ron Schweiger, Mark Mahler, and Bill Dwyer.

Over the long haul, Joe and Anita Conway, John and Wendy Holman, Carolyn and Dave Engle, Patti Caputo, Kadish and Donna, Mike and Barbara Masiello, Fran Augello, Martin Rotundo, John and Cathy Pototsky, Michael and Mary Mirantz. Old compatriots Stanley Davis,

Ben Greif, Larry Lonergan, Mary Torggler, Gini George-Cummins, Krupal Prabhaker, Lucy Newell, Leslie Tobias, Jean Cornin, Heather Smith, Tonee Nelson, Terri DiLemme, Steve Johnson, Vivian Otero, Chris Civello, Ronnie Blackwell, Sonia Burchard, Lori Mullery, James Banks, Melissa Mannese, Donna Colleymore, Carol Hinkley, Mike Kenney, Michael King and his crew, and Rick Baran.

David McCullough, for what he did for the Brooklyn Bridge and Brooklyn, for arriving on the eve of the centennial in a historic church, speaking history the way he writes it, for his graciousness, a kind letter, and his willingness to meet with a young(er) writer twenty years ago; Olga Bloom, who supports the Brooklyn legacy every day; Pete Hamill, who has always understood it.

Giovanni Mosconi, Marco Mosconi, Guido Franceschi, Jose Quizhpe, Rocco Onessimo, Joe Marcolin, Joe O'Connor, and Mary Elizabeth Gavin.

The extended Huggard, Terry, White, Nassoor, Pape, and Porio families; the Birenbaum clan, east and west; Anthony Russo, Philip Sleep, John and Lydia Rosse, and Betty Rosse; Veronica and Victor Marrero and Virginia and David Mahaffey. Also two Connolly families: one in New York and one on Prince Edward Island.

Dorothy Kenny, Overton Tremper, Tommy Henrich, John Kaiser, Jim McElroy, Bill Burdick, Tom Bisky, artist Jim Amore, Drew Holland, Michelle Berdy, Meg Kearney, Joe Kinard, Rahul Mehta, and the crew at 1690 North Point, Bagdhad-by-the-Bay. Thanks and appreciation to all.

The Greatest Ballpark Ever

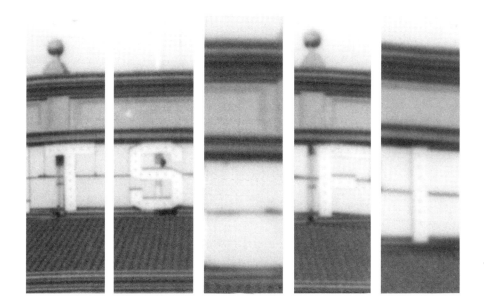

I am going to write somewhat about the world but mostly about you—your home and kiddies, mom and the loved ones, old Doc Smith and the preacher, the Brooklyn Dodgers and the Star-Spangled Banner—in short, the American scene. But I am going to ask you to look at it through my eyes, and through the eyes of certain far wiser men than I, whose sight I have borrowed, as you can.

Philip Wylie, *Generation of Vipers*, 1942

I sing of Brooklyn, city of myth,
stone mother, whose cobbled caress shaped me,
for better or worse, into the man I am today.
Walt Whitman

CHAPTER ONE

Hallowed Ground

It was a mysterious photograph, shot at about a 60-degree angle from the ground up, of an old, bishop's crook New York lamppost. Its decorative flourishes ended in a large glass globe, which poured forth a soft yellow glow rather than today's harsh, blue-white fluorescence. It looked to be an overcast day, but the framed image might have lied, considering it was from an unidentified newspaper roughly three decades old. In the background was a wooden wall that seemed to be about ten feet high, the kind that typically surrounds construction sites. On it were posters: "Kennedy for President." The street signs off the stanchion? Bedford Avenue. Montgomery Street.

Ebbets Field. Or what was left of it by 1960. A wooden fence with posters fronted by a streetlight that soared above it, surrounded by sky. The picture was on a wall in a pizza joint in San Francisco, memorializing a place three thousand miles away, speaking silently of a transition into a new age. For all photograph's simplicity, the stark image was likely to generate only a casual glance and scant recognition from the scores of eyes passing over it. A handful of people, at best, might get the message. Yet for those who knew, the cognition was kinetic, almost as if the wrecking ball itself had burst from the slumber of history to land once again at your feet.

Between 1913, when ball club owner Charles H. Ebbets opened the place, and 1957, the Brooklyn Dodgers, also known early on as the Superbas and then the Robins, played baseball at Ebbets Field, a few blocks east of Flatbush Avenue and the Brooklyn Botanic Garden. The pantheon of characters that populated Ebbets Field's acres during those years have paraded across the pages of American literature—not just sports literature, mind you—creating a mythic and heroic aura surrounding two things Brooklyn: the team and the field upon which they played.

Ebbets Field alive teemed with people, the colors of an artist's palette arrayed around its outfield walls, a bustling Brooklyn neighborhood right over the top of its right-field fence on Bedford Avenue, where a cascading home run ball would occasionally stop traffic while children scrambled in its wake. It was a ballpark established with knit-together parcels, purchased surreptitiously by intermediaries with no awareness of their intended end-use, if only because such information could provide those yet to sell with the leverage of naming their price. In the final analysis, what developed connected the surrounding neighborhoods to the ballpark and its team with an intensity and passion for baseball not known before or since. After two pennant-winning Brooklyn teams played on the ballpark's grounds during Ebbets Field's first eight years, the ball club settled into a close to two-decade pattern of complacent if not downright abysmal play, with only a couple of years proving exceptions. But on Saturdays and holidays—and Sundays after the blue laws were repealed in 1919—the legions came, often jamming the stands, with overflow fans standing behind ropes in the outfield during an era when baseball allowed that practice.

In the decades since Ebbets Field was wiped from the American scene, it has been a name uttered at various junctures when plans for and construction efforts on new stadiums proceed, but not because anyone would ever want to build a ballpark the same way. Too many things were wrong with Ebbets Field to make it a paradigm. Yet the aspiring successors present themselves, whether in Baltimore, Cleveland, Denver, San Francisco, Pittsburgh, San Diego, Cincinnati, Philadelphia, or in Houston or Arlington, Texas, with St. Louis and others to come. Their objective is always the same. They seek to grasp the intimacy that somehow both emits and captures a rollicking, signature sense of pride, reinforcing a wonderful sense of place.

Consider how Ebbets Field created an alchemy that married architecture and the beauty of the game to the grit between the cobblestoned streets around it, how the green symmetry of the diamond and the asymmetry of its concrete, metal, or wooden fences and barricades created elements as intrepid as the outside world it walled away. In another place, the activity within could be thought of as an escape or diversion. In Ebbets Field, it was an immersion. The dramas spawned were recited with greater fervor than the litanies often performed on the sabbath in the Borough of Churches.

In 1931 Ebbets Field underwent significant renovation, when the double-decked stands were extended from just beyond third base further down the third base line and throughout the outfield in left and center field in order to create more seating capacity. The new stands reduced the distance from home plate to the left-, left-center-, and center-field fence, until the new stands finally met the Bedford Avenue wall in an angled corner in the deepest recesses of right-center field. This modified the field and created the so-called bandbox that remains beyond the ken of any of the more modern imitative baseball parks.

The fans eventually took to calling the team's players *Bums*, but they were always *Our Bums*. On this diamond, where anything could happen and often did, no team's lead was safe, least of all one belonging to a visiting club playing against the prodigious Dodger lineups in the early and late 1940s and during the golden years of the 1950s. Helping to create the havoc were the ballpark's right-field fence, a jutting scoreboard with angled sides, and a right-field wall with a slanted lower half. If the ball hit the fence, it fell straight down, and if it hit the concrete wall hard, it careened hard back toward the infield. If the ball hit at an unanticipated angle around the scoreboard or in the deep right-center-field triangle corner, it could create quite an escapade for an outfielder. While incredulously observing one afternoon's events, the federal judge and longtime baseball commissioner Kenesaw Mountain Landis likened the park to a pinball game. And so it was. The result made perfect sense of its fascination for children and adults alike.

"We lived and died with the Robins and the Dodgers as both kids and adults," said Brooklynite Murray Rubin, "and to this day there is a great void in me over that. I can feel for those fans in other cities who also lost their teams but I don't believe their hurt can even closely compare to ours in Brooklyn."

It was at Ebbets Field, of course, where a lanky young slugger by the name of Floyd Caves "Babe" Herman doubled into a double play as one of three Dodgers to arrive on third base at the same time on a summer afternoon in 1926. It was at Ebbets Field's and New York City's first major league night game in 1938 when New Jersey native and Cincinnati Reds pitcher John Vander Meer pitched his second consecutive no-hitter. And it was at Ebbets Field in 1941 where catcher Mickey Owen dropped the third strike that should have ended the fourth game of the World Series with a Dodger victory, but which instead served as the catalyst for a four-run Yankee rally and a critical Dodger loss; at Ebbets

Field in 1947 where Jackie Robinson broke the color line; and at Ebbets Field where, months later, Dodger pinch-hitter Cookie Lavagetto—two outs, bottom of the ninth inning—broke up what would have been the first World Series no-hitter, hitting a fly ball off the wall, driving in the tying and winning base runners, who had reached base courtesy of Bill Bevens's walks.

Nine World Series were played at Ebbets Field, certainly far fewer than were seen uptown with either the Giants at the Polo Grounds or the Yankees at Yankee Stadium. But volume of championship jewelry and pennant flags has more to do with teams and annals and less to do with proximity to the action and the overall experience. For those who traversed New York's boroughs to watch baseball in these bygone days, the assessment was consistent: Ebbets Field was the greatest ballpark ever. Yes, the seats were small, the aisles narrow. Cans and bottles occasionally turned into missiles; the air was said to be charged. Nowhere were fans as close to the field.

It wasn't merely the excitement of being there, it was the significance of being a part of something larger, of having a great, unified presence and a collective pride in where and who you were, even while sitting amid many who were so different from you.[1] Ebbets Field was at once a point of arrival and a spontaneous explosion of calibrated tension and fun, and if results at the end of an afternoon or evening sometimes brought despair, what better paean to struggle could be offered than the dream that someday, some elusive day, the sweetness of total victory would ultimately be yours.

Brooklyn fans were said to know baseball better than any others in either league, as if it were bred in the bone. In a manner of speaking, it was. Baseball's roots in Brooklyn stretched back to before the Civil War, when some seventy baseball "clubs" were there. By comparison, across the river in New York, there were only twenty-five.[2]

Brooklyn stood atop the baseball world as champions of the National League in 1890 and again in 1899 and 1900, albeit in the latter two instances with imported players from Baltimore in an era of syndicate baseball, when owners, looking more like promoters, could own more than one team and move their charges for perceived best advantage seemingly at will. Said triumphs were before the advent of World Series play in 1903, however, and once that institution established the acknowledged supremacy of the victor, it became Brooklyn's magnificent obsession. The great day eventually arrived, even if Brooklyn's finishing touches on the 1955 World Championship were seen to in the Bronx. It unleashed an outpouring of celebration in the Dodgers' home borough on a day when Ebbets Field was otherwise relatively quiet, serving only as a staging ground for the team bus on the way to and from its crucial appointment up at Yankee Stadium. No matter. Brooklyn was the now the official capital of the baseball world, as every Dodger fan who had lived there and elsewhere had known it should rightfully be.

It should then come as no surprise that it was thought unconscionable when the Dodgers were moved to Los Angeles two short years later, after the 1957 season, with Ebbets Field, their citadel of struggle, unceremoniously deserted. Owner Walter O'Malley, who made a reported initial investment of $83,333 for an 8.33 per cent share in 1944 and consolidated his control of the team in 1950, was the sole executor of that decision, for which he is reviled to this day. O'Malley, noted one critic, bore a resemblance to the caricature of capitalism in a labor cartoon, with enormous girth, jowls, and an effete cigarette holder. But his intellectual assets were ample, even if the ends to which they were employed were suspect and his manner often cunningly devious. "Part leprechaun and part literal-minded lawyer," said *Time* magazine, "he disconcerts friends with a Groucho Marxist air of insincerity. Yet he walks among foes with the grave and wary eyes of an honest man lost among a legion of pickpockets."[3]

Walter O'Malley wanted a new ballpark for his team, and over a period of years, was unsuccessful in securing the site in Brooklyn that he desired, at the junction of Atlantic and Flatbush avenues. Between 1903 and 1953 all of major league baseball's franchises had stayed in the same locales, but between 1953 and 1955 three struggling franchises had moved: the Boston Braves to Milwaukee, a switch announced during spring training in 1953; the St. Louis Browns to Baltimore, where they were renamed the Orioles in 1954; and the Philadelphia Athletics to Kansas City in 1955. And so O'Malley threatened to move, announcing during the summer of 1955 that he was scheduling seven games in Jersey City in 1956 as an admonition to the city of New York's civic inaction on his behalf. The notion of Brooklyn without the Dodgers was unthinkable. They were the most profitable franchise in baseball. People couldn't believe that O'Malley would do it. Other teams across baseball were in bad straits, but not the Dodgers.

By 1957 everyone believed the talk was more than talk. Politicians came and went from their secret meetings, letters were exchanged, committees were formed. When Philip Wrigley and Walter O'Malley exchanged notes at the Baseball Writers dinner, agreeing to swap the Cubs' Los Angeles Angels minor league franchise for the Dodgers' Fort Worth minor league franchise, and when the announcement was made public on February 21, 1957, it amounted to handwriting on the wall: the Dodgers would have rights to the Los Angeles territory. As the weather warmed, "Keep the Dodgers in Brooklyn" rallies were held; buttons appeared on shirts and lapels. At Ebbets Field, the season began. The weight of the truth deadened the air. In June Brooklyn congressman Emanuel Cellar convened his Antitrust Subcommittee of the House

Judiciary Committee, querying O'Malley and National League president Warren Giles among others. More obfuscation.

When southpaw Danny McDevitt took the mound to pitch to the Pittsburgh Pirates on September 24, 1957, in what turned out to be the ballpark's last major league game, President Dwight Eisenhower was sending troops down to Little Rock to enforce federal orders to desegregate the schools and confront Arkansas governor Orval Faubus, ten years after Jackie Robinson integrated major league baseball on Ebbets Field's diamond with Dodger president Branch Rickey as architect and advocate. The battle for assimilation that had been waged in the social laboratory of Brooklyn had moved to another stage.

In Brooklyn, the crowd was small—just 6,702—and morose. "It seemed dark that night," said Duke Snider. "It didn't seem like the lights were taking hold. There were a lot more shadows out there. It was an eerie feeling . . . there weren't all that many people, and they weren't very happy."

"It was if the doom had set into the place," remembered pitcher Clem Labine, "because the cheering wasn't cheering, not in the manner that you'd usually get."

"It was like you were going to lose a part of your life," reflected Dodger pitching ace Don Newcombe, "like you were losing your Mom or your Dad who had passed away."[4]

At the time Danny McDevitt pitched this game, he was a rookie, twenty-four years old. "I was living out near the 69th Street Ferry in Bay Ridge," said McDevitt. "We all used to take turns driving. I used to scare the hell out of Pee Wee. My record was 6–1 when Ed Roebuck and Don Bessent took me out to a place called the Rendevouz and introduced me to scotch and water. Then, before I knew it, I was 6–4.

"I didn't know it would be the last game. My only concern was just trying to win it.

"So this was a big game for me. And I really don't remember what the crowd was like that night. When I was doing my best pitching, I was in a trance. I'd just lock in with my catcher; my concentration was such that there wasn't anything else in the world. I didn't hear the fans, didn't hear the players. I blocked everything out when I was doing well. I knew right where every pitch was going. Zip. Zip. Zip."

After Elmer Valo's double drove in the first run for Brooklyn in the first inning, organist Gladys Goodding played "Am I Blue" and "After You're Gone." When Hodges singled in Gino Cimoli in the third, the last run that would be scored, she played "Don't Ask Me Why I'm Leaving." As the game progressed, she played other standards between innings, including "Que Sera Sera," "How Can You Say We're Through," "When I Grow Too Old to Dream," and Bing Crosby's theme song, "When the Blue of the Night Meets the Gold of the Day." At the game's conclusion, after McDevitt's five-hit shutout, Gooding started to play "May the Good Lord Bless You and Keep You," but was lamely interrupted when someone put on the familiar "Follow the Dodgers" recording over the loudspeaker. After it stopped, Gooding concluded with "Auld Lang Syne."

Afterward the ground crew raked the infield smooth and put tarps over the mound and the home plate area.

Later that night, Bill Roeder of the *World-Telegram* and Dave Anderson of the *Journal American* were the last two writers to leave the ballpark. As he was about to step over the threshold, Anderson stepped back courteously and said, "You go ahead, Bill."

Roeder did, Anderson realizing in the moment that he was the last sportswriter to leave a Dodger game at Ebbets Field.

On October 8, 1957, an off day before the sixth game of the World Series between the Yankees and Braves in New York, after O'Malley had been granted an extension on the National League's October 1 deadline to announce a move, the Dodgers made it official with a terse statement that team spokesman Red Patterson handed out at the Waldorf Astoria. It said, "In view of the action of the Los Angeles City Council yesterday and in accordance with the resolution of the National League made October 1, the stockholders and directors of the Brooklyn baseball club have today met and unanimously agreed that the necessary steps be taken to draft the Los Angeles territory."

The Brooklyn Dodgers were no more.

"The Dodgers, you see, had committed an unforgivable crime," Pete Hamill would write thirty-one years later, characterizing "Never Forgive, Never Forget" as "a blood oath shouted from Bay Ridge to Brownsville, from Red Hook to Canarsie, becoming the rallying cry of the Brooklyn jihad. . . . They had destroyed our innocence. In one filthy act, they told us that we fans were just a pack of gullible marks— romantic fools who believed all the myths about America.

"They told us baseball wasn't the most beautiful game ever devised by man nor were the Dodgers its most elegant artists. Baseball was a racket, said That Son of a Bitch O'Malley, a businessman's hustle, like any other. The innocent fable was a lie. Money was everything, greed the ruling principle." [5]

Aside from the fact that O'Malley was slated to get about three hundred acres of downtown Los Angeles in a trade for that city's Wrigley Field, speculation has always abounded about the man's feelings. How could he take an institution out of Brooklyn that was so dear to the hearts of so many people? His aide Fresco Thompson offered an insight in a book he wrote with Cy Rice, first published in 1964 under the title *Every Diamond Doesn't Sparkle*. Walter O'Malley wrote the foreword. In it, he reminded readers that Fresco Thompson had been a valued member of the Dodger organization since 1940. He added that Thompson was a trusted one, and always would be. Thompson characterized Ebbets Field as decrepit. He said the park's girders were rotting and some urinals had been wrenched from their moorings. Eli Barker, the ballpark's plumber, who also was familiar with other maintenance around the park, said he never heard tell of either. But darker and more disturbing are other things that Thompson, then a vice president with O'Malley's Dodgers, wrote.

"When I first played in Brooklyn as a member of the Dodgers," he said, "there were four department stores selling class merchandise. Only one remained in 1957. Newspaper Guild trouble had caused the closing of the *Brooklyn Eagle,* the last of four local newspapers. The loyal and substantial fan, the family man, had moved away. He was now living in Westchester County, out on Long Island, in New Jersey, or in Akron, Ohio.

"He was replaced by the undesirables.

"I brand no race, color, or creed as objectionable," continued Thompson. "They all have their scum. But, unfortunately, the scum was now thick in Brooklyn. The element drifting into decaying Ebbets Field and using unprintable language in catcalling to the players or in the stands would shame women to the extent that on Ladies' Day only a handful of the most rugged and probably deafest of the distaff side could weather the sting of words."[6]

The Dodgers had been the team that had broken the color line. Thompson's remarks were an outrage, a thinly veiled disapproval of the blacks and Puerto Ricans who were migrating to Brooklyn.

"In our Ebbets Field location there were close to 400,000 people within walking distance," Thompson said, "in addition to two subway lines, bus lines, and half a dozen trolley car lines feeding us—yet they would continue to supply us with the same element of people, a pretty indigestible potpourri, at best."[7]

The blockbusting by real estate speculators that tipped the neighborhood racially around the Ebbets Field site would not occur for another five to six years. Yet in Philadelphia, in Shibe Park—renamed Connie Mack Stadium—in a neighborhood that similarly changed and in a ballpark that paralleled Ebbets Field in age, size, and the nature of its location, the Phillies would play until 1970, with Phillies' owner Bob Carpenter working toward a civic solution regarding the ballpark's replacement and waiting patiently while it evolved. Carpenter did so without threatening to move the franchise, even though his team's competitive posture was not nearly as favorable as the Brooklyn team's.

Discussions of a new ballpark for the Phillies and a new ballpark for the Dodgers both began accelerating around 1953.[8] It would take Philadelphia seventeen years to get its municipal stadium built.

The city of New York, ironically, would outstrip that effort, managing to get Shea Stadium in Flushing Meadow built for its new National League franchise by 1964. It was a site O'Malley had rejected years before. It wasn't in Brooklyn, he said.

In March 1958 the Dodgers assembled for spring training at Vero Beach, many of the players feeling strange without the familiar Brooklyn "B" on their caps, readying for their first season in Los Angeles. There they would play baseball on the Los Angeles Coliseum's mis-shapen field, featuring a 250-foot left-field line with a 40-foot screen to mitigate against pop-up home runs, in contrast to a 390-foot distance for a left-handed pull hitter unless he was lucky enough to pull the ball right down the line. It was an interim home that O'Malley preferred for its 93,000 seats as opposed to his other option, Los Angeles' Wrigley Field, which could seat only 22,000 patrons. In the meantime Ebbets Field Productions was established, and over the course of the next two years the Brooklyn ballpark would be used intermittently for professional soccer, demolition derbies, and the like. On June 16, 1959, the Dodgers elected to drop their lease on Ebbets Field.

Twelve days later, at an international soccer match held at the ballpark on Sunday, June 28, three soccer officials were injured and a special patrolman, Pat Imperiale, was knocked out when he was struck across the bridge of the nose with a linesman's flag during a fight. Napoli, which had easily defeated an All-Star team from the American Soccer League a week before, lost to Rapid of Vienna, 1–0. City police had been called into the park to break up a fight in the first half, when, after a foul call against Napoli, some of the 18,512 fans ran onto the field and began swinging at players, officials, and park police.

The following week the two teams played a return match before 13,351 that resulted in a 1–1 tie. The event, calm by comparison, was marred only by a box seat that flew out of the second deck of the left-field stands midway through the second half after a Napoli bid to score failed. It missed any mark.

That fall the Dodgers played in a World Series in Los Angeles. On the day it opened, Matt Burns, who remained behind in Brooklyn as the person in charge of Ebbets Field for the team, looked over a ballpark that stood empty, except for a tall, broad-shouldered man, about seventy years old, who sat in one of the green seats quietly looking out at the empty scoreboard, where a sign said: Dodgers Next Game. . . .

"He comes in here almost every day," said Burns. "He just sits here and looks around, like it was a museum. . . . We get a few every day. They come in to sit in the sun or read the paper on their lunch hour. Or like the old man, they just look."[9]

After the fifth game in Los Angeles, four writers—Jack Mann and Stan Isaacs of *Newsday*, Steve Weller of the *Buffalo News*, and Charles

Sutton of the *Los Angeles Times*—removed the Brooklyn Dodgers' 1955 World's Championship pennant that was hanging in the press hospitality room in the Sheraton-West hotel on Wilshire Boulevard. "The help in the hotel were about to take the pennant down," remembered Mann, "since the World Series was going back to Chicago for the sixth, and what turned out to be the final game. After long and thoughtful consideration, my colleagues and I determined that the pennant did not belong in California but in Brooklyn, because it had been won in Brooklyn by the Brooklyn Dodgers and it was the only World Series pennant that would ever be won by Brooklyn Dodgers.

"Accordingly, with Mr. Sutton as our spokesman, we advised the hotel personnel that the pennant was a curio of too high virtue to be left unattended for even a brief interval, and that it had to be removed forthwith and cherished by persons who clearly understood its merit. The hotel personnel were quite cooperative, bringing ladders and other tools to take down the pennant and help us fold and carry it to Mr. Sutton's car."

Stan Isaacs turned over the banner to Ken Smith of the Baseball Hall of Fame, shaking hands on the deal for the hall to hold the 1955 banner for eventual display in Brooklyn, pending the location of an appropriate place. By the late 1980s, an older and ailing Smith couldn't remember the arrangement. Even after the Brooklyn Historical Society's new museum opened, Bill Guilfoile, the hall's curator, wouldn't surrender it. Instead it again wound up in Dodger hands, back to Dodger president Peter O'Malley, Walter's son, who in 1995 unceremoniously shipped it to the Brooklyn Historical Society, leaving to conjecture whether the act was to assuage some long-held family guilt for his father's misdeeds or simply to soothe some of the remaining bitterness.

Today the banner hangs at the society's building on the corner of Pierrepont and Clinton streets, down the block and around the corner from what had once been the site of the Brooklyn Dodger executive offices at 215 Montague Street.

On January 1, 1960, physical possession of Ebbets Field was turned over to Kratter Corporation, the builder who had purchased it from O'Malley, with Matt Burns and Kratter's Seymour Goldsmith, who lived at opposite ends of Yonkers, driving all the way down to the ballpark merely to stage the photo opportunity of exchanging the keys under the façade. The fait accompli of the Dodgers' departure, the void it left, and the nature of all the business transactions made the destruction of the place seem inevitable; no movement ever developed to keep a vestige of it in place as a tangible touchstone of the past on the city block where it stood. Inside, a solitary set of footprints remained frozen in the dirt, leading from the visitor's bullpen, to the pitching rubber, and off into the visiting dugout. Home plate was still in place; the

Bulova clock was keeping perfect time atop the scoreboard; a soccer goalpost replaced first base. Inside the scoreboard, the numbers and team names remained ready for posting.

The official requiem—ceremonies before beginning the demolition of Ebbets Field—was held seven weeks later on a cold Tuesday morning, February 23, 1960. Outside the ballpark an "Ebbets Field Apartments" sign was tied above the home plate entrance, which port opened into a circular hall eighty feet in diameter known as the Rotunda to two generations of Dodger fans.

In the *New York Times* the next day, Gay Talese, covering the story for the paper, led with an image evoking the abandon of a mercurial Dodger center fielder whose talents blossomed in the summer of 1940: "At Ebbets Field yesterday men swung sledge hammers, the dugout crumbled and an iron ball crashed like Pete Reiser against the wall."

The event began around 11 A.M. The gates were open to anyone; about two hundred people came. A steam shovel was in the home plate area, a little ways up the third base line; a one-ton wrecking ball was at the end of its long cable. The field was all torn up, ruts and tire tracks running in all directions. A trailer with two royal-blue stripes sat at second base. The American flag on the center-field flagpole flew upside down, commonly a signal of distress. Though its position was reported to be unintentional, it seemed so fitting that one could imagine the flag flipping over by itself.

A brass band was on hand. So was Tommy Holmes, the native Brooklynite who played between 1942 and 1952, ten years for the Braves and a year at the end for the Dodgers, setting a National League record for hitting safely in consecutive games along the way. And so was Lucy Monroe, who, as she had at so many regular season baseball games, sang the national anthem that morning. Carl Erskine, who threw two no-hitters and helped anchor the Dodger pitching staff during the 1950s, was there as well; he posed for photographers, standing with his right arm by the wrecking ball as if he was about to give it a toss. And in what turned out to be a great service to history, Erskine took home movies, later used in the film documentary *When It Was a Game.*

Tex Rickards, public-address announcer famous for such gaffes as "Will the fans sitting along the rail in left field please remove their clothes," appropriately made an error in his last intonation: "Ladies and gentlemen, now coming in to pitch for the Dodgers, number 14, Ralph Branca." Branca wore 13 and 12 as a pitcher; 14 did and always will belong to the big first baseman, Gil Hodges. But it didn't matter. Branca, smiling and wearing a camel's hair coat, stepped out of the stands to the cheers of the fans and workers in the crowd.

Roy Campanella turned out, the great Dodger catcher who had been in a wheelchair since the auto accident that paralyzed him and almost claimed his life in January of 1958. Campanella, who had shared catching duties with Joe Pignatano that last night in 1957, was presented with his locker, complete with his number 39 uniform, and an urn full of Ebbets Field dirt dug up from behind home plate. To complete the circle, standing next to him was Otto Miller, the man who had caught the very first ballgame in Ebbets Field on April 5, 1913. Miller had been born in Minden, Nebraska, in 1889, and arrived at the Brooklyn spring training camp in Hot Springs, Arkansas, in 1910. The veterans quickly named him "Moonie," and Brooklyn's star pitcher, a left-hander from Alpharetta, Georgia, named Nap Rucker, got after rookie manager Bill Dahlen to keep him. After fifty years, the catcher-turned-coach-turned-scout-turned-bartender was still in Brooklyn. No one really knew if Otto Miller took his own life intentionally when he fell or jumped out a four-story window at Brooklyn Eye and Ear Hospital two years later in the spring of 1962, but with O'Malley primed to open the new Dodger Stadium at Chavez Ravine in Los Angeles just twelve days after Otto's death, the irony of someone so entwined with Ebbets Field from beginning to end performing such an act of despair was within the realm of plausibility.[10]

Underneath the wry smiles and warm handshakes at the old ballpark that winter's day was a great sadness. This was a funeral for a ballpark. When the ceremonies were over and it was time for the demolition to begin, the observers were asked to return to the stands. Then the wrecking ball's first blow shattered the third base dugout's roof, ripping the bullpen phone from its mooring. No one said a word. If there was even a trace of humor earlier in an attempt to ease the painful passage, it disappeared at that moment.

"Then the big crane headed with the speed of Ernie Lombardi into centerfield," wrote Talese, citing the memory of the slow, lumbering Cincinnati Reds catcher. "When it reached the 376-foot mark, the workman swung back on this iron ball. . . . It came spinning towards the wall and, after a few shots, there was a hole the size of Hugh Casey."

If Talese saw the ghost of the Dodger reliever, one of the heroes of 1941, Carl Erskine also saw some of his own. "You know, when I look at the field now I see the past," he said that morning. "I think of things that happened in this nook and that cranny. I'm remembering bad pitches I made from out there and great days we had. That dugout's empty," he said of the visitor's bench, "but when I look at it, I can see all the men that used to be there."

Jack Mann, who eloquently covered Ebbets Field's demolition for *Newsday*, remembered that day years later, citing a 1990s film that itself used Ebbets Field as context. "You can see it in the early scenes of 'Field of Dreams,'" he said. "Kevin Costner's voice-over of the historic film footage tells of the Dodgers playing baseball in Brooklyn while the camera aloft focuses on the third-base dugout of Ebbets Field. A three-story crane drops a huge weight and the concrete roof of the dugout becomes rubble. It is step one in the demolition of the ballpark.

"For auld lang syne," Mann continued, "the thematic-thinking real estate hucksters had the wrecking ball painted white with the bright red stitches of a baseball. It was to be a fun desecration. It was obvious, long before the ball dropped, that the story was in the cab of the crane: a muscular, middle-aged, Brooklyn-Italian man with abundant chest hair and a stinking black-rope cigar. A prototypical fan from Bensonhurst, who had suffered through all those Next Years before the Dodgers got good, would have to pull the lever to bury them. A strong man would weep, surely.

"The trick was to decoy the other reporters away from the crane operator. Gay Talese, the new kid from the *Times*, was there and he'd be all over it. So temporize: interview people like Tex Rickards, the malaprop public-address announcer, until it was over. And then:

'Sal, it must've hurt to drop that thing on the dugout.'

'Nah. I didn't give a shit. I never cared much about baseball.'"

Even in death, Ebbets Field was rich in the provision of the unexpected.

When Sal's first blow landed on the dugout, Erskine just turned away. So did Tommy Holmes. "As soon as that wrecking ball came down," Holmes said, "I said to myself, 'Let me get the hell out of here. No one wants to see this.' And I left."

A little over a week later, on March 2, 1960, the 1,600 inmates of the City Workhouse on Hart Island got 2,200 of Ebbets Field's seats. A few hundred inmates on the island off the Bronx put them in place around the island's baseball and softball fields, prompting Corrections Commissioner Anna Kross to observe that they wouldn't have to squat on the ground any longer to see a game. Warden Edward Dros's first idea was to get Ebbets Field's abandoned PA system, but as he said, "I found Walter F. O'Malley had gotten there first."[11] As the warden's comments went into print, a Los Angeles Dodgers truck was loading seven thousand of the best box seats. Hart Island did wind up with some of Ebbets Field's lights.

By April 11 the stands had been ripped out on the third base side; only the outside wall and skeletal ironwork remained. The roof, flags, and light towers were gone. The final public moments for Ebbets Field arrived twelve days later, on a sunny spring day, April 23, 1960. The assignment to auction off Ebbets Field devolved upon Saul Leisner, himself an old Brooklyn Dodgers fan, who was equal to, if unhappy with, the task. The ensuing notoriety would bring him and his wife an invitation to appear as contestants on "Who Do You Trust," a quiz show hosted by Johnny Carson and Ed McMahon.

Decades later, Leisner would remember Ebbets Field's last day as "the saddest day of my life."[12] Up for auction were the locker room stool of legendary Dodger shortstop Pee Wee Reese, the bench from the Dodger dugout, team banners that waved from the grandstand, sod, seats, gold-painted bricks, discarded bats, electrical fixtures, ushers' caps, team photos, bronze dedication plaques, autographed balls, old official schedules, and finally the brownstone cornerstone, containing a sealed copper box that served as a time capsule.

A public relations firm was hired to help plan the event; to generate some good will, flowerpots filled with infield dirt were given out free. The PR people also hired a caterer who had prepared sandwiches for the press and invited guests, but before everyone showed up and while the tables were left unattended, a horde of neighborhood urchins managed to sneak in to scoop up much of the spread. Ebbets Field would be classic to the very last.

Estimates of the gathering at the marble rotunda for the event ranged from one hundred to one thousand, depending on the news source; Barney Kremenko of the *New York Journal American*, who had seen enough crowds in and around the old ballpark to know, pegged the crowd at five hundred.

Leisner began the auction at 11:15 A.M., climbing an eight-foot ladder and holding a gavel. The first item, a bat said to have been a model autographed by former Dodger pitcher Clarence "Bud" Podbielan and used by ex-Dodger infielder Don Zimmer, fetched $2 from a sixteen-year-old St. Francis Prep student, William Ferris, of 608 Rugby Road. Other items quickly followed, including large photographs of Jackie Robinson stealing home and another of Gil Hodges stretching to nip a runner at first.

The *New York Times* said the event proceeded "amid much raucous bid-seeking and the exaggerated fall of a hammer." Items worth thousands today, a Braves banner earned $4; another belonging to the hated crosstown rivals, the Giants, drew only $3. The St. Louis Cardinals banner had the lowest winning bid: $1.50. The bench out of the Dodger dugout was sold for $3, while a bench seating two in an upstairs box garnered only 50 cents. Regular grandstand seats, items that now routinely fetch two to three thousand dollars, were sold for a quarter, as were bricks painted gold and stamped "Ebbets Field, 1913–1957." A Roy Campanella banner earned $2 at the auction; Sal Maglie's picked up a buck. A set of original blueprints to the ballpark, which would today require a high-bid auction at Sotheby's, went for $19.

Home plate, originally slated for sale, was given away to bespectacled Mickey McConnell, director of training for Little League Baseball. McConnell, who once had been the Dodgers' director of scouting, said the plate would be used in a Little League field that would be built on the grounds of the 25-story, 1,317-unit, $22.5 million housing project that would follow the demolition of the ballpark. No such field was built.

Ten-year-old Gil Hodges Jr. was given a banner with his father's name on it from an Ebbets Field "Night" in his dad's honor. Kratter Corporation, the builders, bid $300 apiece for the two bronze plaques commemorating the ballpark's construction that had been mounted in the famous Rotunda.

The climactic event was the auction of the cornerstone and the revelation of what was actually hidden inside it. "And to build up to the big moment," wrote Milton Bracker in the *Times*, "a trick hammer on a dummy block set off a real explosion in what was supposed to be the cornerstone. It turned out to be a box filled with five circus clowns, including three midgets. All were wearing Dodger uniforms."

The real cornerstone had been taken out of the wall on the first base side of the Rotunda, where it was originally placed on July 6, 1912. Now it was wheeled up, and off the ladder now, a solemn Leisner held a cumbersome oval-shaped microphone the size of a pixie football in his left hand and the gavel handle in his right. For all intents and purposes, this was the end of the end.

Leisner moved with head bowed, eyes downcast, his arm outstretched to touch the half-ton slab with the gavel, his chin resting on his bow tie. Many of the long, sad faces in the crowd mirrored his, people lost in reminiscence, doubtless thinking of the fathers, sons, and friends who had been a part of this place, and the mothers and daughters who enjoyed it or endured it. Maxie Rosenfeld—a Yankee fan, of course—seemed to take the proceedings lightly, posing for photographers with bat in hand, taking a swing at the cornerstone from the left side.

Leisner announced that the 1912 relic had been sold to National League president Warren Giles, who submitted a $600 bid in absentia. Giles would shortly afterward give the historic marker to the Hall of Fame, where it remains on exhibit.

The copper, rectangular box-vault within the cornerstone was removed with the help of a sledge hammer. Like most of the things that had occurred over the past forty-seven or so years in this place, it didn't come easy. Not exactly laboring with the surgical precision of archaeologists, the workers pounded open a big, jagged gash in the top middle part of the half-ton brownstone, driving down almost to the "s" in Ebbets, in the center of the slab. The vault was supposed to be waterproof, but the ravages of time had made that an empty boast. Moisture had turned the letters, testimonials, and pictures inside soggy, and most of them fell apart at the touch.

Among the contents were missives from President William Howard Taft and Mayor William J. Gaynor, a copy of Admiral Peary's message to the nation upon reaching the North Pole, a picture of Charley Ebbets, a 1912 calendar, a copy of the *New York Morning Post* from January 5, 1912, five 1912 pennies and a single 1811 penny, which was worth about $7.50 at that time. Visitors Joe Duome, wearing a checkered hat and a striped jacket, and little Mitchell Modell, clad in a Little Leaguer's Dodger uniform with a "B" cap, checked the remnants and curios as they tumbled out on the ground. "It was a sad thing to see how much people cared for the field and Dodgers," Saul Leisner recalled years later. "There were coins and rosaries and Stars of David in that cornerstone." 13

The auction raised $2,300 for the Little League, ostensibly for construction of their field on the project site. Leisner, whose credits as an auctioneer stretched back to World War II, when he was said to have sold $375,000 worth of war bonds in an hour and $1 million worth on D-Day, donated his fee for the cause. At one point, Leisner made an announcement that someone had donated $10 to the Little League.

An anonymous voice from the crowd suddenly issued forth in retort: "I bet it wasn't Walter O'Malley!"

The very last moments that Ebbets Field existed as a place—the last day a recognizable remnant of brick or mortar stood—went unrecorded. On the eighth of May, the fence that stood along Bedford Avenue was still up; the Gem Blades, Esquire boot polish, Knothole Gang, Mobilgas, and Bulova signs were still in evidence along a contiguous right-field wall; so was the wire screen above it. Only a dark space remained where the scoreboard once stood, and for the first time in memory, gone was the long, low, dusky-gold rectangular sign that advertised the store of the clothier and tailor-turned-politician that ran the length of the scoreboard at its base: ABE STARK, 1514 Pitkin Avenue, with the triple G clothes trademark on either side, and to the left of the name, a black arrow with white letters inside, beckoning, "Hit Sign, Win Suit."

The expanse where the great center fielder Duke Snider once roamed continued to be left to a watchdog called Angel, a reddish collie-chow mix. A mere puppy when the Dodgers departed, Angel spent the empty days running over what was left of the greensward; many kids over the years would have given their souls to do the same thing.14

On the third Sunday in October, three days after the Pirates beat the Yankees in the World Series' seventh game in Pittsburgh on the strength of Bill Mazeroski's home run, the Dodgers closed their eastern office at 130 Clinton Street in Brooklyn Heights.

By January, as the finishing touches were set for the Kennedy inaugural festivities in Washington, a steam shovel was digging a hole at second base for the Ebbets Field apartments. The last vestiges of the Brooklyn that everyone once knew were the sidewalks' old bishop's crook lampposts.

The rendering of a malevolent ball club owner who failed to see a decent measure of his investment as a public trust instead of a private opportunity remains painfully clear. "It was O'Malley's—and only O'Malley's—decision," said Brooklyn and later Los Angeles Dodger vice president Buzzie Bavasi in 1994 about the move. "Everybody else was hoping something could be worked out."

"He borrowed the money from the Brooklyn Trust Company to buy the team, the nickels and dimes of Brooklyn depositors," said baseball historian Tom Knight. "And then he moved the ball club out of Brooklyn." The gold at the end of O'Malley's rainbow was three hundred centrally located free acres from Los Angeles, and the prospect of making a deal with Skiatron, a pay-TV company that could theoretically generate revenues for the Dodgers that would be significantly higher than television revenues in the short term in New York, since O'Malley was bound there by traditional television contracts through 1959.

The dithering and intransigence of Mayor Robert Wagner and his parks commissioner, Robert Moses, who wielded even more power as head of the independent Triborough Bridge and Tunnel Authority, made the politicians complicit in the untoward developments. "O'Malley did all that he could to secure a site in Brooklyn before he left," *New York Times* sportswriter Leonard Koppett noted. The record shows that O'Malley did try to secure rights to the area at the junction of Atlantic and Flatbush avenues, above the Long Island Railroad terminal, even while vacillating about the extent of favorable terms he required. "The one thing he didn't do," Koppett added, concerning O'Malley's failure to get what he wanted in Brooklyn, "was offer the team for sale."

Charley Ebbets was always an advocate for local ownership of a ball club, if only because he felt a local owner would have the interests of the people in his community in mind. "A man shouldn't get in this business if he's solely interested in receipts," Ebbets said. Walter O'Malley was himself a New Yorker, from Amityville, on Long Island, if not the city. In O'Malley's case, local ownership didn't matter. The quest for profit was the first concern. Branch Rickey called O'Malley's move "a crime against a community of three million"; and one of the country's institutions—the great game of baseball—became perceived quite differently well beyond the defined borders of any particular place.[15] Allegiance meant nothing.

If, as has long been maintained, major league baseball is society's mirror, it needed to be on the West Coast and should have been there years earlier. Given the Pacific Coast League's aspirations, petitions, and other official political overtures, the arrival of major league baseball in California should have been handled differently. As is so often the case in politics or business, a motivated person can shanghai a legitimate issue that provides him or her some usefulness or cover

and exploit a constituency with a calculated, selfish decision that pre-
scribes an unwarranted solution. Nothing visionary in that; it is as old
as the wind. One need only trace the origin of cynicism about baseball
back to O'Malley's quest for profits to see the logical result of unprecedented greed. The stewards of this game can never kill America's
love for baseball, but history shows us it sometimes is hardly for lack
of trying.

The thirty-year-old photograph from the San Francisco pizza parlor
captured both the vestige of an older New York and the avarice that destroyed it, an image poised in time on the precipice of a new age. In the
turbulent decade of the 1960s that followed, with street riots, political
assassinations, and a television war, beliefs in which America felt most
secure—among them the idea of extended kinship inspired by the likes
of Ebbets Field itself—were subject to alteration if not downright
destruction.

That no tangible shred of Ebbets Field remains where it stood is an
insult to history. Whether between the chalk lines or outside them,
Ebbets Field, both as historical institution and as symbol, with all the
commitment between it and its community, offers more lessons for
baseball and America in the twenty-first century than the sentiment it
evoked in the twentieth.

CHAPTER TWO

The Squire
of Flatbush

Charles H. Ebbets's birth was recorded in a flourished handwriting in the New York City ledger on October 29, 1859, just a few months before the city began issuing birth certificates. His parents, John B. and Ann Quick Ebbets, were well established, living on Spring Street in Manhattan's old Eighth Ward. "The family had been in the United States for generations as had the Dutch ancestors on my great-grandmother's side," wrote his granddaughter, Dorothy Ebbets Dollmeyer, in a family memoir she composed in Everett, Washington, in 1982. "They were mainly merchants and landowners."

The world into which Charley Ebbets and his contemporaries were born was hardly an easy one. The dawn of 1860 saw the nation on the brink of a great civil war; the last months of James Buchanan's disastrous and ineffectual presidency wound down as Lincoln squared off against Douglas and Henry Ward Beecher thundered abolitionist sermons from his Plymouth Church pulpit in Brooklyn Heights. The Irish had been arriving hungry for twenty years, the Germans behind them; the rush for gold had sent people west on unfathomable journeys with unpredictable results, traveling shipboard around Cape Horn or through Indian lands across the Continental Divide. Veterans proudly remembered their contributions in a dubious war against Mexico as the South prepared to secede. The hordes of new immigrants had created agglomerations of squalor in places like New York's Five Points; many would shoulder arms during the coming war; some would riot against their new president's government when the draft was instituted. Amid all of this, north and south and points west, was an emerging and burgeoning affection for "base ball."

In Brooklyn, two sites had been among the most notable to baseball fans—called "cranks" in those days—who were interested in watching the best teams play. The first of these, the Union Grounds, opened on May 15, 1862, before Charley, growing up across the river in Manhattan, had reached his third birthday. No mention of Brooklyn's baseball past remains at these early spots. No markers adorn buildings or commemorate significance: they're intersections without fanfare or memorial, their history unknown and forgotten, as if part of some Paleolithic age of Brooklyn baseball.

These first two notable Brooklyn ballparks were on opposite ends of Marcy Avenue; both sites had previously been flooded and used commercially as skating rinks during the winter. The Union Grounds was operated by William Cammeyer, heir to a leather business and a political operative who was friendly with New York's William Marcy "Boss" Tweed. The park was in what is now the borough's Williamsburg neighborhood, in the vicinity of Marcy and Lee avenues along Rutledge Street. The second ball park, opened on May 5, 1864, by Reuben S. Decker and Hamilton Weed in the Bedford area, was between Marcy and Nostrand avenues, along Putnam Avenue.[1] Even with the war diminishing the ranks of Brooklyn's amateur teams by some 60 percent, that parks were built at all served to illustrate the game's growing popularity.[2]

Cammeyer's Union Grounds had the first enclosed baseball field, with a six-foot fence around an outfield that had distances of more than five hundred feet from home plate. Meanwhile Decker and Weed's Capitoline Grounds had a "row of stables—the equivalent of today's parking lot— . . . along Putnam Avenue, behind a restaurant, bandstand, sitting rooms for the female fans and clubhouses."[3] The ballpark also was described as having two sets of bleachers seating a total of five thousand fans along Nostrand Avenue and Halsey Street.[4] Anyone hitting a ball over the circular brick outhouse in right field was rewarded with a bottle of champagne along with his home run, thus establishing the Brooklyn practice of providing a player with an article of value on the basis of the provident flight of a fly ball, a tradition unwittingly carried on by Abe Stark at Ebbets Field a few generations later.[5]

During the war era well-known local teams like the Atlantics, the Eckfords, the Putnams, and the Excelsiors graced Brooklyn's ball fields. In 1864 the Atlantics won the championship of the loosely affiliated group called the National Organization of Baseball Players, a feat they repeated two years later. But Brooklyn's greatest baseball victory during these early years came in 1870, when the Atlantics agreed to meet the Cincinnati Red Stockings, the team responsible for starting professional baseball the year before. On a whirlwind tour of the East and the Midwest, the Cincinnati team remained unbeaten in fifty-seven games during its maiden 1869 season, and then reeled off another twenty-seven consecutive victories at the outset of 1870.

On June 14, in a much anticipated showdown, the Red Stockings swaggered into the Capitoline Grounds and the Atlantics played them to a 5–5 tie over nine innings. Although tie games after nine innings were typically allowed to be recorded as such in those days, the game was played to a conclusion at the insistence of the visitors, who looked as if they would emerge victorious when two runs were scored in the top of the eleventh inning. But the Atlantics took the starch out of the Red Stockings, answering with three runs of their own in the bottom of the eleventh, breaking Cincinnati's streak and giving bragging rights to Brooklyn.

Enthusiasm over that game spread well beyond Brooklyn's borders and would be remembered forty-two years later in the remarks by borough president Alfred E. Steers when ground was broken for Ebbets Field in 1912. Steers had been outside the Capitoline Grounds for that big game in 1870, witnessing the contest through a knothole in the fence.

On St. Patrick's Day the following spring, the National Association of Professional Base Ball Players established a ten-team league after meeting at Collier's Rooms, a hotel at East Thirteenth Street and Broadway in Manhattan.[6] The Brooklyn Eckfords, initially slated to be an entry, declined to participate when the team's representative blanched at the $10 league admission fee. The Eckfords did manage to play some league games during the last months of the season when the Fort Wayne team folded, but at the season's conclusion, after collecting needed gate receipts, the scornful league banished the Eckfords and expunged their games from the record. It wouldn't matter much, for the National Association itself would fall by the wayside by 1875, beset by drunks, gamblers, teams that couldn't finish schedules, and internal bickering.

On a snowy February 2, 1876, a little less than five months shy of Custer's Last Stand, the National League was founded a few blocks east of Washington Square, in New York's Broadway Central Hotel, ostensibly to provide audiences with quality baseball and to uplift the moral standards of the sport. The new league prohibited Sunday games and forbade gambling and liquor on the grounds of its ballparks, rules that were "never strictly applied," according to Charley Ebbets's own reflections on the National League's origins made years later.[7] In any event,

Brooklyn's teams weren't considered well-enough behaved to be admitted into such a league.

In 1881 the American Association was formed to provide the National League with some serious competition. With ballgames scheduled on Sunday and beer served as well, the new league drew ire from the pulpits and some conservatives. But the American Association also had a 25-cent instead of a 50-cent admission, which ironically served to expand the market rather than divide it.

The legacy of the Brooklyn team began when George Taylor, a thirty-year-old night city editor of the *New York Herald*, became convinced that a baseball team would be profitable in Brooklyn, whose population had leaped 40 percent to 600,000 people between 1870 and 1880. Like so many visionaries, Taylor didn't have much money himself, but he knew others who did. In the winter of 1882–83 he found an anonymous backer who provided financial help, allowing him to lease a site located between Fourth and Fifth avenues and Third and Fifth streets in South Brooklyn. The lessor was Edwin Litchfield, an influential force behind Park Slope's residential development.[8]

Taylor's cost estimates for grading the terrain, erecting stands, and signing players became too much for his backer, who offered Taylor the lease in exchange for the privilege of opting out of the deal. Taylor accepted and then turned to John Brice, an attorney, who put Taylor in touch with a real estate dealer, Charles H. Byrne, who had desk space in Brice's Park Row office.

Taylor asked Byrne to consider putting up some cash for the venture. A former journalist and onetime law student, the thirty-nine-year-old Byrne was a slightly older alumnus of Taylor's alma mater, St. Francis Xavier College. After graduation, the intrepid Byrne followed Horace Greeley's advice and went west, entering the purchasing department of the Union Pacific Railroad at its headquarters in Omaha. Byrne became active politically and served as Omaha's county clerk for a time. After his term was up, he decided his future was back east and returned to New York, where he became involved in real estate.

Initially Byrne was skeptical about Taylor's idea and the potential ball club's ability to turn a profit, but he knew Brooklyn had a rich baseball past. The idea appealed to him, and ultimately he turned to a man of greater means: his brother-in-law, Joseph J. Doyle, with whom he also operated a gambling house, legal in those days, on Ann Street in lower Manhattan. With Taylor contributing the lease, the three became partners.

Doyle furnished the preliminary funds to turn the vacant site into a ballpark. After it took $12,000 merely to prepare the ground, Doyle began to get uncomfortable with the amount he'd have to invest, so he enlisted a man with deeper pockets who knew quite a bit about some sports but virtually nothing about baseball: Ferdinand A. Abell, owner and proprietor of Narangansett Pier, a gambling house in the Rhode Island town of the same name. Abell agreed to provide most of the bankroll for the enterprise, and Byrne, becoming more enamored with the new professional team's prospects as time passed, was made president. Despite Byrne's titular role, Doyle and Abell were the ones who had control of the business.[9]

Byrne was said to be a generous man, though quick to respond when provoked; he also tended to be very thorough and a worrier. "Mr. Byrne went into base ball in a business like way and displayed a liberality in securing players and treated them with such justice that he soon made Brooklyn famous among base ball people as a place where employees received better care than anywhere else," the *Brooklyn Daily Eagle* would say about him later.[10]

Byrne opted to buy the group a franchise in the Interstate League, a minor league connected with the American Association, by now the National League's big rival. The loop had teams in Wilmington, Delaware, and in Jersey City, Camden, and other nearby towns. The new ownership group hurried to erect its field, to be called Washington Park, arranging for a single-tier wooden grandstand along with bleachers up the banks of the existing incline, since much of the property sat in a hollowed-out basin some twenty-five feet below the adjacent land and the street.[11]

The ballpark, accommodating several thousand people, was built on historic ground that included the Vechte-Cortelyou House. Built of stone in 1699 to thwart Indian raids, the house once served as Washington's headquarters and also as a centerpiece of the Revolutionary War's Battle of Long Island (now more frequently and accurately referred to as the Battle of Brooklyn) on August 27, 1776. This first battle after the Declaration of Independence was signed was also the war's bloodiest, where 256 of 400 Marylanders of Small's Battalion gave their lives fighting a fierce rearguard action that allowed overwhelmed American forces surrounded on three sides to retreat westward across Gowanus Creek.[12] One hundred and seven years later, Byrne, an otherwise refined gentleman proud of his familiarity with theater and opera, unsentimentally converted Washington's quarters into a ladies' rest room.[13]

By the time Harrisburg baseball team arrived for the opening game slated for May 9, 1883, the park still wasn't complete; as a result the contest was played before a thousand or so fans watching for free on public land at nearby Prospect Park. Taylor managed the team; Brooklyn won 7–1. "Polka Dots" became the Brooklyn team's nickname because of the flashy hosiery they wore their first season; they'd give up the finery before the second campaign because the stockings "were continually fraying," though the nickname held on for a couple of seasons.[14]

Three days after the team's park appearance, and twelve days before President Chester Alan Arthur came to Brooklyn for the Brooklyn Bridge's opening on May 24, 1883, the new baseball franchise had its first game in its Washington Park. Six thousand showed up at the 2,000-seat ball field, a couple of miles due south of the new bridge's Brooklyn anchorage, to watch the home team defeat Trenton, 13 to 6.

One of the charter employees for the new ball club was young Charley Ebbets. He managed to land a job as an assistant secretary and handyman, with charge of all of the park's employees as well as supervision of ticket sales.[15] At twenty-three, he'd already seen a lot of living. He was five and a half years old when the Civil War ended and Lincoln was assassinated. The president's cortege, in its procession through New York, passed not far from the Ebbets house on Spring Street. Aside from that, New York's rich tableau and a walk up or down Broadway made him aware of people in all manner of circumstances. When his parents elected to move to Astoria when he was seven, the young boy found the new environment too quiet.

His education concluded in elementary school, where he was said to have an aptitude for mathematics, and his first job was marking the ends of joists as they were measured on a schooner in Astoria Bay. Over time, baseball became his favorite sport, though he never showed any particular prowess that might have caused him to seriously contemplate becoming a player. To the extent that he decided to pay any attention to politics, and his later involvement suggests he may have, the national political scene featured all the acrimony inherent in any bad time: President Andrew Johnson was impeached and missed conviction by a single vote; President Ulysses Grant's administration was beset by scandal; the Hayes-Tilden election of 1876 was disputed; President James Garfield was assassinated in 1881.

Charley had not yet turned nineteen years old on April 10, 1878, when he married Frances Amelia "Minnie" Broadbent, who was a year younger. Charles Jr. was born in New York City on September 27, 1878. While Charley's father, John, continued to live in Manhattan in Greenwich Village—Charley's mother had died of cancer on July 8, 1871, at around age forty-seven—Charley, Minnie, and Charley Jr. were living on Alexander Avenue between 134th and 135th streets in the Bronx at the time of the 1880 census; with them, too, were Minnie's fifty-five-year-old mother, Amelia, and her twenty-three-year-old sister, Eliza. Living two doors down from them was Charley's older sister, Charlotte, then twenty-nine, and her husband George Bissell, forty-one, a Union Army veteran, who, as a corporal in the Fifth Wisconsin regiment, had heroically forced his retreating company back into a battle that they then won; promoted to sergeant as a result, and eventually promoted to captain, George suffered the loss of his left arm during the Battle of the

Wilderness in 1864 in Spotsylvania County in Virginia. After the war, he became a Customs House clerk, a job that he would keep. The rest of Charley's siblings, except for his brother John, then twenty-seven and a clerk and bookkeeper who favored Manhattan, were living with Charlotte and George: James Tunis Ebbets was then twenty-five; Charley's younger brother, William Snell Ebbets, was eighteen; the youngest, Ada Elizabeth, was listed as fourteen years of age in the 1880 census. George's family also had Kate Stafford, an Irish domestic, living with them. In September of that year, Charley and Minnie had their second child, a daughter, Florence; she died as an infant.[16]

By the early 1880s, now in his early twenties, Charley had already been a draftsman for William T. Beer's architectural firm in Manhattan, where he helped draw up the plans for the Metropolitan Hotel. He also worked on Niblo's Garden, one of New York's more prominent popular amusement centers, and had experience in publishing, first with Dick & Fitzgerald book publishers, and later as a subscription clerk working for Frank Leslie, whose illustrated newspaper had wide circulation in New York.

Ebbets had an entrepreneurial streak, continually striving, trying new things. He went as far as printing inexpensive editions of novels and textbooks on his own, hired salesmen to sell them, and even sold the books door-to-door himself when his salesmen's efforts floundered.

Although it is not clear exactly when Charley and Minnie moved to Brooklyn, their family was growing. Another daughter, Lydia Maie, was born in November 1882. It is also apparent that whatever family harmony existed on Alexander Avenue had to suffer as a result of the actions of Charley's older brother James. James married Mary Elizabeth Moore in January 1881, and on December 8, 1882, he sued all of his siblings and their spouses—and even his own wife—over the distribution of two parcels of land named in the will of his great-grandfather, William Quick. The land in question was at 41 Broad Street and 473 Greenwich. Ted Steele notes in his Ebbets family genealogy, "In December 1883, the New York State Supreme Court ruled in James's favor. Later amended filings in 1883, 1884 and 1885 expanded the defendant list to 22, plus several business enterprises."[17] Whatever the result, there was an accommodation with Charley at some juncture, since James would one day be in his employ with the Dodgers as an assistant secretary of the ball club, and Charley himself would be the source in a reporter's story alluding to how he kept the proceeds from his share of the sale of a family business property on Broad Street in lower Manhattan and added to it until, in 1907, he had saved $125,000.

Charley became involved with the Brooklyn baseball franchise at its inception through his brother John, who was acquainted with the new ownership group. During that first season, the Brooklyn team picked up a number of players from the Camden Merritts after that team disbanded on July 20, 1883. The strength of this new talent allowed Brooklyn to win that year's Interstate League pennant, or what Ebbets would later call a handkerchief as opposed to a real flag.[18] With Byrne handling the political machinations, the development provided a springboard to join the American Association, which, together with the National League, constituted the highest level of play at that time. Brooklyn played in the American Association for the next six seasons. Half the Brooklyn players got married during 1887 and during the course of the following winter, and for the next two years, the fans called the team the Bridegrooms, or simply the Grooms.

Meanwhile young Ebbets was gaining more latitude with his employers, skillfully arranging schedules and assuming increasingly greater supervisory roles in the new enterprise's operations. He drew upon his publishing experience, using a hand press under the bleachers to produce scorecards and initiate their sale; he hawked them in the stands himself, too.

The winter of 1888 featured a mammoth blizzard that immobilized New York between March 11 and March 14. Charley's father, then sixty-four years old and living at 76 MacDougal Street between Bleecker and Houston in the heart of Greenwich Village, died two days later.

Charley had been making a name for himself that winter, managing the Nassau Toboggan Slide amid snow, ice, and hay bales at Washington Park, where a two-hundred-foot chute propelled toboggans clear across an icy field into straw festooned over an incline on the side. Promotional events conjured up by Charley for the kids and teachers of P.S. 39 and for reporters prompted the *Evening Sun* to call him "the best toboggan slide manager in the country."[19]

As the years rolled by and his prominence in baseball increased, the sporting press would often tout Charles Hercules Ebbets; the name seemed to fit him and the enormity of some of the challenges he faced. Charley never signed his name that way; never used it. Actually, the middle initial stood for Henry.[20] But no one ever bothered to let a little detail like that interfere with a good story.

In 1889, while being managed by Bill McGunnigle, the American Association Brooklyn Bridegrooms had their Washington Park destroyed by fire at midnight, Saturday, May 18; it was rebuilt in wood with the capacity upped by an extra 2,000 seats to 4,000—wooden planks with no seat backs—within twelve days.[21] The team went on to win a pennant, and played an acrimonious "world series" with the National League Giants from across the East River in Manhattan. The Giants prevailed in the best-of-eleven series, six games to three, but the victory didn't do anything to quell the enmity the New Yorkers felt for the Brooklyn team, even after besting them: "We will never play your team again," Giants owner John Day said to Byrne. "Your players are dirty. They constantly stall and complain. We've been deprived of three games by trickery," he said, alluding to Brooklyn's stalling while holding a lead so games could be called on account of darkness. "I don't mind losing games on their merits," Day added, "but I do mind being robbed of them." [22]

Day's threat was empty. In 1890 the Brooklyn team, which was considering switching leagues anyway, joined the National League after a clique of owners in the American Association who were jealous of Byrne's standing in the greater baseball community plotted to keep the Brooklyn team—and Cincinnati's as well—off all of the circuit's key committees. [23] The idea was ludicrous, since Byrne was well regarded throughout baseball and considered the game's preeminent statesman.

Manager McGunnigle brought the Brooklyn team home as winners again in the new circuit, winning the regular season race against the Giants and pulling off an unmatched feat of having back-to-back championships with the same team in different leagues. By this time the fans had taken to calling the Brooklyn team the "Trolley Dodgers," since that practice was becoming either an attendant charm or a daunting facet of Brooklyn life.

The ball club's showing also proved fortunate in a battle for the fans' allegiance, since the new Players' League, also known as the Brotherhood, fielded a local entry in 1890 called the Wonders. The new team was backed, among others, by the Flatbush real estate mogul and financier George Chauncey, who had been a player on the old Excelsiors, but part of the money for league interests had also come from the purse of the Kings County Elevated Railroad. [24] Chauncey and an associate, E. F. Linton, saw a chance to build traffic for the line as well as build up a new section of the city that would help expand their businesses. The team played at Eastern Park over in Brooklyn's East New York section, a ballpark featuring a double-deck wooden stand whose roof at each end was finished with a turret topped by a conical spire. Bleachers extended the seating from first base on one side and from third base on the other. Unfortunately, the park's remote location at Eastern Parkway and what was then Vesta (in the vicinity of what is now Van Sinderen) Avenue, was at that time too far from Brooklyn's major population centers, a few miles west.

The new league folded at the end of the year, but Chauncey liked the action. He got together with the Trolley Dodgers ownership group and, even though he had just taken a financial beating in a bellied-up league, bought his way into a position of power with the older, more established franchise. In coming to terms, he convinced the baseball champions to move out of Washington Park in South Brooklyn over to Eastern Park.

Another item on Chauncey's agenda was firing the successful McGunnigle in order to bring in John Montgomery Ward, the former manager of his old Players' League team and largely the architect behind the whole league. Even though McGunnigle had just brought home two consecutive championships, Doyle and his crew shamelessly went along with the summary dismissal of their man. As sportswriter Frank Graham later said, this action probably minted the adage "There is no sentiment in baseball."

The Dodgers, meanwhile, were incorporated as the Brooklyn Baseball Club; the stock of 100 shares capitalized at $250,000 with the Byrne-Doyle-Abell group taking just over 50 percent (Taylor had sold his interest in 1885) and the Chauncey group, with associates E. F. Linton and H. J. Robinson, taking the balance.[25] Thereafter the team went into a tailspin. The sole saving grace of Chauncey's suggestions was that he happened to notice Charley Ebbets. Impressed with Ebbets, who turned thirty-one years old in the fall of 1890, Chauncey offered to sell him stock; when Ebbets went to express his gratitude, Chauncey stopped him. "It isn't because I like you that I am selling you this, although I do like you. I am selling it to you because I know that owning it will be an even greater spur to you—that it will make you work even harder than you have so far, if that's possible. I think I have sized you up rightly as a young man who appreciates an investment like this, who will do his best to improve it. And my investment, too."[26]

But the investment didn't do well. The team fell to sixth in an eight-team league, and fans didn't like making the trip all the way out to East New York. Doyle sold his interest to Abell. Byrne took the team's ill fortunes to heart, and with financial losses increasingly annually, the stress and fret impaired his health. The vaunted John Montgomery Ward left as manager in 1893 and was followed by Dave Foutz, a popular pitcher who unfortunately would be ill for most of the time he managed the team.

Worse yet, the team did poorly while Brooklyn was growing rapidly. Census figures in 1890 revealed that Brooklyn's population had increased within the previous decade by another 33 percent to 800,000 people. In the few short years since its opening, the Brooklyn Bridge had already had far-reaching consequences for Brooklyn. Ice floes in the East River couldn't inhibit transport or commerce anymore, and the linkage of Brooklyn and New York spurred both residential and commercial development in Brooklyn and a greater interdependence between both municipalities.

Within Kings County, the independent towns established in the 1600s were disappearing. In 1894 Flatbush, New Utrecht, and Gravesend incorporated into Brooklyn, even though many of the so-called rural political leaders were opposed. Even in the old Dutch settlement of Flatlands, "progressive ideas" about becoming part of the city of Brooklyn permeated the local talk, to the consternation of those who felt their way of life was better off left alone, with their towns remaining independent. Critics exclaimed that before too long those Brooklyn city leaders would cut a deal and merge with New York, and wondered why they would want to couple their idyllic existence with the public affairs of any entity that large. And while the leaders at Brooklyn City Hall were eyeing and completing the annexation of the smaller independent towns to Brooklyn, they *were* considering plans to merge their city with New York. It was practical; commercial and residential real estate development and Brooklyn's vast potential for further real estate development fueled the need for infrastructure expansion. All of that created a situation in which Brooklyn's municipal government could maximize its borrowing. New York was where all the major businesses were, and its tax coffers, rich by comparison, could build Brooklyn's roads, sewers, and schools.

The pace of Brooklyn life had been changing for some time. Although the trolleys that sped down the borough's roads provided key linkages to jobs and commerce that helped promote economic growth, they also were killing an average of one pedestrian a week. Brooklyn now had a large industrial base with thousands of factories; the Brooklyn Navy Yard was the nation's largest; more meat was dressed in Brooklyn than in any city save Chicago; Coney Island was coveted as a resort destination for the wealthy.

By 1895 Charley and Minnie Ebbets were living at 328 First Street in Brooklyn, just a few blocks from Washington Park, with their four children: Charles Jr. was seventeen; Maie, thirteen; Anna, nine; and Genevieve was three. A live-in servant assisted Minnie. Sometimes there were more than just the in-house chores to contend with. "To help with expenses, the players' uniforms were washed and dried in my grandmother's own home," Dorothy Ebbets Dollmeyer wrote of Minnie Ebbets. "It must have been quite a display for the neighbors to have all those uniforms on the clothes lines in one of the better neighborhoods. My grandmother didn't do the laundry herself; she had people come in and take care of those chores. But when grandfather brought home newspapermen or baseball people, she herself would get out of bed and prepare the midnight suppers rather than waking the cook. She never complained about these inconveniences. She was smart enough to figure that was also her income she was assuring."[27]

Charley was active locally. An avid bowler, he belonged to a number of social clubs and was widely known. Like most of the politically connected with wide business interests, Ebbets favored consolidation not only of the independent towns within Kings County with Brooklyn, but also of Brooklyn with New York. He was a Democrat, but like almost every Brooklynite, he kept a wary eye on Tammany Hall. Given his reputation, popularity, and extensive contacts, and with the urging of backers like Chauncey, he willingly tried his hand at politics, and in doing so opened an even wider reservoir of political, social, and business ties. In 1895 he ran as a Democratic candidate for the State Assembly from the 12th Assembly District, which covered Park Slope. He outpolled Republican C. L. Lincoln in a close race, 4,101 to 3,852, winning 48 percent of the vote compared with his opponent's 45 percent, with four other fringe candidates amassing another 616 votes.

On January 1, 1896, Flatlands was annexed, and the city of Brooklyn included all six of its original towns. Brooklyn had grown into Kings County's borders; the two entities had become synonymous. The rest of the year proved to be a bad one for Ebbets and his team. Doyle, an original investor, died that year, Ebbets succeeding him as club secretary; the team finished tied for ninth in a twelve-team league; old fan favorite and former manager Dave Foutz died after the season at his Baltimore home; and, in a Republican year when William McKinley was swept into the White House, Charley was defeated in his reelection bid. His opponent, Republican Henry H. Abell (apparently no relation to Ferdinand), who would later become a police commissioner, polled 5,420 votes, or 52 percent, to Charley's 4,752 votes, or 46 percent, the remainder split among the Progressive, Socialist-Labor, and Populist candidates.

Charley ran again in 1897, and this time was elected for a four-year City Council term.[28] Another Democrat elected that November, with whom Charley would become more friendly, would play a prominent role with Ebbets and the Dodgers down the road: Stephen W. McKeever.[29] Fifteen years later, Ebbets and the McKeever brothers would become partners in the Brooklyn National League franchise. Ebbets's deliberations with other politicos gave him information quite useful for the day when he would seek a parcel of land for his new ballpark: discussions through the turn of the century were wide-ranging about the upcoming plans for a subway system, and where and how that subway system and the neighborhoods alongside it would grow.

Less than two months afterward, Brooklyn's incorporation into the greater city of New York would become official. On January 1, 1898, the city of Brooklyn would officially disappear, and during the last few hours on New Year's Eve, as the witching hour approached, the omens were evident: at the Common Council Chamber at the flower-bedecked City Hall—soon to become Borough Hall—a silk American flag was dipped in deference to Brooklyn's; a driving rain lashed the streets; and the political oratory was long, sentimental, and warily optimistic. Five former Brooklyn mayors and Frederick Wurster, the current mayor, were present, along with a full contingent from the Society of Old Brooklynites.

"That will be the crucial test of annexation, the fiscal test," thundered St. Clair McKelway, the editor of the *Brooklyn Daily Eagle*, getting to the nub of things. "The honey must henceforth come the way of all who have made it."[30]

It also was on this New Year's, the most notable of Brooklyn's historic days, when Councilman-elect Charles Ebbets took control of the Dodgers. The announcement was made at a dinner at Brooklyn's Clarendon Hotel. Ebbets had purchased 40 percent of the team from the old Brotherhood interests in a deal consummated the previous day in Alfred M. Kiddle's office in New York's Potter Building. By using his savings and borrowing as much as he could, Ebbets had bought up the minority interest. Meanwhile his partner Ferdinand Abell, tired of the losses that had begun with the advent of the Players' League and that had continued throughout the 1890s, was only too happy to give Ebbets an option on his shares until February 1. Although Charley agreed to make the purchase and it would have brought his holdings up to 85 percent, he ultimately wasn't able to swing it. Abell, not anxious to sell to anyone else, held the shares.

When the guests had been seated, Ebbets, by now a handsome thirty-eight-year-old with a close-cropped haircut and sideburns but with a generous handlebar mustache, began by acknowledging an absent friend: "Gentlemen, I know it is not customary to inaugurate affairs of this sort with a toast, but I am going to depart from the usual custom and offer one; I ask you to drink to health of Charles H. Byrne, president of the Brooklyn Baseball Club, who is lying seriously ill, and to his speedy recovery."[31]

Byrne, suffering from a variety of ailments, had rallied and showed some slight improvement, but he slipped into a coma and died three days later at his home at 107 West Eleventh Street in Manhattan. The *Brooklyn Daily Eagle* called him the "Napoleon of Baseball," and in an editorial on January 5 said, "Few men were better known and fewer still are held in the esteem which he enjoyed."

Ferdinand Abell had been a hands-off owner, but the $12,000 in losses that he sustained with his ballclub holdings after the 1896 season exasperated him. Nevertheless, even after Charley failed to exercise his option, Abell, and Chauncey, who retained an interest, were content to let Charley run the club. One of the first things Ebbets decided, with their assent, was to move the ball club back to South Brooklyn. "We have to get back to where it's easy for the fans to get to us," Ebbets said.[32]

Subsequently he announced that a suitable site had been found in South Brooklyn for what would be the "new" Washington Park. The grandstand and bleachers, financed largely by the street railway companies, which recognized that greater attendance was in their interest, were erected in the spring of 1898 between First and Third streets and Third and Fourth avenues. This second Washington Park, located diagonally across the street from the old location at Third Street and Fourth Avenue, was built to the north and west rather than to the south and east like its predecessor. The new Washington Park was just a block away from the First Street Basin off the Gowanus Canal and was susceptible to an occasional malodorous downwind breeze. The field had home plate on the Third Street and Fourth Avenue side, making right field the sun field. The single-tier, covered wooden grandstand went as far as first base along the Fourth Avenue side and just past the skin of the infield on the third base, or Third Street, side.

Past the grandstand, a long set of bleachers in two separate sections was on the first base side; a solo, smaller bleacher section was down the third base line, which had the larger grandstand. Another bleacher stand ran from straightaway center to left-center field.

First Street, behind the right-field fence, was intersected at a perpendicular angle a third of the way down the block by Denton Place, a one-block-long street that coincidentally matched the given name of a phenomenal thirty-year-old pitcher for Cleveland, Denton True "Cy" Young, by then an eight-year veteran with 214 of his 511 career wins amassed. A series of several-story, walk-up apartments were on the north side of First Street, between Denton and another street that ran parallel to it another third of the way down the block, Whitwell Place. The buildings were commonly known as the "guinea flats" after the Italians that lived in them, "guinea" being a slur so frequently applied at the time that it wasn't even thought of as one.

Ebbets and his partners resented the fact that people could watch from their windows across the street for free or, worse yet, could seat people on the roof of any of those buildings to take in the game for a modest fee or for nothing. While inspecting the new 50- and 25-cent seats under construction at the new park, Ebbets made clear his antipathy for giving away the product: "I know it has been the custom in baseball for many years to issue complimentary tickets for the opening game of the season, but the practice has been overdone. We have decided on an innovation this year," he added. "We will issue no invitations.

The grounds will be handsomely decorated, and we will have a concert, but no free tickets.

"On next Friday," he continued, "the new grounds will be thrown open at 1 P.M., and at 2 P.M., the 23rd Regiment Band will begin a concert. At 3:20 P.M. an American flag will be raised by my daughter, Miss Maie Ebbets, after which a photograph will taken of the enclosure, and the game between Brooklyn and Philadelphia will begin at 4 P.M."[33]

Charley's immediate preoccupation in 1898 was twofold: putting a decent product on the field and getting fans in the stands. "The management of the team will remain in the hands of Mr. Barnie," Ebbets said, referring to Billy Barnie, the pilot who had led the team in 1897. "We shall start out afresh, past feelings, if there are any, will be buried."[34] Things didn't stay that way for too long; Charley sacked his manager when the team had a 15–20 record after only thirty-five games. Ebbets, who had never played himself, then went down on the bench to manage. In the dugout, wearing street clothes and a beaver hat, Ebbets did worse. He went 38–68, ending his notion that he might be able to handle the manager's role by finishing tenth in a twelve-team league. It would be his sole effort as a field manager.

The league had a terrible year at the gate in 1898, with the public preoccupied by the Spanish-American War. But over the winter, because of the peculiar ways of syndicate baseball, the Dodgers' fortunes abruptly turned around. In those days, owners could own shares in more than one team. Multiteam owners acted as puppeteers, pulling the strings of fan loyalty to stack one team at the expense of another. Though the conflict of interest inherent in one person's owning a piece of more than one team raised some ire among the ethical, league statutes permitted it. Owners could do whatever they pleased.

The Baltimore Orioles had suffered a drop in attendance, and their owner, Harry B. Von der Horst, was looking for a new deal. Seven years earlier, Baltimore had one of the worst teams in the league. In 1892, after recruiting Ned Hanlon to manage, it developed one of the best. Von der Horst began sizing up the opportunity for profitability in the Brooklyn market, liked Ebbets, and began talking with Abell. Before long, an agreement was reached. Von der Horst received a substantial interest in the Brooklyn team in a stock swap, picking up some of Abell's and Chauncey's stock as well as some of the Byrne and Doyle shares when those heirs disposed of their holdings. Ebbets, still a minor stockholder, picked up some shares in the deal and also was reelected president, while Hanlon was cut in as a minor stockholder.

The Baltimore roster was gutted immediately. Von der Horst sent Hanlon north to manage Brooklyn in 1899, and Hanlon, in turn, took several players with him. The most famous of these was outfielder

Wee Willie "Hit 'em Where They Ain't" Keeler, born on Pulaski Street in Brooklyn's Williamsburg section. Hanlon also brought Hughie Jennings, who would play mostly at first base, and outfielder Joe Kelley.

Two other Baltimore players, a third baseman and a catcher, refused to move to Brooklyn. The third baseman was a short, slight, 5' 7", 155-pound Irish scrapper from upstate New York named John McGraw. The catcher hailed from Bolton, Massachusetts, was an inch and a half taller and about 70 pounds heavier. His name was Wilbert Robinson. The pair were co-owners of Baltimore's Diamond Café, a three-story restaurant and watering hole on North Howard Street that had pool tables, bowling alleys, and a reading room. In the years to come, McGraw and Robinson would make their mark on New York City baseball history and become antagonists in the one of the greatest rivalries in sports, that of the New York Giants and the Brooklyn Dodgers.

For the next two years, in 1899 and 1900, the new players that Hanlon managed brought Brooklyn to the top of the baseball world. Someone in the press box nicknamed them the "Superbas," after a popular vaudeville act known as Hanlon's Superbas. The name caught on quickly and would persist with the fans long after Hanlon was gone. Meanwhile Brooklyn's urbanization was practically complete, reflecting America's rural-to-urban metamorphosis. In 1900, only two years after annexation, the borough of Brooklyn had 1,166,582 residents; the census indicated that of 476,498 workers, only 2,538 (½ of 1 percent) were agricultural.

The Superbas'—and Hanlon's—decline began the following year, when the upstart American League, which was the old Western League aspiring to major league status under the leadership of former sportswriter Ban Johnson, began raiding National League rosters. With the new league plucking some of Brooklyn's most prominent stars, the Superbas slid to third in 1901. Ebbets, preoccupied with baseball and business in general, decided not to seek reelection to the City Council.

The team finished a distant second the following year. After that, its reversal was more acute. The player raids were enough to convince both Von der Horst and Abell to unload their stock. Von der Horst was in poor health and Abell, who had simply had enough, sold his stake to Ebbets. When American League president Ban Johnson had his way and the Baltimore franchise was moved to New York to become the Highlanders in 1903, Brooklyn manager Hanlon became convinced that he should attempt to buy Von der Horst's shares, combine them with his own, and move the Brooklyn club down to Baltimore.

Ebbets refused to consider moving the Superbas out of Brooklyn. All of his money had gone toward purchasing Abell's stock, but now, to outbid Hanlon for Von der Horst's, he turned to a friend, Henry Medicus, who owned a furniture company. Medicus gave Ebbets the cash he needed, and Hanlon's bid to control the team's fortunes and whereabouts was thwarted.

Ebbets made Medicus treasurer and installed his son, Charles Jr., now in his mid-twenties, as club secretary. As for Hanlon, Ebbets allowed him to stay as field manager, though Charley cut his salary from $11,000 to $7,500 when the ownership battle was over. The team grew increasingly worse, finishing fifth, sixth, and eighth between 1903 and 1905. By the end of the 1905 season, the two men were barely on speaking terms. Rather than continue, Hanlon elected to leave to manage the Reds.

By 1907 Ebbets and Medicus had bought out the remaining few shares that still had been held by Hanlon, consolidating their holdings. Charley's attitude as president of the club hadn't changed much since he took over the team in 1898, as he illustrated when defining his current responsibilities as club president to *Eagle* reporter Willis Brooks: "The first is to dodge people who want passes to the baseball games. The next is to look pleasant and say agreeable things when I am cornered by such persons as I have been unable to dodge. And the third is to restrain myself from giving the requested passes. The rest of my duties are merely perfunctory. They give me no trouble whatever." Ebbets said everybody prevailed upon him: elevator boys, bootblacks, card partners, cigar sellers, bartenders, waiters who spilled soup down his back, politicians who regarded themselves as what he called "a constitutionally-privileged class in office or out." He went on, "Rich men ask for passes because they are rich, poor men ask for passes because they are poor. I believe there is only one argument that hasn't yet been advanced by anybody as a means of obtaining a baseball pass. No red-headed man has asked for one on the grounds that he is red-headed. Still, there is time for him yet."[35]

But at least two problems other than freeloaders also preoccupied Ebbets. Not only were his Superbas unable to contend for the pennant; worse yet, the hated New York Giants were perennial contenders and sometime champions. The combative John McGraw, who had taken the job managing the Giants five years earlier, wasn't beyond sticking his defiant chin in the face of any umpire, or of anyone else for that matter, and that included Ebbets. The seeds of their lifelong antipathy were planted by an incident in Washington Park one day in 1905. The Giants were drubbing the home team while Ebbets, sitting in his box, was watching McGraw in an argument with the umpires. Soon Charley himself became entangled in the jawing back and forth, and McGraw hurled an epithet in Ebbets's direction.

At that point an indignant Ebbets got up out of his seat. What McGraw had called him is left to conjecture, since the exact words weren't seen as fit by editors to record. But the tenor of the conversation was such that Ebbets, incredulous, asked McGraw to repeat what he said, whereupon McGraw loudly embellished it with an additional adjective for all within earshot. Ebbets subsequently lodged a protest with the league, but National League president Harry Pulliam preferred to avoid McGraw rather than to deal with him. Nothing came of it. The continuing success of the Giants rankled Charley, who didn't even like to make deals with them; he said he wouldn't give McGraw the smoke off his tea.

Despite Brooklyn's inability to contend for the pennant in those years of the century's first decade, fans were still turning out, especially for big games and holidays. The inadequate capacity of Washington Park on those occasions frustrated Charley, and when he saw fans milling around in the street, unable to get inside, he used his mathematical prowess to glumly do some quick mental calculations to ascertain how much money he was losing.

Before Charley Ebbets could fulfill his dream and build his new ballpark, he had to find a place for it. He first thought about remodeling his team's existing home, but abandoned that idea after contemplating the cost. He had been offered the the Washington Park site between First and Third streets and Third and Fourth avenues in South Brooklyn for $350,000, but thought the amount too much to spend, especially since the ballpark was built on landfill. It would cost him at least $50,000 more to prepare the ground for a concrete stand, especially a double-decked one.

A concrete stand was a priority, too, since wooden ballparks were an ever-present fire hazard, a constant liability and a source of worry. Fire had always been an overwhelming threat to the wooden ballpark: in just one season, 1894, National League parks were either damaged or destroyed by fire in Baltimore, Philadelphia, Boston, and Chicago.[36] Over the years there were still more blazes, and the prospect of a disaster always haunted a team owner's mind.

Charley had kept his share of the proceeds after an old family business property at 41 Broad Street in Manhattan was sold, adding to it assiduously until he had $125,000 saved, a threshold reached in 1907. With the advent of warmer weather, Charley began to devote his attention to his dream of constructing a big new baseball field. Although the Superbas had disturbingly settled into a pattern of second-division mediocrity, Ebbets, keeping his thoughts to himself, began beating the bushes in search of a new site. It took that season and most of the next for him to figure it out.

The specific piece of land that Charley wanted was east of Grand Army Plaza, down the first few blocks of Eastern Parkway and then several streets south on Bedford Avenue. It was bounded by Bedford Avenue on the east, Cedar Place on the west, Montgomery Street on the north, and Sullivan Place, misidentified on later blueprints as Sullivan Street, on the south. (A common mistake; the real Sullivan Street, meanwhile, remains in Red Hook, in the waterfront Brooklyn neighborhood that has the best views of the Statue of Liberty.)

The land was in the southwest part of an area called Crow Hill, just east of the Flatbush Avenue–Eastern Parkway–Washington Avenue triangular tract that was, for the most part, an ash dump, the exception being the portion of the triangle on Eastern Parkway that provided street frontage and grounds for the Brooklyn Institute of Arts and Sciences, or what would later become the Brooklyn Museum.

Even though this was barely a mile and a half east of Washington Park as the crow flies, it was up and over the long incline of the precisely named Park Slope, across and past the eastern side of Prospect Park, difficult to get to via the streets from the westernmost part of Brooklyn, which at that time included some of the borough's more populated neighborhoods like South Brooklyn, Brooklyn Heights, and Red Hook, as well as the commercial areas in downtown Brooklyn. Ebbets's confidantes were somewhat skeptical, reasoning that the site was too far from the borough's population centers.

Although building and land speculators were beginning to buy up parcels or tracts in the area, the neighborhood still had relatively wide-open spaces during the early years of the century, sometimes with only one or two ramshackle houses per block. A spate of colorful characters were living there. A good local contingent, for instance, was in the audience at the Old Golden City Club, several miles to the southeast in Brooklyn's far reaches of Canarsie, where a turn-of-the century bout featured two popular Crow Hill boxers: one, a young law student, Art Rotolo, was attended in his corner by Pop Ludden and Jo Hammond; the other, Pancho the Mexican Peanut Vendor, was sponged down between rounds by Tutty Gianni and Georgie Lee. Pop Jinks was the referee. Although the winner, if any, wasn't mentioned, the contestants and the fight fans all retired to Eddie Yander's Saloon, also known as Chateau Ug, and anyone missing the affair had only to check with Mattie Mathews to determine whether or not it was a good time, since Mattie, nicknamed George Washington, reportedly never lied.[37]

There were others: Squat Gregory, reputed to weigh a ton; Packey Mullins, who was said to be capable of licking his weight in wildcats; Boo Boo Shoe, attracting the girls with "that little dance of his"; Boochie Horseman, who, with Gong Gong Butlerlip, his manager, operated a fish market at Troy and Bergen that was farther to the north and east of Ebbets's secretly targeted ballpark parcel. Local neighborhood ballgames fostered some enthusiasm, too, and were often umpired by Jay Wren, who had a vested interest in the affairs: he had a partnership with Danny Morgan, selling hot clam chowder with tidbits of fresh fish from a peddler's wagon, a partnership that dissolved one Sunday when a foul ball landed in the chowder pot and precipitated an argument between the pair.[38]

It was area targeted for development, till then only a farmlike landscape that was changing as newly laid-down street grids bracketed the bumpy fields and cackling chickens of a passing way of life. The territory across the blocks that Ebbets's gaze fell upon was often casually called Goatville or Pigtown, reflecting the widespread presence of farm animals. Such names were common throughout Brooklyn then, and would persist even into the 1950s in the few places where the animals remained.

There were fourteen wooden buildings in 1908 bordering the western side—Cedar Place—of what would become the Ebbets Field site. Only two structures were officially listed on the Sullivan Place side, though fourteen parcels were apportioned. One block west of the site, on Franklin Avenue, the imposing Consumers Park Brewery took up half a block. The Hygienic Ice Company stood next to the brewery. Unlike populous South Brooklyn, stands of row housing in Crow Hill were few in 1908 and 1909.

Ebbets felt optimistic about his intended site because Brooklyn was growing on each side of it. He knew from his City Council days and through his business contacts just how the land would develop, and he knew that people would be able to get to this spot largely because of the improved service offered by the Brooklyn Rapid Transit Company. A handful of trolleys would pass nearby and so, ultimately, would the Brighton line of the new subway system. Charley was seeing something the others weren't. For now, it would have to remain a tightly held secret if it was to get done.

Charley saw the trip to the great new ballpark he would build almost as a quick, pleasurable excursion. Going around the northern end of Prospect Park from Park Slope, or coming down Flatbush Avenue from the Navy Yard or downtown Brooklyn, the route would be glorious: people would pass the Soldiers and Sailors Arch in Grand Army Plaza, dedicated to the defenders of the Union. Maybe the symbolism of the breathtaking Frederick MacMonnies sculpture atop the arch would rub off on the team's fortunes: Victory in her chariot, flanked by angels.

CHAPTER THREE

A Steward in the Rough

It was a pre-Christmas bacchanal, a lavish fete at the old Waldorf-Astoria at 34th and Fifth, and it would present the opportunity for an utterance that subjected the speaker to ridicule for years. The words, meantime, turned out to be more prescient than any of them could ever dream. The time was December 1909; the affair's host was Pirates owner Barney Dreyfuss, celebrating his team's seven-game World Series victory over the Tigers, an event pitting Detroit's steed of the spikes, Ty Cobb, against Pittsburgh's mythic warhorse, bowlegged Honus Wagner. Neither, of course, had disappointed: Cobb, upon reaching first base, yelled over to shortstop, "I'm coming down, Krauthead," and the Dutchman, beckoning him ahead, obliged the Peach's flashing metal by shoving the horsehide down his gullet, loosening a few teeth in the putout's course.

The *Sporting News* called the dinner "one of the biggest social events ever known in the history of baseball." Cap Anson, Willie Keeler, Christy Mathewson, John McGraw, Charlie Comiskey, and scores of others were there, culminating a year filled with noteworthy events.

The milestones were major. The major leagues' first concrete-and-steel ballpark, Shibe Park, was opened on

April 12 for the Athletics in Philadelphia. Named after team owner Ben Shibe, the field was 340 feet down the right-field line, 378 feet in left, and a whopping 515 feet to straightaway center field; it had a double-deck grandstand from first to third base and bleachers running down the foul lines.

On June 30, the second of its kind, Forbes Field, was opened outside Pittsburgh.[1] The ballpark's grounds were on seven acres of what had formerly been part of Schenley Farms. "Originally," writes baseball historian Lawrence Ritter, "Forbes Field consisted of a roofed double-decked grandstand that curved around home plate and extended 25 to 30 feet past first and third bases. On top of the grandstand was a mini third deck, consisting of a covered row of box seats that stretched from one end of the grandstand roof to the other. The roof boxes were apparently the 1909 equivalent of today's luxury sky boxes."[2] The park had massive amounts of real estate in each direction: 376 feet down the right-field line and 360 feet in left, while center field was 476 feet away.

As much as all of this gave baseball reasons to celebrate, tragedy followed shortly thereafter. On July 29, National League president Harry Pulliam, under extreme stress from the job and suffering from nervous exhaustion, killed himself with a single shot to the head in his room at the New York Athletic Club. His successor, John Heydler, was opposed in enough quarters that he would only last through little more than the season.

Into this gathering marking the year's events came Charley Ebbets, arriving at the dinner's rostrum as a stand-in speaker for Giants owner John T. Brush, who was indisposed. Charley Ebbets had been in baseball for twenty-six years by then and had run the Brooklyn ball club for twelve years, and since the successive championship years atop the National League at the turn of the century, his team had continued to paddle along in underwhelming fashion. Ebbets was fifty years old now, and though his team was coming off a trove of second-division finishes, he'd already provided long and meritorious service to the game.

Like every old politico, Ebbets was tenacious in holding a floor when it was granted him, and on this particular evening, he waxed on about the history of baseball. Finally, he uttered the single line for which he was remembered more than any other. It was a line W. A. Phelon had used in *Sporting Life* a year earlier, but it stuck to Charley like a fly to paper.

"Baseball," he said, "is in its infancy."

He was asked to repeat it for the benefit of someone in the back of the room. He evoked some unintended laughter from the ballplayers, club executives, and assorted hangers-on in the crowd of two hundred, and still more when a heckler yelled, "She's a pretty old infant; she's been toddling around since 1839!"[3] Another well-oiled guest offered, "I ain't heard you right yet," and a somewhat indignant Ebbets sallied forth again with his prophecy.

When he gave that speech, Charley could reveal little about his own grand ambition that fueled his vision of optimism. Fifteen months before, in September 1908, Charley—through two layers of intermediaries—had begun buying up parcels in secret for the purpose of building his own concrete-and-steel baseball park, not even showing his wife, Minnie, the site. His son, Charley Jr., knew, of course, as did another father-and-son team.

Ebbets Sr. knew that it would take an experienced and astute New York hand to help manage the process. His closest associate in mounting his effort to move secretly was an old political and personal friend, Bernard J. "Barney" York. The sixty-seven-year-old attorney for the Brooklyn baseball club had grown up in lower Manhattan, not far from the house on Spring Street that was Ebbets's first home. York had a long and celebrated career in Democratic Party affairs, first appointed as clerk of the Court of Sessions as far back as 1868. York had held that post for twenty-eight years and had served in 1898 as greater New York's first police commissioner. His son Frank, a graduate of Columbia Law School and his law partner, also knew about the site.

The first step in Ebbets's new enterprise was the establishment of a dummy company to purchase the land on which to build. The four men understood that his plans would have to remain a tightly held secret if the ballpark was to become a reality. No one could associate this company with Ebbets or the building of a baseball park, lest holdouts develop among the current landowners, squeezing him for unreasonable or unattainable amounts of cash. Nor could public condemnation efforts be used to help him secure a certain-size, preapportioned parcel; government didn't play such roles then.

The name for the dummy company Ebbets wanted to establish was chosen when Barney and Charley opened a dictionary to a page with the word "Pylon" on the top. York then hired realtor H. C. Pyle to acquire the property without mentioning to Pyle that he was working for Ebbets and with the proviso that his own name be kept out of any negotiations that might ensue. George Gray and Charles Brown were the agents working for Pyle who did the negotiating and buying.

By 1910 the 28,800-seat concrete-and-steel Comiskey Park opened in Chicago.[4] Down in Washington Park, Charley now had Bill Dahlen managing the club, a veteran of the old Chicago White Stockings who came to Brooklyn in time for the two consecutive turn-of-the century championship teams. Out in Crow Hill, two blocks west of the ballpark site Charley secretly coveted, the ash dump bordering Brooklyn's

Washington Avenue was officially designated by its new name: the Brooklyn Botanic Garden. Olmsted Brothers Landscape Architects, the firm co-founded by Frederick Law Olmsted, who co-designed Central Park and Prospect Park, completed a topographical survey for the Botanic Garden's roadways, pathways, and esplanade. By the time construction on the Garden began, the newspapers began referring to the neighboring area as Crown Heights, nothing more than a real estate marketeer's embellishment of the original name. It's a bit easier to sell building lots for "Crown Heights" than it is for "Crow Hill."

Ebbets, meanwhile, also had by now hired an architect to help him with the ballpark plans. Clarence Randall Van Buskirk first had an office on Fulton Street, but by 1910 he had established himself at 180 Montague Street in Brooklyn Heights. Van Buskirk, who hailed from Closter, New Jersey, was by then thirty-eight years old. Some fourteen years earlier—in March 1896—he had married into one of Brooklyn's oldest families, saying his vows with Lillian Van Sicklen in a ceremony in a local Dutch Reformed church near Van Sicklen Street in Brooklyn's Gravesend section. By the time the NYU graduate was working on the ballpark, he and Lillian were still living in the old Dutch homestead with their seven-year-old son, Bertram, and Lillian's father, James.

Ebbets swore Van Buskirk to secrecy and had him work on the plans for a year, telling him only what he needed to know. Ebbets also took a major role in the planning. To ensure that the ballpark design would be state of the art, Van Buskirk and Ebbets visited the newer major league ballparks, seeking to absorb every major and minor detail calculated to enhance patron comfort.

Clarence, unsure as to whether the undertaking would be on the Washington Park site or elsewhere, would sometimes enter or leave Charley's office with the plans fastened in a special pocket inside his jacket, so no one could deduce what was in the works.

The long requiem for wooden ballparks—the change would take time—continued on St. Patrick's Day, 1911, when a plumber's blowtorch ignited a fire that destroyed Washington, D.C.'s American League ballpark. Less than a month later, another spectacular inferno erupted in New York just after midnight on April 14, when the Polo Grounds in upper Manhattan went up in flames. The blaze consumed the left-field bleachers; only the clubhouse, the right-field bleachers, and some of the center-field seats were saved.

The Giants were forced to move their home games to the American League's Highlanders' home field, Hilltop Park, located on what is now the site of Columbia Presbyterian Hospital in upper Manhattan. Meanwhile, owner John Brush planned to replace the destroyed park with a 40,000-seat concrete-and-steel Polo Grounds, which would make it the largest park in baseball. New York's first such ballpark, it opened by

August with a capacity of 16,000, and by the time the Giants appeared in the 1911 World Series, the capacity had been upped to 35,000.

Most people looking at Charley Ebbets in the autumn of 1911 would have thought him a man who had everything other than a winning team. The handlebar mustache and the long sideburns gone and the brown hair turned gray, his was a stately countenance, sometimes dour but often with an open smile. He was a pillar of Brooklyn, the man in charge of running the Brooklyn baseball team since 1898. Most people only saw the surface, however, which was what Charley wanted them to see. In fact, his life was in tumult. It was a mess.

Charley was no longer living with Minnie, his wife of thirty-four years, after she learned he had "committed indiscretions."[5] They were splitting up. A hotel clerk's wife, Grace Slade Nott, had caught Charley's fancy, and they were in too deep to stop. She was some years his junior. To make matters worse, his budgets were so stressed by his effort to accrue land parcels in secret for his ballpark that he was virtually broke.

Things were so bad that he actually had to convince the National League's other owners to stretch the season out until Columbus Day so that he could draw one more big crowd to Washington Park. After that, the sportswriters, who wrote nothing of his personal affairs, started temporarily referring to the man they had dubbed Charles "Hercules" Ebbets as Charles "Holiday" Ebbets.

Meanwhile, speculation abounded about a possible new park for the Brooklyn ball team. As late as October 30, 1911, Ebbets stated publicly that his team might move to Fulton Street and Crescent Street in East New York, but that if Brooklyn did buy the Washington Park site and remain there, a concrete stand would be built. The pundits thought a rebuilt Washington Park made sense; they knew that Ebbets had sunk something like $30,000 into renovations there at the end of the 1907 season. But all of this talk was designed to disguise Charley's real intentions, for he was putting the final pieces together of his new acreage on the fringes of Flatbush.

After filing the deed on December 29, 1911, for the last parcel, the city-owned piece that ran through the property, Ebbets prepared to make his announcement. On Tuesday, January 2, 1912, the *Brooklyn Citizen*, one of the borough's four major papers, alluded to the news in an item printed hours before the story broke. "Just as a warm-up to what he would do in the banquet line if the Superbas ever won a championship," the *Citizen* reported, "President Charles H. Ebbets will tender a dinner to the sporting writers of Greater New York at 5 o'clock this evening."[6]

Ebbets, promising the scribes some sensational news, had sent out invitations the previous week. One of the lines was written in red ink, prompting the *Brooklyn Daily Standard Union* to comment that "a very important piece of news that will deeply interest every fan in Brooklyn, and, too, those outside of Brooklyn, will be announced during the dinner."[7]

The soup-to-nuts affair was Runyonesque enough in character and attitude to command the presence of Damon Runyon himself. Celebrated sportswriter Grantland Rice and the "four kings," Brooklyn's four sports editors—Abe Yager of the *Brooklyn Daily Eagle,* William Granger of the *Brooklyn Citizen,* L. F. Wooster of the *Brooklyn Times,* and William Rafter of the *Brooklyn Standard Union*—were also present. The setting, the downtown social club known as the Brooklyn Club, was an institution that drew its members, Charley among them, from the ranks of Brooklyn's business and legal communities. It was at the Brooklyn Club, then located on the corner of Clinton and Pierrepont streets, on the day after New Year's, 1912, that Charley Ebbets gathered the writers, editors, and baseball luminaries to tell of the grandest of all his plans.

Despite what sportswriter Frank Graham wrote to the contrary in his informal history of the Brooklyn Dodgers sixty years ago, knowledge of the ballpark site had not leaked out beyond a tight circle of Ebbets's associates. Everyone knew Ebbets was looking to buy up land for purposes of constructing a concrete ballpark, but those who were speculating on the whereabouts missed by miles. Although the *Brooklyn Citizen* correctly guessed that Ebbets was about to unveil plans for a ballpark, a subsequent edition just before the press conference said, "The park will, in all likelihood, be built on the site of the present Washington Park. Real estate agents of East New York have long been after Ebbets to locate in their vicinity."[8]

When the big moment came at the dinner, Charley first took a moment to acknowledge his patrons' frustration. "Brooklyn has supported a losing team better than any other city on earth," Ebbets said. "No place has such loyal and cheerful fans, and no one realizes it more thoroughly than myself. Such a patronage deserves every convenience and comfort that can be provided at a baseball park, and that is what I hope to provide. It is a plain case of expressing my appreciation to those who have stuck by me even when the outlook was at its worst. The fans naturally want a pennant winner and that is the goal toward which I am striving. I believe we shall have a winner in Brooklyn, and I shall leave nothing undone toward accomplishing that object."[9]

With that he unveiled the blueprint and diagram for the "Proposed New Grand Stand for the Brooklyn Base Ball Club," which, the *Brooklyn Citizen* reported, would "be located between the Willink entrance of Prospect Park and Nostrand Avenue, on a plot bounded by Montgomery Street, Bedford Avenue, Sullivan Place, and Cedar Place."

Surprise at the location reverberated through Brooklyn. "Every one of the guesses fell short of the mark," the *Standard Union* said the next day. "While it was a forgone conclusion that Ebbets' big piece of news would be the announcing of the purchase of a ground for a new ball park," said William Granger in the *Citizen*, "the location had been so well concealed that [of] all of the guesses made as to the location of the new park not one was even close."

Ebbets introduced several guests, among them the Yorks and the very same G. W. Chauncey who had first given Charley an opportunity to buy into the franchise. Then the testimonials began. "Mr. Ebbets and I have been friends ever since he bought my stock twenty years ago," said Chauncey, "and I have taken a friendly interest in the ball team, although I do not own a cent's worth. He bought from me with cash and notes, and every note was taken up on time. He has been absolutely reliable in all his dealings with me, and so far as I can, I am always willing to help him."[10]

"Had it been known the Brooklyn Baseball Club wished the land for a new park," said Pyle, alluding to potential landowner holdouts, "I imagine some of it would have soared in the clouds."[11]

During the dinner Barney York had suggested that the ballpark be called Ebbets Field, "which, in all probability, will be the name adopted," wrote Granger of the *Citizen* the next day. York also described a large hole in the middle of the acquired property as "a subway to China."[12] Grading, it was noted, was also necessary elsewhere on the plot.

Ebbets had additionally bought lots on the three corners adjacent to the main entrance at the junction of Sullivan and Cedar. Altogether, thirty pieces of property were purchased, the two largest costing $50,000 and $25,000. The total cost for all the parcels was somewhat less than $200,000. Charley had been held up by one piece of property, a 20-by-50-foot parcel in the vicinity of what would become the area around the grandstand on the third base side. The land was said to be worth about $100. The owner was said to be touring Europe but couldn't be found, with Ebbets's agents traipsing through the Alps trying to track him down; then they received word he'd gone to California. Finally they found him in Montclair, New Jersey. Realizing something was up, the owner held out until he was paid $2,000 for his land.[13]

Ebbets discussed many of the planned ballpark's features himself, and with Charles Jr. discussed the varied means of egress and transportation links to the park. A blueprint distributed to the press showed the layout of the stands with the left-field wall facing north and right field facing east. The new ballpark would have "an immense grandstand which will have the afternoon sun in the rear and the summer breezes in front of the stand," the New York Times reported. "The baseball diamond will be in the southwestern part of the plot."

The configuration of the playing field would eventually mirror the irregular shape of the land parcel. City streets bordered each side, but the parcel wasn't square. The Cedar Place street frontage, on the third base side of the park, was longest at 638 feet. The Sullivan Place frontage, on the first base side, was almost 479 feet long and tilted inward toward Bedford Avenue, the site of the soon-to-be right field–center field wall, where the street frontage was almost 475 feet long. The street frontage on the Montgomery Street, behind left field, was 450 feet long.

According to plans, Ebbets Field's double-deck grandstand would begin in foul territory at the right-field wall and wrap around the diamond to just past third base, where a few feet would separate it from a concrete bleacher that would continue out to the left-field wall, in foul territory. No grandstands were slated for construction in fair territory. The blueprints appearing in the following day's papers also featured a small bleacher stand placed diagonally across the depths of dead center field that wasn't built when construction began nor even in the years afterward in the fashion originally planned. As a result, center field would be over 450 feet instead of the planned-for 425.

One of the park's most noteworthy features was not outside the ballpark, on the field, or in the stands. A "semicircular rotunda," ostensibly for the efficient flow of fans into the park, would have a "mosaic tiled floor and white glazed brick side walls" that would be the primary entrance to the park.

"Rugs would be placed over the tile floor," according to Ebbets, with folding chairs set down to allow fans to sit comfortably while attendants fetched their autos from a garage built across the street.

Architect Van Buskirk, talking informally with reporters, claimed that it would be possible to get a crowd of 35,000 out of the new ballpark in five to seven minutes. Press accounts were glowing. "The new baseball park will represent an expenditure of $750,000 and will rank with the best parks in the country," the New York Times wrote. Fifteen links to mass transit would make the new site accessible, including the Brighton Beach subway line, with a nearby "Consumers Park" station that would stop a few blocks from the ballpark.[14]

"These [links] connect with 38 transferring lines," the *Eagle* said. "Even a bigamist could ask no more avenues of escape or approach."

"A megaphone device will inform the fans of every new face in the struggle, where he will play, his favorite author and what he thinks of the tariff," the *Eagle* added. "That will be a tremendous advance over the old way of doing things, when you always asked the man beside you what the umpire said, the man always told you wrong, so that you did not know the difference until you read the papers the next day."

"Brooklyn owes a debt of gratitude to President Ebbets and his associates, in giving to the borough so magnificent a ball field," the *Citizen* editorialized the next day. "The best way for Brooklyn to requite this debt is to patronize the new field in increasing numbers. There is no sport that we can think of that provides at once so much real pleasure and the opportunity for an afternoon's recreation in the open air at so little expense, as the great American game of baseball."

The matter of when the park would be ready was also discussed. "It is part of the battlefield where the British army under Howe clashed with the Continental troops under Washington. For this reason," the *Citizen* noted on its editorial page, "Mr. Ebbets, who is nothing if not patriotic, intends to hurry along the work of construction so that the park will be opened either on Flag Day in June, or if untoward obstacles are met, in August on the anniversary of the Battle of Long Island."[15]

Everyone conveniently ignored that the Superbas were scheduled to be out of town on the August 27 anniversary, probably because they surmised Charley could get the other powers in the league to agree to a switch and change in the schedule if he wanted to for a big date. After all, they'd nicknamed him "Holiday," hadn't they?

A slight oversight was made by those esteemed members of the fourth estate—many of whom were legends in their own right—who failed to recognize that no provision had been made for them. The ballpark that Clarence Van Buskirk designed was, quite unfortunately, without a press box. Until the first one was built off the bottom of the second deck in 1929,[16] reporters attending games at Ebbets Field sat in the first two or three rows in the upper deck.

The ballpark also incorporated a design concept that was new to local fans, and some of them failed to appreciate it. Years later Minnie Ebbets recalled that some people said "Charley was mad" to put a twenty-foot wall around the ballpark, an action undoubtedly inspired by his rancor over people watching the games for free over Washington Park's fence from the so-called Guinea Flats. Putting up such a wall was hardly unprecedented; Philadelphia's Baker Bowl, where the Phillies played, had had a forty-foot wall since 1895.

Van Buskirk's design of the Rotunda, meanwhile, was doubtless influenced in some measure by Philadelphia's new stadium, the home of the American League Athletics. "The Shibe Park cupola had similarities to the Ebbets Field Rotunda in that they both served as entrances and had offices above," sportswriter and historian Leonard Koppett has noted. Shibe Park's distinctive cupola had windows with awnings above three tall portals that provided the main entrance to that park. Essentially, Van Buskirk had taken the design elements of the cupola a step further. The Rotunda's space was bigger and more ornate, as were the offices above, too, where owner Ebbets would have both his office and a private room looking out over Sullivan Place.

The ground-breaking ceremony was both anticipated and heralded, billed as "Spade Day" across all of Brooklyn, scheduled for 1 P.M. at the new ballpark site on March 4, 1912. It began with speeches off a wooden stage festooned with flags and red, white, and blue bunting. The crowd was variously reported at anywhere from five hundred to two thousand and included many neighborhood parents, who propped kids up on their shoulders so the youngsters could get a better look at the speechmakers.

The surroundings were bleak: a couple of shacks and rough terrain, rutted gullies, small hills, cow paths, and goat trails made it hard to imagine graceful Zack Wheat gliding over the landscape in pursuit of a fly ball.

Borough president Alfred E. Steers remarked about looking through a knothole as a child to see the famous 1870 upset when the Brooklyn Atlantics defeated the Cincinnati Red Stockings at the old Capitoline Grounds. He named individual players from that era, too: Bob Ferguson, a catcher; Dickey Pearce, the shortstop; and George Zettlein, a pitcher.

"It is not only because I deem it a pleasure to be with Mr. Ebbets on this occasion that I come here," said Steers, "but also because I deem it my duty as Borough President. Mr. Ebbets is doing a fine thing for Brooklyn in giving the city one of the greatest ballparks in the world. I was born in this neighborhood, and every bit of the ground is dear to me, and it gives me much pleasure to be here, fans and ladies and gentlemen, and to see the start of this proposed magnificent ball grounds."

Steers told his constituents what Ebbets Field would mean to Brooklyn. "In my mind this huge ball field will do much toward developing this section of Brooklyn. Already the trolley, elevated and subway line owners are getting in touch with the situation and are planning to have better transit facilities. By the time the stadium is built, there will be a big change in the transit situation. Just wait and see when the Superbas start playing in their new park."

Steers also commented on the game and its place. "A man who is not interested in baseball is not a human man. Something is wrong with him. We cannot have too much baseball in these strenuous business days. Out of the offices, the factories and the stores there come into the sunshine and open air thousands and thousands of our citizens. It is a great sport, a clean sport, a healthy sport and an honest sport. A healthy interest in such open-air pastimes will assure the welfare of the nation. More power and a long life to the Brooklyn Ball Club and the grand sport which it promotes and fosters.

"I tell you what I want to see," Steers told them, interrupted by the crowd's cheers, "and I know you all want to see it, too, and that is for Brooklyn to proudly take her place at the top of the baseball world, as she did when I was a boy and used to peek through holes in the fence. And I think Mr. Ebbets will give us the best team in the country, and it will play right here on this park."[17]

When the speeches were finished, the honor of turning the first spadeful of earth fell to Ebbets. Clad in a long, fur-lined overcoat and sporting a diamond pin, he had long since given up his bushy mustache. In the fourteen years since he'd run the club, he'd changed from a strapping, dark-haired young man into a round-cheeked, open-faced fifty-two-year-old, white curly hair sneaking out from under his bowler hat. Now, in one of the most important moments in his life, he carefully removed a chamois cloth from a beautiful, solid silver spade with an ebony handle, a gift of the Castle brothers, Walter and Edmund, the contractors who would build the ballpark. Off the platform now, he picked some manageably soft ground in front. From the crowd someone yelled, "Dig up a couple of new players, Charley!"[18] Everyone laughed.

Then, choreographing the act for photographers, Ebbets dug in and let fly. The crowd roared. Proud in that moment, he might also have wondered if he was both figuratively and literally digging a hole for himself.

Afterward, Ebbets and some of the luminaries repaired to Fred Winter's Consumers Park restaurant nearby. That evening, a light snow began to fall over the site, covering it with a blanket of white.

That summer, in an article in *People's Weekly*, Ebbets noted that baseball had undergone a rapid transformation during the past two decades and that patrons wanted comfort, safety, and faster play than ever before. Defending his now-famous infancy remark, Charley noted that at the time he began in baseball in 1883, there was not a perfect fireproof or safe stand in the major leagues, but that since then almost every franchise had a steel-reinforced concrete park, or a "baseball stadium," in the works. "It is the result of the natural growth of baseball and a step toward greater and better sport than the followers of the game have any idea of at the present time," Ebbets said.

"I want to build a structure that will fill all demands upon it for the next thirty years," he added, noting that otherwise he wouldn't invest three quarters of a million dollars in the new park. "It is a very expensive proposition to move and build a new park, and this time I am going to figure in all reasonable growth and demand as I forecast it. I believe that baseball will continue [as] America's most popular sport for centuries to come and will improve both in play, character and attendance for many years yet. It is this steady increase in popularity that I am endeavoring to anticipate."[19]

By 1912 the construction boom under way elsewhere in baseball resulted in a spate of new parks. This was at once seen as a maturation of the game, and for the first time, some seemed to recognize Ebbets's remarks as a harbinger of things to come. Though the new Polo Grounds and its 40,000-seat capacity set a size standard for the times, its design hardly did. The huge double-decked grandstand had the wide-arc curve of the closed end of a horseshoe around home plate, creating plenty of foul territory and keeping the fans farther away from the diamond than necessary.

In Cincinnati, Redland Field opened, a ballpark described by Lawrence Ritter as originally consisting of "a covered double-decked grandstand that curved around home plate and extended about thirty feet past first and third base. Covered single-decked pavilions continued down the length of both foul lines."[20] A separate stand-alone bleacher section behind a nine-foot screen in right field seated 4,500, giving the park a total capacity of 25,000. The park would be renamed Crosley Field in 1935 after a subsequent owner, Powell Crosley.

Up in Boston, the Red Sox were inaugurating 35,000-seat Fenway Park, a ballpark that featured a one-tier concrete-and-steel grandstand stopping, at that time, short of the left-field corner and extending all the way to the right-field corner. The bleachers in right field and the 25-foot wall in left field—somewhat shorter than the 37-foot "Green Monster" today—were made of wood. Aside from the 324-foot left-field line that resembles today's 310-foot marker, the ballpark then had a much more vast 550-foot expanse to deepest right-center, on the far end around the corner of the bleachers, and had at least one other odd feature: a 10-foot-high incline to the left-field wall that quickly became known as Duffy's Cliff, named after Duffy Lewis, the Red Sox left fielder between 1912 and 1917, who learned how to master it defensively.

In Detroit, Bennett Park, the home of the Tigers located at the corner of Michigan and Trumbell, received the first of its three rechristenings in 1912 when it was renamed Navin Field, seating 23,000. Originally the park had been named for Charley Bennett, an 1880s Detroit catcher who lost both legs in a freak train accident. Frank Navin had become principal owner of the Tigers in 1908. The park would become Briggs Stadium after a subsequent owner in 1938 and then Tiger Stadium in 1961.

The new parks in Boston, Cincinnati, and New York illustrated the overwhelming popularity of baseball when there was no doubt about the fact it was the national game. Owners weren't afraid to invest in new and grandiose stadiums for their teams, and they were confident that fans would fill them. By the standards of the day, the parks' accommodations for the fans were luxurious. And consistent with the ballparks built earlier, the outfields were generally expansive, the exception being when a particular foul line was constricted by the size of a lot that an owner had to build upon within a street grid.

Ebbets, meanwhile, was having a tougher time than anticipated getting his new ballpark ready for an opening midway through the 1912 season, having been too optimistic about the ballpark's construction timetable and about his ability to foot the bill alone. Great quantities of lumber, furnished by Johnson Brothers and by Louis Bossert and Sons, the same Bossert of Brooklyn's well-known Montague Street hotel, were used to make forms for the large number of concrete piers and the huge wall that would surround the field. Work progressed, albeit at a slower than expected pace. On July 6, 1912, at 10:30 in the morning, with the stirrings of a scanty, new lawn just beginning amid the newly laid out infield and with some of the steel of the ballpark's frame already in place, the ceremonies to lay the cornerstone began before a large crowd. Ebbets "fondled the trowel with as much pride as a child takes in a new doll," said the *Brooklyn Citizen*.

Barney York was master of ceremonies. Charles Ebbets Jr., now thirty-four, read the testimonials, including the letters of congratulations from President Howard Taft and Mayor William Gaynor. When young Charley got to Giant owner John Brush's wire, he stumbled on the word "perpetuity."

Borough president Steers was the first speaker introduced. "I consider it both a great duty and great pleasure to be present here in the laying of the cornerstone of this great monument to baseball, to Brooklyn, and to New York City. I want to say a word about Brooklyn. Brooklyn is a great borough. In population it is as large as three or four of the great cities of the country put together. It has a greater population than three of the smaller states put together, and it is growing at the rate of four hundred families a week. I have no doubt it will soon be the largest of all the boroughs, and the largest city individually in the United States."[21]

The Reverend James M. Farrar said, "The bleachers alone define pure democracy. Here initiated the initiative, referendum and the recall. . . . Mr. Ebbets has done a great work for Brooklyn and for baseball." Following him, Rabbi Nathan Krass made a heartily met request of three cheers for Ebbets.

When Charley Sr. spoke at last, he said that a derrick couldn't get him out of baseball until he had won the world's title for Flatbush and vicinity. The crowd roared. Charley Jr. and Charles Medicus, son of treasurer Henry Medicus, laid the cornerstone. Then, amid cries of "Brooklyn for the pennant in 1913," all the items that would tumble out of the cut Connecticut granite almost forty-eight years later were deposited, including the mementos and some business cards of those in the crowd.

After the ceremony, as at the ground breaking, Ebbets gave an informal party for a number of his guests over at Consumers Park restaurant. When it was over, everyone went down to Washington Park to see their Superbas lose to the Giants.

A Van Buskirk drawing in the *Brooklyn Times* the next day, illustrating how the ballpark would appear when finished, showed how desolate the area around the ballpark still remained. Only three houses were standing over a five-square-block expanse to the east and northeast behind center and right field. The block behind the left-field barrier had no buildings at all.

Work didn't proceed as quickly as planned, however. By the end of July Ebbets was feeling the pinch from the outflow of cash for construction to finish the job. It wasn't the first time he was short on cash, nor would it be the last. Official estimates still persisted that the ballpark would be ready as early as August 28.

By the time August 27 came along, the *Brooklyn Times* was reporting that it was "probable that Ebbets Field will be opened on Saturday, September 14 when the Pittsburghs begin a series here." The skeletal ironwork had started to rise, but the ballpark was nowhere near complete.

The next day Ebbets was joined by two new principals as he made a big announcement at the new ballpark site. He had struck a deal with Stephen and Edward J. McKeever that allowed them to become stockholders. No terms of the deal were disclosed, but years later it was revealed that in order to complete the deal, Ebbets bought out the 30 percent share of stock of his old friend Henry Medicus, and then sold 50 percent of the ball club to the McKeevers. Speculation about what the McKeevers paid has varied widely in baseball writing over the years, ranging from $100,000 to $500,000. Whatever the exact amount was, it's a safe bet that when the assets the pair afforded to help with construction were added in, their total investment was closer to the higher number.[22]

"My brother and myself have bought an interest in the Brooklyn club because we believe it is a good investment," Ed McKeever said. "Then, too, I am a baseball fan. While I will take an active interest in the club, its management will continue the same. Mr. Ebbets will have absolute charge. We wanted to invest some money and my brother and myself were pleased when we got a chance to place the investment by purchasing stock in the Brooklyn club. We wanted to keep all our money invested in Brooklyn."[23]

The brothers, sons of a shoe dealer, lived in close proximity to each other on Sixth Avenue in Park Slope. Steve was born on October 30, 1854, quit school at age ten, apprenticed with a plumber, and by eighteen was in business for himself. He got his first big contract after a bitter political fight for the plumbing, gas, and steamfitting work being done on the rising Brooklyn Bridge, and later did big jobs on the Kings County and Brooklyn Union elevated railroads, and for manufacturing companies along the riverfront.

Ed, born March 19, 1859, first went to work for a brass company at fourteen, then went into the tea business for himself at nineteen. In 1886 he partnered with Michael Dady in the Hudson River Broken Stone Company. They located their plant on Breakneck Mountain at Storm King on the Hudson, opposite Cornwall. They made money as contractors and builders, the source of most of it coming from rock quarries, where they crushed and furnished rock for the track beds of the New York Central Railroad, supplying the railroad's rock ballast between New York and Buffalo.

Steve won the alderman's post in the 1897 election and was re-elected in 1899, but subsequently decided against a third term, as well as a nomination for the State Senate, even though he would have been a likely winner. He also refused a Tammany-backed nomination for state treasurer during a year when all the Democrats but gubernatorial candidate William Randolph Hearst swept to victory.

In 1899 Ed returned to Brooklyn to go into the building and general contracting business with his older brother. One of their largest enterprises was the erection of over one hundred houses in one season in Brooklyn's upper Greenpoint neighborhood, dubbed McKeeversville. They sold the homes to a syndicate. In the summer of 1910 they built a menhaden oil and fertilizing plant employing 250 workers on Crab Island, twelve miles from Atlantic City, said to be worth half a million dollars.

Although the deal between Ebbets and the McKeevers couldn't compensate for the delays in construction that had taken place up to that point, what the McKeevers provided evidently greased the skids so that the project could go forward more quickly. Two separate corporations were formed with an interlocking directorship: the Ebbets-McKeever Exhibition Company would own the ballpark, and the Brooklyn National Baseball Club would own and operate the ball club. The Exhibition Company had Ed McKeever as president and Steve McKeever as vice president, with the elder Ebbets as treasurer. Charley Sr. ran the ball club as he always had, while Ed McKeever now served as vice president and Steve McKeever as treasurer. Ebbets Jr. served as secretary of both companies.

The same day the news about the new owners was announced, it was revealed that there was no chance the new ballpark would be ready before September 21. "Had it not been for several delays by the slow delivery of the material there is no doubt but what the park would have been completed by this time," reported the *Brooklyn Times* on September 14. "Despite the numerous delays and several attempts on the part of a walking delegate of the Structural Iron Workers Union to call a strike, the work on the field is going ahead steadily."

With the season proceeding drearily, the ballpark's progress was the only news worthy of report. And then something changed that. On September 17, a youngster made a great splash with his Superba debut a day after making a long, overnight journey from Montgomery, Alabama, where his Southern Association team had just concluded its season. His name was Charley Stengel, soon to become better known as Casey, given the initials of his hometown, Kansas City.

Kid Elberfeld, Stengel's manager at Montgomery, had forced his protégé to replace his down-home duds and cardboard suitcase, despite Stengel's protestations that he was saving money for dental school. The Tabasco Kid delivered a withering admonishment urging Casey to part company with a few bucks: "If you get caught in a hard rain with that cardboard suitcase, all that you'll have left will be the handle."[24]

"You're going to the big leagues," Elberfeld told him. "You're not gonna be a dentist."

Stengel won the hearts of Brooklyn's Washington Park fans immediately as the spark in a victory against a tough Pirate team, with four hits, a walk, three stolen bases, and two runs batted in on a sunny, 70-degree, Indian summer day. It was a phenomenal performance, and when the following day's game was rained out, Brooklyn's scribes had another day to write about Casey's feat.

Stengel hit .316 that fall, combining the prospect of a great new player with anticipation of the new park. By September 20 Ebbets announced that "the incomplete condition of the stands would make accidents liable and for that reason the opening will postponed until next year."[25]

Work on the park pressed forward. The lower deck was completed by this time except for seat installations, held up by the ironworkers' efforts on the skeletal structure above. The diamond was in place, including the keyhole from the pitcher's mound to the plate. It didn't come easy. The grounds had been excavated to a depth of three feet, where a layer of six-inch stone was placed, and then a layer of two-inch stone, then one-inch stone. On top of that was placed six inches of clean steamed ashes, then eight inches of topsoil.

Castle Brothers had the contract for filling in the dirt. One of the brothers was impressed with the rich, black color of a load of dirt he saw in a wagon one day, found out where it came from, and offered to buy all he could get at $2 a load. Seventy loads had been poured on the field before landscaper Mike Daly came around. He examined a handful of soil and then went immediately to Ebbets's office, which was then across the street. Ebbets, the McKeevers, and everyone else had approved it; Daly was so agitated "he began chattering in a dialect heard only in Galway 'west of the law.'"[26]

However fine and fertile the soil was for some uses, it would be terrible for a baseball field, holding water like a sponge so that a Christmas shower, according to the papers, wouldn't dry out until the Fourth of July. The seventy truckloads had to be shoveled up, reloaded, and removed. Eight inches of loam, fertilized with fish chum from the McKeever Brothers factory at Egg Harbor, were ultimately used for the field, which had a six-inch fall in all directions for drainage. The drain encircling the field had its lowest point at Bedford Avenue and Sullivan Place, where it connected with the main sewer.

Much of the wall was in place around the perimeter of the outfield now, and the ballpark was visually taking shape. "When Ebbets Field is completed," the *Brooklyn Times* headlined, "Brooklynites may pride themselves on having the finest stadium in the country dedicated to the national game."[27] Three months later, there was a sure sign Ebbets Field would be ready. In January of 1913 the wooden stands at Washington Park were dismantled plank by plank. Only the clubhouse on the Third Avenue side was left standing.[28]

Although Ebbets Field's exterior design has remained a classic, evident by its frequent resurrection in photographs or by the use of similar features in renderings of proposed new stadiums these many years later, other amenities touted by the press would quickly be forgotten. Among them were the "roomy and armless" seating, provision for across-the-street parking, new means of egress, and other features deemed grand by standards in 1912. One of the ballpark's more lasting innovations was that it had the first curved-back stadium seats.

What the sportswriters couldn't know amid all the grandiloquent exclamations, even if they did understand the fans' fervor for their team and the game, was the inimitable way the ballpark would fit in a tightly knit urban neighborhood a generation later, and how the configurations of the field and construction of the barriers would define the excitement in a game played in the confines of this place.

The writers could not know that the team's board of directors would elect to change the left-field bleachers markedly by erecting an expanded double-deck stand across left and center field in 1931, encroaching inward across the outfield's expanse. Those Ebbets Field renovations affected the ballpark's dimensions and had a far greater impact on the field of play than other subsequent measures designed to expand and renovate other ballparks. It was different from Red Sox owner Tom Yawkey's reconstruction of Fenway Park in 1934, different from the impact of the two-year renovation that Walter O. Briggs would undertake when double-decking the entire ballpark in Detroit beginning in 1938. It also differed from Powell Crosley's effort to add a covered upper deck to Crosley Field's one-tier left- and right-field pavilions in 1939, which didn't affect fair territory at that park at all.

Even though Briggs and Yawkey made their ball fields smaller, as was the case in the vast majority of ballparks where renovations were done over the years, Ebbets Field's renovations put the center-field wall 399 feet away from home plate and reduced the left-center power alley to 365 feet. These shortened distances, subjected to tinkering over the years, affected the way pitchers pitched, the hitters' results, and the outcome of many games. And as the Brooklyn writers unquestionably did know back in the dog days of summer in 1912, the people whom they were writing for cared very much about the outcome of the games Brooklyn would play, since a substantial number of people in Brooklyn seemed to believe to some degree that who they were was reflected by the Brooklyn National League team. A half-century before the social sciences would develop theoreticians known as symbolic interactionists, who believe society exists and continues to exist on the basis of significant symbols, the notion in Brooklyn was understood in simpler terms.[29] More than anything, the Brooklynites who would come to bear witness would become Ebbets Field, and Ebbets Field would become them, in return.

CHAPTER FOUR

The New Ballpark

By the beginning of March 1913 the trusswork that had risen over Flatbush the previous fall was now altogether dressed. At the junction of Sullivan Place and Cedar Place, standing high above the ballpark entrance behind home plate, "Ebbets Field," in full caps, now was seen majestically on the façade's setback just below the ballpark's crown, the single design element that would serve to brand the image of the ballpark as an immortal piece of Americana. A flag rose precisely above the center of the name. Along the outside edge of the roof were interval placements of small globes as a finishing touch, likely replicating baseballs, a feature that would disappear within a few years. No one then could imagine that the ballpark's exterior façade, its most definable component, would set a timeless standard.

None of the new ballparks completed by then made as much of a statement: not Shibe Park (as distinctive as Shibe's cupola was) or Forbes Field, certainly not the Polo Grounds, and not the understated entry portal to the new ballpark up in the Fens in Boston.

Ebbets Field's main entrance was at the ballpark's southwest corner. Fourteen rows of small-pane, Federal-style windows, separated by brick pilasters, ran straight from the sidewalk or just above the main gate's galvanized iron marquise above the entryway to the near-top of the streetfront façade. There concrete gargoyles marked the spring line for the crowning semicircular windows above each of those fourteen rows, with each of the windows surrounded by an ornamental half-circle of brick-belt coursing. Between the Fiske and Company bricks surrounding the windows were bas-relief medallions of baseballs, the arc of the ball's stitching running lengthwise.

Farther up the first and third base sides of the park, on Sullivan Place and Cedar Place, respectively, the exterior window-and-brick façade gave way to simple concrete columns above the first-deck floor line, with open spaces between them, allowing natural light to filter through the stands from the sides of the ballpark. Between the columns, Vulcan Rail and Construction installed the pipe and ornamental railings, which also featured designs of baseballs.

The grandstand on the first base side continued all the way down to the right-field wall, but on the third base side went only about forty feet past the infield, where a narrow twelve-foot space separated it from a single-level concrete bleacher. The bleachers that continued out toward the left-field wall were closer to the field than those at old Washington Park. The brand-new Ebbets Field had no seats in fair territory behind the outfielders.

Behind the ballpark's fence in right-center field, an undeveloped Bedford Avenue was undisturbed except for a few of Henry Ford's flivvers. At the outset, only a single small sign adorned the junction of the Ebbets Field exterior wall on the Bedford–Montgomery corner, with the rest of the Bedford Avenue wall white as a cloud, devoid of the advertising that would become a familiar staple years later. Only the black exit-gate doors in deep right-center field, a third of the way down the block, provided a stark color contrast.

Diagonally across Montgomery Street and Bedford Avenue were empty lots with a billboard, while the dirt across the street behind the wall in left-center field had been smoothly crested into a bluff, enabling those standing at the top to see the crescent of the infield.

From that vantage point, the ballpark's double-decked stands stood in full view, neat and empty. The only sign of industry in the Superbas' new neighborhood was one that had already been there: the double smokestacks of the Consumers Park brewery, seen behind the one-deck concrete bleacher running from behind third base to the left-field corner. Few other buildings were around; when one looked east from the brewery, the ballpark loomed as the most imposing structure on the horizon.

It was an optimistic scene in an optimistic country, which at that moment was readying for the inauguration of President-elect Woodrow

Wilson of New Jersey, who had exploited the Roosevelt-Taft feud that had split the Republican Party in the election of 1912, ending a sixteen-year Republican reign in the White House. Industrialized America had taken its place as a world power. The nation had built and opened the Panama Canal, though whether its ships should be required to pay tolls, as the United States had initially agreed years before in its international discussions, was a national political issue. Wilson, the former New Jersey governor who had left a presidency at Princeton University while under fire a few years earlier, had now miraculously managed to become president of the United States. The new president had denounced Taft's Dollar Diplomacy—whereby Washington promoted foreign investment by the commercial sector to expand America's overseas interests—and unlike the Taft administration, was generally unfriendly to bankers and trusts. Although the issue of foreign influence and American investments in China was a concern, as was the political instability and level of American influence in Latin America, the United States seemed far removed from diplomatic storms brewing in Europe; the possibility that war would erupt within a year and eventually become a world war that would require a contribution of American blood wasn't remotely a part of the public discourse.

On March 16, 1913, less than two weeks after the Wilson inauguration, the public got its first glimpse of the virtually completed interior of Ebbets Field. Charley Ebbets, exhausted, wasn't there, however, having sailed for New Orleans for a much-needed vacation on the insistent orders of his doctor; Steve McKeever was off in Philadelphia. But Ed McKeever was there, up in his office, and Charles Ebbets Jr. was there, too, dispensing tickets. The city hadn't yet completed the exterior sidewalks, so the approach to the park was muddy. The gates were opened at nine o'clock in the morning and were kept open till six o'clock. Fifteen thousand came, with two thousand the most in the ballpark at any one time, that being at two o'clock in the afternoon.

Only two days before, Ebbets Sr. had announced that an "electrical" scoreboard would be installed by summer, despite the opposition of Harry M. Stevens, who made some thinly veiled accusations about scoreboards being wrong too often, rather transparently hiding his concern that the new innovation might impair his scorecard sales. An electric scoreboard would be quite an innovation given that numbers were typically dropped manually through slots, but there was no subsequent indication that an electric scoreboard was ever implemented then. A decision was also made by Ebbets around this time not to build the bleachers that had been intended to serve as 25-cent seats out in straightaway center field.

The Rotunda, the entry point into the ballpark at the home plate gate, was one of the ball park's major attractions: a circular room eighty feet in diameter, entirely supported by up to twenty-five-ton trusses at what would be the level of the third floor. Italian marble columns and an apron of marble wall were imported and installed by the Brooklyn Steam Marble Company of 180 Third Avenue. The Rotunda's ceiling was elliptical, curving most evidently around the room's perimeter, reaching a height of twenty-seven feet at the center. It was the largest dome in America made of metal lath and iron furring, constructed by the Troy Metal Lath Company under M. F. Forster at 724 Eighth Avenue in Manhattan.

The Rotunda's aura and charm were further accentuated by a ball-and-bat chandelier, called an "electrolier" by its creators, the Simes Company of 18–20 Rose Street in Manhattan, featuring facsimiles of baseball bats as part of the fixture, suspending illuminated glass baseball globes. A marble mosaic tile floor, which had been completed in the last week, was designed with a stitched baseball in the center and "Ebbets Field" composed in the tile around it.

The main entrance to the Rotunda, under the galvanized-iron, glass-glazed marquise, was fifty-six-feet wide, protected by three curved doors that could slide into pockets in the wall on either side when the ballpark's gates were opened. Once fans were inside, they would find fourteen gilded-cage ticket windows equidistant along the Rotunda's circular walls. Installed during the previous week, each ticket window had doors adjacent and a turnstile behind it, forestalling entry into the caverns underneath the stands. The concrete floor underneath the stands was scheduled for pouring later that week. The ballpark's grandstands were complete save for the placement of a few remaining seats.

Once fans went up through the ramps and through the portals and into the stands, one feature was evident on the field of play. Between the right-field foul line and the two-door exit gate in the deepest recesses of right-center field, the twenty-foot-high wall was bent in the middle. The bottom half of this wall—the bottom ten feet of it—angled outward at a gentle slope, enough to cause havoc with the carom of a fly ball. It would become a notable signature among many of the ballpark's unique features, a quirk that would differentiate Ebbets Field from other parks in an era when grand new parks were being built.

The wall was not without precedent. An earlier ballpark, the fourth Oriole Park where the old Orioles played in 1901 and 1902, had a wall whose bottom two-thirds were similarly angled.

On the whole, the new parks were tailored in their dimensions to the demands of a baseball era when an over-the-fence home run was infrequent and a much less strategic element in generating runs. Most of the parks would have long foul lines and expansive outfields unless a city's urban grid confined one of the fences to a shorter field. That was the case in Ebbets Field, where the right-field line would be confined to just short of 300 feet, thanks to Bedford Avenue on the other side of the wall. The left-field line, in contrast, would be a whopping 419 feet. On opening day, the distance to the center-field wall would be some 450 feet.[1]

Now, in the final days before Ebbets Field was to open and with Ebbets away on doctor's orders, it was up to architect Clarence Van Buskirk and groundskeeper Eugene Parker to finish the details. Van Buskirk did, following up with the Baltimore Enamel and Novelty Company for the interior signs, and with Snyder of Flatbush—there would be another Snider in Flatbush thirty-five years later—for various hardware items.

On March 29 the ballpark was visited by a large delegation from the New York Society of Architects that included President Samuel Sass and Vice President Constantine Schubert. After Van Buskirk toured them around, they all expressed their pleasure and could find no cause for criticism.[2] They too managed to miss the fact that the new field had been constructed without a press box.

When Ebbets's 1913 team broke spring camp in Augusta and finally arrived after wending its way up the East Coast, its members had an opportunity to work out for a couple of days in their new park. "The accommodations quarters for the home team with the ample lounging room made the place so homelike that few of the boys went home for lunch," the *Brooklyn Daily Eagle* reported. "After the morning workout, they loafed around and sent small boys for cans of soup, the ballplayers' favorite diversion in the way of midday food."

Ebbets Field would premiere with two teams whose contests would become an autumnal rite decades later. A Saturday exhibition game on April 5 against the Yankees with their new manager, Frank Chance, would open the new park. Until then the American League club had been known as the Highlanders, or simply as the New York Americans, the team that had been moved from Baltimore in 1903 to put an American League franchise in New York.

Newspapers, merchants, politicos, and people on the street were all promoting or talking about the opening of the new park. The Abraham and Straus (A&S) department store called Ebbets Field a "monument to outdoor sports," congratulating "Brooklyn upon the enterprise which has inspired the erection of the great baseball stadium to be opened Saturday," offering tickets at its theater booth with "no advance box office prices."[3]

A&S advertised baseballs from 19 cents to $1.25, basemen's mitts at 75 cents to $5, and baseball suits, containing shirt, cap, pants, and belt, "the pattern of cloth . . . the same as used in the Big League," at $2.24 each. "Season opens tomorrow! Whoopee! Come on—get your goods," the ad read. "If you cannot go to the great game, play ball yourself with the boys. Everything needed is here and prices are very moderate."[4]

The morning broke overcast, but the clouds gave way to afternoon sunshine. Gates were supposed to open at noon, but because of confusion regarding the hiring and assignment of ticket sellers, it was another hour before things got on track.

"The crowd of a thousand or more early birds stood the delay patiently and took the incident good naturedly," said the *Eagle*. "The expert manipulators of the pasteboards arrived at 1 o'clock, and as soon as they were safely locked in their little concrete cages against the assault of gunmen and grafters they began to turn loose tickets for all who had the price."[5]

Still more confusion stemmed from a ballpark worker unable to locate keys for the gates. Finally that was settled and things moved along more smoothly, but only for a short time. Even though the number of ticket windows at the marble Rotunda far outstripped the several at Washington Park, the windows were inside an eighty-foot-wide circular room, a design that had immediate unforeseen consequences.

All those now streaming toward the ballpark came as Ebbets thought they would come, via the trolleys, from every direction, and quite naturally, walking overland, up Park Slope through Prospect Park. As the crowds pressed inside the fifty-six-foot-wide doorway and the lines from the ticket windows all fanned out toward the Rotunda's center, the crowd-channeling concept proved to be flawed. A gift floral arrangement to Steve and Ed McKeever on display was soon underfoot in the swarm of fans, and the Rotunda was hopelessly jammed.

The arrangement left ticket sellers and ticket takers hard pressed to keep up while the incoming hordes pressed against those already waiting to buy tickets, so the gates were temporarily closed to prevent a panic. The two ranking police officials—Inspector Cohen and Captain Gallagher—had their hands full, even with twenty mounted cops and a regiment on foot.[6]

Charley Ebbets envisioned the Rotunda as a space serving to shield fans from rain or providing a comfortable place to linger after the game. Instead, it was a maelstrom of pregame activity resulting in an unsolicited intimacy not unlike that found on the average subway train at rush hour. Still, the Rotunda's hurly-burly before game time also served to heighten both tension and excitement. The anticipation quickened the pulse and made the moment of that first glimpse of Ebbets Field's diamond all the more delectable.

When the two teams practiced before the game that Saturday, the ballpark was more than filled an hour and a half before the game began.

The bluff across Montgomery Street behind the fence in left-center field, "Deadhead Hill," then higher than the left-field wall, was jammed with people right up to the corner at Bedford Avenue. Although most from that vantage point could look down upon the action for nothing, one opportunistic entrepreneur built an elevated wooden bleacher and sold plank space that was quickly bought up for 50 cents a person. Back from New Orleans in anticipation of the big event, Ebbets promised before the day was out that he'd put up a canvas behind the wall to block the view.

The fans settled in to the sound of Shannon's 23rd Regiment Band, a perennial part of Brooklyn opening day ceremonies and the very same band that had played at the opening ceremonies at the second Washington Park in 1898. Around three o'clock, Ebbets, Ed McKeever, and Ed's wife, Jennie, proceeded to center field so that Mrs. McKeever could have the honor of raising the oversized American flag before the band played the national anthem. But again, things weren't that simple. When they reached the flagpole, there was no flag; it was another minor item that had slipped through the cracks. With the entire ballpark waiting, a groundskeeper was sent to retrieve the flag from an office under the grandstand. He hustled Old Glory out to center field as quickly as possible so the ceremonies could begin.

After the flag was attached to the pole, Jennie McKeever, in her emerald green waistcoat with a hat to match, began hoisting the colors, with an appropriate pause for picture taking. The players, almost all hatless, with arms folded or hands behind their backs, stood behind her. They wore their eight-button sweaters with navy-blue button panels and collars, pin-striped uniforms, and wide-striped white-and-blue socks. Once the banner was run up the mast, the band performed the national anthem.

Only the ceremonial first pitch remained, the honor falling to Charley Ebbets's youngest daughter, twenty-year-old Genevieve. Umpire Tim Hurst had handed her the ball earlier. Now, with the flag raising concluded, she stood in her cerise gown and a big, wide-brimmed hat. She didn't falter, throwing a straight strike to umpire Bob Emslie. And then, to another roar, the Superbas took the field with Nap Rucker, their ace, on the mound.

Rucker retired the Yankees uneventfully in the first. After the first Dodger batter, Casey Stengel, grounded out, second baseman George Cutshaw, a second-year player who had come up through the Pacific Coast League, singled up the middle for the first hit in Ebbets Field. After Benny "Earache" Meyer followed with another single, Zack Wheat inadvertently provoked the first incident in what would ultimately become Ebbets Field's great comic tradition. Induced to hit a foul pop on the third base side, Wheat watched as Yank third sacker Roy Hartzell, in pursuit of the ball, took a header into a bevy of musicians, bonking his head on the bass drum, which in turn resonated obligingly in G. Among those razzing Hartzell, according to the *Eagle*, was "the clerical row back of third base."

Consisting of the Reverend James M. Farrar, Monsignor Edward McCarty, Rabbi Nathan Krass, and the Reverend R. W. McLaughlin, the clerics represented four different faiths. In full ballpark ardor when questioned, they declared the game morally uplifting, "helpful to the writing of sermons," and concurred that with some judicious rooting (not to mention divine intervention), they might actually help Brooklyn win.

In the fifth inning, Stengel hit a long, hard line drive to left-center field that hit the ground and skidded along on a part of the field where the grass had not yet taken. Yankee center-fielder Harry Wolter moved to cut it off but angled the ball badly. As he moved to stab it, he kicked the ball instead, and it rolled to the wall. As Wolter chased the sphere in vain, Stengel sped around the bases for an inside-the-park homer. The late-season hero was picking up where he left off, and the crowd loved it.

The following inning Gentleman Jake Daubert, the fine first baseman who had already shown great talent, hitting .307 and .308 in his second and third major league seasons, also hit a hard shot in Wolter's vicinity for a second inside-the-park homer. Although the Yankees managed to tie it in the ninth with a couple of runs off reliever Frank Allen, Brooklyn properly christened the ballpark with a win in the bottom of the inning when J. Carlisle "Red" Smith drove the ball past the shortstop into center field, bringing Zack Wheat home from third base for a 3–2 Superba win.

"Rejoice, ye Brooklyn fans," said the *Eagle*, "and deliver thanks, for our own Superbas fittingly dedicated Charles Hercules Ebbets' magnificent stadium, the greatest ball park in these United States, by soundly trouncing Frank Chance's Yankees yesterday afternoon to the merry tune of 3 to 2 in the presence of 25,000 wildly enthusiastic rooters who jammed every available inch of space in the immense stadium—the greatest outpouring of baseball fanatics that ever turned out to witness an exhibition game—and at least 7,000 others, who witnessed from the bluffs that loom above the field, over at Montgomery Street and Bedford Avenue."[7]

"As with Rome, so with Brooklyn," boasted the *Brooklyn Daily Standard Union*. "The words 'Ebbets Field' are lettered on the tiled floor of the Rotunda, at the top and bottom of the outline of a baseball. There is no apostrophe after Ebbets's name, because the huge amphitheater, though named after the man who built it, is really dedicated to baseball, the fans and the Brooklyn team. There is nothing personal about the building, except the enterprise of its sponsor. Moreover, it is calculated to outlive by far even those veterans of the diamond to whom life seems to be eternal. Barring accident, the building may last 200 years, or four times as long as the average structure lasts."[8]

The *Standard Union* called it the "handsomest, most complete and modern baseball arena in the world," an opinion reflecting the superlatives that came from every quarter. After that first exhibition, Ebbets was separating five and ten dollar bills late into the night, and when asked what he thought by reporters, he chortled, "It looks like a big season." The win against the Yankees, unfortunately, represented the high point of Brooklyn's year.[9]

The regular season officially opened with Brooklyn facing the Philadelphia Phillies on a cold, nasty day, Wednesday, April 9, with only 10,000 spectators braving the unpleasant weather. The league permitted Brooklyn to open the season a day early in recognition of its new ballpark, and despite all the hoopla of a few days earlier, more ceremony was in order.

Jake Daubert was presented with a gold bat, a brass band was on hand for the big day, and a floral horseshoe was presented to Ebbets as photographers snapped wildly. The players paraded across the field, and borough president Steers threw out the first ball to umpire Bill Klem. Steers, who had been at the ground breaking the previous March, had subsequently complained during an interview that he wouldn't run for borough president again because being in office was too expensive; among other things, he said, he was buying too many baseball tickets for people. And that was before Brooklyn had a new ballpark.

The hometown team's sentimental favorite, Nap Rucker, was tapped to start the official National League opener for Brooklyn. In the first inning, Philadelphia's Dutch Knabe doubled to right with Ebbets Field's first official National League hit. Right-fielder Benny Meyer subsequently muffed both Hans Lobert's foul fly and Sherry Magee's fair fly ball, allowing Knabe to score. The Superbas prevented further damage when Wheat nailed Paskert trying to stretch a single and when Stengel heaved a strike to the plate, cutting down Magee trying to score. But Tom Seaton, who started the game for the Phillies, made the run in the first inning stand up for a 1–0 victory.

When the Giants visited on April 26 for a weekend game, it became clear that the Rotunda was a problem. The Brooklyn Baseball Club had hired a hundred special police, all former soldiers at least six feet tall, and dubbed them the Dohertys, but they were no match when 40,000

descended on Ebbets Field and fought for admission. It was a near riot, and front-page news in the papers, where it was described as "a bitter battle" that "endangered the lives of many women and children."[10] The disorder began early and got worse; in the crush of the crowd a number of women fainted, children were bruised, clothes were torn. Inexplicably, some entrances in the Rotunda were closed, and people already holding reserved-seat tickets fought to pass those waiting on line to buy them.

Fistfights broke out; people were trampled; only the intervention of a few strong men who managed to open some space allowed victims to get to their feet and get out. The city police looked calmly on from outside and failed to lift a finger while the special police were swallowed up in the crowd. The failure of the city cops to act was based on a prior order of former police commissioner Bingham, who had once barred city police from interfering at the Polo Grounds unless specifically called inside the park by management. "When the catastrophe that is inevitable under such idiotic conditions comes to pass, it will be those very same hog-tied policemen who will get the blame for the deaths and injuries," wrote Thomas Rice in the *Eagle*.[11]

Ebbets had already promised that he would provide an outline for a new plan that involved opening new entrances. The next day, he announced that two new gates had been opened on each side of the ballpark. "This should help not a little," critiqued Rice, "but the weak point to the system is that . . . the reserved seat folk crowd through the same turnstiles used by the immediate buyers, and as the turnstiles practically adjoin the windows, any considerable number of people at one gate who already hold tickets not only block off the man who has just bought his, but block the line before the window."[12]

No other ballpark would be constructed that way again. When Yankee Stadium was built in 1923, care was taken to put ticket-buying kiosks outside the ballpark, with a good deal of distance between the kiosks and the entrance gate. This allowed fans holding tickets to gain access to the turnstiles from the right or left or from the ample space between the kiosks.

Ebbets Field's new entrances were opened up and everyone managed to take everything in stride, while Ebbets, feeling the strain of it all, hinted he might retire.[13] In the meantime, each of the papers was running a box in its sports page every day announcing how to get tickets for an honorary dinner for Charley Ebbets on May 10. The event was oversubscribed, held at the Hotel Shelbourne in Brighton Beach, and somewhere between 1,000 and 1,200 people came, overflowing the dining room and extending the seating into adjacent broad piazzas.

The entire Brooklyn, Cincinnati, Chicago, and New York National League baseball teams were on hand, and the cheering for Ebbets was periodically so enthusiastic and prolonged that toastmaster Lewis Pounds, Brooklyn's superintendent of public works, jokingly threatened to throw his gavel into the crowd.

Ebbets was given a diamond pin in the shape of a baseball diamond; when he rose in response to all the tributes, he was almost—but not quite—moved beyond words. "This is the most pleasing moment of my life," he said. "Never in my recollection has any individual in the baseball profession received a demonstration of this character. I wish that I had the tongue of an orator to make suitable reply. I am almost at my wit's end to respond to all the tributes I have received tonight. I will carry this token, with the recollection of this happy evening, to my grave."[14]

Although the fans were able to enjoy new ballpark features like the first scoreboard that showed not only line scores of out-of-town games but who was up in the batting order, the "megaphone device" ballyhooed in initial publicity efforts turned out to be a failure. The promised amplifier was debuted in the form of a microphone left near home plate, so balls and strike calls could be heard. Unfortunately, the epithets frequently tossed around the home plate area were heard as well, and as a result Ebbets did away with the innovation immediately.[15]

Soon after Ebbets Field was opened, two high wooden benches were installed at the rear of the lower stand behind home plate. Ebbets and the McKeevers each took one, and there they would invite and entertain friends, an egalitarian precursor of today's sky box. Steve usually kept a big tumbler of milk on hand during the games, and in later years he had a device to hold the glass attached to his seat. Ebbets and Steve McKeever would hold court with the fans out in the open, sometimes during the games but most often after, when there were either smiles and congratulations from the fans who would gather round or, conversely, sympathies, concerned discussions, arguments, and sometime acrimony if the team lost. Ed McKeever, quieter, preferred to slip into the crowd anonymously, especially if the Superbas had taken a beating.

For the lucky few with the opportunity to find out, the place that could be so full of fun or furor when brimming with people could also be magical when quiet. For Charley Ebbets's granddaughter Dorothy—his son Charles's daughter—Ebbets Field was a private playground. "We would wheel our doll buggies from our home, close to the field, and spend the day playing house in the dugouts. A favorite bit of fun was racing the doll buggies down the runways. Getting into Harry Stevens's refreshment supplies also was a lark and sometimes a cleanup job when we lost drinking straws in a burst of wind. 'No foreign objects on the playing field,' of course." [16]

If Charley Ebbets had an adoring granddaughter and an admiring public to cushion against assorted critics who castigated him for penury, the one thing that everyone seemingly agreed on was the bleak prospect for the world's championship he had promised Brooklyn fans. The 1913 Superbas maintained at least a pale imitation of pennant intentions until July, when the team fell away, sliding into the second division, winning only 65 games and finishing some 34½ games out. Even so, the nucleus of a future pennant winner was beginning to develop: Jake Daubert managed to capture the batting crown, hitting .350; George Cutshaw, solid at second, led the league in putouts at the keystone. In the outfield, Wheat patrolled left and Stengel found his way into the lineup consistently. Even though the National League champion Giants drew 630,000 up at the Polo Grounds, the Superbas' sixth-place team had an acknowledged great year at the gate, boosting its attendance by 104,000 to draw 347,000 into Ebbets Field.[17]

After a sixth-place finish, Ebbets had manager Bill Dahlen in for a meeting on November 20, and the two agreed that it was in the best interests of the ball club for Bill to depart. In his place would come Wilbert Robinson, the Giants coach who'd recently had a falling out with his boss, the legendary manager John McGraw. Ebbets knew of the breach, and after some discussion, he and the McKeevers agreed that they would hire Robinson as a coach while seeking to get another old Oriole, Tiger manager Hughie Jennings, to manage the club. But American League president Ban Johnson managed to surreptitiously block Brooklyn's move toward Jennings, and at that point the Brooklyn owners decided to gamble on Robinson to head the team, even though he had never managed before.

Big and rotund at 5'9" and 230 pounds, Wilbert Robinson lacked the hard edge of a McGraw, and though he could take a ballplayer to task verbally, he'd do it in a way that would build a ballplayer's confidence rather than diminish his skills or run him down. He established expectations of better performance, and tried to keep his players calibrated with critical appraisals when he thought their performance wanting. If his jovial demeanor or his girth allowed observers to think he was soft, they were mistaken. He was rough as a cob. After a foul tip had ripped the nail off his right little finger while he was catching for the Baltimore Orioles at the Polo Grounds in 1896, he continued in the lineup. Only when the finger turned black did he begin to pay attention. When it later became time for doctors down in Louisville to cut the finger off below the first joint to avoid blood poisoning, he watched rather than take anesthetic.[18]

As for his pitchers, he liked them big, and always advocated that they use their best pitch when a situation was critical and called for getting a hitter out. Little Vic Lombardi, a Dodger pitcher in the mid-1940s, never would have gotten in the door of a Wilbert Robinson clubhouse.

Pitchers Raleigh Aitchison and Edward Joseph Pfeffer, called Jeff (he also had a brother, "Big Jeff," who pitched for Chicago and Boston in a six-year career between 1905 and 1911), the now-fading Nap Rucker, and another, younger Georgian by the name of Sherrod Smith all graced Robinson's staff, and together they were capable of giving the Ebbets Field crowd something to cheer about. When it became clear that Robinson and Ebbets were comfortable with each other and that "Uncle Robbie" was likely to be around for a while, the writers began dropping the nickname "Superbas," associated with Hanlon's management of the team going back to 1899, and began calling the team the "Robins" in reference to the team's new manager. They also occasionally referred to the team as the "Flock," as in a flock of birds, but even then, the scribes still occasionally used the team's other older name and earlier established nickname, the Dodgers.

Meanwhile the happy days Ebbets and the McKeevers had enjoyed moneywise in 1913 were quickly coming to an end. The 40 percent spike the team saw in its attendance (to 347,000) with the opening of Ebbets Field was in peril. A competing, "outlaw" third major league had been formed, organizational meetings having taken place around the time Ebbets Field was opening its doors. Now, a year later, the new league was ready to field its teams.

The new Federal League took wing largely on the bankrolls of wealthy industrialists such as Charles H. Weeghman, who had lunchrooms in Chicago, Phil Ball in St. Louis, and Robert B. Ward and his brother Walter, owners of the Tip Top Bakery in Brooklyn. They put franchises in Chicago, St. Louis, Pittsburgh, and Brooklyn, directly opposite major league teams, and in other cities, such as Indianapolis, Baltimore, Kansas City, and Buffalo.

It would be just the luck of the Brooklyn National League Baseball Club that a competing franchise was going to land not only in its backyard but in its old ballyard. Brooklyn's new Federal Leaguers—the Tip Tops or the Brookfeds, as they were called—were slated to play in Washington Park. Renovation plans were designed to make it "an exact counterpart of the North Side Grounds [later Wrigley Field] at Chicago. By adopting the plans of the Windy City park, the Wards saved much time and trouble," the *Eagle* reported. Although the Wards wouldn't provide details regarding the contract awards to either C. B. Comstock, the supervising architect, or the building contractors, "the Chicago park will cost in the neighborhood of $215,000," providing some indication of what the Brooklyn ballpark's renovations would cost. "The grandstand will be a single decker," the news account said, "but will be so erected that an upper tier may be built should occasion require."[19]

The prospect gave Ebbets and the McKeevers a shudder. By the middle of March in 1914, the entire square block between First and Third streets and Third and Fourth avenues was filled with work shanties and material, while two cranes towered over the site. Three hundred workers crawled over the landscape, and the contractors, who were offered incentives, expressed optimism that the work would be completed in time for the Federals' May 2 opener. The major leagues, meanwhile, threatened a lifetime ban for players who made a jump to the Feds. Although the threat intimidated some of them, most were still emboldened enough to linger in their salary demands so they could squeeze a few extra bucks out of the owners.

The natural rivalry and already acerbic relationship between the Dodgers and Giants, given the antipathies of McGraw and Ebbets, were further fueled in 1914 by the private and deeply held rancor that now ran between Robinson and McGraw. Although neither would admit his feelings about the other publicly, the intensity of the two and the way each emphasized the need to win against the other among his players heightened the confrontations. The Giants took the season series, thirteen games to nine, Robinson often muttering about those losses for hours after a game.

By the time the 1914 season concluded, with Brooklyn finishing fifth with a 75–79 record, just slightly under .500, it was clear that Ebbets and the McKeevers had suffered at the hands of the upstart Federal League in ways they preferred not to admit, even though the Brookfeds were only a .500 team, finishing 77–77. The new circuit not only was encroaching on major league markets and imbuing minor league towns with a major league cachet, but also was bidding up the prices of major league players. And attendance at Ebbets Field was awful. In spite of the team's best finish since 1907, only 122,671 wandered through the gates, the worst home attendance for a Brooklyn ball club since the Spanish-American War year of 1898. (Pittsburgh and Philadelphia also had anemic attendance, and Cincinnati's was worse than Brooklyn's.)

Over the winter the Feds put on a push to lure Jake Daubert, and also moved one of their biggest gate attractions, Benny Kauff, to the Tip Tops. The prospects of the Dodgers having to fight the Brookfeds even harder for patrons increased in 1915 with Kauff's arrival. A flashy guy, Kauff had a penchant for loud clothes, check grabbing, and knocking the hell out of a baseball. He led the Federal League the previous season, batting .370 for the Indianapolis Hoosiers, a franchise that was then moved to Newark the next year.

The Federal League, fighting hard to be recognized as a third major league, had filed suit in the United States District Court for Northern Illinois on January 5, 1915. The suit was brought against Organized Baseball, the sixteen club presidents in the American and National Leagues and the three members of the baseball's National Commission (which then governed baseball). The action alleged violation of the Sherman Anti-Trust Act. The Federal League asked the court to declare Organized Baseball's structure null and void and to essentially do the same to the contracts it had with its players, which would make all of them free agents; it also asked that that the court have Organized Baseball refrain from continuing or initiating legal action against players who had jumped to the Federal League in violation of their contracts.

The Federal League brought an eleven-point argument for relief before Judge Kenesaw Mountain Landis in Chicago, and given that Landis had fined Standard Oil $29,000,000 as a trust-busting judge, the case was a matter of some concern. A Cubs fan, Landis listened to four days of testimony and stem-winding legal arguments, and at one point, cautioned them all: "Both sides must understand that any blows at the thing called baseball would be regarded by this court as a blow to a national institution."[20] After hearing the arguments in January, Judge Landis sat on the case for eleven months without rendering a decision, while theories about how he might rule abounded on both sides and in the press.

During the Federal League battle, some sympathetic sportswriters with a newfound beat were willing to go along with the Feds' puffed-up attendance figures. Even though the Robins' crowds had picked up from a year earlier, fans were still going to see the pin-striped Tip Tops and the likes of showboat Benny Kauff, who was still hitting juiced-up baseballs over the wall and holding court in Brooklyn's best bistros and gin mills. Naturally Ebbets was irritated by exaggerated press reports on the size of crowds showing up to see the Federals, but could do little other than question their veracity and mutter about the art of press agentry and the ethics of reporters under his breath.

The extra pressure of the Brookfeds had Charley Ebbets looking to make some extra money with the ballpark when the team was on the road in 1915. He talked about boxing, about setting up tennis courts in the outfield, even about ice hockey in the wintertime.

Initially Marcus Loew showed some movies at Ebbets Field, but these were stopped after a year for violation of the Sunday law. Boxing was the only idea that panned out, inaugurated at the ballpark on May 31, 1915. The headliners on the featured card were 155-pound Mike Gibbons and U.S. Army champion Soldier Bartfield, who weighed in at 148 pounds. Gibbons, from St. Paul, was a very proficient boxer, the kind of fighter called a leather pusher in the trade because he would frequently "carry" opponents that he could put away. He could make good money at the business, but lacked the competitive fire and gritty spirit so often characteristic of champions.

The open-air fight was on a clear day under a warm sun, with a crowd of 11,000 in the stands. The boxing ring was put near home plate on the third base line. "The solid bank of straw-hatted fans in the upper tier of the big baseball stand, the circus seats and canvas walls on the field, the bright hued raiment of the women scattered throughout the big crowd, the boxers dancing about the ring, the referee clad in white flannel, the band and the clicking of the 'movies,' all tended to give real holiday color to the scene," said *New York Times*.[21]

Gibbons's performance was lackluster given that he was the better boxer, but in the fight's last rounds he managed to stagger Bartfield "with his terrific wallops." Without a KO in New York in those days, it was a "no decision" fight, though reporters would often express their opinions in news accounts. Bartfield "easily earned a draw," one headline writer said, while another write-up began, "Gibbons Has Hard Bout," with a subhead "Soldier Bartfield Makes Westerner Hustle to Win." The first knockout at the ballpark was on the same fight card, when an Italian American, Johnny Dundee, dropped John Drummie with a right and a left uppercut in the second round.[22]

The next day the baseball team returned. In an exciting contest, Brooklyn managed to tie the Philadelphia "Quakers" in the bottom of the ninth inning, and Zack Wheat subsequently drove in the winning run in the bottom of the eleventh, but not without inducing a casualty. Local florist W. C. Martin, who had complained of chest pains while exulting in the ninth, let out a final victory shriek in the eleventh before collapsing in his seat dead. What could be better? He was in heaven before he had a chance to go.

By the end of July the Dodgers had reached second place in the jumbled standings. Robinson's team had a shot, something that couldn't be said during the last fifteen years, so Robinson and Ebbets went out and picked up a couple of pitchers: Larry Cheney was purchased from the Cubs, while Rube Marquard, dubbed the "$11,000 Lemon" during his early days with the Giants before then–pitching coach Robinson set him on the right path, was picked up from McGraw on waivers. In the earlier part of the 1915 season and the preceding two seasons, Marquard had pitched in 108 games; he'd gone 9–8 by August after going 12–22 the year before, and McGraw decided he was finished. But none of Brooklyn's pitching replenishments worked during the campaign, and the team's bid faded with an offensive swoon in mid-September as the team sat in second place. The Robins finished third, but delight of delights, the hated Giants finished last. For Brooklyn fans, the only thing better could be winning the pennant.

In late October the Brookfeds owner George Ward, who had five 80-foot poles under construction to serve as light towers that would make night games possible, gathered some semipro ballplayers to play several innings under night lights at Washington Park in the hope that such games could be scheduled the following season. He originally wanted to have night contests for Federal League games during the 1915 season but couldn't finish the project in time. As an experiment, the effort presaged the barnstorming Kansas City Monarchs' system of portable lights on poles with generators on trucks by fifteen years and the major league debut of night baseball by twenty years; while Ward was serious, his upbeat comments belied the nascent stage of the technology. The exercise was pronounced satisfactory after acknowledging some faults "which may easily be remedied by adjusting the screens in front of the lights," making the staging sound more like a photo shoot.

The Federal League drew well, but the high salaries that its owners promulgated were causing as much strain on them as they were on the magnates of the American and National leagues. Meanwhile, by his inaction, Judge Landis encouraged the two opposing parties in the federal lawsuit to consider settling their differences, an effect probably intended.

Late in 1915 the oil mogul Harry Sinclair—the same person who would later be linked with the Teapot Dome Scandal during the Harding administration in the early 1920s—announced plans to bring a Federal League team into Manhattan. Sinclair took an option on property at 144th Street and Lenox Avenue, not far from the Polo Grounds, where the Yankees had become tenants of the Giants. Sinclair also had blueprints displayed in an office window around Times Square detailing the over 42,000-seat park that he said he intended to build, and rented a luxury suite of offices in a Manhattan skyscraper to boot. It was all a bluff, but it worked. It prompted the National Commission— or so-called Organized Baseball—to settle.

Ebbets and the McKeevers got the best Christmas present they could have hoped for when the agreement folded the upstart Federal League in December. The pact allowed Weeghman to buy the Cubs and move them into his new ballpark on the North Side of Chicago, while the St. Louis Federal League franchise owner, Phil Ball, was allowed to buy that city's American League franchise. The Ward brothers were given twenty annual payments of $20,000; Sinclair received ten annual payments of $10,000 for his wooden ballpark in Newark and was permitted to sell players who had jumped contracts back to major league owners.

The only negative item in the sorting out was the destination of Brooklyn favorite Benny Kauff. McGraw forked over $30,000 to acquire the popular Federal League star, cutting off Wilbert Robinson's dream of adding him to his own squad at Ebbets Field. Thus Kauff took his colorful ways across the river.

Ebbets Field, meanwhile, was spurring growth in its immediate area. Housing starts had generally involved several homes at a time, but by 1916 rows of attached row houses—ten or twelve at a time—were rising near the ballpark. Housing had been built by Crown and Carroll streets, one and two blocks north, and also on President Street between Bedford and Rogers avenues, three and a half blocks away. More homes were built two, three, and four blocks south, along Sterling Street and Lefferts Avenue and Lincoln Road, the construction heading east from Bedford toward Rogers, Nostrand, and New York avenues.

The Bedford Avenue block across the street behind the right-field wall was still largely undeveloped, with only a single, small wooden shack. On Montgomery Street by Stoddard Place, one block east, a small brick building stood where a six-story apartment would rise in the 1930s, overlooking the field. A number of the Brooklyn players— especially those with families—had rented apartments near Parkside and Flatbush avenues, and were reportedly often seen pushing their baby carriages on surrounding streets or in Prospect Park.[23]

At the start of the 1916 season, Ebbets Field's right-field wall was bedecked with ads that extolled scotch whiskey and announced that Tanglefoot flypaper caught 50,000,000,000 flies. In an era before a fence was atop Ebbets Field's twenty-foot wall, when balls that bounced fair into the stands were home runs, Robins' second baseman George Cutshaw was fortunate enough to hit a ground ball into right field that hit the angled wall just so, went up into the air, and spun with just enough english over the wall for a home run. Perhaps this was indicative of the Robins' fortunes in 1916, when a Brooklyn team was at last competitive and poised to make a run at a pennant.

The club had great hitters like Wheat and Daubert, but the spark-plug was none other than Casey Stengel. Manager Robinson also used Ivy Olson—who had a short fuse—to replace Ollie O'Mara at short. While Ivy and Robbie hardly got along, sportswriter Frank Graham characterized Olson as "smart and hard and tough, and as game as anybody that ever lived." Robbie himself evidently concluded as much, for Olson wound up playing.

The Robins wore new white uniforms featuring a Brooklyn "B" on the left side over vertical and horizontal stripes that created a window-pane pattern. They played with swagger and stayed ahead most of the way. The majority of baseball prognosticators were waiting for Brooklyn to collapse. The team dropped five games to the third-place Phils in early September, allowing the second-place Boston Braves to creep into the lead, but then the Phils beat the Braves three straight to take first place. However, the Phils then hit the Giants in the midst of their all-time record 26-game winning streak, and lost four in a row, allowing Brooklyn to again take first.

Now the Robins would go head to head against Philadelphia. Ebbets roused the fans' ire when he scheduled a morning–afternoon double-header on Saturday, September 30, in the wake of a rainout, in order to get two separate gates. Seven thousand showed up for the morning encounter; 16,000 came in the afternoon. By losing the morning game, the Robins fell a half game behind the Phillies. But they bounced back and took the second game, 6–1, with Rube Marquard beating the Phillies' 33-game winner that year, Grover Cleveland Alexander, to regain the lead. For the raucous fans at the new ballpark, the fruits of victory were about to assuage the bitterness of a decade and a half.

After a quiet Sunday in observance of the blue laws, Jack Coombs tossed a shutout for Brooklyn at Ebbets Field to beat the Giants, while Philadelphia was splitting a doubleheader in Boston. Brooklyn was now ahead by a full game with three games left to play against the Giants, all at Ebbets Field. The Phillies had only pair remaining in the form of a twin bill on Tuesday. They dropped their first game and were behind in the second as Brooklyn overcame a 4–1 New York lead with four runs in the third.

The Brooks reached Rube Benton and knocked him out of the box, and when McGraw put in Pol Perritt, he was going into a full windup even with runners on base. Grounders that should have been handled were squibbing through, and something about the Giants play wasn't quite up to snuff.

McGraw was outraged; the Little Napoleon felt his team wasn't giving 100 percent. The Giants had already been mathematically eliminated, and many of the players on his squad were old friends of Robbie's from his days as a Giant coach. Additionally, there was some bad blood between the Giants and the Phillies. Although the Giants managed to tie the game in the fifth, the Robins scored a run in the bottom of the inning and also scored single runs in the sixth, seventh, and eighth for a 9–5 lead. McGraw, disgusted, was gone by the end of the game, not banished by the umpires, but of his own volition. The Giants did manage to push one inconsequential run across in the ninth. Wheat, who caught the last fly ball, threw it in the stands as he galloped off the field. It wasn't official yet, but everyone in the crowd was ecstatic. Brooklyn was going to win the pennant.[24]

McGraw didn't like it a bit. He complained to reporters about players disregarding his signals and refusing to obey orders, but had enough sense to keep his mouth shut when asked if he thought his players were throwing the game. When Robinson was told of McGraw's inferences, he said simply, "We beat the Giants fifteen times in twenty-two games. Tell McGraw to stop pissing on my pennant!"[25]

The Brooklyn Robins became official champions while they were in the clubhouse, when the final results of the second Philadelphia game arrived.

Under the stands, in the clubhouse, the players laughed, hugged, yelled, and snake-danced, draping themselves all over Robbie and each other. For Charley Ebbets, it was the first pennant since 1900 and the first in the new ballpark. Charley had a winner in his fourth year in Flatbush, and when the clinching occurred, the joy was unbounded.

"Well, I'm satisfied, boys," Charley said. "I've attained my ambition in baseball, that of winning a pennant, and I'm ready to step down and out. If there's anybody that wants the club, he can have it for what it's worth, because if I go, I'm sure the McKeevers will go with me. We've been like brothers since we became partners and we have no regrets.

"I've worked hard in baseball and I'm 56 years old. I've built a fine baseball stadium for Brooklyn and I've brought a pennant to the borough. It was a big undertaking. I've had my knocks and I've had my boosts. I'm glad it's over, because I need a good long rest, and I'm going to take it. I'm ready to sell out if anybody wants to buy."

"Yes, you are," said a reporter nearby. "You'll wait till you win a world's series."

"Well, that might come right now," Charley said. "But the proposition to sell the Brooklyn Ball Club holds good. I'm willing to hold my share of the Ebbets Field property and take a rental." It was the first of Charley's remarks about selling that he'd make from time to time.

"Anyone with a million or so," wrote one scribe, "can have the Superbas right now."[26]

Above the Rotunda, beginning with the fourth set of double windows on the first base side of the park, Ebbets had both his office and a larger private room behind it, each of the rooms encompassing two sets of double windows. A reception room was outside his main office, and on the morning of October 6, a husky guard was outside, turning away all who would prevail upon Charley for Series tickets.

The Robins had a motorcade out of Brooklyn starting from Ebbets Field at 11 A.M. At the appointed hour, after Ebbets opened his door and gave a brief interview to newspapermen, the team's twenty-three players and seven club officials, including Charley, piled into eighteen touring cars that would take them on their way. They proceeded down Bedford Avenue, stopped at the Bedford branch of the YMCA, turned at Lafayette Avenue, and wended their way downtown. Cheering thousands prefaced the stops at Borough Hall, which had six or seven thousand more people, and in front of the *Eagle* building, with another five hundred fans and a "Hail to the Chief" serenade from the St. John's Orphan Asylum Band. From there it was on to Grand Central, where they also were mobbed, for a one o'clock train up to Boston and an overnight at the Brunswick Hotel before the beginning of the thirteenth World Series.

The Robins dropped the first two games up in Beantown, the second contest a fourteen-inning classic between Sherry Smith and a young Babe Ruth. The contests were held at Braves Field, since the capacity was bigger—40,000 to 35,000—than that of Fenway Park.

While Charley had been up in Boston, the McKeever brothers were supervising World Series ticket orders in the ballpark at home. "Edward McKeever handled the office force," said the *Eagle*, "while Steve McKeever salved the impatient populace clamoring at the sanctum doors." There was one report of scalping, but the McKeevers, knowing who had received the relatively few tickets distributed to that point, followed up quickly to ensure that tickets were not falling into the hands of speculators.

Meanwhile, work had begun on the double rows of field boxes that would extend from the dugouts on both sides of the field. In left field, wooden bleachers had already been erected. In the years ahead they would come to be known as "Wheatsville," in honor of the team's great outfielder.

In the third game, on October 10, the first World Series game in the new park, Carl Mays faced Jack Coombs for the Robins. Before the game, Jake Daubert went over to a field box, rubbed his bat over the bald head of John Geier, a friend from his hometown of Minersville, Pennsylvania. Jake went three for four, his first single in the third with one out setting up the game's first run, which was driven in by George Cutshaw. Brooklyn added another run in the fourth and two in the fifth to chase Mays. Boston scored twice in the sixth and once when Larry Gardner homered in the seventh, but Ed Pfeffer was brought in to nail down the 4–3 win down for Brooklyn.

Finally in the win column, the Brooklyn fans let loose in an area across the street adjacent to the ballpark. "Down on the green patch of territory bounded by Malbone Street [before most of Malbone was renamed Empire Boulevard], Cedar Place and Bedford Avenue, there was a jubilee yesterday afternoon just as the haze of the October day melted into the shadows of evening, which was in many respects the finest ever seen in Brooklyn," said the *Eagle*. "Several hundred frantic men and boys sprang from encircling seats out to the green area of turf and zigzagged about behind a band delirious with joy. For fifteen minutes they wound in and out of the diamond blue pennants fluttering, singing 'Glory, glory hallelujah!' and yelling their heads off. A stranger, unfamiliar with the ways of baseball and the baseball crowd, might have taken the demonstration for an outing of lunatics."

Boston's Royal Rooters stood by with their flags and voices still. After the Brooklyn celebration had finally finished, they piped up with their own procession, and their redcoat-clad band played their anthem, "Tessie."

All at once, the fans parted with their summer headgear. "In another moment friend and foe alike bombarded each other with cushions of straw and the air was filled with the flying discs. This," said the *Eagle*, "was the end of a perfect day."[27] Here, in its fourth year, fans at Ebbets Field saw what would go down in history as one of the Brooklyn ballpark's most celebrated games.

CHAPTER FIVE

Robins' Nest

The sunset parade after the third game of the World Series on October 10, 1916, would be the most glorious moment at Ebbets Field for the rest of the decade. For even though the next morning dawned brilliantly in Brooklyn, with a cloudless sky, a brightly shining sun, and the stands filling quickly, the dream of Charley Ebbets's championship quickly unraveled.

The Brooklyn Robins managed to score two runs off Dutch Leonard of the Boston Red Sox in the first inning in game 4, but in the top half of the second, Red Sox third baseman Larry Gardner came up with two men on, tapped the plate lightly, pulled down the visor of his cap, and smacked a Rube Marquard offering out by the flagpole. After chugging around the bases, he slid into the plate for a three-run, inside-the-park homer as the Red Sox poured out of their dugout to greet him.

The afternoon's sole comfort would be the only Series appearance of Brooklyn's old favorite, southpaw Nap Rucker. The crowd rose to give him a long, rousing cheer as he walked in from the bullpen with Brooklyn behind 6–2 in the eighth. Rucker, who had been sidelined by bursitis much of the year, had announced his intention to retire come season's end. It was the only Series appearance of his career, and he was coming in to pitch for what everyone rightly sensed would be the last time. He obliged by striking out three men in two innings, including the last hitter in the top of the ninth, the last man he ever faced.

For the Ebbets Field and old Washington Park denizens who had waited as long as Rucker to see the team in the Series, it was a touching note, even if it couldn't somehow magically change the results. The two teams went back to Boston, where the Red Sox wrapped up the Series in the fifth game the next day on Ernie Shore's three-hitter.

For all of Brooklyn's success that fall, changes were ahead. Charley Ebbets was still smarting from the higher, multiyear contracts he awarded during the Federal League war, and as they expired, he was cutting salaries by as much as a third. "Ebbets liked a clear line of demarcation kept between baseball's upper classes—the owners, the league officials, the managers—and the lower classes—the players. Today," wrote Robert Creamer in 1984, "when star players make five or ten times as much as the manager, it's difficult to appreciate the inferior position the players held in those days."[1] The holdouts, Daubert, Stengel, and Wheat, were especially angry given their winning season and languished without signed contracts into the spring, leading to a sourness among some players at Ebbets Field, even as the National League pennant was hoisted up the flagpole at the beginning of 1917. The team got off to a slow start.

More important, the nation was preoccupied with the war in Europe, which the United States formally entered on April 6. There was plenty of activity in Brooklyn, but most of it was centered at the Brooklyn Navy Yard rather than at Ebbets Field. At one point, Ebbets agreed to have the Brooklyn club play a ballgame to benefit the war-related "Militia of Mercy" charity as well as the Red Cross.

Although it wouldn't be for much longer, Sunday baseball with admission charges was still outlawed in New York, and since the more conservative religionists were firm about any commercial incursions on the Lord's Day, Charley—and not for the first time—resorted to some duplicity: he announced that when his team played the Phillies on July 1, a band concert would be held before the game, and that attendees could pay for that to benefit the charities and see the game for free.

Admiral Usher, the Navy Yard's commandant, watched from a box as 1,500 sailors paraded as part of the before-game festivities. Of the 15,000 that turned out, about half paid and the other half wandered in after the music, and when it was all over, Ebbets and Uncle Robbie were arrested for flouting the law and then routinely released by cops. Charley, quite pleased, turned over more than $5,000 to charity and put another dent in the Sunday baseball ban.[2]

There was little reason to use the ten rows of wooden-plank bleachers in fair territory—the so-called circus seats—that were extended into left center field the previous fall before the World Series. The Superbas finished a listless seventh, and attendance, as it did in the rest of the league, plummeted, in Brooklyn's case sliding from 447,747 for the previous year to 221,619.[3]

During 1918 many players either enlisted, went to work in war-related businesses, or were taken by the draft. Pitcher Al Mamaux, who came over from Pittsburgh in a five-player deal that involved Brooklyn's sending the beloved Stengel and George Cutshaw westward, wound up taking a draft-exempt job at the Quincy, Massachusetts, shipyard. Provost Marshal General Enoch Crowder's "work-or-fight" order, issued that May, meant that all draft-age men had to be either in the military or in essential industries. Chuck Ward, a shortstop arriving in the Stengel deal, was drafted, and the core of the Brooklyn pitching staff, Jeff Pfeffer, Leon Cadore, and Sherry Smith, had gone off to serve. Remaining, though, via the Pittsburgh deal, was one Burleigh Grimes, a spitballer who over time would play a big role in Brooklyn.

Ebbets, meanwhile, established a fund with a $500 contribution to help take care of the ballplayers' dependents in their absence, offering to equal any amount that was contributed collectively by the players. As a nonessential industry, baseball saw its schedule cut short by the War Department, completing the season in early September. With Brooklyn a central hub of military preparedness and with a raging influenza epidemic, an anemic trickle of 83,831 fans, the lowest in the majors, showed up for the home portion of a truncated 126-game season. (Boston's Braves only drew a little over a thousand more.) Brooklyn finished an uneventful fifth, and afterward the club announced plans to turn Ebbets Field over to the military for use as a storage facility for the duration.

The poor attendance hurt. "Financing was a problem," Dorothy Ebbets Dollmeyer recalled in her memoir. "It was grandfather's only business and he was not in the position of Colonel Ruppert, owner of the Yankees . . . or the others to whom baseball was an avocation and glamour and showmanship were the only goals."

Any misfortune regarding money and all the economic uncertainty had to be kept in perspective. Thousands of Americans had now perished in the Great War as millions of Europeans had before them, much of it in trench warfare that amounted to little more than mass slaughter. And the influenza epidemic was claiming more than a half a million lives in the United States alone.

Then, on November 1, while the First American Army was attacking along a front fifteen miles north of Verdun, a thoughtless, needless disaster rocked Brooklyn, just blocks away from the ballpark. It occurred during the evening rush hour in the Malbone Street tunnel, near the Malbone Street station along the Brighton subway line. Before 7 P.M., an old wooden five-car train driven by twenty-nine-year-old Anthony Lewis, a railroad dispatcher serving as a replacement motorman because of a Brooklyn Rapid Transit strike that began early that morning, went around a curve at seventy miles per hour.

The train jumped the rails, running into a concrete partition between the north and southbound tracks, and nearly everyone in the first car, save the motorman himself, was killed. The left sides of the second and third cars were stripped away, and pillars cut great gashes in the sides of the other cars. Most of those in the second car were also killed or badly injured.

As news of the accident spread quickly over the borough, those who had expected family or friends flocked to the site. For a frantic short while that evening, Charley Jr. was uncertain about his father's fate, since he was supposed to meet him at Ebbets Field about the time the collision occurred. For an hour, Charley Jr. feverishly worked the phone trying to ascertain his dad's whereabouts, finally getting word that Charles Sr. was making a short speech elsewhere for the War Savings Stamp Campaign. Charley Jr. then threw open Ebbets Field's gates for treatment of the less seriously injured. Out of the hundreds who were hurt, about fifty people were treated at the ballpark by doctors volunteering their services. By 11 P.M. that night, eighty-five bodies had been recovered. The death toll would rise to ninety-seven, resulting in a listing in the *World Almanac* under rail disasters. Ten days later, the armistice was signed, ending World War I.

Not long after the accident, the name of Malbone Street was changed to Empire Boulevard, and the Malbone Street subway station became the Prospect Park station. Unlike the war, which everyone would seek to remember and memorialize, the city of New York did everything possible to make everyone forget the events of that night in the tunnel.

Unsure about the postwar economy in 1919, baseball cut back its usual 154-game schedule to 140 games. The Giants franchise changed hands over that winter, not going to candy mogul George Loft, oil mogul Harry Sinclair, or actor George M. Cohan, who were all reported to be interested, but instead to Charles A. Stoneham, who ran what was called a "bucket shop" on Wall Street. A bucket shop took people's stock trade orders but didn't necessarily execute the transactions, hoping to cash in on customers' poor guesses. It was a less-than-savory business, and so was the man who acted as a go-between to help arrange the sale: gambler Arnold Rothstein, who would be implicated in the Black Sox scandal later on. John McGraw was also able to buy a small interest in the ball club as part of the deal.

Once the season began, Casey Stengel, discharged from the navy he had joined the previous June, began picking up where he had left off. It was in Brooklyn at Ebbets Field in late May, while Casey was in his Pirates uniform, that he pulled a stunt for which he'd become renowned.

It was the first year Sunday baseball was permitted in New York State, a development Ebbets had waited to see happen for a long time, and a healthy Sunday crowd of some 20,000 had turned out at the ballpark. Up until then, with the exception of opening days, Ebbets Field had been like a neighborhood ballpark hosting a small-town team during the week, and it was only on Saturdays and holidays when the people from around the borough would come en masse from their neighborhoods to see the games.

Stengel was having a tough time with left-hander Sherry Smith that day, striking out twice and grounding to short, with the crowd razzing him each time as an easy out. "It was the custom during Ebbets Field's 45 years of existence for right fielders of both teams to occasionally stop in the Dodger bullpen, which was in foul territory near the right-field wall, and stay there between innings when it was unlikely that they'd be coming to bat, instead of making the long jog into the dugout and back," writes Robert Creamer. It was there where Stengel stopped, visiting with his friend Leon Cadore. The pitcher liked to do magic tricks, and happened to be holding a sparrow.

"Let me have it," Casey said.

Stengel covered the sparrow with his cap, brought it to his dugout, and then put it under his cap on his head before he went up to hit. It was then quite literally that he gave the crowd the bird. "The crowd greeted him with mock applause and a round of good-natured boos," says Creamer. "Casey turned towards the stands, bowed and lifted his cap, and there was the sparrow, which immediately fluttered away. The crowd howled, and even the plate umpire, Cy Rigler, joined in the laughter."[4] The hat stunt secured Casey's place as the game's reigning comic genius.

Surveying the day's events afterward, Wilbert Robinson said, "Hell, he always did have birds in his garrett."[5]

If other laughter was reserved for Robinson's fifth-place team, baseball's fears about the economy proved to be unfounded. Attendance picked up everywhere. At Ebbets Field, buoyed by Sunday baseball and a desire for a return to normalcy, attendance more than quadrupled to 360,721, fourth highest in the league. Meanwhile McGraw's Giants, up till then the biggest drawing card in baseball, drew over 700,000—almost twice what the Robins had—up at the Polo Grounds.

Yet the sense of sacrifice and sadness that accompanied the losses in the war was still very much with everyone, and it would stay that way for a long time. Up on Eastern Parkway, known then for its beautiful homes and apartment houses and its elegant tree-lined thoroughfare, the names of soldiers who had died in the Great War would be fastened below each tree.

The private life of a baseball magnate hardly ever made news, but it did in the case of Charley Ebbets, whose marital problems hit the press in September 1919. Minnie filed for divorce, and this story was followed by snippets of news that kept appearing through December. Minnie asked the court that the papers be sealed. When reporters came around to ask Charley about it, he said, "Yes, it's so, but I wonder if you can't refrain from mentioning, in connection with this affair, that I own the Dodgers."[6] The scribes, quite naturally, recorded every word and promptly printed it. Actually, Minnie was acting in collusion with Charley, since he paid for her attorney. Charley himself would only admit that Mrs. Ebbets wanted her freedom.

The Ebbets divorce papers revealed the other woman in Charley's life, Mrs. Grace Slade Nott. Anna Marie Ebbets Booth, Charley's middle daughter, testified before court referee William H. Ford that she asked her father to give Mrs. Nott up; Charley, in turn, told Anna to "mind your own business."[7] Anna also told of another occasion when she put Mrs. Nott out of the Ebbets Field grandstand, only to have Charley come down and give his daughter the same treatment.

The referee's report recommended that the court grant Mrs. Ebbets's request for a divorce. Divorce laws were tougher in those days, however, and Justice Benedict, the presiding judge, quickly assessed that things were proceeding too smoothly in the case, found the collusion, and wouldn't grant the decree. Minnie had to settle for seeking a legal separation in December.

It also was an eventful off-season in other respects. Babe Ruth was purchased the day after Christmas by the Yankees, and the sale changed the game of baseball indelibly and forever. On Friday, January 16, 1920, prohibition on alcoholic beverages began nationwide, something that would certainly have an impact on Harry M. Stevens's catering business at Ebbets Field. The spitball was outlawed, too, before the start of the 1920 season, with a caveat: the active major league veteran pitchers who had always thrown a spitter could continue to use it for the balance of their careers.

Brooklyn had two of the seventeen pitchers who were "grandfathered" by the edict—Burleigh Grimes and Clarence Mitchell—and both of them helped give the Robins the mound depth that arguably made their staff the best in the league going into the 1920 season. Aside from the Robins' spitballers, they still had left-handers Sherry Smith and Rube Marquard, as well as right-handers Pfeffer, Cadore, and Mamaux.

Leon Cadore became known for one of the most famous baseball games ever played. Ebbets Field hosted the middle game of three consecutive extra-inning marathons in May that featured pitching performances that are inconceivable today. Cadore and Joe Oeschger of the Braves made history pitching all twenty-six innings on a nippy, overcast day, Saturday, May 1, when the Robins and the Braves wound up in a 1–1 tie in Boston, the game finally called on account of darkness. Cadore, who was never the same pitcher again, went back to the hotel, went to bed, and stayed there.

The Robins, meanwhile, grabbed a midnight train to Brooklyn to meet the Phillies on Sunday, seeing as how Sunday baseball was still illegal in Pennsylvania. It took all of thirteen innings to lose to the Phillies, 4–3, at Ebbets Field, with Burleigh Grimes and George Smith also pitching complete games. To add insult to injury, the Brooklyn team took another night train back to Boston, found Cadore still in the sack the next day, and then went out only to drop a nineteen-inning contest, 2–1, with Sherry Smith and Boston's Dana Fillingim also pitching the entire contests.

In three days, Uncle Robbie's team had played fifty-eight innings, scored five runs, and had nothing to show for it. And when the twenty-six-inning tie game Cadore and Oeschger pitched was continued on June 25 from where the two teams left off, the Braves scored in the first inning to win. Nevertheless Grimes was having a great year and Zack Wheat, Hy Myers, and Ed Konetchy were carrying the team at the plate.

While the Robins seesawed with the Reds for the league lead, taking and losing first place in June and again in July 1920, two black baseball teams had booked a date at Ebbets Field, with the Bacharach Giants, an Atlantic City–based team that played between 1916 and 1929, pitted against the New York Lincoln Giants, a white-owned team that operated between 1911 and 1930.

"Cannonball" Dick Redding was on the mound for the B's against an old teammate, Smokey Joe Williams, and 16,000 fans showed up for the occasion. The only time Redding was in any trouble against the Lincoln Giants was when Fats Jenkins, who would play regularly in Ebbets Field in 1935 with another black team, the Brooklyn Eagles, tripled. But Redding went on to retire the next three men he faced, the last one on a called strike, en route to a 5–0 shutout victory.

Black baseball and the Negro Leagues were created as an enterprise in the wake of segregation; there hadn't been a black player playing with a team in the so-called major leagues since before the turn of the century, despite John McGraw's unsuccessful efforts to pass off Charlie Grant as Chief Tokohama, a Cherokee Indian, in 1901. The move drew the ire of White Sox owner Charlie Comiskey after a spring training exhibition game, when he observed, "the Cherokee of McGraw's is really Grant, the crack Negro second baseman, fixed up with war paint and a bunch of feathers."[8]

Black teams emerged in the period between 1890 and 1916 out of the large black communities up and down the East Coast and through-, out the Midwest and South. The success of the teams commercially swelled with the black migration northward around the time of World War I and in the years afterward, before the onset of acutely difficult economic periods within the communities themselves. Black teams played each other and white semiprofessional teams, with teams operating independently and setting up dates where they could, often playing without a permanent home base.

"Typically, a team's extensive travel, nearly constant schedule of games, and payment of players determined its professional status," writes historian Neil Lanctot.

> Yet black professional teams remained unorganized, lacking league affiliation and the formal contracts employed in white Organized Baseball, which bound players to individual clubs.
>
> Black professional teams also contended with limited financial backing, and like other African American institutions, seldom operated without direct or indirect white assistance. Few black entrepreneurs possessed the necessary capital, and even those with adequate resources were unenthusiastic about investing in something as uncertain as a professional baseball team. Moreover, because of rampant prejudice, blacks at least initially needed whites to lease playing fields and arrange games with white opponents, and white booking agents, controlling parks and schedules, soon became a permanent yet controversial fixture in black baseball.[9]

A big Texan by the name of Andrew "Rube" Foster, a pitcher with a submarine delivery, whipping the ball in with a low, below-the-belt sidearm motion, was the son of a minister. He had gotten his nickname when he outdueled major league pitcher Rube Waddell in a barnstorming game in 1903. After starting with the Waco Yellow Jackets at age seventeen, Foster starred with the Chicago Union Giants, the Cuban X Giants, and the Leland Giants before partnering with white businessman John Schorling to become a co-owner, manager, and player for the Chicago American Giants. Foster went on to form the Negro National League with eight teams based in the Midwest in 1920; in December 1922, he helped Edward Bolden, a postal employee who had started and led the Hilldale club in Darby, Pennsylvania, in 1910, form the Eastern Colored League in time for the 1923 season. The league would have six teams, including the Bachrach Giants, the New York Lincoln Giants, the Hilldale club, the Baltimore Black Sox, the Cuban Stars, and the Brooklyn Royal Giants. The Brooklyn Royal Giants played at Dexter Park in Woodhaven on the Brooklyn–Queens border, just on the Queens side of the county line. Dexter Park served as the home of the Brooklyn Bushwicks, one of the country's finest white semiprofessional teams, who would sometimes field moonlighting major league ballplayers playing under different names.

The owner of the Brooklyn Royal Giants was Nat Strong, forty-nine, a white New York City native who had been a booking agent and in the promotions business since the late 1890s; Strong co-owned Dexter Park with Max Rosner and ran the Bushwicks, and also controlled a number of other semipro parks in the New York metropolitan area. He routinely booked black teams in the 1920s, "offering a flat guarantee of $500 to $600 and refusing to offer visiting clubs the common option of a percentage of the profits," according to Lanctot.[10] The relationships between and among all of those involved in running the business of black baseball were interdependent and complex; Strong's policy regarding barnstorming teams often infuriated the black owners, yet in hard times they were happy the dates could be had. In either case, most, but not all, preferred such terms rather than having a team remain idle.

Strong's participation in the Eastern Colored League is described as tepid by Lanctot, and he notes that by the 1930s, Strong was "openly hostile to any organization that might potentially cut his bookings by weaning black teams away from their reliance on independent games with white semipros."[11] As such, an Ebbets Field that attracted black teams was a competing venue for Strong, and for that matter, the Bushwicks' and the black teams' caliber of play was good enough to keep neighborhood crowds entertained for a long afternoon doubleheader. Those who lived nearby didn't even have to spend a nickel for carfare to get to Ebbets Field.

Brooklyn climbed back on top in the 1920 National League race in the middle of August, and then the Giants jumped in the race as well. Brooklyn began September with an auspicious start: back-to-back shutout victories by Grimes and Cadore to slip into first. But Pfeffer and Grimes were beaten in Philadelphia on Labor Day, and Brooklyn fell back to second place. Good hitting won the next three games against the Phils, and Grimes opened a homestand against the Cardinals with a 4–2 victory. This last win put the Robins back into first.

The next day, in what was probably the most exciting game all season long, Brooklyn trailed St. Louis 5–3 going into the bottom of the ninth before tying the game. In the eleventh, the Cardinals scored three runs to make it 8–5, but then Brooklyn rallied for four in its half to win the game, 9–8, and retain its lead in the standings.

Uncle Robbie's flock won five more games in the next three days to run their winning streak to ten. And then they whipped the slumping Reds two out of three. When the Robins shellacked the Cubs at Ebbets Field in both ends of a doubleheader on September 14, the *Eagle* headlined that it was "all over now but the shouting," while sports reporter Thomas Rice, probably the victim of a straw-hat snatcher, bewailed "the juvenile straw hat bashers of alien origin whose assaults upon citizens have been treated by magistrates as a merry jest."

When Marquard shut the Giants out at Ebbets Field on September 26, it clinched a tie for the pennant. "Robbie was so excited that, as he came out of the park, he kissed a strange woman, thinking it was Ma," said sportswriter Frank Graham in his informal history of the Brooklyn Dodgers. "At least, that's what he told his startled wife, who was standing a few feet away, waiting for him." [12]

Brooklyn won the pennant the following day, an off-day, when the Braves' third baseman Norman "Tony" Boeckel beat the Giants with a home run into the left-field stands at the Polo Grounds. Brooklyn's season-ending margin would be a comfortable seven games over the Giants, giving their fans their second World Series at Ebbets Field in five years.

Over 800,000 fans came out to Ebbets Field that season, the second-highest draw in the National League to McGraw's Giants, the men turning out most often in jackets and ties and wearing caps or hats, even in the bleachers behind the three-foot-high wooden fence in left field. Women came too, though they were many fewer in number, arriving most often but not always escorted. When the crowds were heavy, people would stand in front of the scoreboard placed between sections of the bleachers in left-center field, obscuring the inning-by-inning line scores of the games. The only thing electric about the scoreboard was the round "Boston Garter" clock, situated in the center on a pediment that rose a few feet higher than the ballpark's original exterior wall, which stood a few feet behind it. Advertisements promoted Safetee Shaving Razors and Gem Damaskeene Blades at seven for 50 cents.

The lettering for strikes, balls, and outs, posted above the line scores for each of the league's games, was twice as big as the names of the teams' cities, which were all abbreviated except for Boston and

St. Louis. Batting orders were listed vertically on the left side of the board, but since the players didn't wear numbers then, those who were in the batting order were identified by matching the number posted on the board to the player's name in the scorecard, which, more often than not, mirrored the spot he had in the batting order anyway.[13]

Over in the American League, attendance records were being shattered; the Yankees became the first team to surpass the million mark in a single season. The Ruthian era had begun: the Babe was in the process of launching a season record of 54 home runs, eclipsing his own record of 29. Despite that, it was not the Yankees but the Indians, led by the great Tris Speaker, who were edging out the reigning American League champion White Sox, who had other problems as well. Toward the end of the 1920 campaign, the conspiracy on the part of some members of the Chicago White Sox to throw the previous year's Series against the Cincinnati Reds at the behest of gamblers was coming to light. After September 23, each day's headlines revealed a new piece of information from the Chicago grand jury investigation.

To add to all the attention, several days before Cleveland clinched the pennant and the Brooklyn–Cleveland World Series began, Brooklyn district attorney Harry E. Lewis called in twelve Brooklyn players over the course of two days to examine them regarding rumors suggesting that players had been approached by gamblers to fix the upcoming World Series. The investigation revealed no wrongdoing.

When baseball's National Commission met, it was originally reported that the World Series would begin with three games in the home of the American League park, then the middle four games in Brooklyn, with the last two, if necessary, alternating between the two sites. (The World Series was a best-of-nine affair requiring five wins between 1919 and 1921.) But then plans changed and Brooklyn drew the first three contests.

Brooklyn was favored by virtue of the team's pitching, but public sentiment across the nation seemed to rest with Cleveland and its player-manager Tris Speaker in sympathy for an unthinkable tragedy: the death of the team's shortstop, Ray Chapman, the morning after he was beaned by submarine pitcher Carl Mays's fastball in a contest with the Yankees up at the Polo Grounds during the dog days of August. Before that incident, scuffed baseballs browned from bouncing in the dirt were often kept in games; those balls were tougher to see, especially in shadows, and pitchers could make a scuffed ball move in different ways. Afterward, the leagues mandated that only new, relatively unmarred baseballs could be kept in play.

The Series opened at Ebbets Field on Tuesday, October 5, amid all the conjecture and prognostications that pre-Series hoopla typically engenders, with the thinking that Brooklyn had four terrific pitchers to Cleveland's two. The writers also had time to focus on two brothers out of Cleveland, Tennessee, who were on opposing sides: Doc Johnston, thirty-three years old and a first baseman, played for Cleveland; brother Jimmy of the Dodgers was a third baseman two years his junior.

It was a cold, windy day for the Series opener, which forced Brooklynites to wear overcoats to the ballpark. Always hospitable to the press, Ebbets passed out half-pint bottles of rye to reporters in the outdoor press box, notwithstanding Prohibition.[14] Mayor John Hylan, a Brooklynite from Bushwick, did first-ball honors after entering Ebbets Field from the center-field gate with a Dodger pennant in hand, heralded by the trumpets of the N.Y.P.D.'s band.[15]

Bleachers had been built in front of the scoreboard in left-center field, obscuring all but its very top from view. Instead, to monitor balls, strikes, and outs, a minuscule inning-by-inning scoreboard was attached to the three-foot-high outfield fence at the front of the bleachers. It was so small a space that instead of putting the visiting team's line score above the home team, the inning-by-inning account of runs for each team ran side-by-side. Unfortunately, the scoreboard revealed at the end of the game that Brooklyn had lost, 3–1, with Cleveland's wily, sinewy spitballer Stan Coveleski besting Brooklyn southpaw Rube Marquard, after the Indians had taken a 2–0 lead in the second inning on an error, walk, single, and double.

People gathered as early as nine o'clock the next morning for the second game, with plainclothesmen breaking up more than a few dice games while people waited. "Most of the crowd that congregated around the entrances was composed of policemen and firemen," said the *Eagle*. "The police came early to ensure themselves entrance to the game. The firemen's delegation was a surprise to those who thought they knew mathematics. It was reported at headquarters that a detail of 50 men would guard the aisles. The delegation that arrived congested the streets."

It was cold again, but 10,000 of the 22,559 who would ultimately be in attendance had entered the park by noon. They weren't the only ones who decided to show up: so did the Feds. One of the reporters hinted in his story at the libations supplied by Ebbets, and it prompted agents looking for a spectacular score to show up and raid Charley's office. But he'd evidently been tipped off they were coming, and the hootch had been hidden in a dim Ebbets Field attic.[16]

Meanwhile Wilbert Robinson put his team through an extended batting practice in an attempt to break a week-long slump. Jim Bagby, Cleveland's other ace, was pitted against Brooklyn's master spitballer

Burleigh Grimes, who sprinkled seven hits in the course of pitching a masterful 3–0 shutout.

The weather was perfect the next day, and the Standing Room Only signs were up by one o'clock. Those in the seats shed their overcoats and sweaters and used them as seat cushions. Brooklyn scored twice in the first inning; and it was all the team needed. Sherry Smith won the third game on a brilliant three-hitter, 2–1, to give Brooklyn the Series lead as they left Ebbets Field. "I feel greatly encouraged," Wilbert Robinson said. "The Superbas are the gamest bunch of men I have ever seen." [17]

It was the high-water mark for Brooklyn baseball since the Dodgers had moved to Ebbets Field; they wouldn't again see a two-games-to-one advantage in a World Series for the next thirty-two years. Once the Indians got back to League Park in Cleveland, Brooklyn's fortunes changed.

Coveleski scattered five Brooklyn hits, allowing only a single run in a 5–1 whipping in game four, while Brooklyn hurler Leon Cadore left the game in the second inning after falling behind 2–0. In the fifth inning of game 5, Cleveland second sacker Billy Wambsganss made an unassisted triple play en route to an 8–1 Indians win. Even though Zack Wheat hit .333 and Ivy Olson hit .320, the rest of the Brooklyn regulars were anemic with the bat, and the Robins failed to score in their last eighteen innings of Series play. Cleveland took both those games at home, 1–0 and 3–0, to send the Brooklynites home as losers, five games to two.

If Charley Ebbets had reasons to be happy amid the dispiriting loss to Cleveland, he wasn't, largely because he hadn't been feeling well since the 1920 pennant celebration, afflicted with a buzzing in his head that wouldn't go away. "The buzz has been so intense," he said, "I fear I must have broken a blood vessel in the excitement attending the last of the pennant campaign." [18] Ebbets's affliction went undiagnosed, but his granddaughter Dorothy suffered from what was most likely the same thing beginning in her sixties: tic douloureux, which can cause extreme headaches, discomfort, and pain.[19] Charley would suffer with it the rest of his life.

"I've got everything," Charley said, referring to his largesse, "except enthusiasm that a major league club owner needs. My ailment has chased enthusiasm out of my system. No man belongs in baseball who is in the game solely from the box office standpoint," he said, in an admonition that might have served subsequent stewards of the game well had they been thoughtful enough to follow the advice.[20]

Ebbets Field began to develop a more variegated identity in the first half of the Roaring Twenties as a destination for things other than baseball, including football and—good God!—opera, though quite naturally it remained overwhelmingly linked to the Dodgers. Big-time fights staged by Humbert Fugazy became commonplace at the ballpark. In one battle, Pete Herman regained his bantamweight championship from Joe Lynch, besting Lynch in fifteen rounds on July 25, 1921, after losing his crown at Madison Square Garden the previous December. Steve "Kid" Sullivan lost three different grudge matches with his longtime nemesis Vincent "Pepper" Martin at the ballpark in 1922. Pancho Villa, the ferocious Filipino flyweight, beat Johnny Buff on September 14, 1922, at the park, just a few weeks after dropping a ten-rounder to Frankie Genaro in the same venue.

The place was colorful, Coney Island in a can, its own movable feast. Charlie Knapp, who went to his first game at Ebbets Field then, remembers a story that circulated among fans during the early days. "Ebbets Field's roof was pitched, and occasionally a foul ball would go up there and someone nearby would always say, 'There's one for the office.' The story was that the slant of the roof actually funneled balls down to a certain chute and from there on down right into Ebbets's office. About half the people in the stands believed it."

Even though the successful season in 1920 put Charley Ebbets's financial troubles behind him, he'd retained his penny-pinching reputation earned in his acrimonious salary quarrels with players, and in his bickering with suppliers in lean years over the prices of services, baseball equipment, and apparel. "Even before I started going to the games the story of Charles Ebbets was well known," Knapp recalled. "How he had spent every dollar he had and every dollar he could borrow from every friend he had to buy the land and build a stadium."

In tough years, Ebbets was tougher to deal with, putting off his creditors for as long as possible, watching carefully over every last nickel and zealously lecturing his employees about thrift. "There are people in Brooklyn or men who played ball for him who will tell you he was niggardly and by way of proving it . . . cite you chapter and verse," Frank Graham wrote. "A foolish pride prevented him from admitting that if he seemed stingy, it was only because he didn't have the money to spend. . . . Actually—although it could never be truthfully said of him that he liked to throw money around—he was generous when he had it, and more than one charitable agency in Brooklyn could testify that to call on him for help was not to call in vain."[21]

Coming from Graham this was faint praise, for if there was one thing Ebbets *did* spend freely on, it was the press. "The newspapermen had to be handled cautiously and entertained regularly," Dorothy

Ebbets Dollmeyer recalled, and to do so was expensive on both counts. A case in point was Ebbets's approach with Bill Rafter, editor of the *Brooklyn Standard Union*. Ebbets would take the Rafters out, and the ritual was almost always the same. After a big dinner, the Rafters would repair to the rest rooms and, while they were away from the table, the check would come, and Ebbets would pay it. One time, when the Rafters had left their little daughter at the table, she overheard Ebbets muttering, "He ought to have a 'G' in front of his name."

Trouble was, the little girl was precocious enough to repeat what he'd uttered when her parents got back. "Bet the team got a panning the next day," Dorothy said, when recounting the story in her memoir.

However hard-hearted Charley Ebbets was in dealing with his players in negotiations that were amplified in the press, or however long he stiffed a creditor when things weren't going well, he wasn't beyond ensuring opportunities for charities to collect within the confines of the park, and also, when flush, saw fit to provide for some needy locals outside it. "At every ball game there would be one of the Sisters of the Poor, a begging order of nuns," Dollmeyer said. "The patient little women who gave their lives to this quiet sort of charity never knew that a plainclothesman was assigned to unobtrusively protect them from any possible unpleasantness. As far as I know, there was never such an occasion. Baseball fans are usually above that kind of heckling. Grandfather was not a Catholic but he had respect for everyone's religion."

Beyond that, Ebbets did good deeds that were good for his business, and he knew it. "Another altruistic gesture for which grandfather was remembered was his kindness to the underprivileged little guys in Brooklyn. On weekdays, after the third inning or so of a game when no more paid attendance was anticipated, he would allow these little urchins to come into the bleachers to see the rest of the game. The kids were there by the hundreds and probably many had walked some distance to get there, lacking carfare. Bob the Bouncer—Big Bob Blau— would usher them in with the constant admonition of 'No fightin' and no doity woids.' When people complimented grandfather on his thoughtfulness toward these kids, he would smile and say he was just assuring himself of future baseball fans.

"'No fightin' and no doity woids' became a family joke."[22]

It was during this period that the ballpark itself was becoming defined as a haven for madcap zaniness and acknowledged as a comfortable home for those for whom a straitjacket was not out of the question. Wilbert Robinson, who would retreat to his beloved Dover Hall in Georgia to recover from the baseball season every winter, was himself largely responsible. For after 1920, his reign over the franchise became legend from the standpoint not of establishing a winning tradition, but of creating a hilarious one.

Only in two of the next eleven campaigns would his team challenge with any seriousness for the National League flag. On the streets, "Uncle Robbie" argued strategy with cops, cab drivers, barbers, and Navy Yard workers. Sometimes he let them pick the lineup; once, desperate, he allowed the baseball writers to pick it. With kids, he was warm and patient: "He was wonderful," Charlie Knapp said. "He would spend time with us. He would discuss his moves with the kids, tell us what he'd do and why."

He could also get testy: one day he started a rookie pitcher who got shellacked and just left him in. Finally, he walked over to the box where Ma Robinson was sitting, and said, "I hope you're satisfied now. I started that kid like you suggested. Maybe now you'll do less second guessin'."

Another time, after Zack Taylor started off the ninth inning in a scoreless tie with a resounding three-base hit, Robinson, coaching at third, extended his hand, saying "Put 'er there, kid," whereupon Taylor leaned off the bag and was picked off.

Once during spring training in Florida, Robinson loaded his team on the bus and rode from Clearwater to Lakeland for an exhibition game with the Indians, and while rolling down the road in Lakeland passed the Indians relaxing on a hotel porch. Robinson stopped the bus.

"Hello Robbie," a surprised Tris Speaker said. "What're you guys doing here?"

"We came over to play you guys this afternoon," said the Brooklyn skipper.

"Gosh, Robbie," Speaker replied, "that game isn't scheduled until tomorrow."

Problems with signals, lineups, and runners winding up on the same base added to the glorious tales. Once Robbie was so exasperated with the way his players performed that he issued an executive order: "From now on we'll play without signs." The Robins promptly went on a winning streak.[23]

If there was a day Uncle Robbie shouldn't have given a sign, it was a game against the Phils when Jacques Fournier had six hits and was standing in the batter's box going for a seventh straight. Uncle Robbie sent the runner at first, who was gunned down for the third out. The Robins were far enough ahead that they didn't need the run, and since it was their last chance to hit, Fournier missed a chance to tie the record—seven hits—set back in 1892. The record holder? Wilbert Robinson. Frank Graham wrote that Jacques felt cheated, and never forgave Uncle Robbie.[24]

Ebbets Field wasn't only the home of the unexpected on the diamond; it also provided surprises in the stands. Charlie Knapp took his younger brother to see a Robins-Giants game, recalling it to be 1922 or '23. It was before game time, and they were in a fairly remote section of the stands when a vendor came up to them and gave them two bags of peanuts. As Charlie started to push the bags away, saying that he didn't have the money for them, the vendor told him, "No, that's all right, they're already paid for by the two ladies up there, Mrs. Robinson and Mrs. McGraw. They think it's nice that you took the little guy out to the park with you." For all the bad blood that supposedly ran between John McGraw and Uncle Robbie, Blanche McGraw and Mary were still friendly enough to sit together at the games.

And Charley Ebbets, who once said he wouldn't give McGraw the smoke off his tea, occasionally played an overt role in that ritualized conflict. "Sometimes the unexpected and unplanned developments offered more excitement than the scheduled game," Dorothy Ebbets Dollmeyer wrote. "John McGraw, and our manager, Wilbert Robinson, were always at odds, but one day grandfather got into the argument and Robinson stepped back. I have never known an owner to get into the act but that day grandfather came down from his accustomed bench at the top of the stands and he and McGraw went the rounds. I will say politely that they were hurling invectives and casting aspersions—just the two of them. They were purple in the face and stomping and waving fists and it was beautiful and the fans loved it. I was frightened for grandfather but knew the ushers, players and fans would not let anything happen to him. Finally, someone separated them before either had a stroke or heart attack, and McGraw went back to the visitors' dugout. For Ebbets a standing ovation and for the guy from Coogan's bluff—the Bronx cheer. It was probably the finest rhubarb ever to take place in Ebbets Field and not one umpire was involved. I'm sure McGraw had police protection to get him out of the field that day."

In the fall of 1923, the third consecutive World Series between the Yankees and the Giants preempted the Army–Notre Dame game originally scheduled for the Polo Grounds. As a result, the contest was moved to Ebbets Field in the first big-time football game seen at the ballpark. The gridiron was laid out with the near sideline running through the middle of the infield, roughly parallel to the third base line. A ten-row wooden bleacher was on the far side of the field, relatively close to the sideline and as far in front of the right-field wall's advertisements as possible.

While the Yanks were drubbing the Giants 8–4 up at Coogan's Bluff to tie the Series at two games apiece, Notre Dame was turning loose a diversified offense under Knute Rockne good enough to score two touchdowns—one in the second quarter and one in the fourth quarter—during a 13–0 victory over Army in Brooklyn. Thirty thousand crammed Ebbets Field for the occasion.

Something else had happened during that summer, however, that went largely unnoticed and unreported but that would have a major impact on Brooklyn and Ebbets Field. If there was a single point at which cohesion would break in the life of the Brooklyn franchise, it was traceable to the events of July 8, 1923. Although details are sketchy, an incident occurred at Ebbets Field that became known as "the fight," spawning an enmity between Steve McKeever and Charles Ebbets Jr. that culminated in Steve's throwing Charley Jr. out of the ballpark. This act, which would significantly affect the future of the club—and in the next decade and a half, the condition of the ballpark and each family's finances—was the traceable beginning of the Ebbets–McKeever schism. It ultimately led to internal chaos and finally, twenty years later, to the realignment of ownership that eventually resulted in control of the ball club falling to Walter O'Malley.

Charles Ebbets Jr. had been having intermittent problems with alcohol for some time, and his behavior could be intemperate and erratic. Whether or not this affected the day's contretemps is uncertain, but events that occurred at the ballpark that afternoon created an irreparable breach between Ebbets Jr. and Steve McKeever. They were never able to patch up their differences.

Charley Jr. continued along in his provocative ways, even when he wasn't really doing anything wrong. Later that year, on September 28, he would be involved in a minor scrape with the law when a patrolman named Scheider in Traffic Squad B had arrested a cab driver for a traffic infraction near Grand Central Station.[25] Charley Jr. didn't like the way it happened and offered the cabbie his card and said he could call him as a witness if he pleased; while a crowd was collecting, the cop decided to arrest Ebbets Jr. too. Since Charley Jr. didn't have enough money with him, friends had to come and bail him out.

Buzz in his head, trouble with a weakening heart, and within a week of the fight between his son and his business partner, sixty-three-year-old Charley Sr. was swimming off Manhattan Beach with Grace in early July 1923 when he became an unwitting hero. To his perhaps even greater credit, he shunned any spotlight and attention. Harry Margol of 1463 Bedford Avenue was seized with cramps and was crying for help when Charley swam over to him and held him up until Eddie Zimmerman, a life guard, arrived in a boat and pulled Margol aboard. Ebbets swam back to the beach and hurried away, and it wasn't until days later that the incident was reported in the *New York Herald*.[26]

After the season Ebbets Sr. had made arrangements to build a winter home in Clearwater. Given his health problems, Florida beckoned as a nice alternative to the northern winter. The place was opened by the middle of December, and there also was some talk that he might soon build a small hotel for the Dodgers' spring training seasons in Clearwater. For Charley Sr., Florida's warmth was a tonic and also provided a respite from some of the unpleasantness surrounding the incident in July.

Although Steve and Ed McKeever still had a high regard for Charley Sr., their rift with Ebbets Jr. festered unproductively. For one thing, Steve McKeever was the club's treasurer, and young Ebbets hadn't been paid for his duties as the ball club's secretary since the ruckus.

The *Eagle* reported in July 1924 that Charley Ebbets Jr. was suing the team his father half-owned for $4,270 in back pay.[27] The McKeevers had blocked his salary for more than six months, stating that young Ebbets didn't earn the money and was therefore not entitled to it. The new action revealed that as of April 24, 1924, Charley Jr. had been replaced as the club's secretary by his brother-in-law Joe Gilleaudeau, an attorney and the husband of his youngest sister, Genevieve.

Charley Jr. maintained that he was entitled to his $5,000 annual pay up through the time he completed his term of service as the ball club's secretary. Frank York, the team's counsel, noted that the younger Ebbets was still a director of the club. Both York and Ebbets Sr. tried to persuade the McKeevers to pay Charley Jr.'s wages up to the time of his ousting, but the brothers objected. Regardless of the resolution of the pay issue, it was the end of Charley Jr.'s active day-to-day role as one of the team's officers.

Disagreements in councils above the Rotunda were easily matched and routinely surpassed by those in the stands. Sometimes one could find you while you were just standing around. Such was the case for Jackie Farrell. One of the earliest rabid Dodger fans was a weatherbeaten old lady known as Apple Annie. She dated back to sometime before 1920, and typically sat in the upper stands around third base, yelling and screaming at the players below as the spirit moved her. The ballpark and what happened within it were her province.[28] She took it seriously. And she took what was written about the ball club very much to heart as well. In 1924 Annie read a story that displeased her about the Robins in the *Daily News.*

Not one to keep her opinions about such matters to herself, she took a walk over to the press area, which still failed to feature a closed-off press box. She politely inquired after the *News*'s reporter. The story had been written by a second-year man, a twenty-seven-year-old reporter named Paul Gallico, a strapping specimen, 6' 3½" and 195 pounds.

He'd been on the crew team at Columbia, and was gutsy or dumb enough to get in a ring with Jack Dempsey for the sole purpose of writing a first-person news story about what it was like. But Gallico wasn't there that day. The *News*'s tiny boxing writer, Jackie Farrell, was.

Farrell acknowledged her question, which turned out to be mistake. Apple Annie took after him instantly, using her umbrella to bat him about the ears while spewing invective about the paper's story. After she cuffed Farrell around to her satisfaction, she went back to her perch by third base.

Yet there *was* something to be excited about that summer; the Robins were making a serious bid for the National League pennant. And then, the last weekend in August, while in the midst of a fifteen-game winning streak, the Robins swept the Giants. By September 6 Brooklyn reached first place, if only for three hours, while the Giants lost the first game of a doubleheader against the Phillies before winning the second game.

The next day, September 7, 1924, was a mob scene. The ballpark was sold out and the gates closed some two and a half hours before game time; it was so crowded that even people who had tickets couldn't get in. Some of the thousands turned away elected to get in by scaling the walls, with some injured in falls. When a score of others got in by using a telephone pole to crash through the street-exit gate in right-center field, thousands of freebies rushed into the ballpark behind them.

The cops were called to disperse the fans from around the gate and to keep others from getting in. It was so crowded that umpire Bill Klem and his crew needed a police escort to get on the field. Gate-crashers were estimated at 6,000 to 15,000, and fans were seated all around the outfield. As often happened in those days when the Giants or Cardinals came to town, the outfield areas where fans sat were roped off from play, the consequence being that eleven ground-rule doubles that day would fly into the throngs of on-field spectators.

With Brooklyn behind 8–4, Jack Fournier led off the bottom of the ninth with a single up the middle. Eddie Brown sent a fly ball into center, which Hack Wilson was unable to reach because of an encroaching crowd. The Giants demanded the batter be called out due to interference, but umpire Bill Klem said no, instead ordering the Brooklyn ball club to move its crowd back or risk forfeiting the game. After a ten-minute delay, with arguments from both teams and police pushing people back, the game resumed.

With men on second and third and nobody out, McGraw changed pitchers, bringing on right-hander Hugh McQuillan to pitch to third baseman Milt Stock. Stock came through with a base hit to score Fournier, making it 8–5, and then Tommy Griffith flied out for the first out as Brown tagged and scored from third, making the score 8–6.

When Zack Taylor flied out to left for the critical second out, Brooklyn's hopes rested with Burleigh Grimes, a good-hitting pitcher. Burleigh didn't disappoint, delivering his second single in two innings; Stock was now on third. Andy High then doubled into the standees in right field, bringing home Stock.

The score was now 8–7, and Brooklyn had the tying run on third and the winning run on second, and an outfield ringed with people into which a plunked double would win the game.

The roaring Faithful were beside themselves. In a year of improbabilities and miracles, they were ready for another. Uncle Robbie elected to send Dutch Ruether, another good-hitting pitcher, up to hit for Mitchell. Virtually everybody was primed for a double into the crowd and a raucous Brooklyn victory celebration. Judge Landis, peering from his seat near the dugout, leaned against his cane, waiting for the final denouement.

McQuillan set himself on the mound and threw a curve. Ruether swung and missed. Again McQuillan peered in; he set. The pitch was another curve; swing and a miss, strike two. After McQuillan looked for the sign and set, he delivered; the pitch to Ruether was another curve ball. Ruether went down swinging. The ballgame was over.

A silence fell over Ebbets Field, with the exception of a few Giants fans unable to contain themselves, undoubtedly risking some bodily harm to express their sentiments. Brooklyn fell a game and a half behind the Giants, the bid to take first place foiled.

The Giants kept a step ahead of Brooklyn for the rest of the way, and the Robins ultimately finished second, just one and a half games behind. The Giants went on to lose to the Senators in the Series, but the Dodgers drew 818,883—less than 26,000 behind McGraw. In 1920 the Dodgers earned $189,785 in net profit: the following three seasons they netted $151,604; $146,372; and $116,539. Now, in 1924, the team netted $265,669; the season had made Ebbets a free-and-clear millionaire.[29]

At the 1924 baseball meetings, in another of his contributions to baseball, Ebbets proposed abandoning the tradition of settling the site of the first World Series game with a coin toss, in favor of an alternating year-to-year schedule. Ebbets's plan advocated having two home games, three away, followed by the last two at home (as needed) for games 1 through 7, with the American League opening the series one year, the National League the next. The plan was put into effect two years later. Fans had previously been skeptical about the coin toss when the park with the larger seating capacity was chosen for the opening game.

With his health slipping due to a weak heart and other associated ailments, Charley went down to Clearwater that winter in the hope that the warmer weather might help. It did somewhat, but then he made a decision to go north with the team during the first week of

April. It was a rough trip. Upon arriving in New York, he went immediately to his apartment in the old Waldorf Astoria on 34th Street and Fifth Avenue and was confined to bed. Soon after he received word that his old friend Barney York had passed away, but Charley was too weak himself to attend the service.

He was thought to be doing satisfactorily for several days, but on the afternoon of April 17, 1925, his health took a precipitous turn for the worse. He died at 6 A.M. the following morning, with his wife, Grace, his sister, Ada, and daughters Genevieve and Maie and son Charles Jr. at his side. Charley Sr. was sixty-five years old.

The word traveled through New York City like a flash fire. The Waldorf was busy that morning. Led by Uncle Robbie, in tears as he boarded the elevator, many of the ballplayers—among them Grimes, Vance, Fournier, Wheat, and Taylor—visited the hotel in the first few hours. The Giants and Dodgers were scheduled to play that afternoon; there was some discussion between National League president John Heydler and the McKeever brothers about what to do. Charley Ebbets, after all, was the dean of baseball owners, had been in the game forty-two years, and was beloved by his colleagues and the fans. A distraught Uncle Robbie, speaking as if his old boss was temporarily indisposed, said, "Charley wouldn't want anybody to miss a Dodgers-Giants game just because he died." It was a perfectly logical opinion.[30]

The decision was made that the day's game and others in the National League should go on as scheduled to avoid confusion that might otherwise result with fans a few hours away from arriving at the park. The players on both the Dodgers and the Giants, it was decided, would wear mourning bands on their sleeves. That game was still under way when the hearse carrying Charley's remains passed by the ballpark later that afternoon in a circuitous route to the family's home at 1406 Glenwood Road for the wake. Games also would be played on Sunday and Monday, but on Tuesday, the day of the funeral, all the National League games would be canceled. Heydler immediately ordered all the flags at National League grounds to half mast for thirty days; American League president Ban Johnson ordered flags in his circuit's ballparks to be similarly cast, but only for the day of the funeral.

Charley's funeral was fit for a king. With an N.Y.P.D. motorcycle escort leading a motorcade that circled Ebbets Field, the procession wended its way several miles through Brooklyn neighborhoods, passing both Ebbets Field and old Washington Park on the way to St. Ann and the Holy Trinity in Brooklyn Heights. Tom Shannon's 23rd Regiment Band played Chopin's Funeral March as the cops opened a lane amid the waiting throngs down Montague Street. A who's who of the baseball establishment and New York City politics was in attendance, while 100,000 Brooklynites lined the streets to pay their respects.

The man who was Ebbets's successor as team president, Ed Mc-
Keever, who had knocked the wood on his desk at Ebbets Field a few
weeks before when mentioning he'd never been sick a day in his life,
had complained of a cold while at Charley's wake at the Ebbets home.[31]
It was raining by the time the mourning party got to Greenwood Cemetery the day of the funeral, and Ed, aged sixty-six, caught more of a chill
at the graveside while cemetery workers worked to widen the grave to
accommodate the oversized casket. In the days following the service,
Ed contracted pneumonia. Eleven days after Charley, Ed McKeever died.

The fact that he passed away so quickly created other problems.
Ebbets's heirs, headed by Joe Gilleaudeau, would not agree to have Ed's
brother, Steve McKeever, as president, stemming from Steve's differences with Charley Jr.

Finally Wilbert Robinson was elected as the team's president.
Whatever his skills were as a field manager—and evidence would soon
accumulate that he was becoming more and more complacent in that
regard—the ball club's directors couldn't have made a worse choice to
head the organization. In mid-June Robinson decided that he couldn't
serve as both president and manager, so he made Zack Wheat an "assistant manager" and put him in charge of the bench. But Zack had neither the authority nor the demeanor for the role, and over the course of
the next six weeks, the team slid.

By the time Uncle Robbie went back to the dugout in midseason,
claiming his absence was only due to the need to acclimate himself to
his new responsibilities as president, the team was out of the running
and failed to respond to his leadership, too.

If there was one saving grace, it was Dazzy Vance.

Vance. It became a magic name in Brooklyn.

On July 20, 1925, he struck out seventeen Cards in ten innings.
Just under two months later, on September 8, the Dazzler pitched a
one-hitter against the Phillies, facing the twenty-seven-batter mini-
mum, with Nelson "Chicken" Hawks erased trying to steal after his
second-inning single. In Dazzy's next outing five days later at Ebbets
Field, he was fabulous again. He held the Phils hitless through eight.
The score, oddly, was 10–1; Vance had walked one man and lost the
shutout when left-fielder Jimmy Johnston made a double error.

With 20,000 fans yelling at the top of their lungs on every pitch,
Vance began the final inning without wasting a pitch, coming right at
pinch-hitter Lew Fonseca. Fonseca fouled off the first two pitches, and
then hit a pop foul off first base, but Charlie Hargreaves, a catcher who
was playing one of only two games that season at first base, dropped
the ball. A groan echoed through the stands. But the Dazzler came
back with an off-speed curve ball to strike Fonseca out. Then, with the
crowd roaring incessantly the rest of the way, he fanned pinch-hitter

Wally Kimmick on three pitches for the second out. Center-fielder Freddie Leach stepped in, Vance delivered, and Leach hit a short, sinking liner over near the left-field line, Johnston just managing to get to it and put it away for the final out. Amid the crescendo in celebration of the no-hitter, fans launched their straw hats from all quarters of the ballpark.

With all the drama and tragedy, perhaps it was appropriate that opera debuted that summer at that ballpark that Charley had undertaken to build and that Ed McKeever helped him finish. The opera was free, with tickets distributed through the city's park commissioners or obtainable at the Municipal Building on a first-come, first-served basis at the city chamberlain's office. Seats were arranged on the field, too, bringing the park's capacity to 40,000 for each of the three performances—*Aida; Cavaliera Rusticana* and *Pagliacci;* and *Faust*—during the first eight days in August. Because of demand, people were restricted to two seats for only one of the nights.

Josiah Zuro, the director of the Free Municipal Open Air Opera season, directed; Charles Marshall, the leading tenor of the Chicago Opera, led a cast of American singers. The performances were broadcast on the radio; City Chamberlain Philip Berolzheimer announced subsequently that he'd received a radiogram that brought word of *Aida's* improbable reception over the airwaves in France.

During the performances, the mayor was there in person, walking up and down the aisles: "Are you having fun? Are you having fun?" he asked. "It's courtesy of your mayor, John F. Hylan," he'd say in the next breath, "and don't you forget it!"[32]

Seventy-one years later, while talking to *New Yorker* editor Roger Angell in a Broadway shoe shop in 1996, the social and literary critic Alfred Kazin could remember seeing *Faust* at Ebbets Field, but he couldn't recall whether the performance was any good.[33] But Kazin remembered the most important thing, the thing that everyone remembers about going to Ebbets Field: he was there with his father.

CHAPTER SIX

The Daffiness Boys

The Roaring Twenties were famous for the Charleston, Charles Lindbergh, Babe Ruth, speakeasies, flivvers, and flappers; famous for gangsters, rum-runners, daredevils, flagpole sitters, and marathon dancers; famous for flashy clothes, bicycle racers, bankrolls, and daring aviators with long scarves that whipped in the breeze; famous for an expansion of the American Dream. A chicken in every pot; a car in every garage. Amusement parks abounded; Coney Island was the only Disneyland. The Roaring Twenties were an event at Ebbets Field, too, but people were roaring for a different reason.

Any number of stories illustrate Wilbert Robinson's loosening grip on his Robins from the middle twenties onward. In one episode, frustrated by the players' poor performance, he established a "Bonehead Club": any player who made an error or stupid play had to kick money into a kitty. The first act that warranted the fine was Robinson's: he mixed up the hitters on his lineup card and sent up the wrong hitter during a game.

Robinson's central on-field figure in the litany of mayhem was a lanky left-handed slugger named Floyd "Caves" Babe Herman, one of the greatest natural hitters of his day, who could smite a baseball with equal ferocity to all fields.

Unfortunately, he had trouble catching baseballs. With a sometimes dazed and confused Uncle Robbie at the helm, Herman helped the team define a new brand of baseball with antics that prompted the writers to label them the "Daffy Dodgers" or the "Daffiness Boys."

Herman's first day in a career that would earn him an indelible place in the hearts of Brooklynites was April 14, 1926. Two months into the season, he was hitting at a .360 clip and trailing only Kiki Cuyler and Pie Traynor among the National League's leaders. Around the same time, a less-than-diplomatic Uncle Robbie was about to get a lesson on getting into arguments with people who buy their ink by the barrel.

This particular event in the disassembly of the Brooklyn franchise began inauspiciously on Saturday, June 5, 1926, when a Feg Murray cartoon appeared in the *New York Sun* with likenesses of Zack Wheat, Jacques Fournier, Dazzy Vance, and Burleigh Grimes, listing their "big" salaries of $15,000 to $16,000. Included was a large illustration of thirty-one-year-old, second-year pitcher Jess Petty, showing the favorable merits of his performance thus far that year compared with that of the veterans, implying that his earnings would have to be elevated the following year and that the others were overpaid.

When Wilbert Robinson saw the cartoon and read the accompanying column, he was outraged. He held the *Sun's* Joe Vila responsible, but sat on his feelings for a couple of days before calling Vila's managing editor, Keats Speed. It was a mistake. Robinson unloaded on Speed, who tried to calm him down to no avail. Robbie continued his harangue, and its consequences included the paper's policy reversal on calling the team the Robins. The paper never used the nickname again, reverting to "Dodgers," and thereafter only referred to Robinson as "the manager of the Dodgers," never using his name.

"It sparked a bitter feud with old Steve McKeever, who thought Robbie behaved like an ass; it damaged the club's relations with the press; and it hurt Robbie's standing with many fans," writes Svein Arber.[1] And quite literally, everything else began to fall apart as well. On August 5, Zack Wheat hit a ball out of the park but pulled a leg muscle rounding first base. He limped into second, where he sat down on the bag. After five minutes while the game was delayed with Wheat unable to move, Robinson came out. So did Rabbit Maranville, who was ready to run for him, but Wheat waved him off and limped the rest of the way around the bases. It would be Zack's last home run in Ebbets Field.

It was ten days later, on August 15, when Herman was involved in the classic incident in which three Dodgers wound up on third base at the same time. Over the years, Herman was given the blame for this and occasionally credited with tripling into a triple play, while he actually doubled into a double play. Somewhat lost in history is that he also batted in the game-winning run with that hit.

With the Braves up on the Dodgers 1–0 in the seventh inning, good old Otto Miller, now the third base coach, complained to Uncle Robbie that he was tired of walking out to the third base coaching box since nothing ever seemed to happen out there. Mickey O'Neil, a veteran catcher in his eighth season who would catch seventy-four games that season for Brooklyn and who'd spent all his previous seasons with the Braves, volunteered to coach for an inning.[2]

The Robins quickly evened the game after Johnny Butler singled off Johnny Wertz and Hank DeBerry doubled, driving Butler in. Dazzy Vance singled with DeBerry stopping at third, and after Chick Fewster was hit by a pitch, the right-handed rookie, Wertz, was yanked by Boston manager Dave Bancroft in favor of lefty George Mogridge, a thirty-seven-year-old, fourteen-year major league veteran, who would face Merwyn "Jake" Jacobson, a left-handed, light-hitting outfielder, who'd be followed by the rookie Herman.

Now, with the bases loaded, Mogridge induced Jacobson to pop out. Up came Herman. Umpire Beans Reardon recalled it this way: "I had a play one day in Brooklyn that was unbelievable. . . . The Dodgers had the bases loaded. Hank DeBerry was at third, Dazzy Vance on second, and Chick Fewster on first. 'Turkey Neck'—that's what I called Herman—hit one off the fence in right-center field. DeBerry scored. Vance should have, too, but for some reason he stopped and went back to third. Fewster, figuring Vance would score, went on to third. Herman, seeing the ball bouncing around out there, rounds second and comes into third. Now I got three men standing on third, and every one of them is being tagged. I said, 'Damn it, wait a minute. I got to figure this out.' Finally I said, 'The bag belongs to Vance, so Fewster, you're out, and so are you, Turkey Neck, for passing a runner on the baselines. That's it. The side's out. Let's play ball, fellas.'"[3] Fans in the stands were incredulous, pointing, laughing, yelling, slapping their foreheads, groaning. Of the conclave at third, Robinson said, "It was the only time them guys have got together on anything the entire year."

The event was a watershed, becoming legend overnight. And the jokes began about both the team and Babe Herman. Man to cab driver: "The Dodgers have three men on base." Cab driver: "Which base?" Herman, later trying to defend his fielding, would tell reporter Tom Meany that he would quit if a fly ball ever hit him on the head. But when asked about his shoulder, Herman said, "The shoulder don't count." Another time Herman had almost convinced a member of the fourth estate to stop portraying him as a clown in print, lamenting that he was just a family man trying to make a buck and contending that the reporter's caustic comments would ultimately hurt his paycheck. When the scribe demurred for a bit, Herman pulled a lit cigar out of his suit pocket and started puffing on it, restoring the reporter's trust in his gut instincts. End of lobbying effort.[4]

The club was now drawing around 650,000 at Ebbets Field, typically fourth or fifth in league attendance, but the fans had little to watch. After the team finished seventh in 1925, it seemed for the rest of the decade as if the Dodgers had gone to live in a country named Sixth Place. But there were other reasons to come out to Ebbets Field: Humberto Fugazy continued to put on his fight cards, and some of the bouts were stellar. The largest nonheavyweight gate for over two decades was from a fight held at Ebbets Field in 1926: the Jack Delaney–Paul Berlenbach light-heavyweight championship battle for a title that Delaney regained on points over the course of fifteen rounds. The July 16 fight grossed $461,789, with 49,186 fight fans taking up every available seat in the stands and on the field.

Professional football came to Ebbets Field that fall, though it wasn't originally showcasing the borough's best professional team or the best professional league. The National Football League had by then established itself as the premier professional league, and a fellow named Eddie Butler put up the money for an NFL team called the Lions. Red Grange, who began operating his American Football League in competition with the NFL, established a Brooklyn AFL team with Harry Stuhldreher, dubbing them the Horsemen in a marketing ploy to take advantage of Stuhldreher's role as one of Notre Dame's legendary "Four Horsemen." Although the NFL team was better, the Horsemen were playing in the best venue in Ebbets Field. Both teams struggled at the box office and in the standings, and before the season ended, they merged as an NFL team. The mixed amalgam was called the Horse-Lions. "Thankfully, 'it' disbanded after the season," commented writer Stan Grosshandler, "saving the world from a potentially horrifying logo."[5]

From 1920 on, the neighborhood was gradually built up with more families and kids. Ebbets Field would become a central part of their lives. The land across the street from the left-field wall, referred to as Deadhead Hill or jokingly called McKeever's Bluff, was bought by the ball club in the twenties and flattened out. Kids played touch football, roller hockey, and even set up nets for tennis.

All of the small saloons that bordered the ballpark were offshoots of the old brewery on Franklin Avenue, where Charley Ebbets had taken reporters and guests after the ground breaking and other early ceremonies at the park. The Consumers Park Brewery became the Interborough Brewery, a mattress factory, and then a spice importing company, which it remains today.

In the middle twenties, single- and multifamily homes were being built by land development companies all across Brooklyn's Flatbush and Crown Heights neighborhoods. Just a block south from the ballpark, down the gently sloping hill, Bedford Avenue intersected with Empire Boulevard, which had become a row of automobile businesses. But the most famous auto business in Brooklyn was a Socony-Mobil gas station, which prospered for many years just across Bedford Avenue behind Ebbets Field's right-field wall. The gas station, opened in October 1922, was the first retail outlet for gasoline ever established for Socony, which was an acronym for Standard Oil Company of New York.

In 1927 both Babe Ruth and Charles Lindbergh established themselves as the first superheroes in American culture, thanks to radio and theater newsreels supplementing print media. Then as now, there was wonder in the common experience of the moment: "I was at Ebbets Field when the word of the Lindbergh flight's success came," recalled Richard Lecds, who grew up in the neighborhood and went to P.S. 161 near Crown and Nostrand. "All the fans started to cheer."

Even with film giving greater currency to celebrity, something was fundamentally part of the game then that is absent today. With an eight-team league in which every team would play each of the others twenty-two times, eleven at home and eleven away, and with players bound to the same team, even the visitors would become familiar. Leeds had the autographs of everybody who came through. "Pie Traynor would recognize me; he'd walk with me all the way to the Franklin Avenue subway when the Pirates were in town," said Leeds. And then, unfathomable as it seems today, Pie Traynor would *get on* the subway.

One time the great Traynor even tapped an unsuspecting young man on the shoulder while the lad was intently looking through his player-picture-autograph book. "Would you like me to sign?" Traynor asked, smiling kindly at young Arthur Harrow, who then lived nearby on Carroll Street between Washington and Franklin avenues.

"I was stunned," remembers Harrow. "My brother Alan and I would split up to cover the two different subway stops to get the players coming out. For thirteen years, my entire life was baseball and the Brooklyn Dodgers."

Not all the ballplayers were as accommodating as Traynor. "One time later on I gave Tex Carleton my book to sign," said Harrow, "and he took it in the cab like he was going to make off with it. I went right in after him and got it back."

The games started after three o'clock in those days. "On rainy days, you could check to see if the flag was up," Richard Leeds said.

"That was the indicator of whether or not there would be a game that day. No flag, no game. You could see the flag from the Boys' Room on the third floor of P.S. 161," Leeds remembered almost seventy years later. "One of my teachers would occasionally send me in to check."

He wasn't the only kid that had to keep the adults apprised. "We Ebbets kids had been the weather watchers for the Brooklyn Dodgers," Dorothy Ebbets Dollmeyer recalled in her memoir. Charley Jr.'s family lived close to the field. "From our back porch, we could see the flagpole in the outfield. On an unsettled day—rain or clouds—we had constant calls to our home, presumably because the phones at the field were busy." Since not everyone had radios and there was no television, the Ebbets kids had to pass the word. "Mother would station one kid on the back porch and another at the phone." The flag watcher would relay whether or not the game was still on.

"Our telephone was busy with other calls concerning the team: 'Why is Robbie going to pitch Grimes tomorrow?' 'Why doesn't Vance let somebody other than DeBerry catch for him?' 'Take so-and-so out for good. He's no help.'

"We were taught to be polite always," she said, "and answer something like, 'That's a good idea. We'll pass it on.' We kids should have been on the payroll."

The tie with the team transcended the differences between the neighborhoods, and the sentiment for the team permeated each neighborhood. Whether fans were young or old, they were always preoccupied with how the team was doing, and the word found its way to every corner of the borough through newspapers. "One of my early memories," Murray Rubin recalled, "was coming home from school at 3 P.M. and, together with some of the kids on the block, making a beeline for the corner candy store on Sutter Avenue to glance at the evening newspapers. In those days the papers—the *Journal, Telegram,* and the *Brooklyn Eagle,* among others—carried the partial line scores of games in progress. Because there were several editions, the final one at 6 P.M. usually had the completed home games of the Robins, Giants, and Yankees.

"Radios were nonexistent then—at least on our blocks—and since we were not allowed in the pool room where inning by inning scores came in by ticker, the corner candy store was our only source. I don't remember what we did on weekends when evening editions were not always available, but there were always the night editions of the *News* and the *Mirror,* two of the morning papers, that always contained the final results. Incidentally, once we reached the age, any age, when we started to wear long pants instead of knickers, we were then permitted into the poolroom and were able to watch the scores as they were posted on a large blackboard."

Even though the Brooklyn teams weren't contending in the late twenties, their fans were rabidly competitive. "After more than seventy years," Edgar Feldman recalled, "it is clear that things believed to have happened never occurred, but I am perfectly sure of one particular episode that smacked of comedy. It's a bleachers story. At this particular game with Dazzy Vance on the mound, the men in center field removed their jackets, so the pitch came at the batter from a field of white. But when our men came to bat, the jackets were again donned but with the fronts to rear so that the ball was fired out of a decipherable background. I don't remember the game being halted but I never ever did see this like again. The Dodger fans stopped at virtually nothing but it was all mischievous and bones were left unbroken."

The fervent backing combined with all that energy and enthusiasm focused in one place posed a great marketing opportunity for an entrepreneur able to figure out how to create an effective impression. One individual managed to do this better than anybody else. Four words on the outfield wall accomplished it: "Hit Sign, Win Suit." Abe Stark was born in Manhattan in 1893 to Russian immigrant parents; he was six when his parents moved to Brownsville, when the neighborhood was still mostly farms. His father, three sisters, and a brother all worked in sweatshops. By the time Abe finished the seventh grade at P.S. 109 and quit to work full-time in a clothing store—seven days a week for $2.50 a week—he had already sold newspapers, lemonade, and "everything from flypaper to toothpicks," as he recalled. "One of the earliest things I remember about home," he said, "is the 'puschkas' nailed on the wall. The puschkas were little boxes that different charities used to leave at people's houses to be filled. Every month or so somebody'd come around and empty them. Well, my mother and father would put coins in the puschkas, even when it meant having less food."[6]

Abe opened his own clothing store in Brownsville at age twenty-two, in 1915, two years after Ebbets Field opened. He took over the sign space on the outfield wall once rented by Bull Durham Tobacco, and offered players a suit if they could hit the sign with a fly ball. Overton Tremper, a Penn grad who played with the Dodgers as a reserve outfielder in 1927 and 1928 and who later played and managed the semipro Bushwicks, remembered the original Abe Stark sign, which was much larger than the famous one erected later on at the base of a new scoreboard. Tremper, by the way, once had the ignominious distinction of being paddled as a freshman at Penn for failing to wear a beanie, with the punishment administered at the direction of Walter O'Malley, then head of Penn's sophomore vigilance committee.[7]

"It was up in 1927," Tremper said of Stark's original sign, "and it covered the right field wall, top to bottom, from the sideline to about

150 feet or so to right center." Murray Rubin's father worked for Abe Stark from 1919 until Stark gave up the store in 1959. "Many balls hit the original Stark sign," Rubin remembered. "My father told me that on some evenings, he altered more suits for players than for paying customers."

Over its many years, the sign was good enough to fuel Stark's business in Brownsville, but it indicated only one dimension of the man. "When the Depression hit, and hit hard, there were a lot of people, and a lot of tailors, out of work in the neighborhood," Rubin said. "Abe Stark hired a lot of them, even if only for a day a week, and even if there wasn't much work. He'd make work for them, and he'd do it in such a way that it wasn't obvious. He knew that it was important psychologically for someone to have some money coming in, even if it was only a little bit. It's just the way he was. He cared about people."

It was that kind of demeanor, coupled with his constant stream of philanthropic activities, that ultimately ensured a successful political career for Abe Stark. In 1931 it was just beginning, with Abe undertaking the successful management of George Blumberg's state senate campaign.[8]

When Ebbets Field was renovated in 1931, Abe Stark's "Hit Sign, Win Suit" offer was moved. Placed at the bottom of the new scoreboard, it was now a difficult target, yet not totally impossible to hit: a three-foot-high, thirty-foot-long sign that any outfielder could run in front of to pull in a fly ball, providing that it hadn't been scorched on a line by the hitter. Mel Ott was the first to oblige, winning the first two suits during the 1931 season.

"After Mr. Stark transferred his offer to a small sign under the scoreboard in right center," said Murray Rubin of the suit alterations his father performed in Stark's Pitkin Avenue haberdashery, "my dad rarely saw any players."

Before the renovation, while Ebbets Field was still expansive, the batting practice backstop was stowed during games in deep right center by the far reaches of the wall near the flagpole. Photographers who cared to could snap a picture a few feet away from the batter's box. Kids ran on the field after the game for the last ball, which a player would often flip to them. Charlie Knapp recounted how one day, as all the kids were running toward catcher Hank DeBerry after Dazzy Vance chalked up a game-ending strikeout, Vance motioned to Hank, who tossed the ball back to Dazzy, who then tossed it to young Knapp. Another time, running on the field after a game, Knapp recalled passing Rogers Hornsby close enough to see the sweat on his forehead. "What I remember was the sheer size of him. Big hands, big arms. A big man."

During the week, Ebbets Field seemed like a laid-back, neighborhood ballpark with small crowds. But on big holidays and weekends the throngs that showed up pleased the Ebbets and McKeever ownership factions no end, even if it was frustrating when the ballpark overflowed its capacity. Writing in the *Sporting News*, the *Eagle* reporter Thomas Rice contended in a 1927 season postmortem that an Ebbets Field bounded on four sides by the street grid could never be expanded to adequately satisfy "a borough of Brooklyn's size and enthusiasm," concluding, "It all seems to prove that the late Charles H. Ebbets was a conservative man, after all." After declaring that baseball was still in its infancy, Ebbets "went out and built a ball park that went out of date within 15 years."[9]

By the late twenties, the Depression that had not yet struck the rest of the country had already begun for Brooklyn baseball. The franchise was in trouble and everyone could sense it. In January 1928, a story floated in the papers that New York mayor Jimmy Walker was part of a group that intended to buy the Dodgers. When asked about it, the mayor said, "I have enough duties to take up all my waking hours right here in connection with City Hall. I am not seeking anything else at present."[10]

McKeever, for his part, wasn't interested. "It seems to me that somebody seems bent on selling the Robins every other week. I don't know what the attitude of the owners of the other half of the club are, but you can say for me that I never will sell my share. Baseball is my life hobby, and I propose to remain in it as long as I live."[11]

McKeever initially started commissioning plans beginning in 1928 in anticipation of remodeling Ebbets Field into a larger-capacity ballpark sometime in the near future. Meanwhile, concerning on-field events, the rancor in the Dodger front office couldn't be camouflaged any longer when McKeever himself delivered a bitter tirade against Robinson and demanded that he be fired as manager that summer, even though he had another year at $25,000 on his contract. But the Ebbets faction paid no attention and Robinson kept his job.

Even so, Robinson himself was open to change. "It is no secret that affairs in the Brooklyn club have been very unpleasant the past year or so," Robinson said after the season. "Now if it would help the situation any for me to step down as manager, I am ready to do it. Remaining as president, which I must do to fulfill my contract, I would do everything in my power to help whoever is named manager. I would make the building of a thorough scouting system my first job. Brooklyn never can compete with other clubs in getting young players from the minors. Right now I have only two scouts, and while I have no fault to find with their work it is plain to see they cannot cover the ground the scouts of McGraw and other managers do."[12]

The effects of discordant ownership left everything at an impasse. Even though everyone theoretically agreed that the ballpark should be enlarged, the two factions couldn't reach agreement about something as basic as the team's manager, so the architectural plans remained in McKeever's rolltop desk. Such haplessness was not only evident in the team on the field; it was also evident on the field itself. The Ebbets Field diamond was beginning to show wear: the field was practically bald in spots and was full of ruts and holes, thanks in part to the Fugazy fight nights, to the football of the Manhattan College Jaspers, whose first Ebbets Field dates began in 1928, and to other events that had seating on the grass.

Before the 1929 season McKeever took the lead to ensure the field was freshly sodded. He also directed other changes at the park: "What looks to be a running track 20 feet wide extends just outside both foul lines," said the *Eagle,* which also noted that "all the numbers and names on the scoreboard have been freshly painted so that it is possible to read them without the aid of a pair of binoculars."[13]

Bulbous Brooklyn Democratic boss John McCooey came out on opening day to toss out the first ball; Jack Dempsey, standing next to him in pregame cordialities, provided a perfect physical contrast. Nothing made a difference; the Robins would again finish sixth. The relentless drumbeat of mediocrity led Brooklyn fans to hang out "Wait 'til Next Year" banners after an opening day loss.

The Dodgers had four members on the team's board of directors charged with running the business: Joseph Gilleaudeau, Wilbert Robinson, Steve McKeever, and Frank York. With McKeever and Robinson snarling at each other in the offices above the Rotunda, and with the Ebbets and McKeever factions in a deadlock, something had to give. Commissioner Landis tried to no avail to broker some agreement between the two ownership groups at the Hotel Commodore during the two-day annual winter meetings in December 1929. When the representatives of the National League sat for a picture, Steve McKeever and Wilbert Robinson placed themselves about as far away from each other as they could. Steve, wearing a bow tie and with his blackthorn stick, sat between the Pirates' Sam Dreyfuss and the Giants' John McGraw on the extreme left of the lower row, with six people between him and Robbie, who sat on the extreme right. Joseph Gilleaudeau, who headed the Ebbets faction, stood over Uncle Robbie's shoulder. In the back row, in the middle between them and all the other National League owners, stood the Brooklyn ball club's bespectacled attorney, Frank B. York.

The impasse within the Brooklyn team's leadership was also causing concern around the rest of the National League. Finally, in

February 1930, after league president John Heydler called both sides to another meeting at the Commodore to try to break the deadlock, a compromise that satisfied neither faction was hammered out over the course of four hours. In it, Wilbert Robinson would step down as president and as a board member but would receive a two-year baseball contract as well as a civil contract to manage the team.

Frank York, son of the late Barney and friend of the late Charley Sr., as well as an old associate of Steve McKeever, one of the same pair of Yorks involved with Pylon Construction, became the club's next president. Harry DeMott, a banker involved with the club, became a vice president. Heydler also added another neutral director to break deadlocks on the board in the future: Walter "Dutch" Carter, a Brooklynite who had once pitched at Yale and who was a brother-in-law and one-time law partner of former Supreme Court justice and presidential candidate Charles Evans Hughes.

"Money will not stand in the way of giving the fans Brooklyn players, who, if properly handled, will comprise a championship ball team," said York. "When the time arrives we hope to provide a modern baseball plant—an enlarged Ebbets Field—with a seating capacity of 50,000.

"The Brooklyn club owns the property on the north side of Montgomery Street, which runs behind the left center field wall of Ebbets Field," York continued. "It is our plan to petition the city to move Montgomery Street back onto our land so that there will be ample room to extend the double deck grandstand clear around to the exit gate on Bedford Avenue.

"Ebbets Field, with temporary stands, cannot seat more than 25,000 persons. We would find ourselves in a sad mess if the team should get into a world series before plans to increase the size of the grandstand could be put through. With this idea in mind, the Brooklyn club hopes to begin building early next year.

"These improvements involve a large sum of money, but the club will have no trouble getting it from the banks. Good work by the team coupled with accommodations for 50,000 spectators, would double the club's business at home, especially on Sundays, when in the past thousands of fans have been turned away."[14]

York's vision for such a capacity—an Ebbets Field with 50,000 spectators—turned out to be a pipe dream. Yet by July 1930 Steve McKeever had decided to put up a fence over the right-field wall, after fearing for too long that a screaming line-drive home run over the twenty-foot barrier could strike and seriously injure some old lady who might be walking on the other side of Bedford Avenue. The new fence would not necessarily prevent someone from getting hit, but it would ensure that the arc of the ball would be greater, theoretically allowing for a lazier trajectory and more warning.

The work began after the Robins left on a road trip in the middle of August, and was completed while they were away. When the Dodgers returned home to Ebbets Field in September, the new screen was in place. For the remainder of the season, any ball that hit the new screen was still to be a home run, since a rule existed to guard against teams changing field configurations in midseason. The following year, the erection of the new scoreboard would cover portions of both the wall and the fence.

Meanwhile the architectural plans for the expansion of the stands were being brushed off. Finally, in February 1931, the team's new board member, Dutch Carter, announced that the work on expanding Ebbets Field would begin the following week. Even with Steve McKeever's longtime political connections and his anticipation of cutting through the red tape, the expected swap of Dodger land across the street behind the left-field wall for a deeded exchange with the city to re-route Montgomery Street never materialized; the city wouldn't agree to it. Instead, in a decision of great future consequence, the team elected to make renovations entirely within the confines of the ballpark's existing lot. It would be tight and the ballpark's field would become considerably smaller, offering left-field stands that would now become inviting targets for hitters and make the place much less hospitable to southpaw pitchers.

The ball club's original architect, Clarence Van Buskirk, who had worked so assiduously on Ebbets Field during the ballpark's original construction, was out of the picture; no one had heard anything of him in years. Van Buskirk was sixty years old at that time, but he had departed for Michigan after his wife sued him for divorce in 1914. The break was so complete that he didn't even respond three years later when the couple's only child, Bertram, then fourteen, wrote, pleading for help with his terminally ill mother's medical bills after she had been struck by tuberculosis.

Destitute, the boy went to work creosoting railroad ties in upstate New York, where his mother was hospitalized, the situation leaving him unable to pursue the college education his father had. Years later, working for the Dime Savings Bank, then one of Brooklyn's foremost institutions, Bertram Van Buskirk took his own son, Douglas, to Ebbets Field's Rotunda, showed him the dedication plaque and pointed to a name. "That was your grandfather," he said of the man he never saw again, the man his son never met.

The architectural plan for the ballpark's new addition was drafted by Otto C. Poderwils of Richmond Hill in Queens. It called for replacing the concrete bleachers down the left-field line and the wooden "circus seats" in fair territory in left field. In their place would be an extension of the double-decked grandstand from behind third base, into the left-field corner, following into fair territory out to center field.

The optimism York originally had in projecting a capacity of 50,000 seats was quickly replaced by realism. The construction program originally called for 10,000 more seats, but once work began it was clear that the greater width of the seats would disappoint those expectations. In fact, the construction would only increase capacity from 25,000 to a little over 31,000, a figure that would still be regularly eclipsed during big games and holidays when fans found their way into the park by any means necessary.

On the morning of Friday, February 17, 1931, Steve McKeever walked out on the field and broke ground for the new addition, cheered on by about one hundred people, including his three-year-old grandson, Bud. The renovation was to cost $450,000.

The skeletal ironwork of the new addition loomed over Ebbets Field as the games began that spring. As the iron latticework went up, it was apparent that the view from the buildings directly across the street from the center-field fence would now have much of the field obstructed by the new stands. "The new left field wing of the grandstand, which circles around to where the centerfield flagpole used to be, is taking form," noted sportswriter Tommy Holmes. "Some of the new 9,000 seats [sic] are already rooted, most of the rest of the reconstruction work is in concrete form and the skeleton steel outline of the rest gives a real idea of how the enlarged park will appear when completed." Holmes said the new grandstand under construction looked like something a hurricane left in its wake, though he thought the contractors had done "nobly" since the club's directors made the decision to go ahead and build just a couple of months before. The makeover of Ebbets Field also extended to the ushers' uniforms, but their new garb was critically panned. The crew was "richly bedecked in flaming scarlet," looking like "part of an animal act." "And then there's the new scoreboard," wrote Holmes. "It looks like a modern one. The Judge [Steve McKeever] says it will be operated with high efficiency. Last year," he went on, "the numbers of last week's umpires invariably hung on the old board and created great confusion in the stands."[15]

On May 1, 1931, the Empire State Building opened. Governor Franklin Delano Roosevelt, Mayor Jimmy Walker, and former governor Al Smith, who was president of the Empire State Building Corporation, were there. The same day, the Dodgers' business manager, Dave Driscoll, announced that all save the last section of the new stands would be open to the public when the Giants invaded Ebbets Field the following day. Attendance records were expected to be shattered.

The gates were closed at 2:30 for the 3 o'clock contest when all the seating and standing room had been sold. Several thousand disappointed fans were still milling about in the streets. The fence in left field was now 353 feet away, in left-center, 365, and to straightaway center field, about 400 feet. The second-deck addition now entirely double-decked Ebbets Field on three sides, and in deepest center field, the ballpark's roof was markedly raised and pitched backward at a different angle from the roof covering the rest of the park. This design was simply to squeeze in the maximum number of rows.

The center-field portion of the alteration created a jutting second deck and an interesting nook and cranny in the lower stand where the wall angling across center field approached the right-field wall but didn't quite meet it. Instead, the wall angled straight back in order to accommodate the Bedford Avenue exit gate.

On the field in 1930, Brooklyn had made its first big pennant bid in six years. The Robins had recalled catcher Al Lopez from Atlanta, and shortstop Glenn Wright had rounded into form after suffering through arm troubles the year before.

The team moved into first place on Memorial Day and managed to stay ahead of the league champion Cubs for much of June and July. One of the reasons was the acquisition of pitcher Dolf Luque, a dark-skinned Cuban right-hander who was picked up from Cincinnati in a trade. His presence at Ebbets Field prompted an incident crisply described by Dorothy Ebbets Dollmeyer in her memoir: "At one game the wife of Adolf Luque was sitting a couple of rows ahead of me. In front of her, an obnoxious individual was giving Luque a bad time verbally—'Get that foreigner off the mound; I came to see Vance or Grimes pitch.' Mrs. Luque very calmly stood up, reached over and pulled the man's straw hat over his ears. He looked so funny with the crown of his hat on the top of his head and the brim around his neck, and the fans were so amused he had no alternative but to get the remains of his hat off his head and throw them under the seat. He didn't even turn around. I don't think he knew who had ruined his hat. Moral of the story—never razz a ball player. His wife might be right back of you."

The Robins faded in August, losing seven of eight and falling to fourth place. Yet in September, they reeled off eleven wins in a row and reclaimed first before losing three in a row to the Cardinals at home and four more after that. They ultimately finished in fourth place, six games back of the Cardinals, who won the pennant by two games over the Cubs, and a game behind the third-place Giants. Nonetheless, 1930 turned out to be an exciting and profitable year. Babe Herman hit .393 in 614 at-bats and the club drew over a million fans for the first time, the final tally being 1,097,329. The figure placed Brooklyn second in league attendance to the Cubs. Oddly, the Giants had never tallied a million at the Polo Grounds and wouldn't until 1945.

Lefty O'Doul was acquired from Philadelphia for 1931, but the season began disastrously, Brooklyn losing ten of its first twelve games. In the season's second game, rookie outfielder Alta Cohen hit in both the number three and the number nine spots in the lineup after manager Robinson instituted a double switch during a pitching change. The Braves missed the mistake when he batted out of turn in the first instance, hitting a single; later, in the nine spot, he singled again.

On May 2, hosting the Giants the day the new, renovated stands were opened, the Robins' winning tally came home in the seventh inning after Fresco Thompson, the new second baseman who worked at J. C. Penney in the wintertime, walked, stole second, and then came all the way around on a grounder to Bill Terry at first, after Carl Hubbell raced across from the mound to take the throw. The crowd of 35,316 went home happy.

On the Fourth of July, 42,500 fans jammed Ebbets Field, ten thousand more than the capacity of the renovated ballpark. The Robins obliged their fans by shutting out the Giants twice. Other than listening to pitcher Pea Ridge Day make hog calls from the mound, the games served as the year's highlight en route to a fourth-place finish. When the baseball club's directors convened for a board meeting in the team's offices above the Rotunda on October 23, some of the waiting reporters played craps to kill time. After the board members emerged four hours later, Frank York announced that Wilbert Robinson had been replaced as manager by Max Carey, a great hitter and the leading all-time National League base thief, who spent many years with the Pirates before finishing as an active player in Brooklyn in 1929. After eighteen years at the helm, Uncle Robbie, when reached, said Max's appointment was all right with him.

Since Carey's real name was Carnarius, Tommy Holmes suggested in the *Eagle* that Brooklyn consider changing the team's nickname from the Robins to the Canaries, but no one else was singing; instead, the team decided just to emphasize its old nickname, the Dodgers.[16]

The club didn't stand still during the spring of 1932, purchasing the power-packed Hack Wilson from the Cardinals. Short but with an immense, oversized torso, Wilson hit 56 home runs for the Cubs in 1930, but his liability was a proclivity for the bottle; he would hit 23 home runs for Brooklyn. Attempting to signal an end to the Daffiness Days, the Dodgers also dealt Babe Herman to the Reds, a move that shocked and saddened fans.

New York's baseball landscape changed markedly in early June when, on the same day that Lou Gehrig belted four home runs in a single game against the Philadelphia Athletics, news broke of John McGraw's retirement from baseball. The Little Napoleon, plagued by prostate problems and in declining health, offered the Giants' managing job to Bill Terry; even though their relationship was caustic, McGraw had a measure of respect for his thirty-three-year-old first baseman. The Giants would finish sixth, but over at Ebbets Field, Max Carey piloted his new team into a third-place finish.

The Depression had hit in full measure, and attendance at Ebbets Field dropped off for the second consecutive year; the decline at the Polo Grounds and elsewhere was also evident, though it would take another year before the impact was felt at Yankee Stadium. For Frank York, the strain of running the Brooklyn team in conjunction with running his life was too much, and on October 11, 1932, he went to lunch and never came back; Steve McKeever waited all day for him in the offices up in the Rotunda. "He was like a soft wind blowing through the office," one of York's colleagues said, according to Frank Graham. "He came in one door and went out the other and you could never hold him." York was never again seen around Ebbets Field, virtually vanishing into thin air. An announcement was made that he had stepped down as president, ostensibly to devote all his time to his law firm. Within nine months, his actions as an attorney drew critical oversight when it was revealed that he improperly allocated almost $100,000 of a woman's estate to himself as an estate executor; the court ordered the money repaid.[17]

Steve McKeever, seventy-eight years old, succeeded York as president and elected not to give up his favorite seat in the unreserved grandstand in favor of an owner's box. At this point McKeever effectively controlled 50 percent of the ball club himself, while the Ebbets shares were split among fifteen heirs. During McKeever's tenure as president, the Brooklyn ball club moved its executive offices from the Ebbets Field Rotunda to 215 Montague Street, at the corner of Court Street in Brooklyn Heights. (The original "215" building is no longer standing.) The Montague Street office was located centrally in the civic and financial heart of the borough; the proximity eased arrangement of face-to-face meetings with the team's banker-creditors, an increasingly frequent need.

The baseball Dodgers continued to suffer, falling to sixth place in 1933 with yet another decline in attendance at Ebbets Field to 526,815, or half of what they'd drawn in 1930 and the lowest since 1922. The pitching staff included Walter "Boom-Boom" Beck, so named for the quick reversal of his offerings and the sound they made when careening off the outfield walls. He would win twelve but lose twenty. As Stengel would one day say of Roger Craig when he managed Craig with the Mets and Craig went 9–24, you have to be good to lose that many.

The Brooklyn franchise was now in full disarray. Not only were the Ebbets heirs and the McKeever faction still at odds; the Ebbets heirs were in court with one another, prompted by the fact that income from the ball club had stopped. Charley Jr. and his sisters Maie and

Anna wanted the estate's trustees examined with regard to a June 15, 1933, accounting, and named three people in the court action: Charley's widow, Grace; the Brooklyn Trust Company; and ball club director Joseph Gilleaudeau, the husband of their youngest sister, Genevieve.[18]

When Grace took the stand in court in February 1934, she said she left all the workings of the estate to the bank and denied knowing anything about the plans to enlarge the mortgage on Ebbets Field to build additional stands.[19] It took another four years before the case was resolved.

Circumstances were such that Brooklyn's team was regarded as little more than a joke. Giants player-manager Bill Terry had given an interview to a group of reporters a month earlier, assessing his team's chances against those of the other National League contenders. Roscoe McGowen, the Dodgers' beat writer for the *New York Times*, popped what became the famous question: "How about Brooklyn, Bill?" Terry thought a moment, grinned, and said, "Brooklyn? I haven't heard a peep out of there. Is Brooklyn still in the league?"[20]

The quip quickly stoked the hot stove league's fire. The Dodgers' general manager, Bob Quinn, read it in the newspaper and, knowing an opportunity when he saw one, pretended to blow a gasket. He took off after Terry in the press, lambasting him for demeaning Brooklyn, bemoaning how Terry's pronouncements might serve to diminish fan interest in the Dodgers and leave empty seats at Ebbets Field. Quinn was more than a little displeased when Max Carey failed to weigh in from his home in Florida to add to the abuse heaped on Terry, and before Carey could even pack to get to training camp, he was out of a job.

The Dodgers offered the manager's slot to Casey Stengel, the colorful old Superba and one of Carey's coaches. Stengel refused to take the job unless his old boss was paid on his contract, which was good through 1934. Max, after getting assurances he'd get paid the remainder of his contract, urged Casey to take the job. So Casey signed a two-year contract on February 23, 1934. Two days later, John McGraw, one of Casey's managerial mentors, died at sixty. Wilbert Robinson called it "the saddest news that ever came to me."[21]

Stengel, meanwhile, was loaded with retorts for Terry when he met the writers, for whom he always provided entertaining copy. "The first thing I want to say is, the Dodgers are still in the league. You can tell that to Mr. Terry. I'll let Mr. Mungo do a lot of the talking for me against the Giants this summer," said Casey of his star hurler, Van Lingle Mungo. "When he starts heaving that fastball, he won't be easy to contradict."[22]

Later that summer, on August 8, long after an overflow crowd with 5,000 turned away came out to Ebbets Field for a Memorial Day doubleheader to boo Terry and the Giants, only to see the Dodgers lose both,

Van Lingle Mungo would shut out their arch rivals 2–0. But on that very same day, Stengel's other managerial mentor, Wilbert Robinson, Brooklyn's beloved Uncle Robbie, felt dizzy at a minor league meeting of the Southern Association. He went up to his hotel room, hit his head on the bathtub, and died later that evening of a brain hemmorhage. He was seventy-one. Within a few short months, the two leaders, who had led the great rivals in so many memorable battles, were gone.[23]

On the field, not much had changed. The Dodgers spent virtually the entire season mired in sixth place; they had even managed to slip to seventh for a time in July, while the Giants moved into first place on June 8 and stayed there all summer. By September 7 the Giants were up by seven games. All year long, Brooklyn fans had lashed out at Bill Terry for his "still in the league" quip. And now St. Louis, with the Dean brothers, Pepper Martin, Joe Medwick, and slick-fielding Leo Durocher, began to close the gap. On September 21 the Cardinals were at Ebbets Field for a doubleheader. Dizzy Dean, on his way to a thirty-win season, pitched the opener and allowed only three hits, as St. Louis romped 13–0. In the second game, his brother Paul threw a no-hitter, with the Cardinals 3–0 victors. "If I'da known Paul was gonna throw a no-hitter," Diz said, "I'da throwed one, too."

On the last Friday in September, the Cards caught the Giants, so the pennant race, down to its final two days, was in a dead heat. The Cards were hosting Cincinnati in St. Louis. And the Giants? They were scheduled to finish at the Polo Grounds—against the Dodgers, whom they had already beaten in fourteen out of twenty games. A heavy rain dampened the turnout, but 13,774 fans—mostly from Brooklyn—took the subway uptown to Coogan's Bluff, where Bill Terry was greeted with hoots and catcalls at every turn, and Mungo pitched the Dodgers to a 5–1 victory. Meanwhile Paul Dean was beating the Reds, 6–1.

On Sunday, while the Cards were drubbing the Reds, 9–0, the Dodgers were finishing the Giants, rubbing it in with an 8–5 victory after the Giants had broken on top, 4–0. Sweeter yet, Terry brought on his ace, Carl Hubbell, in relief when the score was tied at 5–5, but Brooklyn put three across to whip him. After the game, Stengel and Terry saw each other in the hallway behind the Polo Grounds' center-field clubhouses. As author Robert Creamer describes, Terry had "a surly way of talking," and the pair almost mixed it up.

"If your ballclub had played all season the way you did the last two days, you wouldn't have finished sixth," Big Bill said to Casey.

"No," said Casey. "And if your fellas had played all season long the way you did the last two, you wouldn't have finished second."

Terry started for Stengel but then walked away.

Casey was his usual voluble self with the press. "The Giants thought we gave 'em a beating Saturday and yesterday," said Stengel.

"Well, they were right. But I'm still sorry for them when I think of the beating they still have to take. Wait until those wives realize they're not going to get those new fur coats this year. I've been through it. I know."[24]

The victory was reminiscent of the end of the 1927 season, when the Giants came to an overflowing Ebbets Field on September 25 while making a move on the first-place Pirates, the fans from overflowing stands held behind outfield ropes. The game was called on account of darkness with the contest knotted in a scoreless tie at the end of seven innings, but a week later, when the game was made up, Brooklyn had trounced the Giants 10–5 behind Vance to eliminate them from the race. Even if Brooklyn finished sixth, 28½ games out, any season was within redemption if the Giants could be knocked off.

Nothing really changed over the winter and into the 1935 campaign, except for the arrival of Frenchy Bordagaray. He was the perfect foil for Stengel. Given the team's performance, the madcap stories carried the fans. On the field, the best yarns involved Bordagaray, a California native who variously sported a mustache, goatee, or both, in contrast to the clean-shaven legions of the day. Bordagaray came to Brooklyn in 1935 after a cup of coffee with the Chicago White Sox the year before. "He could run, was a good hitter, was a good outfielder, a good ballplayer," remembered Buddy Hassett, a first baseman on the team.

And he also was a character. One time Bordagaray went into home plate standing up and was tagged out; when Stengel asked him why he didn't slide, he said he had some cigars in his back pocket. Stengel fined him $100 for that. The next day Bordagaray hit a ball over the fence, and circled the diamond by sliding into every base, including home plate. Stengel, who once told him, "There'll only be one clown on this club, and that'll be me," fined him another hundred. Another time Frenchy was picked off while standing on second, and as Stengel charged out to argue, Bordagaray confessed the ump was right; he'd been tapping his foot at second base and must have been caught while his foot was up in the air. Another day, chasing a batted ball in the outfield during a game, his cap flew off; he stopped to pick it up, and then caught the fly. Another time, representing the tying run with two out, he stole third while Stengel was coaching there, even though Casey urged him to stay put.

"I ought to fine you for that," Stengel said.

"With the lead I had," Frenchy fired back, "you ought to fine yourself for not inviting me over."[25]

"One day in batting practice," Robert Creamer writes, "Frenchy accidentally caromed a ball off Stengel's head. The Dodgers had been in a losing streak but that day they won. Bordargaray went to Stengel afterward and said, 'Case, I think we can keep on winning if I can just hit you on the head with a ball every day for luck.'"[26]

Bordagaray's dedication to creating spectacles or being the life of the party was hardly limited to the playing field. "One time," Hassett added, "he ran against a racing horse."

By 1936 the Brooklyn National League baseball team was getting turn-off notices for electricity at the club's offices at 215 Montague Street, and staff members were doing their best to put off bill collectors of any stripe.

On March 23, while Brooklyn was losing an exhibition game to Allentown, business manager John Gorman announced that a loud-speaker system would be installed at Ebbets Field in time for opening day, thanks to a contract that had been inked with the Electro-Acoustics Company of Fort Wayne. The amplifiers would be set atop the scoreboard. Ebbets Field had been one of the last of the major league ballparks—the ultimate distinction falling to Yankee Stadium—without a public address system. The Polo Grounds had abandoned megaphones back in 1929.

The Giants and Yankees faced each other in the World Series that October, while the Brooklyn front office was in chaos. The Brooklyn Trust Company, to whom the ball club now owed over half a million dollars, was asserting more and more influence over the club. Yet the team's business manager, John Gorman, made a move that defied fiscal prudence when he fired Casey Stengel with a year to go on his contract, which meant that Stengel would have to be paid $13,000 not to manage.

The Brooklyn team made the announcement on October 4 from the World Series press headquarters at the Commodore, and the front office didn't tell Stengel ahead of time. Buddy Hassett was with Stengel in the hotel's lobby when one of the writers approached them, and he remembered that Casey took it hard.

"I stayed with him the whole evening—he and his wife—and he took it very badly," Hassett recalled. "Even though there was a year remaining on his contract, those jobs were hard to come by, and it was the deepest part of the Depression."

Stengel's firing wasn't popular with the sportswriters. Just a few weeks earlier, Gorman and McKeever had given Stengel a vote of confidence. Gorman said the reason for the dismissal was that Stengel hadn't shown "sufficiently successful results with the Dodgers," but the scribes regarded the team as woefully lacking in talent. Casey had been great copy since the days at Washington Park, and his deftness was so appreciated by the writers, they threw him a party after he'd been canned. "This must be the first time," Football Giants coach Steve Owen observed, "anyone was given a party for being fired."

Times were tough, economic hardship casting a deepening despair. The Depression was also continuing to weigh heavily on the Ebbets heirs, who were still receiving no money from the Ebbets trust. Less than two weeks before Christmas in 1936, Charley Sr.'s oldest daughter, Maie Ebbets Cadore, now fifty-four years old, said that she might have to apply for a job as a scrub woman at Ebbets Field. Ill and impoverished to the point where she was without money to see a doctor, Maie said she had written to the front office to try to get her husband, Leon, the former pitcher, a job as a scout. But her letters went unanswered.

Instead Cadore had been working as a salesman on commission for a drug house. "It's entirely out of his line," Maie said. "He earns a little and sometimes not that. I had to apply for home relief about a year ago. The home relief people said: 'This is a queer case. We've never seen anything like it before. Here you are part owner of an estate of $1,000,000 or more and you're asking for relief.' I told them I couldn't eat the benches at Ebbets Field.

"I'm an heiress all right," Maie complained bitterly, "but right now I've got to get enough to eat on."[27]

Over the winter before the 1937 season began, rumors surfaced that Brooklyn might sign pitcher Satchel Paige of the Pittsburgh Crawfords of the Negro National League, with the *New York Amsterdam News* reporting, "Those close to the Brooklyn management said the club was sending out feelers to the other teams to get their reaction to playing against the Negro star." A number of major league players during that era, Carl Hubbell and Dizzy Dean among them, expressed surprise that teams hadn't moved to sign players like Paige or Josh Gibson. When reached by the *Amsterdam News*, Steve McKeever said he'd be perfectly willing to sign Paige—provided the new man in Brooklyn's managerial revolving door, Burleigh "Boily" Grimes, the crusty old pitcher—okayed such a deal. But Grimes, when reached in Missouri, was mum on the matter. Had it ever come to pass, and had the color line been smashed ten years before that momentous event actually took place, different names and story lines would adorn the history books, and Brooklyn's Dodgers would have been a better team—with a better accounting ledger—sooner.[28]

The team that took the field on opening day in 1937 could have used the help. They were, at least, wearing new uniforms, perhaps in the hope that a change of finery could shake them out of the doldrums. The Dodgers had new green hats with a plain unadorned "B" on the caps; the new flannels had "Brooklyn" printed across the front in plain block letters in kelly green on white flannel, instead of blue or blue-red trim on white, as they had in the past. On the road they wore kelly green and tan, which looked awful. The change made about as much difference as anything ever did.

Deals brought a twenty-four-year-old three-year veteran, Harry "Cookie" Lavagetto, and thirty-five-year-old outfielder Heinie Manush, a fourteen-year veteran and a .330 lifetime hitter, to Brooklyn. But fundamentally the team wasn't any different, and the ballpark, between broken seats, mildew in the Rotunda, need of a paint job, and otherwise spotty maintenance, was on par with the team.

Also arriving in a deal for Lonnie Frey was infield veteran Woody English, who was playing third base for the Cubs back in 1932 when Ruth hit his "called shot." (Woody told me in a telephone conversation that the Babe didn't call it.) Woody was a right-handed hitter who would slice the ball such that opposing outfielders would play him close to the right-field line, opening up more of a hole in right-center. One time, on a gray day when the field was wet from the rain, Woody's good fortune was aided when Paul Waner fell down in the outfield, allowing his line drive to hit Abe Stark's sign.

"The ball had to hit the sign on a fly, and the official scorer had to verify it," Woody remembered. "By the end of the season I had hit the sign three times, so I went down to pick up my suits. A tailor was there—it wasn't Abe Stark—and he went over to the counter and looked it up and sure enough, he saw that I had three coming. He said, 'Right this way, Woody' and brought me over to this rack. He showed me these three pretty cheap lookin' things . . . and I said, 'Listen, just give me . . . one . . . good . . . suit.'

"He chuckled and said, 'All right, Woody, c'mon back here.'

"He took me to the back, where the good suits were. And that's what I got; one good suit."

Johnny Hudson, another Dodger infielder who was on the team between 1937 and 1940, playing most of his games in 1938 and 1939, also had the knack; Abe Stark would recall some years later that Hudson too hit the sign three times. "And I don't run out there and try to catch those balls, either," the haberdasher said.[29]

Even if the team had failed to turn things around on the field, its haplessness was embraced in the genesis of two enduring creations beginning in 1937. It was the year *World-Telegram* cartoonist Willard Mullin first drew the famous Brooklyn Bum. For the next twenty years, the Bum would become the indelible symbol of the Brooklyn franchise. And the Brooklyn Dodgers Band—not yet called the Sym-Phony—began when a bunch of friends from the Williamsburg section of Brooklyn set out to have a picnic at Alley Pond Park in Queens. When the weather turned bad, they called the picnic off, but as they were going home, the skies cleared, and they decided to head for Ebbets Field. They had musical instruments with them, and were stopped at the gate.

"You can't bring those instruments in here," a guard said. They retreated, and then came up with an alternate strategy. One of them went in, went up a ramp where he was visible from the outside, and then lowered some cord down to the street, where the instruments were tied one by one and hoisted into the stands.

Within a few years, the Brooklyn Dodgers Band—the Sym–Phony—was an officially sanctioned part of the ballpark experience. Eventually the members got seats in Section 8, Row A, numbers 1 through 7, or even sometimes co-opted as many as ten or twelve seats with friends. Initially the band's zany, off-key performances—employing a tuba, snare drum, bass drum, old trombone, and trumpet—seemed very much in step with Ebbets Field's tradition of other sloppy renditions, most notably of baseball on the diamond. When the latter changed, the band became all the more treasured.

The fans could get a charge out of anything. "I was at the first game Dizzy Dean played, at Ebbets Field, coming back after his broken toe in the 1937 All-Star Game," recalled onetime neighborhood kid John Nichols, remembering Dean's too-early return that caused him to change his pitching motion, favoring his injury, which consequently hurt his arm and ruined his career. "Diz was on second base, and on a hit that drove him in, everybody in the stands was yelling, 'Hip, hip, hip, hip,' as Diz chugged home with his limp."

If Grimes was frustrated by only managing to move the baseball team up a single notch to the familiar environs of sixth place, a glimmer of hope would hover later in the fall.

Mere mention of the name "Bedford Avenue" by that time meant "home run" for legions of young Dodger fans who would wait patiently during games for a fly ball that would clear the wall. Others would lie flat on the sidewalk and peer through the crack where Bedford Avenue's exit gate didn't quite meet the ground, offering a view of the action.

Common was the experience of Sam Winchell: "One of my earliest memories of the Brooklyn Dodgers and Ebbets Field goes back to the '30s. As a teenager during the Depression, I couldn't afford to pay to get in. As crazy young kids, we would hang out at the Mobil station on Bedford Avenue right across the street from the field. When we heard a roar, we knew a home run had been hit, and we all fought for the ball. By presenting the ball at the gate, the possessor would be admitted to the game. How nutty! Sometimes it was a shutout or no homers were hit, and we waited nine innings in vain."

It was around this time when a young Jack Kavanaugh had his first experience with Ebbets Field. He recounted his initial discovery of the ballpark and his astonishing luck in a memoir entitled "A Dodger

Boyhood." He and another ten-year-old boy began walking toward Grand Army Plaza on a sunny, weekend morning from his home on 12th Street near the southwest end of Prospect Park. When they got to Grand Army Plaza, the pair were asked by a young man to pass out handbills, with remuneration set at 50 cents apiece, paid in advance.

"We could have pocketed our half dollars and dumped the handbills down a sewer or into a trash basket. We didn't. We disposed of them all. . . . Then, instead of turning back, we pushed on along Eastern Parkway going past the Brooklyn Museum looking for a candy store where we could spend some of the money we had just earned. When we reached Bedford Avenue, I saw Ebbets Field for the first time. I probably had heard about it. Boys assimilate such knowledge. Still, in memory it looms as Camelot.

"If an event was needed to fix the moment in my mind," continued Kavanaugh, "it happened as we walked behind the cement right field wall. Suddenly the street swarmed with other boys running toward us. A baseball, having cleared the screen atop the wall, came bounding toward me. I like to think I fielded it with the grace of Glenn Wright, the Dodgers' star shortstop. I clutched it with suddenly sweaty palms. But it was mine! In a few days the ball disappeared into pickup games played with other small boys on diamonds we improvised on the meadows of Prospect Park. It probably ended its usefulness wrapped in black friction tape. Small boys don't become collectors of baseball artifacts until they grow up and can buy back the talismans of their youth."[30]

For all that was changing in Brooklyn, a sense of wonder still surrounded ballplayers for the kids, and Ebbets Field remained a penetrable bastion. "I was a true Knothole Kid," John Nichols remembers. "In 1933 and 1934, I would sneak into the field about the eighth inning when gates opened on the side street. I would hide in the wooden ticket booths and peek, so help me, through a knothole, waiting for the players to come from the dressing rooms. I would then run out, get an autograph, and duck back into the booth. The chief security guard, a big guy named Joe Moore, would bellow out that we had better vacate the premises, or else. It never happened."

It was typical for Ebbets Field's doors to be opened to various youth groups all through the Depression. On June 26, 1936, two thousand kids from eleven different orphan homes arrived in forty buses as the guests of Dodger president Steve McKeever. They were a reflection of the melting pot that was Brooklyn, coming from the Kallman Home, the Norwegian Home, the Brooklyn Hebrew Orphan Asylum, the Brooklyn Protestant Orphan Home, the Pride of Judea Home, the St. Peter Claver, the St. John, St. Vincent's, and St. Charles homes, as well as the Brooklyn Baptist Home.

Some young fans weren't willing to wait for the ball club's benevolence. John Loughran, who would become a Jesuit priest and a provost at Fordham, reported that he had an "infallible way of sneaking into Ebbets Field," slithering through a slight gap by the side of the sliding doors in front of the Rotunda. "During the mid-1930s," wrote Max Israelite, "I was one of a small number of teenaged boys who made it a practice to sneak into Ebbets Field. Sneaking into a ballpark—without being apprehended—was a highly esoteric skill possessed only by the few. It was a skill developed by careful observation of the cardinal principles of unauthorized entry as taught to us postulants by older, more experienced gate crashers.

"In Ebbets Field, the procedure was this: We would get to the ball park early, about 9 A.M., when the service gates were open to permit the delivery of the food and beverages for the day's game. At this hour, a boy could wander in and about, unchallenged. When we were certain we were not being watched, we made a beeline for a previously selected hiding place.

"I had two favorite hiding places: one was atop the roof of the men's room in dead center field, a spot accessible only by means of a steel ladder affixed to the wall inside the facility. The second was behind an old water heater, no longer in use, which had been disposed of by stowing it under the stands, leaving enough room behind it for two somewhat undersized teenagers.

"We would lie in our places of concealment, silently and virtually motionless, until shortly after the gates were opened to admit the paying customers, exiting our hideaway only after the ballpark was partially filled. One tried to be inconspicuous—invisible would have been better—as he selected a seat in the bleachers, where none of the seats were reserved. We never sat in the first several rows. Foremost in our consciousness was the necessity to avoid attracting the attention of the 'specials,' the private cops hired by management to maintain order in the ballpark, and, especially, we were certain, to track down, seize, and expel illegals like ourselves, all the while vilifying us and our antecedents.

"We would split up and try to find seats next to a fatherly-looking gentleman, then engage him in conversation from time to time, to make it appear, to any curious special, that this was a boy whose dad had taken him to see a ball game on a Sunday afternoon. A special was not likely to ask to see the raincheck of such a boy. Possession of a raincheck was the ultimate test of legitimacy.

"If the gentleman seemed to be simpatico," continued Israelite, "the boy would confess that he had sneaked in, that he was in imminent danger of being tossed out on his fanny, and could he have the man's raincheck for a security blanket? More often than not, the gentleman would find the lad's story fascinating, would judge him to be an enterprising young fellow, and was glad to conspire with him to outwit the authorities. Never once, in all our joint experiences, did an older man summon a special to eject a boy!"

Sometimes kids tried to sneak in when no one was playing. On February 9, 1936, a day that was cold and damp with a mixture of snow, sleet, and rain, Patrolmen Herman Moeller and Herman Nagle were cruising by the ballpark late in the afternoon when they saw something suspicious. Six baseball bats and a pair of baseball knickers were being dropped over the right-field wall and into the street.

Right behind the bats and knickers came fifteen-year-old Solomon Cohen and his friend Ronald Goldfarb. The cops apprehended them, but a third boy got away. Investigations showed that the Dodger locker room underneath the stands had been entered, and that some equipment had been taken. The baseball bats were owned by a minor league farm unit of the Brooklyn club. The knickers belonged to Brooklyn outfielder Ralph Boyle. Not that stealing his pants was the reason, but Boyle never played again in the major leagues. In Children's Court, young Cohen was ordered to Bellevue Hospital for observation. Goldfarb was arraigned in Adolescents' Court.[31]

The best situation, of course, was to possess a legitimate ticket for a game. If you had one in advance, you could talk with anticipation with your friends about what you were likely to see. Attending a game was a big deal, especially since regular season radio broadcasts of games were not yet a reality in the New York market. "When you went to a game, you were it," remembers Tom Knight, who attended his first game in 1936. "When you'd come back to your block, a crowd of people would gather around, adults *and* kids, and they'd want to know who did what and how they moved out there. And they'd want details."

Other attractions held the thrall of sports enthusiasts at Ebbets Field. One of the most surprising fights ever at the ballpark occurred when a former welterweight and middleweight champ, little Mickey Walker, "The Toy Bulldog," held heavyweight Jack Sharkey to a fifteen-round draw on July 22, 1931. Sharkey fought again at the ballpark that fall, this time besting the Italian giant Primo Carnera in a fifteen-round decision.[32] The big boxing cards eventually petered out, with most of the action gravitating across the river. Brooklyn was left with its club fights that provided great entertainment in the neighborhoods. The more avid fight fans would traipse between the neighborhoods for the bouts.

As for baseball, Ebbets Field had a second home team during the summer of 1935. The Brooklyn Brown Eagles, a black team, were a part of the new Negro National League that had been launched in 1933 by Pittsburgh's Gus Greenlee. Greenlee, a North Carolinian by birth and whose mother was half-white, became a numbers impresario and a partner of the white Latrobe Brewery owner, Joe Tito.[33] Greenlee's bootlegging with Tito enabled him to finance hotels, a restaurant, and other businesses. He also invested in boxers and, in 1931, organized one of the great black teams of legend, the Pittsburgh Crawfords, a suitable rival at that time to Cumberland Posey's Homestead Grays. Not long after the death in December 1930 of league founder and the first pillar of black baseball, Rube Foster, the original Negro National League folded in the throes of the Depression in 1932. The same fate was also befalling several minor leagues in Organized Baseball at the same time, and a number of major league franchises were in trouble as well.

Greenlee's new Negro National League got off to a shaky start in 1933, but the East-West All-Star game between black stars staged in Chicago that year was a major success in both sustaining the league's teams and establishing the linchpin of the league's identity. Some Negro National League promotions had been scheduled at both Yankee Stadium and Ebbets Field in the 1930s, but after the 1934 season, with a desire to penetrate the New York market with a consistent rather than an intermittent presence, the league decided to put a team in Brooklyn. Such a team would compete directly with promoter Nat Strong, Dexter Park, and the control Strong exercised over black baseball bookings in the entire metropolitan area.[34]

The events at Dexter Park could draw a good crowd. "The white ballplayers at that time were always glad to play against our Negro ballplayers," the great Negro league third baseman, Judy Johnson, remembered, "because there weren't the salaries like there are today. They made almost as much playing against us after the World Series was over as they would make almost the whole season. I played against every big leaguer, from Babe Ruth on down. On Sundays we'd go up to New York and play the Bushwicks, a white team in Brooklyn, and they had some major leaguers on that club. It got so for a while we'd play the Bushwicks on the first and last Sunday of the every month. We were drawing more people with the Bushwicks than the Dodgers in Ebbets Field sometimes."[35]

Although the move to put a black team in Ebbets Field was thought by some to be an ominous challenge for a fledgling league against the entrenched power of Nat Strong, especially given the high level of unemployment and hardship facing the black populous the league was counting on for support, the question of Strong's individual influence and the impediments he might create became moot with his death from a heart attack at age sixty-one in January 1935.[36] In a related development the Cuban promoter Alex Pompez, blocked successfully by Strong in the past, now managed to secure and renovate a home ground for his Cuban Stars that had previously eluded him. He located in the uppermost reaches of Manhattan, at 204th Street and Dyckman Oval.

The Brooklyn Brown Eagles were run by Abe and Effa Manley, a couple who had met at Yankee Stadium at a World Series game in 1932, and who would become prominent in black baseball. Abe Manley, like Greenlee a North Carolina native, also had a numbers business with a couple of legitimate offshoots, though his were based largely in New Jersey, where he had started the semipro Camden Leafs in 1929. Abe was black but Effa was white, raised "in an interracial environment by a white mother of German/Native American descent and a black step-father. She viewed herself as an African American throughout much of her life and in a rare reversal passed as black rather than white," writes Neil Lanctot.[37]

The Eagles, an antecedent to the famous Eagle teams that began playing in Newark the following year, were a middling team. They went 15–15, finishing fourth in the eight-team Negro National League in the first half of the 1935 season, and went 13–16, finishing sixth, in the second half.

One of the team's standouts was Leon Day, a nineteen-year-old pitcher. "I didn't see anybody in the major leagues that was better than Leon Day," said Larry Doby, the first black player in the American League. "If you want to compare him with Bob Gibson, stuff-wise, Day had just as good stuff. Tremendous curve ball, and a fast ball at least 90–95 miles an hour. You talk about Satchel; I didn't see any better than Day." Monte Irvin, who also came up through the Negro Leagues before playing with the New York Giants, echoed the sentiment: "He was as good or better than Bob Gibson. He was a better fielder, a better hitter, could run like a deer."[38]

The Eagles lost $30,000 that first year, with part of the loss attributed to the owners' inexperience in the role. The team drew poorly, with Ebbets Field's distance from Harlem thought to be one of the reasons. The franchise was shifted to Newark in 1936, but the Eagles would still have dates in the future at Ebbets Field.

In what would have to be considered a largely orphaned sport in Brooklyn, professional grid action commenced again at Ebbets Field in 1930 after a four-year hiatus, thanks to Big Bill Dwyer, who owned the New York Americans, the NHL team that wore red, white, and blue jerseys and vied with the Rangers for the affections of the Madison Square Garden fans. Dwyer, referred to as a "Brooklyn businessman," owned the Keeney Park racetrack in Florida and also was one of the biggest bootleggers around, a man whose hootch was highly regarded by speakeasy patrons.

Dwyer and John Depler bought the Dayton Triangles for $2,500 from Carl Storck, who between 1939 and 1941 would become commissioner of the league. The proud owners then moved the NFL franchise to Brooklyn. Depler, a former Illinois captain, coached what became the first Brooklyn Football Dodgers team, featuring Father Lumpkin, Izzy "Indian" Yablock, Wild Bill Kelly, Rex Thomas, Ollie Samson, Al Jolley, Hec Garvey, Swede Hagberg, ex-Giant Jack McBride, and Georgia Tech's Stumpy Thomason, whose fumble was taken the wrong way by Roy Reigles in the 1929 Rose Bowl. The Brooklyn team would finish a respectable fourth, with a 7–4–1 record, and even managed to beat the New York Football Giants by a nip-and-tuck 7–6 at the Polo Grounds in late November, but they lost in a December return match at Ebbets Field.[39]

With the new stands across the back of one of its end zones because of the ballpark renovations in 1931, the Football Dodgers had more seats to sell and less distance between the gridiron's end zone and the seats. They weren't able to come close to filling them, even with their newest attraction: the agile 5'10", 240-pound lineman Herman Hickman, a Tennessean known as the poet laureate of the Volunteer State. The team was dismal, arriving at Ebbets Field with a 1–4 record after its first five games on the road, finishing 2–12, a sudden and alarmingly appropriate counterpart for their baseball namesakes.

Dwyer, $30,000 in hock on his football investment by the end of the 1932 season, sold out in the new year to Chris Cagle and Shipwreck Kelly. Cagle came from money, had a swashbuckling man-about-town playboy image, and to buttress his three-season experience with the New York Football Giants, was a West Point All-American for good measure. Kelly, a running back out of the University of Kentucky, had also played with the Giants. The Football Dodgers managed to eke out a winning 5–4–1 record in 1933 when the NFL split into two divisions and the rules on passing were relaxed, but missed a chance to finish first with a key Thanksgiving home loss to the Giants. Dan Topping, who married Norwegian figure-skating champion Sonja Henie and who was later to gain fame after World War II as owner of the Yankees, bought Cagle's half of the franchise in 1934, but the development didn't change the team's mediocre play.

"The best Brooklyn 'offense' was Ralph Kercheval's long punts," writes football historian Stan Grosshandler, but "the old college offense of 'a punt, a pass and a prayer' didn't make it in Brooklyn, where they had a punt but never a pass and, consequently, the team seldom had a prayer."[40]

The arrival of former Detroit Lion coach Potsy Clark in 1937 didn't change things, especially the anemic offense, until later that

season when Clark found an Ace—Ace Parker, a Duke All-American—
to quarterback the team. Yet even then, the transformation failed to
produce winning seasons overnight. By the time it did, in 1940, Clark
would be gone, replaced as coach by Jock Sutherland, a dentist from
Pittsburgh and a single-wing offense proponent who benefited too from
Clark's 1938 addition of the highly touted Mississippi tackle Bruiser
Kinard. In 1940, the Football Dodgers ran up an 8–3 record, with four
straight wins at season's end, finishing only a game behind the Redskins, who went on to lose to the Western Division champ Chicago
Bears 73–0. The lopsided loss left rueful sentiments in Brooklyn, since
the Football Dodgers would have been hard pressed to perform worse in
the NFL championship game than the 'Skins.

Other football was played during Ebbets Field autumns: Manhattan College concluded the last of thirteen games played at Ebbets Field
between 1928 and 1937; St. John's had played football games at Ebbets
Field, as well as Dexter Park, until it began a forty-year hiatus with its
football program in 1931;[41] the high schools from the Public School
Athletic League also played regularly, whether for baseball or for football. In one of the more memorable games in Public School Athletic
League history, a face-off between Erasmus and Madison high schools
at Ebbets Field in the mid-1930s featured quarterbacks Sid Luckman for
Erasmus and Marty Glickman for Madison. Madison won. Luckman
would later gain fame as quarterback for the Chicago Bears; Glickman
would gain his first as a sprinter and later as a longtime broadcaster.[42]

The Catholic high schools played at Ebbets Field, too: Brooklyn
Prep and St. John's Prep met in an annual Thanksgiving morning classic, sometimes drawing as many as 10,000 to the ballpark.

Whatever the level of play, the venue was important. Ebbets Field
was a shrine for many of Brooklyn's parents and schoolkids who strove,
scrimped, saved, studied, and played, as well as for those who just
worked or worried. Its place in the culture was confirmed in Arthur
Miller's *Death of a Salesman*, when Willy Loman, the main character,
preens about his son's playing on the fabled ballpark's gridiron: "God . . .
remember that Ebbets Field game? The championship of the city? . . .
When that team came out, he was the tallest, remember? . . . Like a
young god. Hercules, something like that. And the sun, the sun all
around him. Remember how he waved to me? Right up from the field,
with the representatives from the three colleges standing by? And the
buyers I brought, and the cheers when he came out—Loman, Loman,
Loman! God Almighty, he'll be great yet. A star like that, magnificent,
can never really fade away."

CHAPTER SEVEN

Larry and Leo
Lights, Camera, Action

E bbets Field was a different ballpark in the spring of
1938, and though no one knew it at the time, within
six months and without a single pitch thrown, the
Depression had ended for Brooklyn baseball.

The chief causes were threefold. First, Leo Durocher
was acquired by the Dodgers from St. Louis just before the
second consecutive World Series between the Yankees and
Giants in October 1937. Brooklyn dealt four players to get
the aging, weak-hitting shortstop, and the deal made no
sense whatsoever unless someone in the front office was
envisioning him as a manager.

Second, a month later, the longstanding lawsuit
brought by Charles Ebbets Jr. and his sisters Maie and Anna
against Charles Sr.'s second wife, Grace, their brother-in-
law Joe (and through him their sister Genevieve), and the
Brooklyn Trust Company, was dismissed. The court found
the ball club's leaders were not paid excessive salaries,
found no fault with the decision making surrounding the
bank's 1931 loan to double-deck the stands at Ebbets Field,
and determined that the trustees best conserved the
estate's assets by not selling the interest in the ball club at
a "ridiculously low price" during the Depression's lean
years.[1]

Third, George V. McLaughlin of the Brooklyn Trust Company, nicknamed "George the Fifth" by the press for the combination of his middle initial and imperial demeanor, was fishing around for new executive leadership for the ball club. He talked with Ford Frick, president of the National League, and tried to interest Branch Rickey, who was running the St. Louis franchise. Rickey recommended Larry MacPhail, the dynamic, volcanic, alcoholic, irrepressible, brilliant, and often unreasonable character in charge of the Cincinnati franchise.

MacPhail had introduced night baseball to the major leagues in Cincinnati in 1935; painted and spruced up Crosley Field; and put the building blocks of a pennant contender in place. His biggest escapade had been years before, after the Armistice, when he led a group of fellow officers into Holland in an aborted attempt to kidnap the Kaiser. They managed to penetrate the castle where he was staying before being discovered. As MacPhail and his cronies fled, he copped a Hohenzollern ashtray, which he subsequently took pains to display prominently on his desk. Most important, he made things happen, a very good thing in a place where they aren't.

When MacPhail met McLaughlin, he mentioned his terms, looked at his watch, banged his open palm on the table, and said he had business elsewhere if he couldn't do it here.[2] On January 19, 1938, the Brooklyn Dodgers announced that Leland Stanford MacPhail, better known as Larry, had agreed to become the club's new executive vice president. MacPhail took the job on the conditions that the old leadership would stay out of his way and that the bank would give him money to effect operating improvements. The statement announcing MacPhail's appointment was signed by Steve McKeever.

Before long, MacPhail had bank officers sweating, worried that he was spending their good money after bad. When he looked at the offices at 215 Montague Street, he talked of making alterations by knocking down the walls. The stands at Ebbets Field were "rusty and dusty and in need of paint, and there were broken seats that had to be replaced. The dugouts were crumbling, and the clubhouses needed cleaning and freshening."[3] MacPhail went in and told McLaughlin he wanted $200,000 for ballpark improvements, and got it; he knew Phillies owner Gerry Nugent was always in need of cash, so he told McLaughlin he needed $50,000 to buy Dolph Camilli, the Phillies' star first baseman, and got Camilli.

On March 7, the day after MacPhail spent the fifty grand on Camilli, Steve McKeever suddenly died. Reports in the paper said he succumbed to pneumonia, but a neighbor, who lived a few doors down from the McKeever family, heard that at the end eighty-three-year old Steve had a heart attack when he heard that MacPhail had spent all that dough on a first baseman.

The Judge was memorialized widely, and was buried out of St. Saviour's in Park Slope, with every pew in the church taken and mourners kneeling outside in the snow during the service. Mayor Fiorello La Guardia and other dignitaries walked next to the slow-moving hearse as flurries fell.

Within a month after Steve McKeever's death, the New York City Council, prodded by Tax Collector Dave Soden, Democratic leader Frank V. Kelly, and Councilman Joseph Sharkey, who introduced the measure, voted to change the name of the street alongside the third base side of the ballpark from Cedar Place to McKeever Place. It wasn't the only thing that had changed around Ebbets Field. The ballpark had a fresh coat of paint on the inside walls and posts, and the seats had been painted, too. The walls above and around the refreshment stands had photo murals; the bathrooms had new fixtures. The ushers had new uniforms, wearing green and gold, and so did the Dodgers, for the first time wearing the white flannel with the now familiar blue script of the team's name across the chest. On the ballplayers' left sleeve was a patch of the trylon and perisphere (the Giants and Yankees wore one, too), the symbol of the next year's New York World's Fair. At home, the team wore a white cap with a blue brim, a blue Brooklyn "B," with blue piping coming down off the blue bean of the cap. On the road, they wore the all-blue cap with a white bean and white Brooklyn "B" that would become the club's standard both home and away the following season.

When MacPhail first arrived in Brooklyn, he said that he had no plans to install lights at Ebbets Field, but soon after the start of the season, he changed his mind. After petitioning McLauglin for more money—another $110,000—he got permission from the league to schedule seven night games.

The first night game was to be June 15, 1938. Minnie Ebbets, crippled by arthritis at the age of eighty, left her Brooklyn apartment near Grand Army Plaza, reportedly for the first time in three years, to sit in a field box near third base. Her arrival prompted the *Eagle* to note that the "grand old lady of baseball," the "ex-wife of the former part owner and president of the Brooklyn Baseball Club . . . was back at her favorite diversion of 56 years ago." The original Mrs. Ebbets recalled the day in 1912 when Charley said, "Here's where it's going to be, Minnie," when goats were grazing where the diamond was now etched on the landscape. "When I saw those little towels they put on the back of the seats, I had to laugh when I remembered the bare boards I once had to sit on long ago," she added.[4]

Johnny Vander Meer, the Dutch Master, had pitched a no-hitter in his last outing against Boston in Cincinnati, and would be going for the Reds against Max Butcher for Brooklyn. Edie McCaslin, a teenager at the time who went to the game with her husband-to-be, remembered the historic night: "We went out to the ballpark, but I was afraid we weren't going to be able to get in. But we got a spot fairly close. The place was jammed. It was a pleasant evening. We sat on the stairs; I don't think that would be permitted now. You couldn't live in Brooklyn without being a Dodger fan; there was an electricity to the place that just hit you in the face. I can still feel the electricity and excitement inside of me as I think of it today."

The fire marshal had closed the gates at 8:36 P.M., with some 38,748 managing to shoehorn their way into Ebbets Field and another 20,000 turned away. The fans were hanging from the rafters.

With dusk falling and the lights still not on, a rocket was shot into the air while bands struck up the national anthem. At 8:37 P.M., the seven light towers with their 615 floodlights, generating 92 million in candlepower, were turned on to a roar from the crowd. The imperial showman, MacPhail, had arranged for some pregame entertainment. Olympic champion Jesse Owens gave a broad jump demonstration and ran a couple of races, once spotting the fastest runners on the Dodgers and Reds ten yards in a hundred-yard dash. Owens wound up just shy of overcoming Ernie Koy, Brooklyn's fleet center fielder.

The game began at 9:23 P.M. By the end of the fourth inning, Cincinnati was already four runs up, Butcher had been chased, and Vander Meer still hadn't allowed a hit. He had his own cheering section of some five hundred family and friends who had come over from his home town of Midland Park, New Jersey, to see him pitch. By the seventh inning, with the score now 5–0 and the Dodgers still hitless, the Brooklyn fans sensed that they might be seeing something momentous. "Around the seventh inning," Edie McCaslin said of a possible no-hitter, "everyone wanted to see him do it."

By the bottom of the ninth, the old orchard was in crescendo. With one out, Vander Meer got into trouble, walking both Babe Phelps and Cookie Lavagetto. After Grimes sent Goody Rosen in to pinch-run for Phelps, Vander Meer walked Camilli, loading the bases. Vander Meer then induced Ernie Koy to hit a grounder to Riggs at third, who went to home for the force. Up stepped Durocher, who had been dubbed "the All-American Out" years before by Babe Ruth, during Durocher's brief stay with the Yankees. After Vander Meer worked the count to 1–2, Durocher hit a loud foul. On the next pitch, he lofted the ball on a line over second base.

It looked as if it had a chance to drop.

The roaring crowd, already on its feet, seemed to surge and yell at a decibel level high enough to drive the roof off the house. Harry Craft, the center fielder, charging hard, finally caught the ball, and Vander Meer had his second no-hitter in a row, a feat that has never been duplicated.

Babe Ruth had been to the game with his wife, Claire, and his presence early in the evening stirred the crowd, with fans surrounding him, excited to see him. Larry MacPhail, who had put on a Babe Ruth Day in Cincinnati during the Babe's final, brief tour with the Boston Braves, got an idea. The next day, after meeting with MacPhail, Grimes, and Durocher, who been named team captain in May, the Babe signed a $15,000 contract to coach first base for the rest of the year. Three days later, he was out at Ebbets Field. Now the fans and photographers were showing up to see Babe hit batting practice homers onto Bedford Avenue. Even though MacPhail made clear to the Babe that he wasn't going to be considered to manage the club, some speculated about whether Ruth or Durocher would eventually take the manager's job from Grimes, who was seen as inevitably destined for the exit. For despite all the hoopla, the Dodgers were still headed for seventh place.

Ruth's desire to become a major league manager was well known. Babe made no secret about wanting to succeed manager Joe McCarthy while with the Yankees, who opted to release their marquee player and waning star after the 1934 season in order to allow him to become a Boston Braves "vice president and assistant manager"—a nebulous title at best—while playing what would perhaps be his final season before ostensibly succeeding Bill McKechnie to manage that team. The situation soured, and Babe played his last game on Memorial Day of 1935, a few days after hitting three homers in Pittsburgh, the last one, in proportion to the myth that will always follow him, over Forbes Field's double-decked stands in right field, something no one else had ever done.

Ruth's reputation for excess made him a questionable prospect as a manager. If the buttoned-down Yankee owner Jacob Ruppert speculated about how Ruth could manage a team if he couldn't manage himself, the irrepressible MacPhail, running the Dodgers, also had the same problem as Ruth, so one could reasonably conclude that he might not hold that against the Babe. Now, three years later, the Sultan of Swat was in a baseball uniform again, that of the Brooklyn Dodgers, a team comfortably accessible from his place on Riverside Drive.

Babe kept the players loose, would often drive Buddy Hassett to and from the ballpark, was great with the fans and with kids, and seemed to connect with everyone but Durocher. Before the 1938 season was out, the pair had an argument in the clubhouse stemming from a discussion after a young reporter mistakenly gave Babe undeserved credit in a sports story for calling a hit-and-run play to win a game. The story upset both Grimes and Durocher, who let the reporter know about it. Babe wasn't involved in relaying signs, and though Grimes always let him in on the changes, it didn't matter much. The argument with Durocher was really more about their underlying antipathy. Grimes got between

Durocher and Ruth as they were jawing at each other, but as word of the dispute leaked out, any thoughts of Babe assuming the helm—if MacPhail had even ever contemplated it—began to evaporate.

In July, the pain of being a Dodger fan and the impact of a generation of losing teams led to violence and tragedy. The episode began in a Park Slope bar, Diamond's Café, when barkeeper Bill Diamond, the son of bar owner and Tammany politician Pat Diamond, joined a number of other patrons in needling his friend Robert Joyce, a Dodger fan and postal worker. Increasingly drunk, embarrassed, and slighted, Joyce had talked glowingly of Larry MacPhail and a recent trade. After more than an hour of mocking, Joyce got up and left, mumbling something about "getting even."

Joyce went back to the post office, opened it with a key, went over to the gun locker, broke it open, and took a couple of revolvers. He returned to the bar after midnight, walked in, and fired two shots at the younger Diamond, who was hit in the left side, mortally wounded. Another shot went awry as Albany visitor Frank Krug and waiter Charlie Miller jumped on Joyce and pulled him down. Miller grabbed the gun and went out into the street to summon a cop. But then Joyce suddenly got up and pulled out the other handgun, killing Krug and threatening another patron, Bob Eagan, before fleeing into the street. The police picked him up a block away from the scene.

On August 2, the largest weekday crowd of the season, 18,567, showed up for a doubleheader against the St. Louis Cardinals and, in the words of Roscoe McGowen of the *New York Times*, "got a tremendous amount of entertainment for its money.

"Chief items of interest," continued McGowen, "were the playing of the opener with yellow balls, Dolph Camilli's fourteenth and fifteenth home runs in the nightcap and the banishing of Onkel Franz Frisch and catcher Mickey Owen by Bill Stewart, plate umpire, in the second contest." The Dodgers managed to cop the pair from the Gas House Gang. The experimental yellow balls got good reviews as "easier to follow in flight," a theory tested by Johnny Mize's deposit of the first yellow ball on Bedford Avenue for the first run scored off pitcher Fat Freddy Fitzsimmons, who won the first game.

The excitement at Ebbets Field that summer managed to boost attendance by some 180,000 to 663,087, good enough for fourth best in the league. In December, MacPhail hired Leo Durocher to be his new manager, prompting Babe Ruth to send in a letter resigning as a coach.

After hiring Leo, MacPhail decided to break the radio blackout previously agreed to by New York's three major league teams whereby radio broadcasts of games were banned, the theory being that they were giving away the product for nothing. MacPhail felt differently. He believed that such broadcasts would popularize the product, and to that end, he brought Red Barber to Brooklyn. MacPhail had brought Barber to Cincinnati, where he'd been a rousing success, and now Barber's southern locutions would expand Brooklyn's vernacular. The Ol' Redhead was "sitting in the catbird seat" before James Thurber ever appropriated the phrase, and describing the "rhubarb in the pea patch" propagated by Durocher for those at the ballpark.

The venture was an enormous success. Red Barber brought Ebbets Field to life with the immediacy of "now" over the crackling airwaves, before the evening papers or one-star editions of the *News* brought tale of the scores. His word arrived before those coming home from the game were stopped by neighbors, friends, and strangers, all of whom wanted to know what happened and just how it happened. Through the multitude of Philcos and Crosleys in people's parlors, Red Barber created a curious evolution in people's consciousness. He made Brooklyn first. Not in the standings, but on the airwaves and in people's hearts.

MacPhail had a clear idea of how he wanted things to be. He liked the ushering crews in Chicago that were trained and directed by Andy Frain, so he hired a Frain assistant, an energetic man named Jack Haines, to recruit and train a new corps of Ebbets Field ushers. One of them was Jack Kavanaugh, who got the job thanks to the intercession of his cousin, who knew the nephew of Jack Collins, the Dodgers' business manager.

"The fellows just ahead of me were turned away," Kavanaugh recalled, remembering the long line of applicants that stretched outside the entrance to Ebbets Field's Rotunda. "My name got me inside. I joined a growing group sitting in the lower grandstand behind first base. When about 100 of us were in place Jack Haines addressed us. We were hired, he told us, to be ushers. Not everybody would work every game; it would depend on the size of the crowd. For next week's opening day, we would all be used. Come back wearing a white shirt with a detachable collar. A green tie was required and black shoes."[5]

Perhaps the most perceptible difference about Ebbets Field in 1939 was that the Dodgers seemed like they were starting to become winners again, jumping up to second place in May behind the pitching of Hugh Casey, Whitlow Wyatt (who had been picked up from the minor league Milwaukee Brewers), and Luke Hamlin. Regular Ladies' Days also had been instituted on the Dodger schedule. "My music class from Brooklyn College would go to Ladies' Day on Fridays, including our professor," Brooklynite Arnold Lapiner recalled. "I still remember the hot dog vendor yelling, 'They're skinless and boneless and harmless and homeless.'" Women rooters weren't shrinking violets, either. "The shrill cries of the female rooters pierced the ears of passers-by blocks away," wrote Frank Graham.[6]

The Dodgers fell back but then revived again to play .500 ball through the heart of the summer. A highlight was the acquisition of Dixie Walker, who had knocked around the American League, beginning with the Yankees in 1931, shuffling between the majors and minors for a few years before going on to Chicago and then Detroit. He'd hit .300 with both midwestern teams but had trouble with his shoulder; when Brooklyn picked him up on waivers from the Tigers, the local fans seemed to bond with him instantly. In late August MacPhail gave the green light for another baseball first: Red Barber broadcast the very first televised baseball game, the first game of a doubleheader on August 26, 1939, against the Cincinnati Reds.

There were no scripts, cue cards, or rehearsals for the live commercials. "Nobody ever thought about a thing like that," Red said. W2XBS, the NBC flagship station that would later change its call letters to WRCA and then WNBC, had two cameras, one on the ground level behind home plate, the other in the upper stands, back of third base, right out with the fans.

"I was sittin' right there with 'em," Red said. "And I guarantee you I had hundreds of helpers."

There were no monitors and no assistant directors.

"We had three radio sponsors: Ivory soap, Mobil gas and Wheaties," Red remembered. "I just put on a filling station cap, held up a can of oil and ad-libbed a little bit. Did the same thing for a bar of Ivory soap. Poured some Wheaties in a bowl, sliced a banana, put some milk on it and said, 'This is the breakfast of champions.'"[7]

Six days later World War II began. A young Leonard Koppett remembered the precise moment he received that news. He walked out of Ebbets Field on September 1 after the Dodgers and Cubs had played each game of the doubleheader split in under two hours, only to see headlines on Flatbush Avenue blaring word of the Nazi invasion of Poland. It was an ominous time.

The Dodgers, meanwhile, would go on to win 23 games while losing only 13 in September, finishing with an 84–69 record. While the Reds had been in first place since the end of May and would win the pennant with the Cardinals finishing four games behind them in the loss column, the Dodgers managed to secure a distant third-place finish during the last couple of days of what, overall, was a very satisfying season. Later that fall, on October 22, the first televised professional football game was broadcast from Ebbets Field, on a day the Football Dodgers managed to prevail over Philadelphia, 23–14.

Six days after that—and on a day earlier than usual, since October 29 landed on a Sunday—old friends of Charley Ebbets gathered as they always had to celebrate his birthday. That the celebration would continue posthumously in such grand style was Charley's doing.

"It all began," former New York State Supreme Court justice Joseph Aspinall once recalled, "during one of the birthday parties Charley held 'most every year. He brought in a few bottles of old stuff and we asked him why he was such a tightwad. He came back with a denial and said to prove it he would leave $5,000 in his will to provide a get-together every year on his birthday. We thought it was a joke and forgot about it, but when his will came out, he'd left the money all right."[8]

A provision in the Ebbets will filed in 1925 stipulated that the interest from a $5,000 bequest should be spent annually for a bash in one of the dining rooms of the Brooklyn Club in Brooklyn Heights. Less than a month after Charley Sr. passed away, Surrogate Judge George Wingate disqualified himself to act on the Ebbets will since he was serving as the Brooklyn Club's president. In a friendly action before the court while the will was in probate, Grace Slade Ebbets, Charley's second wife, asked that the money be set aside for the banquet. At the end of December 1927, Justice Dunne of the New York State Supreme Court cleared the $5,000 item.

Justice Aspinall was one of the three named in the will to form a banquet committee, the other two being George W. Chauncey and John Remsen. For years, the bequest remained the only part of the estate that cleared. Subsequently, every October 29, the surviving members of the original select group of seventeen chosen by the banquet committee would gather and raise their toasts to the Squire of Flatbush. Their parties, from champagne, through several gourmet courses, to liqueurs, continued until at least 1941, held in the Coal Hole, a basement room in the club. The room was named after the restaurant along the Strand in London, from which an old Brooklyn Club member, Justice John Woodward, had retrieved a sign—it would hardly be becoming to say that Justice Woodward had pinched the sign—some thirty years before.

In 1939 twelve Brooklyn Club members toasted Charley's eightieth birthday, with a vacant seat set in his honor, as usual. Justice Aspinall had recently died, leaving thirteen of the original group. "Three club members were invited," the *New York Times* noted, referring to Brooklyn Club members outside the circle of Charley's old friends. "Colonel A.W.J. Pohl, treasurer, Walter E. Trum, chairman of the House committee, and Walter O'Malley, the attorney who replaced

James P. Judge, one of the original Coal-Holers when he died three years ago."[9]

One wonders what Charley Ebbets might say today had he known that Walter O'Malley pulled up a seat to eat at his table.

Larry MacPhail wasn't a man to stand still. Boston Red Sox shortstop and player-manager Joe Cronin wanted to play a bit longer, and his self-interest may have cost the Red Sox a player who could've made a pivotal difference on their subsequent contending teams. On the Louisville Colonels, controlled by the Red Sox, there was a young twenty-one-year-old shortstop who Dodger scouts felt was something special. MacPhail spent $50,000 over the winter of 1940 to get him: Harold "Pee Wee" Reese.

Following his success with Whit Wyatt, MacPhail also moved to pick yet another major league pitching castoff, Tex Carleton, from the minor league Milwaukee Brewers. At the beginning of the season, the Dodgers clicked immediately, winning their first eight games. They won their ninth game when Tex Carleton pitched a no-hitter at Crosley Field against the Reds. When MacPhail had the team flown home after finishing its western trip on May 9 with a 12–2 record, 30,000 people met the two planes that carried them to Floyd Bennett Field.

MacPhail wasn't done. In June, he swung a deal for Durocher's old friend, Joe Medwick, paying $125,000 to Branch Rickey and the Cardinals and also throwing in four players, getting Medwick and pitcher Curt Davis in return. In truth, some of cash represented value MacPhail received when Branch Rickey asked Larry to hide a player by the name of Pete Reiser for him, during a period when Commisioner Kenesaw Mountain Landis ordered Rickey to release seventy-three young prospects for running afoul of regulations concerning the Cardinals' operation of their farm system, upon which Landis had long cast a bilious eye. MacPhail picked up Reiser for $100, and after a subsequent spring-training showing when Reiser hit everything in sight, when Durocher tried to keep him, Larry ordered him sent down to Elmira, ostensibly for more seasoning. Hiding Pete Reiser wasn't going to work; the word on his talent was already out. Even from Larry to Branch as a favor to an old friend, protégé to mentor, there was no way Pete Reiser could ever be returned in some multiplayer deal. He was too good. In 1940 Reiser would begin to have an impact at the big league level.

MacPhail had his eye on everything.

At Ebbets Field, MacPhail's team in the stands—the ushering corps—remained largely intact, though Jack Haines returned to

Chicago. "A younger man by the name of Jack Jordan, blond and handsome as a matinee idol, replaced him," remembered Kavanaugh. "The theatrical good looks were a family trait: he was a brother of the stage and screen actress Helen Twelvetrees. Unlike Haines, who rarely donned the gold-braided white jacket of chief usher, Jordan preened in his. Four others wore white jackets to indicate they had the rank of captain. Oddly, there was little envy among the green-uniformed ushers. A white jacket denied its wearer the opportunity to pick up tips by dusting off seats, and the position was too important to risk by hustling standees for a buck."

Another who wore the white coat was a young man named Johnny Freund. "As good-looking as Jordan in a darker way, Johnny Freund's voice earned him the role of announcing over the P.A. system," said Kavanaugh. "Other than irritating umpire Larry Goetz one day by identifying him as 'Goats,' Freund did his job effectively. One day we ushers were asked to audition to replace him for the summer months, as Johnny would be acting in summer stock somewhere. During that theatrical engagement, he changed his name. He left as Johnny Freund but came back as John Forsythe."[10]

On June 16, one of the quirkiest hits ever—inimitably Ebbets Field—won a game for the Reds. In the first game of a twin bill, the Brooks' Whitlow Wyatt was locked in a scoreless, masterfully pitched duel with Cincinnati's Paul Derringer. With two out in the ninth inning, former Dodger Lonnie Frey hit a liner to right field that hit at the base of the screen above the scoreboard, went straight up in the air, came straight down, and disappeared from view somewhere atop the scoreboard. Right-fielder Joe Vosmik waited. Frey, assured of a double, saw Vosmik still standing there, looking up, pounding his glove, so he kept on going.

Joe Pollack, who grew up in Flatbush and who would one day become a reporter for the *St. Louis Post Dispatch*, was at the game. "Everybody just sat there stunned," he remembered. "The third base coach waved Frey on and he trotted in. It was the only run of the game."

"He could have circled the bases all afternoon," said Jack Kavanaugh. "The ball never came down. The newspaper writers decided the ball had remained on a shelf formed by a wing on the right side of the scoreboard where the part that protruded angled back to meet the wall. The press box consensus was that the ball became stuck at the foot of the screen. Not so. My view was from Section 1 of the upper grandstand, next to the right field wall. I was looking down at the small, triangular platform toward which the ball had dropped. The ball didn't become stuck, it disappeared.

"Before the game," he continued, "a workman had climbed up to replace some rotted boards. As the game was about to begin, he was nailing new 2 x 4s into place on the shelf when the umpires spotted him. Beans Reardon trotted out and ordered him down off the scoreboard. Apparently intending to go back and finish after the game, the carpenter left his toolbox behind. He also left the space for one board uncovered. That's where Frey's ball went, plummeting cleanly through the narrow opening."[11]

The Reds were close to clinching the 1940 National League pennant when they met the Dodgers in the last meeting between the two clubs on September 16 in Brooklyn. The score was tied 3–3 after nine. In the tenth, Cincinnati had men on first and second with one out when Reds first baseman Frank McCormick hit a grounder to Johnny Hudson at short. Hudson flipped the ball to second baseman Pete Coscarart, who held on to it for a second and dropped it. "Umpire Bill Stewart called the runner out at second as he whirled to call the play at first and did not see the ball drop," writes Brooklyn baseball historian Tom Knight, noting that there were three umpires on the field. "[Umpire George] Magerkurth overruled Stewart and declared the runner safe at second."[12]

Durocher was out of the dugout like a shot. Leo and Maje had little regard for each other under normal circumstances, and now Durocher raged into furor. Before long Leo was given the heave-ho. When the game continued, Bill Baker hit a sacrifice fly. The run stood up and the Reds won.

After the last out, the 6'3", 230-pound Magerkurth was jumped from behind on his way off the field by a short, stocky irate fan, who had leaped out of the stands. His name was Frank Germano, all of twenty-one years old. Somehow Germano managed to trip Magerkurth, and the photo that appeared prominently the next day in the *Daily News* showed Germano with fists cocked, astride the on-his-back arbiter. The picture ultimately made papers all around the country and would work its way into baseball's history books.

The other two umpires pulled Germano off, and shortly thereafter he was taken into custody. "Frank was an ex-convict out on parole," Svein Arber writes. "Some sympathetic fans hired an attorney to defend him; only in Brooklyn would the lawyer's name turn out to be Louis J. Wacke. Despite the legal aid, Germano's misadventure put him right back into the clink."[13]

In the picture of the fracas, an usher can be seen twenty or thirty feet away, in the background, watching the episode unfold. The usher's name was George Phillips. "Larry MacPhail was outraged," usher Jack

Kavanaugh later wrote. "It was bad enough that his ushers hadn't intervened, the one whose picture was in the paper actually seemed to be enjoying the fight. When he arrived at the ballpark [the next day], Phillips was told not to bother putting on his uniform. Instead he was to report directly to Larry MacPhail so that MacPhail could fire him personally. If we'd worn epaulets, MacPhail would have snipped them off Phillips's uniform and handed him a white feather for cowardice.

"Soon Phillips was back and putting on his uniform. We crowded around as he buttoned the coat and straightened his hat. Then we saw his swollen and blackened eye. No, MacPhail hadn't done it. In fact, it saved Phillips's job. MacPhail, having been told the picture had been snapped just as the usher had turned to investigate what was happening behind him, assumed Phillips had been slugged in the following melee. Actually, Phillips had gotten the shiner hours after the game was over. He had been the second choice of a young lady he had offered to escort home from a bar. But in stepping outside to settle the issue with his rival, Phillips had caught a roundhouse thrown by a different antagonist for a different purpose. However, he accepted MacPhail's interpretation and assurance of future assignments of choice ushering locations that went with it."[14]

Several years later, a defendant appeared in a Brooklyn courtroom. "There was no question of guilt or innocence," Red Smith wrote. "The dip was no special credit to his profession. His level of skill was approximately that of the pickpocket acquaintance of the late Wilson Mizner, of whom Mizner said, 'He couldn't dip his hand into the Hudson without knocking over the Palisades.'"[15]

The judge, Samuel Liebowitz, faintly recognized the accused. After a couple of questions regarding team allegiance, Liebowitz put it together.

"You," the judge said, "are the fellow who jumped George Magerkurth that day! I thought I recognized you."

"That was me," Germano said, beaming, reliving, as Smith noted, his hour of glory.

"Well," the judge said, "I'm giving you three years. You won't find it so bad. They've got a ball team up there, a pretty good one, I'm told.

"But tell me something," the judge said. "I'm a Dodger fan, myself, and I know what the umpires can do to us. But to jump out on the field and slug one of them! Are you really as hot a fan as that? Did that decision—I forgot what it was—did it make you lose your head altogether?"

The pickpocket smiled tolerantly, Smith reported.

"I'm a good fan," he said. "I can get excited. And I was sore that day. I was sore as hell. It was a lousy decision and it burned me up.

"But to tell you the truth, Judge, I had a partner working in the stands that day."[16]

The year 1941 may have been the most exciting season in baseball history. Baseball was set against the backdrop of an uncertain world, and as the months went on, the likelihood increased that America would become involved in a war the size of which the world had never seen. The war in Europe was already a year and a half old; France had fallen; the British armies had escaped at Dunkirk and the Royal Air Force had beaten the Luftwaffe over the skies of London in the Battle of Britain. Arguments in the United States raged between the "America First" isolationists and those who wanted to come to the aid of Britain.

At Ebbets Field, the ballpark was readied for the season with an advertising strip across the top of the scoreboard that proclaimed "Edison's 1941 Combination Bargain $2.25 a month." Gruen Watch Time above the scoreboard featured a bigger clock face than the Bulova clock face that fans would so often see in photographs from subsequent years. Gruen's clock face protruded another ten or twelve feet over the top of the Bedford Avenue fence.

The slanted part of the scoreboard closer to the right-field line was used as an extension of the Gem Razor ad, featuring a full-length image of a safety razor. The Stark sign cast a sense of stability among the changing outfield advertisements from year to year, although Botany, Lifebuoy, and Gem also were regulars. And the Dodgers were now good enough that the fans stopped using the joke in reference to the Lifebuoy ad that was perennial in Philadelphia: How the Phillies use Lifebuoy but they still stink.

After the Dodgers had spring training in Havana, team management began the season with fans threatening to boycott because of Durocher's intentions to start the season without Dixie Walker in the lineup, going instead with Paul Waner in right and Pete Reiser in center. Walker had become enormously popular, but neither Durocher nor MacPhail expected the response they got. Five thousand Brooklyn fans signed a single telegram, threatening to boycott Ebbets Field if the management didn't put "the peepul's cherce" back in the lineup. A huge throng filled Ebbets Field for the opener anyway, but the Dodgers lost to the Giants, who then also took the following two games.

Five days after the season started, the rookie phenom Reiser was beaned by a sidearm fastball served by Ike Pearson of the Phillies. He came to at 11:30 that night at Peck Memorial Hospital.

"I was lying in bed with my uniform on," he told writer W. C. Heinz, "and I couldn't figure it out. The room was dark, with just a little night light, and then I saw a mirror and I walked over to it and lit the light and I had a black eye and black streak down the side of my nose. I said to myself, 'What happened to me?' Then I remembered."

Reiser took a shower, walked around the room, and went back to bed. When the doctor came in the morning, he said they'd keep him another five or six days for observation. When Reiser asked why, the doctor said, "You've had a serious head injury. If you tried to get out of bed right now, you'd fall down." Reiser asked, "If I can get up and walk around this room, can I get out?" The doctor said he wouldn't be able to do it, and prepared to catch him, but of course Reiser could walk and did, explaining that he'd been walking the floor during the night. Before he let him go, the doctor made him promise he wouldn't play ball for a week.

When he showed up at Ebbets Field that night and took a seat behind the Brooklyn dugout, Durocher asked him how he felt.

"Not bad," Pete replied.

"Get your uniform on."

"I'm not supposed to play."

"I'm not gonna play you. Just sit on the bench. It'll make our guys feel better to see you're not hurt."

And so he sat. Until the score was tied 7–7 in the eighth, when the Dodgers had the bases loaded and Ike Pearson was coming out of the bullpen.

"Pistol," Leo said, "get the bat."

"In the press box," Heinz wrote, "the baseball writers watched Pete. They wanted to see if he'd stand in there. After a beaning they are all entitled to shy, and many of them do. Pete hit the first pitch into the center-field stands, and Brooklyn won, 11 to 7."

"I could just barely trot around the bases," Reiser would later tell Heinz. "I sure was dizzy." [17]

The Bums righted themselves, and now ran off a stunning stretch where they won 15 of 17.

At Ebbets Field, Brooklyn fans, sensing victory, were on the edge of their seats, involved in every pitch, every game. Billy Herman, newly acquired from the Cubs to play second base, said playing in Ebbets Field was like playing in a World Series every day. Ann Lee remembered a time when her girlfriends wanted to leave a game early. "This is a Dodger game," she said. "You don't leave a Dodger game early."

The games were exciting whether they were tight or not. And of course when they were, the crowds were wild. On July 14 Kirby Higbe, who had pitched brilliantly, was locked up in a 0–0 pitching duel against Verne Olsen of the Cubs going into the bottom of the ninth. With the bases loaded and Higbe scheduled to hit, Durocher risked the crowd's wrath by pulling him, and sending up a pinch hitter: himself. But Leo delivered, bunting past the mound and bringing Ducky Medwick home from third base with the winning run.

At Ebbets Field, the fans enjoyed it to the hilt. The Brooklyn Dodgers Band paraded through the ballpark, a garrulous, leather-lunged woman, Hilda Chester, rang her bell in the bleachers, and restauranteur Jack Pierce blew up balloons and bellowed "Coo-ooooookie" after Lavagetto, his favorite player. Eddie Bettan wore a pith helmet and blew a whistle, "Number 1 Fan" Shorty Laurice paraded in his top hat, and *Daily Mirror* sports editor Dan Parker wrote the poem "Leave Us Go Root for the Dodgers, Rodgers." In it Murgatroyd Darcy ("a broad from Canarsie") speaks to her beau, Rodge, saying, "Dancin' the shag or rumba is silly / When we can be rooting for Adolf Camilli, / So leave us go root for the Dodgers, Rodgers, / Them Dodgers is my gallant knights." Frank Graham wrote that "Bud Green and Ted Berkman later collaborated in setting the poem with a few changes to music, and it became the marching song of all the Murgatroyds and Rodgers in the borough."[18]

And it was no wonder Dolph Camilli's name was set to music and verse; he continued to pound the ball on his way to a 34-homer, 120 RBI season. "I'm the only player that ever hit three home runs in the upper deck in dead center in three consecutive years," he recalled in 1994. "Fred Fitzsimmons swore that I hit one over the top of a pitcher's head that was so low he ducked, and the ball just kept rising."

Durocher kept the place alive. "Leo was a fiery type of manager," Dolph said. "He kept the players steamed up all the time. He played hunches. But he had experienced guys, guys who could do things, like Lavagetto and Billy Herman. It was a made-to-order club. And the fans, the fans were great; they hadn't had a winner in so many years. Even today, if they're gone, their children come up to me and tell me how much it meant to their parents, how much it means to them."

And then, of course, there was MacPhail. To whom Camilli, for one, was not endeared.

"MacPhail was a blowhard, a reeee-al asshole; he'd flare up and blow his top all the time, sticking his head in on the players."

Durocher brought an eclectic mix of stage and screen stars and gamblers to the ballpark. As often as not, they made their way into the clubhouse. And many got to be friends with the players. "Danny Kaye, who was quite a fan, used to sit with my family," said Camilli. "He's a wonderful person. And he went to the games because he loved baseball."

As summer wore on, it was turning out to be a surreal season. Over in the American League, with the Yankees on the way to a pennant,

Joe DiMaggio was hitting in 56 straight games, while Ted Williams was flirting with hitting .400.

In the National League, Branch Rickey's Cardinals were the main opponents in Brooklyn's quest to capture its first flag in twenty-one years. They had Johnny Mize, Marty Marion, Enos Slaughter, and, toward the end of the year, a rookie by the name of Stan Musial, who would become the single most feared visiting hitter at Ebbets Field over the next sixteen years.

But Brooklyn wasn't to be denied. On September 25, after Pittsburgh had trounced St. Louis, 3–1, the Dodgers needed just one more win to clinch the pennant. The borough held its breath as Whitlow Wyatt worked his way toward a 6–0 shutout victory over the Bees in Boston, as the Braves were called for a number of years. Taxi drivers had no fares; no one was going anywhere. This was before the days of transistor radios, so trolley motormen lingered at stops where radios blared. In the Williamsburg section of Brooklyn, a barkeep was so preoccupied with the radio that he allowed an open beer tap to overfill a mug to the point that the beer's foam was sloshing over his shoes.

Judge Samuel Liebowitz and a jury were hearing testimony in a grand larceny case in County Court when the jurist's secretary quietly made her way up to the bench and handed the judge a piece of paper. As Assistant District Attorney John J. Rooney was in the process of examining a witness, the good judge interrupted: "Here is news of great moment in Brooklyn. Brooklyn has defeated Boston. Pittsburgh has defeated St. Louis. The pennant is ours. Trial adjourned." [19]

At once the streets were filled; impromptu parades started by children were followed by adults. At the site of the original Washington Park, several hundred people gathered as an effigy of the Yankees was burned. There were rounds on the house all over the bars and restaurants of Brooklyn. People gathered under the windows of the Dodger offices on Montague Street. Larry MacPhail had an open house, and reveled in the glory. Bar business was described as a "flood tide." Thousands upon thousands joined the celebration.

At Borough Hall, borough president John Cashmore issued a proclamation pronouncing September 29 Brooklyn Dodgers Day. "The people of Brooklyn are hereby urged to do their part in making this day one to be remembered by hanging out flags and joining in the demonstration for Brooklyn's heroes of 1941," said Cashmore.

On WOR Radio, Red Barber let slip the arrival time of the Dodgers train at Grand Central. When the train arrived at the station, Barber knew instantly that making the announcement was a mistake. The place was mobbed.

Radio bulletins had been flashed on the progress of the train through Rhode Island and Connecticut towns. Inside the train, the scene was as wild and raucous as it had been in the stands at Ebbets Field throughout the year.

MacPhail, meanwhile, decided that he wanted to be on the train as it roared into its berth amid the crowd, so he hopped a cab and went up to the 125th Street station in Harlem, the final stop before Grand Central. But Durocher, knowing nothing of MacPhail's plans, ordered the engineer not to stop, feeling some of his players might elect to get off and take cabs, ducking the fans' assuredly-out-of-control celebration. Leo wanted a full contingent off that train on this long-awaited day.

Grand Central was at once wildly ebullient and partially hysterical, players getting out through the ebbing movement of back-slapping crowds or behind wedges of cops.

Durocher, after making his way through the crowd, headed over to the New Yorker Hotel to meet MacPhail, who, unbeknownst to Leo, was flushed with rage at being passed by at 125th Street.

"There was another crowd waiting in the lobby of the New Yorker, and as Medwick and I were trying to get through, the word was passed to me that the newsreel cameras were waiting upstairs in one of the club's suites," Durocher recalled. "It seemed that they wanted to take some pictures of me before I shaved. When we got to the elevator, who did we find standing there but Larry MacPhail. Redder than a beet and breathing heavily. He didn't say Hello, Goodbye or Congratulations. Just a red, red face and breathing hard and not looking at anybody or anything.

"Didn't say a word in the suite either. Not until the cameras were being taken away. 'I want to see you,' he said, pointing to [traveling secretary John] McDonald. 'And [pointing to Durocher] you. Come with me, both of you.'

"The three of us went into the bedroom and he closed the door and we were sitting in a tight little threesome," Durocher continued. MacPhil asked McDonald why the train hadn't been stopped at 125th Street as Larry had ordered in his wire, which was the first Leo had heard about it, and Durocher interrupted before McDonald could answer, telling Larry what happened. MacPhail glared. When Leo was done, Larry blurted, "You're not satisfied being the manager of this club, you want to be the president."

"No such thing," Leo replied. "I figured the fans hadn't had a pennant winner in twenty-one years and they were entitled to see the players."

"You're fired!"[20]

It was one of many of MacPhail's impromptu announcements, firings that would typically last several hours or until the next morning, as this one did.

The *Eagle* headline was a classic, a keeper. "WE WIN," it said in block letters across the front page.[21] Days later, people thronged the streets, sat atop fire boxes, wrapped themselves around lamp poles, and leaned out windows, police estimating "easily more than a million," while the celebratory parade proceeded from Grand Army Plaza up to Borough Hall. "Million Roar Salute to Parading Dodgers," the *Eagle's* headline blared in full caps. Mounted police headed the cavalcade, trumpets and horns blaring behind them. Reiser, Durocher, Camilli, Reese, Hugh Casey, Higbe, and the others followed, riding in open cars down Flatbush Avenue. The Band, Hilda Chester, and Shorty Laurice were all there, with sixty thousand fans marching behind them on foot.

One of the things MacPhail did to ready Ebbets Field for the World Series was to construct another press box. This second press box hung off the ballpark's roof behind home plate. "The original press box, built around 1930 off the front of the second deck, was relatively small," remembers Leonard Koppett. "Barber had one corner of the box; it didn't accommodate many people—maybe 25 or so—and led directly back to a set of rooms where Larry MacPhail opened a set of offices. The area included a bar that MacPhail opened that was known as 'Larry's Saloon.'"

The bar was first administered by Hymie Green, who, as the sole dispenser of Larry MacPhail's free liquor, inspired a strong sense of loyalty among the press corps. Unfortunately, Hymie also occasionally had Larry MacPhail as a patron, and on one such occasion, after having a couple of pops and a play on the radio went against the Dodgers, MacPhail directed his irascibility at Hymie, who would have none of it. He removed his apron, walked out, and took a job across the street tending bar at Flynn's.[22]

The bartending later fell to Bill Boylan, a former minor league hurler, who doubled around Ebbets Field as a batting practice pitcher. If that wasn't enough, Boylan had a wee-hours-of-the-morning job as a milkman.

"The downstairs press box became exclusively the radio and TV booth later on," added Koppett. "After the '41 pennant, MacPhail built a new press box hanging under the roof. The new press box upstairs was very roomy, very long. But it didn't have a toilet; you had to walk and take a passageway out the back to an elevator and go to the old press box."

Trucking themselves between levels was somewhere between an inconvenience and a liability for those in the upstairs press box, depending on either the tightness of a deadline or one's propensity for beer. "When the games lengthened after World War II," Koppett recalled, "Carl Lundquist, who worked for the UPI, complained that a one-piss ballgame had now become a two-piss ballgame." Although proximity of facilities is never an issue in a modern-day stadium, baseball has exacerbated one aspect of the equation with longer games. "Now, of course," Koppett added, "I've lived long enough to see the three-piss ballgame."

Bob Cooke of the *Herald Tribune* believed no recollection of the Brooklyn ballpark would be complete without a mention of press box attaché Benny Weinrig, who spoke, as Cooke put it, "clear distinct Brooklynese with unfailing accuracy. His vocabulary was an argot unto itself. When something would go wrong in the press area, Weinrig's broad shoulders would suffer the wounds.

"'Why,' he would ask, 'do I always get the blunt of the blame?'

"Once," Cooke added, "Weinrig was presented with a gift at season's end by the baseball writers. Obviously touched, he had additional comment. He didn't like Hymie, the press room bartender. Said Weinrig: 'I hope you guys didn't give anything to that other phony.'"[23]

Weinrig's pièce de resistance would come years later, after reporters in the press box asked him to go down to the clubhouse to check on a player injury. Returning, he reached for the press box microphone and reported, "There are no broken bones. He only sprained a linament in his leg."[24]

Over at Yankee Stadium, the teams split the first two games before rain delayed the resumption of the Series at Ebbets Field for a day. The starting pitchers for game 3, the Dodgers' Fred Fitzsimmons and the Yankees' Marius Russo, dueled beautifully, keeping the game scoreless into the seventh inning. With two out in the top of the seventh, Russo, at the plate, smashed a low liner back at Freddie. It hit Fitz on the left kneecap and ricocheted, still in the air, into the glove of Reese for the third out. Fitzsimmons, meanwhile, was hobbled and had to be helped off the field, while Mrs. Fitzsimmons, behind the Dodger dugout, hid her tears. Fitzsimmons, who had an apartment in the neighborhood and whose bowling alley near the ballpark was part of the neighborhood scene, had pitched nineteen years in the big leagues, but he was 0–3 lifetime in three different World Series. This would be his last and best opportunity to win a game.

Hugh Casey was brought on in relief in the eighth and retired Johnny Sturm, but then was hammered for four singles and two runs, the Yankee protagonists being Red Rolfe, Tommy Henrich, Joe DiMaggio, and Charley Keller before Larry French came on to quell the rally. The Dodgers answered with a single run in the bottom half of the eighth on Dixie Walker's double and Pee Wee's run-scoring single. But after that Russo bore down, and the Yankees had a 2–1 Series edge.

Jack Kavanaugh was ushering behind the plate for the fourth game. He knew the way the wind was blowing for him, knew that military service was around the corner, knew he'd be changing his usher's uniform for Uncle Sam's. "Randolph Scott and Groucho Marx led large parties, effusively greeting everyone but ignoring the usher trying to get one last tip with his soon to be retired seat-dusting rag," he wrote. Also sitting in his section was Casey Stengel, who was now manager of Boston's National League club. Stengel's wife, Edna, failed to make the game, and so, after a number of innings, Kavanaugh, who would have normally put a fan in the seat for a couple of bucks on the sly, took the seat himself.

"I remembered him as the Dodgers manager when I had been a kid getting autographs. His was the hardest to get. Then, one day, while the others were chasing someone down Sullivan Place, I waited with my back to him, then wheeled around and held out my book. 'Sign for me, Casey,' I said, 'before the others see you.' He did."

Stengel saw Kavanaugh's usher's uniform and accepted him as company, carrying on "a nonstop analysis of the game," as Jack remembers. "He managed for both teams. Like all Brooklyn fans, I had thought I knew everything there was to know about baseball strategy. Casey dazzled me with his anticipation of coming circumstances. He didn't second-guess Leo Durocher or Joe McCarthy, and he was two and three innings ahead of the action as he outlined all pending strategy moves."[25]

In the top of the ninth, with the Dodgers ahead 4–3, Johnny Sturm grounded to second; Rolfe hit back to the box. Two away. The third hitter was Henrich. Dodger reliever Hugh Casey worked him carefully, finally running the count out full. The Dodgers were a single strike away from tying up the Series. Casey wound and delivered, pulled the string, and Henrich went for it, a swing and a miss. Strike three! But no! The ball got away from Mickey Owen, rolling back to the backstop near the Dodger dugout. Owen ripped off his mask and went in pursuit of the ball, to no avail. Tommy Henrich made his way down to first base.

Owen recalled later that Casey had two curves. "He had the big sweeping curve that he'd tried a couple of times earlier in the game, but it had hung," Mickey said. "Then he had the quick curve that was working real good. When I called for the curve, I was looking for the quick one, but Casey rolled off that big one, and it really broke."[26]

Tommy Henrich remembered it that way, too. "With the count against me," Henrich said, "I'm just guarding the plate. It came in chest high, and that ball broke like no curve I'd ever seen Casey throw. As I start to swing I think: 'No good. Hold up.' That thing broke so sharp, though, that as I tried to hold up, my mind said: 'He [Owen] might have trouble with it.' If you take a look at the picture of it, you'll see that I'm already looking back over my shoulder. I'm expecting him to lose that ball." Remembering the pitch again fifty-four years later, Henrich reiterated that it wasn't a spitter. "Daniel [the sportswriter] said it was a spitter; what did he know? The ball was in a smooth arc that broke very much. A curve. A spitter jumps. This ball didn't jump."

"I just didn't get my glove turned enough," Owen said, "and the ball bounced off the heel and rolled over to the Brooklyn dugout."

"I can still recall that look on Henrich's face when he struck out," Phil Rizzuto recalled. "He was looking back. He couldn't believe that Owen had missed it. I was sitting on the bench. I was holding the gloves of the guys who were batting that inning—DiMaggio, Keller, Dickey and Gordon. In Brooklyn those kids would run down after the third out and take anything they could. When Henrich swung and missed that pitch, we all started for the runway in the dugout. Then all of a sudden—I couldn't believe it—people were jumping over the stands, Brooklyn fans. It looked like Brooklyn had won."[27]

At the foot of the dugout was Charlie Clark, who had succeeded John Forsythe as the ballpark's announcer. He looked at the ball as it rolled toward the dugout. He had an almost irresistible urge to touch it, to kick it back to Owen, but he knew full well it would be interference and it wouldn't gain him or the Dodgers anything.

"By the time I got it," Owen said, "there was no play on Henrich at first base." After that, Joe DiMaggio hit a hard single to left. "The savvy Leo Durocher and his brainy assistants, Chuck Dressen and Red Corridon, let a red-faced Hugh Casey go on uninterruptedly trying to overpower the Yankee batters," Kavanaugh remembers. "Owen, the catcher, in shock himself for the passed ball, didn't go to the mound to confer with Casey. No one called time. The carnage went on." With two strikes, Charley Keller doubled off the right-field fence, scoring the two runners. "Casey Stengel was nearly out of his mind with frustration as Durocher remained, out of sight, on the bench," Kavanaugh recorded. "At one point, Stengel had his leg over the low railing. I thought he was going to go out and stop the action himself. Actually, he was trying to get the attention of the Dodger bench. The side of the dugout blocked him from the view of players like blinders on a horse."[28]

Hugh Casey walked Bill Dickey to get to Joe Gordon, but Gordon doubled to drive Keller and Dickey home. "What shots they hit," Phil Rizzuto said. "I've never seen such shots in my life."[29] The beleaguered Dodger reliever finally got out of the inning by retiring Yankee pitcher Johnny Murphy.

The Dodgers went through the motions in the bottom of the ninth. They were done. The Yankees won the game, 7–4. "I guess I said good-bye to Casey Stengel as I went off to my postgame assignment," said Kavanaugh. "The loss had left me numb. I don't recall leaving Ebbets Field." [30]

"My first feeling," Owen told W. C. Heinz, "was surprise and then disgust. After that I was kinda numb, like I'd been hit with a real good right-hand punch. I kept asking myself: 'How did I do it? How did I do it?' Then I made up my mind I'd have to live with it. I'd always been able to take adversity pretty good, and I reasoned that I'd been trying my best. At other times I'd dwell for weeks on a pop fly I hadn't gone back on, or if I hadn't backed up first, but this time I had tried."

"Mickey Owen took it in stride about the third strike," recalls Dolph Camilli. "He told a story about being in the shower when MacPhail came in the clubhouse hollering like a madman. 'I didn't know what to do,' Mickey recounted, 'so . . . I . . . just . . . crawled . . . down . . . the . . . drain.'"

"They came to interview the goat of the series," Arthur E. Patterson wrote in the *New York Herald Tribune*, "and many of them left with the feeling that the battered catcher was a hero—heroic in the courage he showed by taking all the blame for the latest misfortune of his teammates." [31]

"As a child I often heard adults discussing baseball and the progress of the pennant races," said Larry Block, who was ten years old in 1941, "but the names meant little to me. My earliest memory which relates to the Dodgers was of Rosh Hoshanah in October of 1941. Of this high holy day Jews the world over eschew worldly thoughts, concentrating instead on the state of their soul and their relationship with the Almighty. However this was Brooklyn. I was walking home from the synagogue with my mother when we encountered a group of men on the way to the subway who had obviously just come from Ebbets Field. My mother asked the question, 'Did they win?'

"'No,' came the reply, 'they lost. Two out in the ninth and the damn catcher can't catch the ball!'

"The fact that my mother had spoken to perfect strangers, that they had replied, and that there was no need to define, 'they,' stuck in my memory." That moment made an impression on young Larry. He would have time to ponder the game over the winter, and would be ready by spring. "Intrigued by the fact that grown men were taking a kid's game so seriously I began to take an interest, scanning the sports pages of the *New York Sun*, which my mother brought home from work every day, and before long, I was hooked on the Dodgers."

The next day the Yankees won 3 to 1 and closed the Series. "That was exciting in itself," Phil Rizzuto said of the game of the dropped third strike. "But I'll never forget the next day when Owen came out to bat. The hand those Brooklyn fans gave him was unbelievable. They were telling him they didn't blame him. They stood and cheered. It rocked old Ebbets Field."[32] In fact, Owen was given an ovation each time he came to the plate that day.

Owen reminisced years later about the response. "The people were nice. I got about 4,000 wires and letters from all over. I had offers of jobs and proposals of marriage. Some girls sent their pictures in bathing suits, and my wife tore 'em up. Actually, I was a better ballplayer after that, because I knew I could take it—like a fighter takes a fella's best punch—and maybe a better man too."

"I don't know what kind of a man he was before it happened," Heinz wondered in the *Saturday Evening Post* in 1965, "but I have a pretty good idea of what kind of man he's been since. I mean, we all drop a third strike at some time, but most of us do it, the worst, in semiprivacy. On that hot and humid Sunday afternoon, though, the Mick dropped his on the big stage of sport with the whole country knowing it and never forgetting, and that kind of thing could take a permanent tuck in a man's try."

"Not with me," Owen said. "I don't know but maybe it made me try even harder. Dizzy Dean once taught me something that I never forgot. We had this pitcher with the Cardinals who wasn't going too good, and he said to Diz, 'What changes should I make?' Old Diz said, 'Don't change a thing about your pitchin'. The reason you don't win is that you're afraid to lose. As long as you're afraid of losin', you'll never be a winner.' I'm not afraid of losing."

"Shortly after Mickey Owen's gaffe," said Larry Block, "the nation was at war with the Axis. The character of the neighborhood changed as it did all over America: there were no young men to be seen and flags with blue stars began to appear in windows. Brooklyn seemed populated by old men, women, and little kids like me."

CHAPTER EIGHT

Football, Fatigues, 4Fs, and FDR

Baseball's history lends itself to literature and rapture; it is easily available and readily revealed by any number among a given generation's best writers for those engaged in its pursuit. In the first half of the twentieth century, this was generally not the case with professional football and certainly not the case for the Brooklyn Football Dodgers, who were and remain as largely unheralded as their baseball counterparts were celebrated. The 1940 and 1941 seasons were the Football Dodgers' most successful. Early in the fall of the latter year, before baseball had wound up what was perhaps its greatest season—courtesy of DiMaggio, Williams, and Brooklyn's winning a National League pennant for the first time in twenty-one years—the Football Dodgers had already played two games at Ebbets Field. They lost narrowly to the world champion Chicago Bears, 14–9, before 27,000 in an exhibition. And they won their home opener against the Detroit Lions, 14–7, after knocking out Detroit's offensive threat, Whizzer White, a future Supreme Court justice, midway through the game.

After the baseball Yankees concluded the 1941 World Series against the Dodgers, Larry MacPhail made the decision to resod Ebbets Field immediately for the 1942 baseball season, rather than wait until spring. As a result, he insisted that the football players wear sneakers during their practices and quit if it began to rain, in order that the new sod might better take hold.

While Football Dodgers team owner Dan Topping looked around for high school practice fields and placekickers practiced off the field in cleats, aiming at imaginary goalposts, the Football Dodgers won their second game and then lost three in a row. The last of them was to the Chicago Cardinals, 20–6 before only 12,054 fans, even with the added attraction of Glenn Miller's orchestra playing at halftime.

On October 26, an undefeated Football Giants squad came into Ebbets Field to face the 2–3 Football Dodgers. A crowd of 28,675 turned out at the ballpark. Brooklyn shocked the football fans and prevailed, thanks to a five-yard run by Pug Manders, followed by a subsequent Manders interception of an Ed Danowski pass.

Afterward, on subsequent weekends at Ebbets Field, the Football Dodgers defeated Philadelphia, 15–6, and Washington, 13–7. At that point, sporting a 5–3 record, the Football Dodgers were a single game behind the Football Giants for the NFL Eastern Division lead. But then they lost to a 0–7–1 Pittsburgh Steeler team by the score of 14–7 on the road, and with that their title hopes disappeared.

The following week, back home at Ebbets Field, the two teams played again, and this time the Football Dodgers routed the Steelers 35–7, to lift their record to 6–4. By the time December 7 rolled around, when the Football Dodgers would play the Football Giants, coach Steve Owen of the Giants had prepared his team as coach Jock Sutherland did the Dodgers, as if the title were on the line, even though the only thing at stake was pride. And since that itself was enough, the fans turned out, with 55,051 filling the Polo Grounds on a cold day. The Football Giants were honoring Tuffy Leemans, whom Giants' owner Wellington Mara had signed out of George Washington University after the 1935 season. Leemans became the NFL's leading rusher in his first season and became one of the best ball carriers in Giants' history. On this day, however, the Football Dodgers ruined the Giants' celebration, sending four New Yorkers, including legendary center Mel Hein, off to the hospital in the course of administering a 21–7 beating. Manders scored all three touchdowns, including one on a 65–yard interception runback.

But something else was going on. Throughout the game, military and civilian officials had been paged over the PA system, and when the game was over, there was an announcement that all servicemen should report immediately to their duty stations.

With good reason. For at 1:53 P.M. New York time, 7:53 A.M. Honolulu time, the Japanese had conducted an air attack on Pearl Harbor. It was the date of infamy. Nothing would ever be the same again.

Earlier that autumn, on November 1, 1941, shortly before that year's mayoral election when Mayor Fiorello LaGuardia would withstand a challenge from Brooklyn district attorney William O'Dwyer, an elevated highway was opened down a fifty-block stretch of Third Avenue in Brooklyn, some three miles east of Ebbets Field. Less than a month after the ball hit off the heel of Mickey Owen's glove, an expressway officially opened that knifed up the western side of Brooklyn. Its construction had sliced a widened traffic artery that cut off a piece of a neighborhood and the old Brooklyn that everyone knew, transforming it forever, and not for the better. The highway arched over a part of South Brooklyn and Sunset Park known as the Gowanus, at one point just a few blocks away from where the second Washington Park stood. The man responsible for the road was Robert Moses.

Around the same time that Ebbets Field was first built, Robert Moses was kicking off his career in public service after an academic effort that brought him through Yale, on to Oxford, and back stateside to Columbia. During those early years in New York, he would walk through Manhattan brimming with ideas, and took up the mantle of a reformer focusing on civil service. It was during Governor Al Smith's tenure in the 1920s that Moses became known as the "best bill drafter in Albany." After Jones Beach State Park, a triumphant public work, was built under his aegis, and after an unsuccessful gubernatorial candidacy as a Republican in 1934, Moses continued his work on parks, projects that helped transform neighborhoods that were sometimes otherwise devoid of parkland.

He also controlled the building of highways by virtue of his leadership of the Triborough Bridge and Tunnel Authority, an instrument of his creation that was designed to insulate him from political oversight. And it was here where his penchant for accomplishment collided with the protestations of those who were in the way of his projects, here where the arrogance of his larger design sacrificed the quality of life and the future of whole neighborhoods. This, in turn, also undermined the future cohesiveness of the larger city that his projects were supposedly creating. Sunset Park's residents "had pleaded with Moses to build the parkway not along Third Avenue but along Second, one block to the west, along the waterfront," contends Moses biographer Robert Caro.

"Second Avenue ran not through the middle of a neighborhood but through the middle of Bush Terminal, a 200-acre agglomeration of piers, railroad sidings, lofts and factories that was already so noisy . . . that the noise generated by a few more lanes of traffic would hardly be noticed."[1] Over sixty years after the highway was opened, Caro's observation that the road should be farther to the west—and inside the industrial area—still applies.

New York City's comptroller, Joseph D. McGoldrick, a resident of Sunset Park, agreed with his neighbor-critics at the time, pointing out that the city had been planning to tear down the elevated rail line that already existed along Third Avenue because a new parallel subway had been built under Fourth Avenue. As he and other neighborhood people said, the elevated at least let some light in. The parkway, which would be wider than the elevated, would come right up to the windows of the buildings, leaving Third Avenue in almost complete darkness. So it wasn't surprising that local critics felt the highway would "permanently blight" their neighborhood. Moses replied to their objections by telling the Board of Estimate that Sunset Park wasn't particularly worth saving because it was a "slum."[2]

Moses's characterization was egregious. The thriving neighborhood of blue-collar families, mostly Norwegians, with Finns, Danes, Irish, and Germans, extended from the homes between Second and Third avenues all the way up to Eighth Avenue. But its heart, as Caro wrote, was Third Avenue, with its "seven movie theaters, dozens of tiny restaurants run by couples and featuring recipes from the old countries . . . and scores of small friendly 'Mama and Papa' stores."[3] But Moses would not be denied his highway, and before long the neighborhood began to die.

With the oppressiveness of the hulking overhead and the array of street-level roadways "wider than a football field" sideline to sideline, as Caro describes it, pedestrian traffic dried up. Stores on one side of the street were demolished to make way for the highway; soon, most of the stores that had brought people to Third Avenue, even on the other side of the street, were gone. A local community organizer, Kathy Wylde, later described what the elevated highway created for the world below: "Noise, dirt, accidents, not lighted, a garbage dump, drag races along it in the night, wild kids, something totally negative . . . a tremendous psychological barrier."[4]

Centralized public policy was now changing Brooklyn's landscape. And if some of it—such as the tearing down of the Fulton Street El— was changing the borough for the better, the monolithic Gowanus Expressway changed it for the worse. After the war, when those returning made choices about where they would live and build their new lives, this would matter.

Ebbets Field, neighborhoods away, still might have been a world away. Yet social policy and emerging trends whose results were not immediately apparent were inextricably linked to an urban landscape's evolutionary development—and destruction. Robert Moses had declared war on a Brooklyn neighborhood and he had won.

Moses's actions had implications for the social fabric of Brooklyn as they would later for the Bronx, whether the matter at hand was his Cross Bronx Expressway ripping the guts out of the middle of that borough in the fifties, or the Brooklyn Heights Association's success at thwarting Moses's ill-conceived plan to smash the contiguity of that neighborhood by running his Brooklyn-Queens Expressway through the brownstones of Hicks Street, even if he managed to do exactly that in the areas south of Atlantic Avenue in Brooklyn, better known today as Cobble Hill and Carroll Gardens. Power over matters like these also enabled Moses to hold fast on matters concerning where new ballparks would be placed. As caustic as he was toward the empowered and disenfranchised alike in the process of destroying homes and neighborhoods to fulfill a vision of civic egress, he was nevertheless a builder most skilled at procuring massive amounts of federal funds and just as adept at dispensing them, with little regard for sentiments other than his own.

For kids in Crown Heights and Flatbush, who were unknowingly growing up in a city that Robert Moses was constructing for them, matters of the realm were far less esoteric. Larry Block, the same ten-year-old who remembered carrying his mother's groceries the day Mickey Owen dropped the ball, lived in an apartment on the corner of Eastern Parkway and Franklin Avenue, five blocks from Ebbets Field. His grandmother also shared the place, his father having passed away when he was an infant. "This part of Brooklyn was known as Crown Heights, but this was long before it ever made the news by becoming an ethnic battleground," remembers Block. "It was a peaceful, pleasant middle-class community containing Prospect Park, the Botanic Gardens, the Brooklyn Museum, and the Brooklyn Public Library. All in all, I remember it as a lovely place in which to grow up.

"The area in which we lived," Block continues, "was basically a Jewish neighborhood judging from my memory of my classmates in P.S. 241, of whom only one was Christian. He was a super athlete, much admired and envied by all of us boys and the subject of much giggling and whispers by the girls. The stores that lined Franklin Avenue, a block west of what was once Cedar Place and what became McKeever Place, were the neighborhood social center, since the now commonplace supermarket was unknown there. I can recall going shopping with my grandmother by going from the grocery to the bakery and to the kosher butcher, then perhaps to the delicatessen or the fish store. As we went from store to store, we would meet familiar faces and always stopped to chat or pass the time of day. Since I was brought along only to carry bundles I found these pauses unbearable, but I now realize that despite living in a big city our life was basically that of a small town, where everyone knew everyone else, including the cop on the beat."

With the advent of the war, every small town was quickly focused on a wider world, and inevitably the question of whether baseball should continue was raised—a matter quickly put to rest in the "My dear Judge" correspondence between President Roosevelt to Commissioner Landis. The commander-in-chief felt it best that baseball be kept going for the recreational outlet it would provide to everyone who would be working so hard on the home front in the production end of war-related industries. Advantage Dodgers: they would be able to build, at least theoretically, on the previous season's successes, even if they'd fallen short of the ultimate goal.

The Brooklyn team got off to a great start in 1942, both financially and on the field. The Dodgers' 1,214,910 Ebbets Field attendance in 1941 led the major leagues; it was 250,000 more than that of the American League–leading Yankees and over 450,000 more than the Giants, the National League's second-biggest home drawing card. For the first time in years, the ball club was free of debt. The Brooklyn Trust Company had petitioned the courts to resign as an executor of the Ebbets estate in February, calling the financial rehabilitation of ball club "a fact."[5]

Even with all those getting into the park, others who wanted to be inside couldn't always manage it. "With Ebbets Field being practically on our doorstep one would think that there were plenty of opportunities to go to see the Dodgers play," remembers Larry Block. "However, putting things in perspective, the local movie house charged 11 cents on Saturday mornings. That's what it cost me to see 'Gunga Din.' The cheapest seat in the bleachers cost 55 cents in those days, which to a ten-year-old bordered on the astronomical. I had to be satisfied with listening to Red Barber on the radio, as did everyone. On hot summer days everyone had their windows open. Walking along Bedford Avenue one could follow the progress of the game.

"In an effort to show they were supporting the war effort," says Block, "the Dodgers not only let servicemen in for free, but on some days you could get in by bringing ten pounds of scrap metal. What a sight to see armies of kids carrying buckets filled with junk down Franklin Avenue! I'm sure that many a Brooklyn housewife searched in vain for the family washtub after a doubleheader. Try as I might, however, I never saved up enough junk to get into the ballpark."

Aside from the youngsters collecting scrap metal to get into a game for free, truck and taxi owners descended upon Ebbets Field's box offices, which served as a distributor hub during the war years for gasoline coupons. A large "V" for "Victory"—two to three stories high—was put up on the ballpark's façade, above the entrance to the Rotunda. Everyone knew that the baseball they were seeing was far from the real article, given the number of able-bodied major leaguers who became a part of the war effort, but throughout those years, this fact didn't diminish the spirit, enthusiasm, fun, or even the emotional release surrounding what was happening at Ebbets Field. Since those in the service were admitted free, many people from faraway places who normally would have little reason to be in Brooklyn got to see Ebbets Field, and they took their memories home with them.

One Saturday afternoon dubbed "Kitchen Fat Day," 4,512 women got in free, bringing 5,002 pounds of grease; a pound provided enough glycerin to produce black powder for six 75-millimeter shells. Signs urging fans to "Buy War Bonds" hung from the side photo and press boxes. A soldier was stationed at one dugout and a sailor at the other, stewards of red, white, and blue wire baskets that were used to hold foul balls hit into the stands; fans were expected to turn back the balls so they could be sent to military camps for recreational use.

Fashion shows were even held at Ebbets Field on some Ladies' Days, with the proceeds for war relief. "It was a 10-cent admission," remembers Thelma Habib. "Ladies would parade across the field during the seventh inning break. Men were in the service and the Dodgers were trying to attract more women to the games; it was mostly 4Fs and women in the stands."

Another woman, not a fashion model, joined the scene in 1942 when an organ was installed at Ebbets Field, and she made a far more indelible impression. Along with the famous fan Hilda Chester, whose ear-splitting yells and ringing bell harangued friend and foe alike, the organist Gladys Goodding became one of the best-known women in all of Ebbets Field's annals.

Gladys Goodding was born in Macon, Missouri, and reared in the Masonic Home in St. Louis. She came to New York in 1923, and for many years played the organ in Loew's and RKO theaters. It wasn't long before she became the answer to a trivia question as the only person who ever played for the Dodgers, Rangers, and the Knicks. She had two children, had divorced her husband years before, and lived in a hotel around the corner from Madison Square Garden at Eighth Avenue and West Fiftieth Street. Gladys rode the subway to Ebbets Field; later on, she would be accompanied by her fox terrier pup, who sat beside her at the organ during games.

As for Hilda Chester, her leather lungs and renown among fans and players afforded her a wide berth. "That Hilda Chester was something," umpire Beans Reardon recalled. "She'd sit there in Ebbets Field ringing that bell and yelling at the umps all the time. One time I asked her what she yelled at us. She said, 'Open your other eye, joik; you've got noive like a toothache."[6] With a voice described by Joe Garagiola as akin to the buzzer at Madison Square Garden, she cobbled together a living by moving peanuts from their fifty-pound sacks into smaller bags for the fabled concessionaires, the Stevens Brothers, or by selling hot dogs for them at racetracks. She had grown up on Manhattan's East Side, and as a young girl "was willing to sock any boy who wouldn't let her play on the baseball teams that made the neighborhood's vacant lots uproarious," said reporter Margaret Case Harriman.

When Harriman wondered whether Hilda moved to Brooklyn because she liked the Dodgers and asked why she crossed the East River and moved to Eastern Parkway, Hilda replied she "liked da climate." The matter of an ex-husband's role in Hilda's whereabouts remained unclear, though a daughter was produced who liked to play softball "up at that school she don't go to no more." The recounting was part of an evening Harriman spent with Hilda at her province in the bleachers, the subject herself proving to be a baffling conversationalist to the reporter once her heroes diverted her attention. Their presence on the field also had consequent physiological effects: a large body that visibly swelled, Hilda's somewhat long, gray, celluloid-butterfly-pinned hair framing fired-up, darting eyes distending as she emanated into a bounce, her stout pink face turning first scarlet and then purple, her "teeth so perfect and prominent that her lips seem always parted and shaped for speech," with encouragement or invective emerging "in a husky, decibel-shattering roar."[7]

It took an initial heart attack for a doctor to instruct her to cut out the yelling, an order which, though not followed, inspired her instead to emphasize her attendance by banging a frying pan with a ladle. In the late 1930s, the Dodger players decided to give her a bell, perhaps with the idea that it made less of a racket. Stories about Hilda always refer to a cowbell, but the pictures show her ringing a school bell, which she stood and waved to ring "high, wide and handsome . . . swishing it from one hand to the other as her arms tire . . . making as much noise as a small fire engine: 'C'mon, yuh crumb you, yuh sorehead, yuh pretzel bender . . . STRIKE!'" For their part, bleacher fans urged her to "Woik the bell, Hilda, woik the bell!"[8]

When she fell ill again with more heart problems in 1941, the players went to see her. She had a charm bracelet from the team and eschewed the grandstand-seat pass that Durocher provided for her, favoring the bleachers instead. Her devotion to the team was as demonstrative as a child's: she bounded hurriedly down the stairs and ramps after a game to get into the best possible position to see and yell a hello to the players up close, and even more so to Leo, who was always kind to her; after Leo was fired years later, she followed him over to the Polo Grounds for a time.

Among the funniest stories involving Hilda concerns the time she leaned over the stands to give Pete Reiser in center field a folded note with instructions to deliver it to Durocher. On the way into the dugout after the inning was over, Reiser paused momentarily by Larry MacPhail's box when beckoned, then went into the dugout and handed Durocher the note. Leo looked at it; it said simply, "Wyatt's losing it. Get Casey hot." Which Leo promptly did, bringing Casey into the game. Afterward, stomping around the clubhouse, Leo went over to Reiser, saying, "Don't you ever give me a note from MacPhail again."

"MacPhail?" said Reiser, looking up quizzically. "That note was from Hilda."

"Hilda!" screamed Durocher, blowing his stack.

Only at Ebbets Field would a woman residing in the bleachers command a pitching change.[9]

At the beginning of 1942, the Dodgers were considered an aging but talented ball club, with Dixie Walker, Dolph Camilli, Joe Medwick, Billy Herman, and Arky Vaughan all over thirty. As the summer began, it looked like they would coast to another pennant. On July 19, 1942, in the eleventh inning of the second game of a doubleheader in St. Louis, Pete Reiser gave everyone a scare by crashing into the bleacher wall going after a ball hit by Enos "Country" Slaughter. Reiser caught the ball, but it was jarred loose when he hit the wall. Slaughter came around the bases to score the game-winner on an inside-the-park homer. The Cardinals swept the pair.

The Dodgers were up by ten games in August when MacPhail came down into the Ebbets Field clubhouse and told them that they were too cocky and would blow it. But on August 16, Brooklyn was still nine and a half games in front.

MacPhail was right.

The crucial series was at Ebbets Field beginning Friday, September 11, when the Cardinals arrived in Brooklyn for games on Friday and Saturday, with Brooklyn's lead down to two games. If the Dodgers could win both, they could put St. Louis away; if they got a split, they'd hold them at bay. But they lost Friday, 3–0, when Walker Cooper shut them out on three hits, and Max Lanier beat them the following day, 2–1. The race was all tied up.

On Sunday, Cincinnati came to Ebbets Field for a doubleheader. The Reds beat Brooklyn twice before a capacity crowd while St. Louis split a pair with Philadelphia, leaving the Cards in sole possession of first place. Though the race remained tight the rest of the way, St. Louis kept an edge as the season wound down, with Brooklyn running out of time to mount a comeback. On the last day of the season, the Dodgers still had a chance to tie for first if they beat the Phils while the Cards lost a doubleheader to the Cubs. The Dodgers won their game, finishing the season with an eight-game winning streak and a stunning record of 104–50. But the Cardinals, who swept Chicago, 9–2 and 4–1, were better, winning the pennant by two games with a record of 106–48.

A week before the 1942 season ended, Larry MacPhail, not content to sit on the laurels of his World War I exploits, accepted a commission as a lieutenant colonel in the army. In his five short, tumultuous years in Brooklyn, not only had he gotten the club out of debt, he'd won a pennant. In his last year, Brooklyn again led the major leagues in attendance, the only team to draw over a million.

Once the flamboyant MacPhail had left, Brooklyn pursued Branch Rickey, whose five-year deal in St. Louis was concluding. Wesley Branch Rickey was now sixty-one years old and comfortable in the Midwest, and he took the Dodger job largely because he and Cardinal owner Sam Breadon weren't seeing eye to eye. "He was Victorian in manner, rumpled Churchillian in appearance," Rickey's grandson, Branch B. Rickey, recalled in 1997. "He was the kind of person who always had something creative and exciting going on around him. Whatever he did, he did with zeal—and it was contagious. The scope of his thinking constantly surprised even those who knew him well—he blended philosophy, politics, economics, decades of baseball and, reliably, a dose of religion. His ability to discover the unseen facts of otherwise ordinary issues was mesmerizing. He relished digging into and then sharing his insights with others who had scratched the surface." [10]

Rickey was born in 1881 to a rural Ohio farming family in Pike County, forty miles north of the Ohio River, in country described as "hilly and barren" by his biographer, Murray Polner. The place was then called Little California, later renamed Stockdale. When Branch was two years old, his father Frank bought 102.8 acres in a place called Duck Run, six miles out of Lucasville, with money borrowed from his father, and the family packed their wagon and moved. The family grew corn and sorghum, raised a few cows, and the boys grew up with a credo that called for thrift and wasting nothing.

The Rickeys originally were Baptists, but after Frank and Emily Rickey were married, they gravitated, as Polner describes, toward the Wesleyite Methodists, a more tolerant church in which no heretic had ever been tried and where John Wesley's words "Think and let think" were the guiding inspiration. [11]

"Years after," says Polner, "Rickey remembered that when his father wasn't farming he was wandering about the region, provoking religious disputations, organizing competing churches based upon shades of barely discernible doctrinal differences, forming or reforming them whenever he felt the pastor had gone too far or done too little." [12] It was his mother, Emily, though, described as outspoken, vigorous, and assured, whom Polner credits with fueling Rickey's ambitions.

His older brother became a teacher and a ballplayer, and Branch followed in his footsteps. Branch attended Ohio Wesleyan, and he became a ballplayer, one who wouldn't play on Sunday, and stuck to his convictions on the matter without regard for how they might affect his fortunes as a professional. He played a bit for the St. Louis Browns and the New York Highlanders, managed three years for the Browns beginning in 1913 and another seven for the Cardinals beginning in 1919, but built his renown as a baseball executive and creator of the farm system, which ultimately provided the Cardinals with a great array of talent and Rickey with a great deal of money.

The best summary of Rickey may have been delivered in the succinct language of Red Smith, whose economy with words created its own legend among those who labor at the craft: "Branch Rickey was a player, manager, executive, lawyer, preacher, horse-trader, spellbinder, innovator, husband and father and grandfather, farmer, logician, obscurantist, reformer, financier, sociologist, crusader, sharper, father confessor, checker shark, friend and fighter. Judas Priest!" continued Smith, using Rickey's favorite expletive, "what a character."

Rickey's behind-the-scenes front office maneuverings for the Dodgers during the war years were as interesting as anything happening on the field. One of the first things he did was get into an acrimonious contract negotiation with Babe Dahlgren, the slick-fielding first baseman who had replaced Lou Gehrig on the field at first base for the Yankees when the famous 2,130-consecutive-game streak ended in 1939. In 1942, Dahlgren, since dealt to the Cubs, had moved from there to the Browns, to the Brooks, and, over the winter, Rickey turned against him in negotiations over the matter of a few hundred bucks and shipped him off to the Phillies. More important, Babe blamed Rickey as the source of a subsequent malicious rumor to derail his career. "He said I was smoking marijuana," remembered Dahlgren in 1986, "and in those days, marijuana was a dirty word."

Upon hearing the rumors, Dahlgren went to Judge Landis and demanded to be drug tested by his office. The judge, sympathetic to Dahlgren and always suspicious of Rickey's machinations, agreed. Dahlgren's test was clear and the matter ended there, except that Babe would harbor bitterness toward Rickey for the rest of his life. "I was the first player drug tested in baseball," he recalled, "and I'm the one who asked for it." The Dahlgren episode underscores how complicated Rickey's—or any individual's—legacy can be, and how untidily a life can evolve despite the world's eagerness for a nicely bracketed story where character traits are consistent, as if part of a morality play.

As they would for the rest of the war, the baseball Dodgers took spring training an hour and a half north of New York City up at Bear Mountain in 1943 because of war restrictions on travel. While the Dodgers slipped to third in 1943 with players coming and going because of the war, Rickey began planning for the day the war would end and the postwar team he wanted to build. He had gone to the Dodger directors and told them that he was thinking of bringing a Negro player to the team. When he mentioned the recruitment of black players to George McLaughlin of the Brooklyn Trust Company, McLaughlin responded favorably but also said, "If you find the man who is better than the others, you will beat it; and if you don't, you're sunk." [13]

As historian Robert Peterson notes, one problem in breaking down the color bar was the reluctance of baseball's leaders to admit officially that it even existed. Doubtless aware that roughly a third of major leaguers were southerners who had grown up with Jim Crow in a segregated environment and might object to playing with or against blacks, baseball's titular heads claimed not to recall "one instance where baseball has allowed either race, creed or color to enter into its selection of players." This canard was increasingly assailed as drivel, and some of the assailants were part of the mainstream media of the day: Westbrook Pegler, Jimmy Powers, Heywood Broun, and Shirley Povich, to name a few. Added to that were stalwarts of the black press, like Wendell Smith, Sam Lacy, and Frank Young.[14]

The added voice of the communist *Daily Worker* could be construed as either help or hindrance. Given its position on the political left and what it symbolized, conservatives then characterized baseball integration efforts as the work of radical agitators and sought to marginalize what others saw as a legitimate mainstream issue for those with moderate views. Well-intentioned conservatives also made their arguments, most notably that Negro baseball was a million-dollar black commercial enterprise that would be poorly served by major league teams raiding its rosters for a few select men, wrecking the league, with the result that hundreds of other black players would not have any opportunity to play at all. Larry MacPhail had articulated this point of view, and black sportswriter Joe Bostic agreed with it for a time, saying that entry of a single Negro player into the majors would divert attention of both black and white followers of Negro baseball entirely away from black leagues. Neil Lanctot comments that if some black owners were resistant to integration, "their response was typical of other black entrepreneurs who recognized the long-term social benefits of integration but feared its immediate negative ramifications."[15]

It was increasingly clear, however, that it was the coterie of major league owners, the league presidents, and the commissioner who controlled the decision, given that managers Gabby Hartnett of the Cubs, Bill McKechnie of the Reds, and the Dodgers' Durocher all indicated that they believed blacks should be given a chance. As Hartnett said, "there'd be a mad rush to sign up Negroes," if there were permission to do so.

Bill Veeck claimed in his 1962 autobiography that he sought to buy the moribund Phillies from Jerry Nugent in 1942 and then recruit some of the greatest talent in the Negro Leagues. "With Satchel Paige, Roy Campanella, Luke Easter, Monte Irvin, and countless others in action and available, I had not the slightest doubt that in . . . a war year, the Phils would have leaped from seventh place to the pennant," said Veeck. His contention that he was thwarted by Commissioner Landis who, in Veeck's words, "wasn't exactly shocked but . . . wasn't exactly overjoyed either. His first reaction, in fact, was that I was kidding him" was debunked by a 1998 article in *The National Pastime*.[16]

What assuredly happened is that Nugent had turned the team back to the National League. Ford Frick, the ex-sportswriter who had ghost-written Babe Ruth's articles and was now the league's president, arranged the Phillies' sale to William Cox, a Yale-educated New York lumberman who liked the horses and who had once caught for the Yale nine. Cox's price: half of what Veeck claimed he had been willing to pay. It was hardly a sagacious decision: after Cox's first season as the president of the Phillies, Judge Landis banned him from baseball after it was revealed he bet on his own team.

The public's view of segregation was summed up by Robert Peterson, who noted subtle changes in the nation's racial attitudes and characterized the practice as a "shaky bulwark against the steady pricking of white America's conscience by the social and economic changes wrought by Roosevelt's New Deal, the Negro's improving educational and living standards, and perhaps most of all, by World War II."[17]

For as white and black Americans fought for their nation in segregated units within the armed forces, they shed their blood and died without discrimination to uphold democracy and principles of liberty in a world threatened by fascism and tyranny. Fighting for such principles abroad made them easier to fight for at home; the hypocrisy of the segregated American reality when compared with the notion of the democratic American ideal was increasingly hard to ignore.

By the time the 1944 baseball season began, even though outward optimism greeted the generally favorable war dispatches, gnawing anxiety still existed for the men and women in harm's way. The home front war effort was evident in the little things that were happening all the time, such as when Frank Sinatra came to Ebbets Field in April to raise money for war bonds, and a photographer snapped a picture of an ostensible duet featuring Sinatra and Dodger coach Charlie Dressen. Everyone knew the war's tide had turned and the allies were winning. But an allied invasion of Europe was still to come, and, at that point, the same kind of effort was anticipated for the Japanese mainland, too.

On May 15 news came that Charley Ebbets Jr. had died. Charley Jr. had been living in a small, fourth-floor tenement apartment at 3852 Tenth Avenue, at 206th Street in the Inwood section of upper Manhattan, his financial condition "not of the best," according to his attorney, David Fultz. Charley Jr. hadn't collected any of the $2,000 annually left for him by his father since 1933 because of the trust-income problems with the estate, and he had been working as an employee of the Ansell-Simplex ticket company in lower Manhattan, an association he began after he leaving the Dodgers. He left two-thirds of his $10,000 estate to his housekeeper, Henrietta Sherwood; one-third to his wife, Martha, who was living in South Hempstead on Long Island. Like Charles Sr., he was sixty-five years old when he died; his life span was three weeks longer than his father's. He was buried in the family plot in Greenwood Cemetery.[18]

And unbeknownst to anyone, Ebbets Field architect Clarence Van Buskirk had died the previous year, January 29, 1943, in Pontiac, Michigan. His son in New York had not been contacted and he was buried locally in Michigan. Van Buskirk's debts exceeded the value of his $900 estate. The architect of Ebbets Field left behind only surveying instruments and a used car to a local friend, a woman whose husband owned the boarding house where he lived.

On the morning of June 6, 1944, the news of the D-Day invasion reached the nation. Church and school bells tolled. All athletic events were canceled. President Roosevelt addressed America with a prayer. "Let our hearts be stout," he told the nation, "to wait out the long travail, to bear sorrows that may come, to impart our courage unto our sons wheresoever they may be."[19]

In the evening, the Manhattan skyline erupted magically in light— one end to the other in a single moment—for the first time since the war blackout had been imposed. On the rooftops, crowds cheered as Liberty's torch and the lights of Gotham once again stared back at the borough of Brooklyn.

Out at Ebbets Field, the Brooklyn roster was akin to a wartime railroad station, players continuing to come and go. The team lost a club-record fifteen in a row in July and sank to finish in seventh place.

In the fall, still nominally in the NFL, the Football Dodgers team took to the gridiron renamed the Brooklyn Tigers. Once the war began changing the football rosters markedly, the Football Dodgers suffered mightily, failing to be a factor in any subsequent campaign. They finished 3–8 in 1942 under coach Mike Getto and 2–8 in 1943 under Pete Cawthorn, when they were shut out their first four games. Now, in 1944, under three different coaches, they failed to win a single game. Even though many of their games were close, with the team losing seven of its games by a touchdown or less, they finished with a 0–10–0 record.[20]

And that was the last of NFL football at Ebbets Field; the following year, the Brooklyn Tigers were merged with the Boston Yanks, a team that played four home games in Boston and one in New York. When a reconstituted Brooklyn Football Dodger team would appear at Ebbets Field in 1946, it would be part of the All America Football Conference. Unlike the NFL of 1934–1946, the new conference would allow black players, breaking the league's racist policy that had been implemented shortly after George Preston Marshall's purchase of a newly awarded Boston NFL franchise in 1932. The policy's major proponent and a virulent segregationist, Marshall would first have his team play at Braves Field in Boston as the Braves, then, in 1936, at Fenway Park for a year as the Redskins, only to move them to Washington a year later. Marshall would not integrate his team until pressured to do so in 1962, when the Kennedy administration's secretary of the interior, Stewart Udall, threatened to keep the team from using the newly completed D.C. Stadium, subsequently renamed for Robert Kennedy after his assassination six years later.

President Roosevelt was running for a fourth term against New York governor Tom Dewey in 1944, and Ebbets Field was on his itinerary. "It was rumored," recounts historian Doris Kearns Goodwin, "that Roosevelt had suffered a stroke, that he had had a major heart attack, that he had undergone a secret operation for cancer."[21] To allay the public's fears, Roosevelt decided to campaign before as many people as possible, allowing them to make up their own minds about the state of his health.

The president made a trip to New York on Saturday, October 21, traveling through four boroughs of the city in an open Packard. In the morning, he was scheduled to give a speech at Ebbets Field. The tail end of a hurricane lashed the city with rain and diminished the waiting streetside crowds. Despite his doctor's repeated requests, FDR was insistent on standing and riding with the top down so that his public could see him. A crowd of 10,000 was waiting inside the ballpark to see the president, most of them huddled under the grandstand. The president's car arrived at 10:55 A.M. and drove around the field right up to a platform behind second base, where, to a rousing ovation, the president "hoisted himself to a standing position and hobbled toward a lectern."[22] The president acknowledged that even though he practiced law in New York and had been governor of New York, and even though he rooted for the Dodgers, it was his first time to Ebbets Field, evoking a roar from the crowd. FDR promised to return to see a game, something that would never happen before his death the following April.

When his talk was finished, his car was driven to a Coast Guard motor pool nearby, where he changed his clothes while inside the car. The green Packard continued throughout Queens, where the crowds were thinner, and the Bronx, where they swelled, then on through Harlem, down Broadway, and into the garment district. Hundreds of thousands of New Yorkers saw FDR that day.[23] For virtually all of them, it turned out to be the last chance. He was reelected in November, of course, which turned out to be the same month in which stock in the Dodger ball club changed hands in a sale for the first time since 1912.

The club's ownership had still been divided evenly between the descendants of Charley Ebbets and those of the McKeever brothers. Fifty percent of the stock was held in trust by the Brooklyn Trust Company for the fifteen Ebbets heirs, 25 percent was owned by Ed McKeever's heirs, and 25 percent was held by Dearie Mulvey, Steve McKeever's daughter.

There were three buyers, and they bought the 25 percent share belonging to Ed McKeever's heirs for a reported $250,000. The foremost member of the trio was Branch Rickey, president of the ball club. Then there was the attorney who handled the ball club's legal affairs at the suggestion of George McLaughlin after MacPhail left, Walter O'Malley. And there was a silent partner whom no one heard about, a Brooklyn insurance executive, Andrew Schmitz.

O'Malley was born in the Bronx on October 9, 1903, the only child of a Manhattan politician, Edwin J. O'Malley, a commissioner of public markets who traced his ancestry to County Mayo. Walter's mother was Alma Feltner O'Malley, who was of German descent. He grew up in what he termed "above-average" circumstances. The only place he ever played baseball was at Culver Military Academy in Indiana, where a ball hit him in the nose, prompting him to quit playing the game forever. He reportedly grew up a Giant fan who occasionally visited the Polo Grounds.

1. Charles H. Ebbets in about 1898 (Baseball Hall of Fame Library, Cooperstown, NY) and circa 1912 (Ebbets family photo). His middle name was Henry, but the writers preferred Hercules, perhaps in deference to the tasks he'd undertake.

2. The main entrance and home plate gate for the second Washington Park, the Dodgers' home from 1898 to 1912, at the northwest corner of Fourth Avenue and Third Street, Brooklyn, circa 1903. The wooden planks across the avenue are for the cut-and-cover construction of the Fourth Avenue subway line under way at the time. (Merlis Collection—*brooklynpics.com*)

3. Ebbets Field architect Clarence Randall Van Buskirk, who would sometimes enter or leave Charley's office with the plans concealed in a special pocket inside his jacket so no one would deduce what was in the works. (Douglas Van Buskirk)

4. Charles H. Ebbets Jr. in the early 1900s. His father and the McKeever brothers were amicable until the end, but Charles Jr.'s fight with Steve McKeever at Ebbets Field in July 1923 was the beginning of a lasting schism that later deadlocked the ownership. (Library of Congress)

5. Spade Day in Brooklyn, March 4, 1912, when Charley, clad in a fur-lined over-coat and a bowler hat and sporting a diamond pin, used a solid silver spade with an ebony handle to turn some manageably soft ground to begin construction on Ebbets Field. A voice in the crowd: "Dig up a couple of new players, Charley!" Everyone laughed. (*Brooklyn Eagle*)

6. Ebbets Field as it was readied for opening in1913, with the sidewalks not yet poured and the name not yet placed in the ballpark's crown. (Library of Congress)

7. On the day Ebbets Field opened, Jennie McKeever, Ed's wife, who had to wait a while for the flag to arrive, finally does the honors, hoisting the colors as the team looks on. (Baseball Hall of Fame Library, Cooperstown, NY)

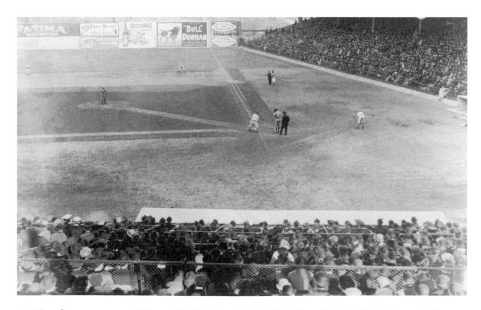

8. The first game at Ebbets Field, April 5, 1913. (Baseball Hall of Fame Library, Cooperstown, NY)

9. Ebbets Field before 1931, when the double-decked grandstand on the third base side extended not much farther than the infield. After the new double-deck addition was constructed in 1931, the railing of the seats in deepest left field had the foul line running atop it for the last ten or fifteen feet as the foul line approached the left-field wall. A ball hitting the rail before the wall and bouncing into the stands was a double. (Merlis Collection—*brooklynpix.com*)

10. The so-called "circus seats" in left field, which were built in time for the 1916 World Series. (Mark Mahler Collection)

11. Charley Ebbets, manager Wilbert Robinson, and Steve and Ed McKeever *(l to r)* in a good moment. (Baseball Hall of Fame Library, Cooperstown, NY)

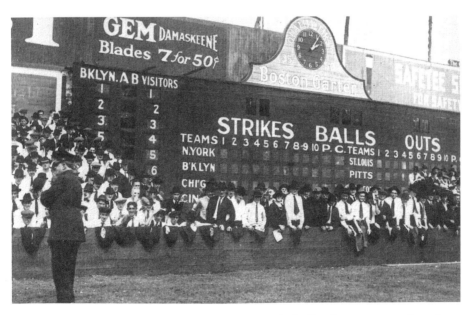

12. The old left field scoreboard, which stood as the ballpark's main scoreboard until it was razed to make way for the expansion of the double-decked stands in 1931. On days the ballpark was jammed, spectators stood right in front of it. (Author's collection)

13. The Ebbets Field press box hanging from the top of the upper deck. It was constructed under the auspices of Larry MacPhail, who wasn't beyond taking a poke at a writer when liquid spirits and his eroded sensibility conspired in tandem. (Baseball Hall of Fame Library, Cooperstown, NY)

14. The Ebbets Field press room, behind the upstairs press box, where bartenders Hymie Green and Bill Boylan presided over what also was informally known as Larry's saloon, in honor of the florid MacPhail. Boylan, a onetime minor league hurler, doubled as a batting practice pitcher and also had an early-morning job as a milkman. (Library of Congress)

15. Frank York, the son of Barney York and, like his father, a longtime associate of both the Ebbets and the McKeever families, became president of the club in February 1930, after Wilbert Robinson was relieved of his presidential duties but was kept on to manage. In October 1932, York went to lunch one day and never came back. (Baseball Hall of Fame Library, Cooperstown, NY)

16. One of the most famous baseball pictures ever taken: hurler Hugh Casey's big curve third strike on Tommy Henrich that would have ended game 4 of the 1941 World Series gets by Mickey Owen, a great defensive catcher, allowing Henrich to get to first base and sparking a Yankee rally that toppled the Dodgers, giving the Yankees a 3–1 Series lead. The next day, Brooklyn fans symbolically absolved Owen of blame with a thunderous ovation that rocked Ebbets Field. (Library of Congress)

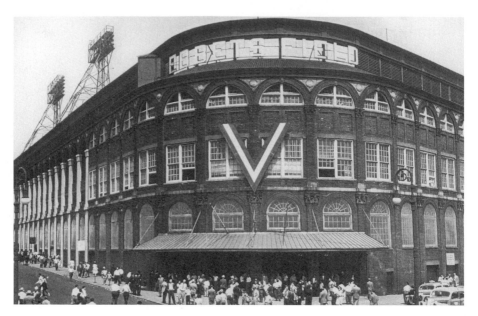

17. Ebbets Field on V-E Day, May 8, 1945. (Collection of Ronald Schweiger)

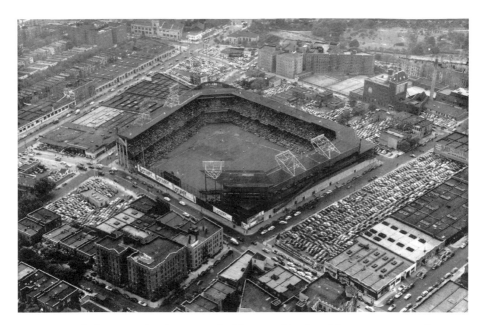

18. An aerial photograph of a jammed Ebbets Field. The old Consumers Park Brewery building is visible in the upper right portion of the picture; the sliver of parkland above it, or to the west of the old brewery building, is a small portion of the Brooklyn Botanic Garden. (Merlis Collection—*brooklynpix.com*)

19. Dexter Park on opening day in 1946, when Queens borough president James Burke threw out the first ball. Located in Woodhaven, just on the Queens side of the Brooklyn–Queens county line, Dexter Park was home of the semipro Bushwicks, who played against many Negro League teams of the day. (Merlis Collection—*brooklynpix.com*)

DI MAGGIO
PINELLI
STIRNWEISS
HENRICH
McQUINN
McGOWAN
RIZZUTO
MIKSIS
PITLER
GIONFRIDDO
BEVENS
BERRA
LAVAGETTO
SLADES

20. Cookie Lavagetto's two-out, ninth-inning hit breaks up Bill Beven's no-hitter in the fourth game of the 1947 World Series against the Yankees, allowing Al Gionfriddo and Eddie Miksis to score, giving the Dodgers a 3–2 victory and evening up the Series at two games apiece.

21. The Brooklyn Dodger clubhouse man, "Senator" John Griffin, always with a fat cigar and a choice headdress, in this instance a top hat, entertaining Gil Hodges and Pee Wee Reese in the Dodger locker room. Note the size of Gil's extraordinary hands, which helped make him a nonpareil first baseman. (Merlis Collection—*brooklyn pix.com*)

22. The famed Ebbets Field Rotunda, with its marble walls, tiled floor, and ball-and-bat chandelier, with ticket windows next to entry portals that created problems when ticket queues fanned out in all directions and obstructed easy entry for those already holding tickets. The circular, eighty-foot-diameter room had an elliptical ceiling that billowed to a height of twenty-eight feet at the center. (Los Angeles Dodgers)

23. September 30, 1950, the second-to-last game of the season with the Dodgers just two games behind, going head-to-head against the first-place Phillies, with the prospect of two consecutive victories forcing a National League playoff. The Duke of Flatbush has just delighted the fans with a key fifth-inning home run that would lead Brooklyn to a 7–3 victory. (Brooklyn Public Library, Brooklyn Collection)

24. The next day, the final game of the 1950 season at Ebbets Field against the Phillies, a young fan is creeps out on top of the right-field wall to retrieve a ball hit by Pee Wee Reese in the sixth inning. The ball hit the screen and dropped straight down, bobbing and finally settling on the ledge while Pee Wee circled the bases for an inside-the-park home run, tying the game at 1–1 after the Phils had scored in the top of the sixth. The game went ten innings, when the Phillies captured the National League pennant, 4–1, on the strength of Dick Sisler's three-run homer. (Brooklyn Public Library, Brooklyn Collection)

25. On September 23, 1951, World War I vet Samuel Maxwell, sixty-two, of 31 North Oxford Street, camped out to be first on line at Ebbets Field, intending to stay in place to purchase tickets when the World Series began. When the Dodgers lost the three-game playoff to the Giants on October 3, he went home, but the next year he was first on line again. (Brooklyn Public Library, Brooklyn Collection)

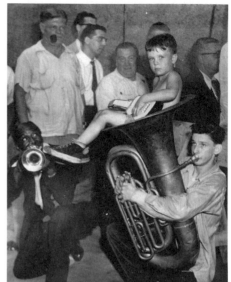

26. August 13, 1951, "Music Appreciation Night" at Ebbets Field, when fans bearing a musical instrument were admitted free. Over two thousand were admitted with every manner of noisemaker. The event was the Dodgers' way of supporting the Sym-Phony Band, which had encountered difficulties with the musicians union. The local wanted its members with union cards to play only for union-scale wages. The union? Fuhgeddaboutit. (Brooklyn Public Library, Brooklyn Collection)

27. A mock display of "Dressen No Head" at Bud and Packy's Bar, 199 Richards Street in Brooklyn, on October 3, 1951, after the Dodger manager executed his ninth inning pitching change in the final game of the 1951 National League play-off and Bobby Thomson hit his pennant-winning homer. (Brooklyn Public Library, Brooklyn Collection)

28. Ebbets Field, lower right, with the Botanic Garden in the triangular-shaped plot to the east of Flatbush Avenue, which runs center to center-left in the photo, with Prospect Park on its left, or western side. Park Slope and the area known as South Brooklyn, moving out toward Red Hook, are beyond the park in the upper left, with the tip of Manhattan island visible at the top. The Grand Army Plaza arch is visible near the junction of Flatbush Avenue and Eastern Parkway, by the entrance to Prospect Park. The site O'Malley wanted for a new ballpark, at Atlantic and Flatbush avenues, was next to the Williamsburgh Bank building, the tallest building in Brooklyn, visible further down Flatbush Avenue on the right side. (Brooklyn Public Library, Brooklyn Collection)

29. Repatriated prisoner of war Rafael Movarosa has the honor of throwing out the first ball to open the game between the Dodgers and the Reds on August 29, 1953. (Brooklyn Public Library, Brooklyn Collection)

30. The Boys of Summer, immortal even before being lionized in literature by Roger Kahn. From left, Reese, Furillo, Robinson, Erskine, Hodges, Newcombe, Snider, and Campanella. (Sport Collection, Copyright Sport Media Enterprises, Inc.)

31. Duke Snider, the magestic Duke of Flatbush, who Branch Rickey said had "legs with steel springs," is shown full extension here pulling one down where the wall angled in center field. Note the padding on the wall added after Pete Reiser made a habit of running into outfield barriers. (Brooklyn Public Library, Brooklyn Collection)

32. Ebbets Field under demolition. (Library of Congress)

33. Auctioneer Saul Leisner's gavel comes down on the Ebbets Field cornerstone, purchased by National League president Warren Giles, who submitted a $600 bid in absentia. Giles later gave the historic marker to the Hall of Fame, where it remains on exhibit today. (Baseball Hall of Fame Library, Cooperstown, NY)

34. September 24, 1957, at 10:15 P.M. The final game at Ebbets Field has concluded, a Danny McDevitt gem, a five-hit shutout of the Pittsburgh Pirates. Abe Stark's offer persisted to the last. (Baseball Hall of Fame Library, Cooperstown, NY)

(Brooklyn Public Library, Brooklyn Collection)

At the University of Pennsylvania, a school his son, Peter, would also attend, he eschewed sports in favor of school politics. He was the first ever to become the president of both his junior and his senior class. He came from money; after graduation his father—who O'Malley said later was hard hit by the Depression—gave him a boat large enough to sleep eight people. In Brooklyn parlance, that meant a yacht: many people there couldn't comfortably sleep that many in their apartments.

He enrolled at Columbia Law School after graduating Penn, but when his father was hit hard by the stock market crash he switched over to Fordham Law at night, utilizing his undergraduate degree in engineering to get a job with New York City's Board of Transportation as a junior engineer. He also immediately embarked on his own entrepreneurial pursuits, starting his own surveying company and publishing a Sub-Contractors Register as well as a Law Guide to the city's building code. Each of those enterprises was directed at securing business from builders.

In 1931 he married Kay Hanson, three years his junior, the lovely girl next door he had been smitten with for some time. She had been stricken with cancer of the larynx several years before, and the surgery that thwarted it left her virtually without her voice. Edwin O'Malley protested his son's plans, fearing she would hold him back, but his son understood that the same girl who was barely able to speak was also the same one he had grown to love. He was undeterred.

Shifting to the law in 1933, O'Malley began working on collections, aiming to put moribund bond and mortgage companies in the black, and it was here that his larger design began to manifest. And his relationship with George McLaughlin and the Brooklyn Trust Company, who had gotten him involved with Brooklyn's National League team, paid off; now he was a part owner of the Dodgers.

With the passing of crusty old Kenesaw Mountain Landis on November 25, 1944, several days after his seventy-eighth birthday, the way was cleared for Branch Rickey's grand design. Late in March 1945, Rickey took Red Barber to lunch at Joe's Restaurant, a large eatery at 326–334 Fulton Street in Brooklyn. The restaurant was famous in Brooklyn, with huge, six-foot green letters spelling out "Joe's" above the entryway of the long two-story corner building. A prodigious green sign with yellow letters also hung at the corner, the restaurant dominating the intersection. "The place was empty," Barber wrote. "The lunch hour was over. Rickey led the way to a table in the back corner. There was no one near us. We gave our orders and were left alone. He obviously had something on his mind. He took a hard roll and began breaking it into small pieces as he talked."

"I'm going to tell you something only the board of directors of the Brooklyn ballclub and my family know," Rickey said. "You will tell your wife, of course, but no one else.

"In my third year as a student at Ohio Wesleyan University I was also the baseball coach. In the spring of 1904, I took my squad down to South Bend, Indiana, for a series with Notre Dame. We were staying at the Oliver Hotel.

"One by one the players came to the desk and signed the register. My catcher, Charley Thomas, the only Negro on the squad, started to register. He was a fine young man, fine family, good student, and my best player. As Charley picked up the pen the clerk jerked the register back and said in a loud voice, 'We do not register Negroes here.' I said, 'You don't understand . . . this is the Ohio Wesleyan University baseball team . . . this young man is our catcher . . . we are the guests of the University of Notre Dame.'

"The clerk said, 'I don't care who you are . . . We do not register Negroes at this hotel.' I said, 'Suppose he doesn't register . . . can he sleep in the other bed in my room? The clerk grudgingly agreed. I handed Charley the key to my room, told him to go there and wait for me . . . that I'd be up just as soon as I got the rest of the team settled.

"When I opened the door I saw Charley. He was sitting on the edge of a chair. He was crying. He was pulling at his hands as though he would tear the skin off."

"'It's my skin, Mr. Rickey . . . it's my skin! If I could just pull it off I'd be like everybody else . . . It's my skin.'

"That was forty-one years ago, and for these forty-one years I have heard that fine young man crying, 'It's my skin, Mr. Rickey . . . If I could just pull it off . . . It's my skin.'

"Now I'm going to do something about it. Mrs. Rickey and my family tell me that I'm too old at sixty-four and that my health is not up to it. They say that I've gone through enough in baseball and from the newspapers. That every hand in baseball will be against me. But I'm going to do it."

Red Barber remembered that Branch Rickey looked him straight in the eyes. With this story and his next few words, Branch Rickey wrote the most important ballad, inspired the greatest legacy around the sense of place that was Ebbets Field. For it was here, "in this crummy, flyblown park," as Durocher would call it, all the while loving it, that extra-special meaning would be attached to a single enveloping word: home.

"I'm going to bring a Negro," Branch Rickey said, "to the Brooklyn Dodgers."

"He didn't ask me to respond," Barber said. "He broke the roll again, dabbled some butter on it, put the broken piece in his mouth. He had told me."[24]

For Barber, a native of Columbus, Mississippi, who also grew up in central Florida, the revelation created problems. He went home, told his wife what transpired, and said he was going to quit. "You don't have to quit tonight," she told him. "You can do it tomorrow. . . . Let's have a martini."

Barber didn't quit the next day, or the day after that, or the day after that. "I started looking into myself. I had time. Rickey had given me time. There was no hurry, but I knew I had to come to a decision of what to think and what to do.

"I made myself realize that I had had no choice in the parents I was born to, no choice in the place of my birth or the time of it. I was born white just as a Negro was born black. I had been given a fortunate set of circumstances, none of which I had done anything to merit, and therefore I had best be careful about being puffed up over my color. Chance, sheer chance."[25]

"I've put a team in the Negro Leagues called the Brooklyn Brown Dodgers," Rickey had told Barber. "They will play at Ebbets Field when the regular Dodgers are on the road. I've got my best scouts—Clyde Sukeforth, George Sisler, Wid Mathews, Andy High—combing the Negro Leagues, studying the players in the Caribbean League, searching for the best Negro players. They think they are scouting for the Brown Dodgers. They don't know what they are really searching for is the first black player I can put on the white Dodgers. . . . I don't know who he is or where he is," he added, "but he is coming."[26]

The pressure wasn't just merely coming from Rickey; it was also emanating from the political structure. That same month, the Ives-Quinn bill passed the New York State Legislature and was signed into law by Governor Dewey. Introduced in 1944 by Republican assemblyman Irving Ives and Democratic state senator Elmer Quinn, the legislation was designed to forbid employment discrimination on the basis of race, creed, color, or national origin, establishing a state agency modeled on the U.S. Fair Employment Practices Commission (FEPC), which had been established as the result of an executive order of the president back in 1941.[27]

Soon after, on Friday, April 6, Joe Bostic, then sports editor of the black paper *People's Voice,* showed up at the Dodgers' training camp at Bear Mountain unannounced with two black players, thirty-nine-year-old New York Cubans first baseman Dave "Showboat" Thomas and thirty-six-year-old Newark Eagles pitcher Terris McDuffie, wanting tryouts for both. Although it wouldn't take effect until July, the Ives-Quinn legislation provided for a State Commission Against Discrimination (SCAD), which theoretically could receive a complaint if a white team were to refuse to grant a tryout to competent black players. Ambushed Dodger officials couldn't fit the players into their schedule that day, but made arrangements to do so the following day. In the process, Rickey invited the group to lunch and angrily rebuked Bostic for his confrontational move. The next day, the players worked out for an hour in front of Rickey and Durocher, who were unimpressed. Nothing came of the effort.[28]

Up in Boston, Councilman Isadore H. Y. Muchnick, who had a large African-American constituency, threatened to revoke the Sunday permits for the Braves and Red Sox unless the teams permitted some black players to try out. *Pittsburgh Courier* writer Wendell Smith made arrangements and brought along three Negro League players: Jackie Robinson, Sam Jethroe, and Marvin Williams. Although Red Sox manager Joe Cronin and his coach Hugh Duffy were impressed with the talent, team officials said that they couldn't be hired on the basis of a short tryout, asked them to fill out forms, told them they would be contacted, and generally gave them the brush-off. After that was over, Robinson and the others packed up and left town, not bothering to go through a similar charade with the Braves.

On Monday, May 7, 1945, the same day Germany surrendered, Branch Rickey announced his involvement with a black league with a press conference at the Dodger offices at 215 Montague Street. Rickey had been involved in secret discussions with Gus Greenlee, who had started the new United States Baseball League back in December and January. The new league would have the Greenlee's own Pittsburgh Crawfords, the Brooklyn Brown Dodgers, managed by Oscar Charleston, the Chicago Brown Bombers, the Toledo Rays, and the Detroit Motor City Giants.

At the press conference, Rickey announced his plans to lease Ebbets Field to the Brown Dodgers and read a prepared statement criticizing the existing Negro American and Negro National leagues for weak contracts, the use of booking agents, referring to the leagues as mere "fronts for monopolistic game-booking enterprises that were 'in the zone of a racket,'" remarks that drew fire from different quarters, whether from the black press, the Negro Leagues, and even other major league owners.

Effa Manley was the only owner present from either of the two established Negro leagues, and she asked Rickey why he had failed to contact either of those leagues—they only had been notified of his press conference that day—before proceeding with his plans. Rickey did not answer, instead referring her question to the United States League's new commissioner, Cleveland attorney John Shackelford, who noted that NNL and NAL officials had spurned the United States League's earlier efforts to arrange a meeting. Rickey went on to intimate that with his help "the new league would be run on a businesslike basis and might eventually join organized baseball."

Although details were not discussed, what Rickey would provide was the use of Ebbets Field and uniforms. The team was not owned by Rickey or the Brooklyn Dodgers, and there was no commitment from either Rickey or the club to guarantee the club would operate, though Rickey did arrange for the team to receive a loan of $6,000 to assist in its difficult fledgling operation.[29]

Exactly what Rickey was up to was a matter of public debate, given that the Yankees and Giants both had split regular rentals from local Negro League teams up at the Yankee Stadium and the Polo Grounds. Perhaps Rickey wanted a slice of outside revenue that could flow to major league teams locally, perhaps he was seeking to be another white operator who sought to buttress the operation of the Negro Leagues while profiting by it as well (unlike others who cared merely about profits), or perhaps—just perhaps—Rickey was only seeking to mask his real intent of finding ballplayers who could break the color barrier with the Brooklyn Dodgers.

What was clear was that he had criticized people who had been involved in sustaining Negro League baseball for years. "Mr. Rickey is attempting to destroy two well organized leagues, which have been in existence for some time and in which colored people . . . have faith and confidence," said Washington Senators' owner Clark Griffith, who also collected rentals from Negro League teams.[30]

The Brown Dodgers opened their season successfully, beating the Philadelphia Hilldales 3–2 before a crowd of 2,000 that came out for a night game at Ebbets Field on May 24. Yet the USL failed to take off. "The actual operation of the USL proved to be anticlimactic," writes Neil Lanctot. "As anticipated, the level of play was mediocre, featuring only a few established players. Moreover, promotions in major league parks drew poorly, and league games were soon being scheduled in smaller venues. By July, the much-touted yet poorly promoted Brooklyn Brown Dodgers collapsed and reorganized under Webster McDonald, who replaced the duo of Joseph Hall and Oscar Charleston. Irving Mazzer's Hilldale team was equally unimpressive, playing rarely if ever in Philadelphia, and eventually disappearing after the first half-season. League publicity was also subpar; by September few African Americans were aware that only four franchises had completed the season."[31]

A transformation was under way. The war was ending, men were coming home, the world would be very different. Pressure was ratcheting up, change was being thrust upon baseball. After the Yankees home opener with the Red Sox was picketed by baseball integration advocates, major league owners appointed two people to study the interlocking questions of major league integration and how to deal with the Negro Leagues: one was Larry MacPhail, who had returned from the

war and who was now the managing partner in a Yankee ownership triumvirate that included Dan Topping and Del Webb; the other was
Branch Rickey.

A. B. "Happy" Chandler, the former U.S. senator from Kentucky
named baseball commissioner in April, stated, "I don't believe in
barring Negroes from baseball just because they are Negroes."[32] That
same month—the month when FDR died at Warm Springs while the
Americans were crossing the Elbe in Germany—Congressman Vito
Marcantonio of the American Labor Party, who represented East
Harlem, said he would introduce a resolution recommending an investigation of baseball's hiring practices. Other politicians and groups were
planning moves to bring pressure to bear: a black city councilman, Ben
Davis, wanted to invoke the Ives-Quinn law, urging the involvement of
the State Commission Against Discrimination; the End Jim Crow in
Baseball Committee was formed by the Metropolitan Interfaith Coor-
dinating Council, which preferred to employ visible tactics like pick-
eting that were favored by the Congress of Racial Equality (CORE).

The committee made plans to demonstrate in front of Ebbets Field
and the Polo Grounds on August 18, but the Giants contacted Mayor
La Guardia, who headed off the demonstrations by convincing the
group to allow a subcommittee of La Guardia's own interracial Committee on Unity to study the problem. La Guardia's committee, established in 1943 to create better race relations in the wake of a Harlem
race riot, already had begun its own investigation into baseball and its
exclusionary policies, and as the mayor explained to a leader of the
picketers, a demonstration at this point that prompted a public incident could be counterproductive in achieving the organization's goal.

During the rest of the summer of 1945, the very young, the infirm, and
the too-old were prominently sprinkled through the big league rosters.
The illustrious Babe Herman, who by this time was forty-two years old
and who had been out of the major leagues for seven years, returned to
the Dodgers on Sunday, July 9, and the anticipation of seeing him again
in Brooklyn's flannels helped squeeze 36,000 into the ballpark. He'd
been playing for Hollywood out in the Pacific Coast League, so he was
still in shape.

True to form, with a man on third and his left cheek loaded with a
chaw of tobacco, Herman came up to pinch-hit for Eddie Stanky in the
first game of a doubleheader against the Cardinals and lined a clean
single to right, only to stumble over first base in the process of delivering the run. He had to dive back to the bag. Herman patrolled the

outfield pastures on only three occasions that season, his other thirty-four appearances casting him in a pinch-hitting role. He hit .265 and poled one home run during this stint and was always warmly received by Brooklyn's fans.

On the other end of the spectrum was Tommy Brown. He had joined the club at age sixteen the year before. At Ebbets Field, a carton of Old Gold cigarettes was slid down the steep incline of the screen from the press box when a Dodger player hit a home run. When Brown hit his first homer, Durocher took the carton instead, saying his player was "too young to smoke."

On August 13, 1945, Rickey, O'Malley, and John L. Smith, a vice president of Pfizer Chemical who would later become president of the prominent Brooklyn pharmaceutical company, purchased the 50 percent share of the Brooklyn Dodgers belonging to the Ebbets heirs for $830,000. With Schmitz also selling his shares, it raised the new trio's holdings to 75 percent, with each holding a one-quarter interest. The remaining 25 percent stayed in the hands of Ed McKeever's daughter, Dearie Mulvey. Rickey also signed a contract to be the managing partner for the next five seasons.

The most significant but unheralded development in baseball that summer may well have occurred on August 28. Brooklyn scout Clyde Sukeforth had gone to Chicago to invite Jackie Robinson to meet with the Dodger president, and now, with Robinson before him at the Dodger offices at 215 Montague Street, Branch Rickey told him what he'd been thinking all along. "The truth is you are not a candidate for the Brooklyn Brown Dodgers," Rickey told Robinson. "I've sent for you because I'm interested in you for the Brooklyn National League Club."[33]

For more than three hours, Rickey first carefully explained the momentous task at hand and then grilled Robinson, predicting the invective he'd have to endure and explaining that the only way he could fight back was through his performance.

As the year wore on, each of the New York teams was being urged to sign an agreement not to discriminate by the state's Fair Employment Practices Commission. La Guardia, for his part, spoke of his Anti-Discrimination Committee's work in radio broadcasts. In the middle of October, in a year when the Detroit Tigers and the Chicago Cubs would play in a World Series, La Guardia asked Rickey if he could publicly state that organized baseball would soon begin signing Negro players. Rickey asked the "Little Flower" to wait one week.

Not wanting it to appear as if he was responding to political pressure, and in order to ensure that the spotlight remained on the athlete and his athletic prowess, Rickey told Robinson to fly to Montreal. On October 23, 1945, Jackie Robinson, pen in hand, sat next to Montreal Royal president Hector Racine, with Branch Rickey Jr., the head of the

Dodgers' farm system, between both men, standing over their shoulders. There Jack Roosevelt Robinson signed a contract with the minor league Montreal Royals, a photograph shortly thereafter distributed on the wire.

It was a moment that was lauded in some quarters and disparaged in others: Judge William G. Bramhan, who headed the organized minor leagues, said he would of course approve Robinson's perfectly legal contract, while wondering why the ranks of the Negro Leagues should be cherry-picked, putting the player selected, his Negro League employers and teammates, and, in the judge's estimation, the player's entire race in a position that would inevitably prove harmful. "Father Divine [a black religious leader] will have to look to his laurels, for we can expect the Rickey Temple to be in the course of construction in Harlem soon," the judge snorted.[34]

This was the crux of Robinson's challenge, confronting the contempt that accompanied acknowledgment, earning respect. It was an effort he would have to go alone, one that would make history in the United States and beyond, not just among black men but among all who tell tales of courage, perseverance, and justice. Jackie Robinson became the name flashed across America, at once the culmination and yet only the beginning of the struggle. He would spend the following season in Montreal, but eventually, as everyone knew, he would be coming to the world's greatest social laboratory.

He would be coming to Brooklyn. The heart of Brooklyn.

Ebbets Field.

CHAPTER NINE

Quicksilver and Thwarted Gold

I n those postwar years, when the Dodger teams became great, when Jackie Robinson fiercely strode across the canvas of the American consciousness, Ebbets Field assumed an even greater significance in the American imagination. During baseball's golden age of the late 1940s and the 1950s, a sense of purpose and history revolved around the game. At Yankee Stadium, where you had a sense of "witnessing" a game, this purpose was cast in dignity and achievement. At Ebbets Field, you actually felt as if you were a part of the game itself. In all the seats you were close to the action; the roof of the ballpark was only eighty feet in the air.

In left field, the foul line didn't just abut the seats that ran along the third base side. For the last twelve or so feet before the foul line reached the fence, the painted white line ran right up on top of the seat railing before reaching the foul pole and the wall. A ball that glanced off the rail and bounced into the stands before reaching the foul pole was a double; a ball going the other way, on the field, was in play.

The close proximity of the stands to the field and the nearness of the fans to the players was well demonstrated by a story that had its beginning in the spring of 1945.

During the early part of that season, a noisy but avowed Dodger fan named John Christian had been sitting in the second deck on the third base side. John Christian developed a fondness for baiting Leo Durocher, which did not make Durocher too fond of him. During the middle innings of a night game on Saturday, June 9, while the Dodgers were playing the Phillies, big Joe Moore, the Ebbets Field special cop who worked at the ballpark for two decades, tapped Christian on the shoulder and told him he was wanted "in the office."

Christian reluctantly followed Moore downstairs. Finally they arrived at the dirt runway that led from the dugout to the clubhouse, where Durocher, who was waiting, asked Christian, "How would you like someone calling *your* mother names?"[1] Christian alleged in a police report filed the next day that Moore and Durocher then took turns pummeling him with a blunt instrument. At some point Christian managed to break away from the pair and ran for the exit, and then went off to Kings County Hospital, where X-rays revealed a broken jaw. Durocher and Moore were arrested the following day. The story and pictures of Christian's badly swollen face appeared in the papers. But now, some ten months later in April 1946, a jury took less than an hour to acquit Durocher and Moore in a criminal courtroom that rang with cheers at the verdict. Eventually Christian received a $6,750 civil suit payoff.

In 1946, the first postwar season, fans were hungry for baseball: servicemen were getting processed out of the military and coming home in droves; housing shortages were acute. Across the Hudson River in Jersey City, the Montreal Royals played their season-opening International League game on the road with their new Negro second baseman, Jackie Robinson. Branch Rickey's noble experiment began well. With two men on in the third inning, Jackie hit a ball 340 feet over the left-field fence. He also had three singles and stole two bases: a nice welcome to organized baseball.

Over in Brooklyn, fans were anxious to get to Ebbets Field to reunite with the returning heroes that they hadn't seen for a while. Pee Wee Reese, Cookie Lavagetto, Hugh Casey, and Pete Reiser were all in uniform—a Brooklyn uniform. On April 23, shortly after the 1946 season began, they had another hero to celebrate: a twenty-eight-year-old from Selma, Louisiana, Ed Head, pitched a no-hitter against the Boston Braves, winning the game 5–0.

On May 30, another of those "only in Ebbets Field" events occurred that ultimately served both literature and cinema. Bama Rowell of the Braves, who signed his first contract on the fence post of the family farm in Citronelle, Alabama, where he would also go to live when his playing days were over, hit a ball that broke the Bulova clock atop the Ebbets Field scoreboard.

It happened in the second inning of a doubleheader nightcap against the Braves, at 4:25 in the afternoon. The ball stayed there, inside the clock, and was ruled a double, the inspiration, of course, for the scene in the movie version of Bernard Malamud's book *The Natural.* An hour later, the clock stopped. For this deed Bama was supposed to get a Bulova watch, but he went into the service for an abbreviated hitch shortly thereafter and it didn't happen—until thirty-nine years later, in 1985. When the Bulova people called to arrange the presentation at his home, he thought it was a prank. But then when assignment editors from Channel 5 and Channel 10 in Mobile called about sending cameras over, Carvel "Bama" Rowell called his wife, Estelle, and asked her to come home from work to be there to share the moment.

The Cardinals and Dodgers were each other's main competition through the early part of 1946, but in late June, Brooklyn took six of seven, while St. Louis stumbled. By July 4, Brooklyn was seven games ahead. The next evening Red Barber was talking with Durocher up at the Polo Grounds, where the Giants and Dodgers had split a doubleheader the day before. Barber asked Durocher about all the homers the Giants hit in those games, and when Leo assailed them as pop flies that would have been caught elsewhere, Red said, "Come on, Leo, why don't you admit they were real homers? Why don't you be a nice guy for a change?"

"A nice guy!" shouted Leo. "I never saw a nice guy who was any good when you needed him. Go up to one of those nice guys some time when you need a hundred to get you out of a jam. Ya know what he's gonna say? He's gonna say, 'Sorry pal, I'd like to help, but things aren't going so good back at the ranch.' I'll take the guys who ain't nice, the guys who would put you in a cement mixer if they felt like it. But just you get in a bind. You don't have to come to them. They'll come looking for you and ask, 'How much do you need?' Look over there," Durocher said, pointing to the Giant bench. "Do you know a nicer guy than Mel Ott? Or any of the other Giants? Why they're the nicest guys in the world. And where are they? In last place!"[2]

Such was the genesis of the famous quote "Nice guys finish last."

The Cards took the league lead after the All-Star Game, but Brooklyn fought back and regained it. Durocher had the team scrapping, and he was scrapping too. An incident during the dog days of August—August 14—was vintage Durocher, an antithesis of the "nice guy" parallel he drew for Red Barber.

It began when Durocher and umpire George Magerkurth got into one of their classic rhubarbs over a foul ball call down the third base line while the Dodgers were at bat. Durocher called Maje a cement head, and in his rebuttal, the arbiter sprayed Leo with some tobacco juice from the chaw he'd been working on. Leo reared back and let fly with spit in Magerkuth's face.

"You're out of the game!" Maje yelled.

"Out of the game? What for?" asked Leo, playing dumb in wise-ass fashion.

"Because you spit in my face!" said Maje, wiping himself with a handkerchief.

"I spit in *your* face?!" came Leo's retort. "What do you think this is on my face—measles?"

That one cost Durocher $500.[3]

The Dodgers stayed in first place till St. Louis surpassed them at the end of August. On September 11, in an extraordinary game at Brooklyn, the Dodgers and Reds went inning after inning without plating a run. Johnny "Double No-Hit" Vander Meer struck out fourteen Dodgers while pitching fifteen innings, scattering seven hits. He was removed from the game after getting a base hit in the sixteenth inning, turning pitching duties over to Harry Gumbert. Meanwhile, Hal Gregg went ten innings for the Bums before yielding to Hugh Casey, followed by Art Herring in the fifteenth and Hank Behrman in the nineteenth. Throws from Dixie Walker and a Pete Reiser–Pee Wee Reese relay combination to Bruce Edwards at home kept the Dodgers in the game, managing to cut down the Reds' Eddie Lukon and Dain "Ding-a-Ling" Clay at the plate. After nineteen innings were played, all in four hours and forty minutes, the game was called on account of darkness, even though light towers sat atop the Ebbets Field roof. In those days unless a night game was scheduled, the lights weren't used.

Because the race between the Dodgers and Cardinals was so tight, the Reds had to make a special trip back into town so the game could be replayed on September 20. This time, a big three-run homer by Dixie Walker capped a four-run fifth inning, leading to a 5–3 Brooklyn win. Since Vander Meer had started again, he managed to extend his scoreless streak against the Dodgers to twenty-eight innings before the Brooks' eruption.

When the season's final day began on September 29, the Cardinals and Dodgers were knotted. But then the Dodgers fell a half game behind the Cardinals as they lost to the Braves, 4–0. Even while their team was losing, the fans at Ebbets Field were intermittently cheering, because they were getting reports over their portable radios that the Cubs were rallying in the sixth inning in St. Louis, where the Cardinals had taken an early 2–0 and then a 2–1 lead.

While the Dodgers listened to the broadcast of the Cards-Cubs contest in the Ebbets Field clubhouse, lingering fans covered the grass in the outfield, milling by the scoreboard that marked the moment with its line scores and the advertisement atop that announced "ELEC-TRICITY more for your money in 1946." There the fans listened to the remainder of the Cubs-Cards game and watched the numbers connected with that game fall through the inning scoreboard slots. The Cubs scored five in the sixth and two in the eighth to trounce 'em. Now the fans had tickets to buy — for a Dodgers-Cardinals National League playoff series.

The contest for the pennant would be best-of-three, the first game in St. Louis, with a return thereafter to Ebbets Field for the final one or two games. The Dodgers hopped on a train, went out to Sportsman's Park and lost the opener, 4–2, prompting Durocher to growl, "Things will not be that way when we get back to dear old Ebbets Field." He knew the Flatbush Faithful would be waiting.

After a day of travel, the playoffs resumed in Brooklyn. The Dodgers, a tired team, were behind 8–1 in the ninth when they staged a rally, knocking out Murray Dickson, pushing three runs across, and loading the bases with two out. Tantalizingly, the tying run was at the plate in Howie Schultz, who had homered the day before. Now, as the Faithful had so many times in the past, fans jumped, stomped, and applauded wildly in encouragement, crossing their fingers and praying for a miracle. But it wasn't to be. Harry "The Cat" Brecheen struck out the tall first baseman, and the season was over.

Yes, it was disappointing, but it had been a great year for the Brooklyn Dodgers. Fully 1,746,824 had come out to Ebbets Field. It was a National League record, and the second-best attendance in baseball behind the Yankees. The Dodgers netted over $451,000. It was a far cry from the poorhouse they were in only a scant few years before.

"Wait till next year," the fans said.

Given the professional grid entertainment at the ballpark that fall, waiting till next year was good advice. By 1946 Dan Topping had left the NFL and decided to take his team up to Yankee Stadium and the new All-America Football Conference. The old Football Dodgers became the new AAFC New York Yankees, featuring old heroes like Ace Parker. They started winning, while the AAFC planted a new and completely unrelated franchise in Brooklyn, calling that team the Football Dodgers. In the great tradition of professional football in Brooklyn, the team went largely unsupported, even though they had Glenn Dobbs passing and Cliff Battles coaching. In their final game of the season, Paul Brown's Cleveland Browns routed the Football Dodgers 66–14 before all of 14,000 fans. The team finished with a 3–9–1 record.[4]

At the beginning of February 1947, word came that Minnie Ebbets had died at her residence at the Hotel Granada in Brooklyn. She was eighty-nine and had been ill since the previous July. The news about the grand dame who dated back to the Superbas' early days at Washington Park merited a paragraph in most of the papers.

Meanwhile the stage was being set for Jackie Robinson's assault on the color barrier in what would become one of the most stirring stories not only in sports history but also in social history, a precursor to the major events of the civil rights movement and events as significant as President Truman's desegregation of the armed forces, the landmark Supreme Court case of *Brown v. Board of Education*, and of individually inspired acts like Rosa Parks's refusal to move to the back of a bus.

In the International League, the Jackie Robinson experiment had turned out to be a wonderful success. Jackie won both the 1946 batting title and the Most Valuable Player award, and the Dodgers also had other black prospects behind him, like Roy Campanella and Don Newcombe.

This major change would normally be enough to fuel any wintertime discussion of the upcoming baseball season. But more so than usual, a pastiche of bizarre events was serving to bring hot stove activities to a boil. As events unfolded, the panoply of sideshows was worthy of a five-ring circus. They would create more anticipation about the 1947 season than about any other in the history of baseball, before or since. In the end, what would happen over the winter would result in a one-year suspension of Leo Durocher, which in turn would make things much more difficult for Jackie Robinson, since if nothing else, Durocher was a fierce advocate for his players. The man who would be Durocher's replacement for that year, Burt Shotton, was not the same kind of firebrand and was in fact much the opposite; he managed in street clothes like Connie Mack, and never left the dugout.

The contretemps began in November 1946, when conservative columnist Westbrook Pegler targeted Leo Durocher. He called and asked Branch Rickey if he intended to get rid of Leo, calling Leo a moral delinquent. Yes, there was acknowledgment that Durocher had had a gambling ball club—poker playing—in the early forties, but Rickey put an end to that. And the actor George Raft did have a craps game going on in Leo's apartment while Leo was up at spring training at Bear Mountain in 1944, and one of the dice players later complained that he was swindled out of $12,000, but Leo wasn't there. And yes, there had been the incident with the fan Christian under the stands, and Leo spitting in Magerkurth's face.

But Rickey defended Leo. And at the same time, Branch Rickey decided that he wanted to impress upon Leo that people like George Raft, at whose house Leo was now staying during that off-season of 1946–47 out in Hollywood, might not be the best company. So Rickey sent his assistant, Arthur Mann, out to Cincinnati for a secret meeting to brief the new commissioner, Happy Chandler, in the hope that a word—just a word—might nudge Leo in the right direction.

Rickey's maneuver proved a mistake, since Chandler threw himself into the situation in full measure. The insistent commissioner reached Durocher while Leo was rehearsing for the *Jack Benny Show*—after first being told, without Durocher's knowledge, that Leo couldn't be disturbed. Chandler ordered Leo to come up to Northern California, to the Claremont Country Club in Berkeley, where they could have a discussion the following Friday. Durocher tried to beg off, claiming personal business in Texas, but Happy would have none of it.

At that meeting, during a walk on the golf course in the midst of a cold drizzle, Durocher was given a list of people he was told not to associate with. Joe Adonis and Bugsy Siegel were on the list, but they weren't Leo's friends. Racing tout Memphis Engelberg was, and so was Havana casino manager Connie Immerman. Chandler also told Leo to move out of Raft's house at once. Leo wasn't happy about any of this. "They'll call me a louse," he said, "but I'll do it."

Complicating all of this was an announcement on November 5 by Larry MacPhail that Bucky Harris would be the new Yankee manager and Charlie Dressen would be a Yankee coach. Dressen had quit the Dodgers after coming to an oral agreement on a contract with Rickey a few weeks earlier. At the time, Rickey and Dressen agreed that only a managerial offer could release Charlie from his duties as a Dodger coach for two more years, but Charlie jumped to the Yankees anyway. Then MacPhail really ignited the fire. He said Durocher approached him about becoming the new Yankee manager. "I didn't seek him out," MacPhail said. "He came to me. I didn't think Leo was exactly the man to lead the Yankees, although I do think he's a great manager and he did a wonderful job in Brooklyn last year."[5]

Leo denied it, of course, saying MacPhail had approached him not once but several times about the Yankees job. While the barbs were going back and forth, MacPhail made a deal and picked up another Dodger coach, Red Corriden, for the Yankee fold.

In the midst of all this, Pegler began blazing away at Durocher in his columns. "If a man dropped down from Mars and read nothing but Pegler's columns for a month," Durocher wrote in his autobiography, "he couldn't help but believe the two great enemies of the Republic were Eleanor Roosevelt and Frank Sinatra." And of course Leo was a friend of Frank's.

Pegler repeated the stories about Durocher, said Leo continued to live in Raft's house even though Leo had already moved out, linked Raft to the underworld characters Leo didn't know, and took aim at Chandler as a do-nothing commissioner.

To complicate matters further, Durocher was also involved with and planning to marry actress Laraine Day, a devout Mormon who neither smoked nor drank and who—minor detail—still happened to be married to someone else. But hold on! What about Leo's girl Edna Ryan, the beauteous, leggy blond from the Copacabana's stage line who was capable of arching even Branch Rickey's eyebrows, "the one-girl traffic jam," as Harold Parrott referred to her, the one who was at Leo's apartment over on East Sixty-first Street, near the Pierre Hotel, right now? She was Leo's regular, if he could be said to have a regular, since, as Parrott would later note when reminiscing about the Durocher trot line, "Leo kept all these lovelies moving from stop to stop as skillfully as he herded his runners around the bases or signaled for one to go from first to third. The ladies never crossed paths, and no two of them ever arrived embarrassingly at the same place at one time, the way early Dodgers like Babe Herman and Dazzy Vance had."[6]

If the tabloids were sizzling, it got better yet. The *Los Angeles Herald Examiner* ran the headline "Durocher Branded Love Thief" after accusations were made by Laraine's estranged husband, Ray Hendricks. In reality, that marriage had been dead for some time, and the ex soon gave Laraine permission to arrange what she wanted. She was granted an interlocutory divorce in California with the stipulation that she not remarry for a year in California, though she was free to marry elsewhere. Leo and Laraine then went to Juarez, where she got a quickie divorce, and crossed the border again and went to El Paso, where they were married. At the suggestion of Laraine's lawyer, who thought it best to placate the California judge, George Dockweiler, Leo set up another meeting with the judge, the judge tipped off the press, and the tempest started again, this time with Dockweiler castigating Durocher for making the court look bad. Leo said he and Laraine had no intention of living together in California, where the judge had jurisdiction, and said that the judge was holding him up to greater scrutiny and a higher standard and was really only interested in publicity for himself.

Now the Catholic Church, to which O'Malley had strong ties, became involved. Father Vincent Powell, director of the Catholic Youth Organization (CYO), on the basis of his disapproval of Durocher's conduct and with demands for his dismissal, threatened to remove the 50,000-member CYO from the Dodgers' Knothole Club, a means of getting kids free admission to Ebbets Field. Rickey, the devout, Bible-thumping Protestant, began discussions with the young Father Powell and then called on O'Malley to help.

It was inconceivable that O'Malley's influence within the Church could not defuse this situation, if O'Malley was interested in quelling it. But the fact was O'Malley didn't much care for Rickey or Durocher and enjoyed their difficulty.

Harold Parrott, the former *Brooklyn Eagle* writer and by then the Dodgers' traveling secretary and himself a Catholic, whose kids knew the tunnels and pathways and crannies of Ebbets Field as well as anyone, had this observation:

> O'Malley, the original Smiling Irishman when it came to blarney, carried a large prayerbook in the Catholic Church. He was respected by the clergy and was in all ways a powerful Catholic who could have stopped all this anti-Durocher nonsense had he wanted to. His best pal was Judge Henry Ughetta, head of the Sons of Italy and Knight of St. Gregory, which meant his connections went all the way to Rome. One word from them both and the Reverend Powell, as well as Monsignor Edward Lodge Curran, another anti-Leo scold, would have piped down, and so would their Catholic Youth Organization.
>
> But the Big Oom never gave the word.
>
> Rickey had reasons to wonder who had put the churchmen up to this. The Catholics never boycotted Hitler or Mussolini the way they went after Leo.[7]

On March 1, the day spring training was to begin, Father Powell withdrew the CYO from the Knothole Club, saying of Durocher that the "effect of his example will be a powerful force for undermining the moral and spiritual training of our young boys."[8]

Meanwhile, after initially giving some thought to Santa Ana, California, Rickey had chosen Havana as the site of the Dodgers' 1947 spring training, with exhibition games also scheduled for Venezuela and Panama. Although some observers suspected that it was just Branch Rickey's way of saving money—and it was, since Havana made a lucrative offer to have the Dodgers train there—it was also Branch Rickey's way of shielding Jackie Robinson from the racist reality of southern segregation and the storm that would follow the last step of his ascension into the major leagues.

The Brooklyn organization had leased the naval air station in Pensacola as a minor league training camp; the Dodgers, though, were training on a single field in El Gran Stadium in Havana, with games scheduled in Venezuela against the Yankees and with twelve days slated in the Panama Canal Zone, where the Dodgers would face their Montreal farm club. Vero Beach, the modern training complex that Rickey was envisioning, was still a few years away. In Havana, the team worked out at the 35,000-seat ballpark and slept at the Hotel Nacional, its old stucco walls bullet-pocked from the revolutionary days.

Once spring training started, Harold Parrott, ghosting an article in the *Brooklyn Eagle* for Durocher, baited the Yankees with a "declaration of war" because of MacPhail's recruitment of the Dodger coaches.

The piece was designed to stoke some interest and create some talk, and Parrott knew MacPhail was easy to bait. Larry and Harold had a bit of their own history dating back to when a drunken MacPhail, disapproving of one of Harold's newspaper stories when Harold was an *Eagle* reporter in 1940, punched Parrott in nose—"MacPhail Bops Parrott Beak," as the other scribes would have it—while the latter was "sauntering out of the press box, quite unsuspecting." As Parrott would later recount, "That's the way Lucifer Sulphurious popped me, too . . . right in front of a few hundred fans who were still in the upper deck behind home plate. . . . The man moved in fits and spurts, weaving in and out of trouble. He seldom did things the easy way."[9]

After the first Yankee-Dodger exhibition game in Venezuela, which the Yankees won 17–6, the teams returned to Havana to play, where, sitting in Larry MacPhail's box, were two of the gamblers—Memphis Engelberg and Connie Immerman—whom Durocher was forbidden to associate with. Branch Rickey was steaming about that later at the hotel, and Herb Goren of the *Sun* and Arch Murray of the *Post* picked up on it. The next day, the same thing happened again with Engelberg and Immerman, and this time Dick Young of the *News* got a quote from Leo, who said, "Are there two sets of rules, one applying to managers and one applying to club owners? Where does MacPhail come off, flaunting his company with known gamblers in the players' faces? If I ever said 'Hello' to one of those guys, I'd be called before Commissioner Chandler and probably barred."[10]

When Young went to MacPhail, another round of stories resulted. Later, reacting to what he construed to be Leo's aspersions, MacPhail tried to get Chandler to investigate Leo for conduct detrimental to baseball. Over the course of the next few weeks, several hearings were held.

Meanwhile, as it would many times in a variety of different ways, the specter of breaking the color line was affecting the team. Several of the Dodgers from the South—including Dixie Walker, Ed Head, Eddie Stanky, and Bobby Bragan—had grown up with the standard regional prejudice of their time and were uncomfortable with playing with an African American—a "colored" player—on their team. Another Dodger initially said to object was Carl Furillo, a native of Reading, Pennsylvania.

The Dodgers were in Panama to face the Caribbean All-Stars when the situation began to play out. "We had been there almost a week," Durocher said, "when one of my coaches, Clyde Sukeforth, reported he was picking up talk that the players, led by Dixie Walker and Eddie Stanky, were getting up a petition to warn us they would never play with Robinson." Durocher decided how he was going to handle it while lying in bed one night, unable to sleep. "I suddenly asked myself why I was being so cute about it. Hell, I was getting as bad as Rickey. The thing to do, I could see, was to nip it in the bud, step on them hard before they had taken the irretrievable step of signing the petition and presenting it to anybody."

Durocher jumped out of bed and told his coaches to round up his players. He had them meet in a huge, empty kitchen behind the mess hall, and they all trickled in. Some were in their underwear, some, like Leo, in pajamas, others were buttoning their trousers.

"I hear some of you fellows don't want to play with Robinson and that you have a petition drawn up that you are going to sign," Leo said. "Well, boys, you know what you can do with that petition. You can wipe your ass with it. Mr. Rickey is on his way down here and all you have to do is tell him about it. I'm sure he'll be happy to make other arrangements for you.

"I hear Dixie Walker is going to send Mr. Rickey a letter asking to be traded. Just hand him the letter, Dixie, and you're gone. GONE! If this fellow is good enough to play on this ballclub—and from what I've seen and heard, he is,—he is going to play on this ballclub and he is going to play for me."[11]

Durocher told them that there'd be other players behind Robinson, too, and that if those standing there were interested in playing, they'd better perform. Soon afterward, they were all sent back to bed.

Rickey arrived in Panama the next morning.

He called the players involved into a makeshift office individually, with a door across some boxes serving as a desk.

Bobby Bragan was one of the people he called in.

Almost five decades later, Bobby Bragan counts both Branch Rickey and Jackie Robinson as two of the most important people in his life. He became very close to both of them, as he did to scores of African-American and Latin ballplayers whom he subsequently played with and managed. He also extolled Leo Durocher as a great manager, an opinion not universally held among the men who played for him.

"Some of the other Dodgers didn't seem to mind the idea of having a black teammate, but I sure did," Bragan recalled. "Growing up in Birmingham, Alabama, I never mixed much with blacks. The only ones I ever talked to were the maid who helped my mother around the house and the men who'd come over every once in a while to ask my father, who ran a road-grading crew, for an advance. That's what I was going to have to do if Jackie joined the Dodgers, and I just wasn't going to stand for that."

When Rickey had Bobby in the office, he said, "It's been suggested there is a move on to keep Jackie Robinson off the Brooklyn club, that there's dissatisfaction among some of the players. I want to get to the root of this. That's why I sent for you. Let me tell you, in the first place nobody else is going to tell me who to play. If Jackie Robinson can do the job better than another player, then regardless of the color of his skin Jackie Robinson is going to play. Do you understand, Bobby?"

"Yes, sir," came the reply.

"And how do you feel about this?"

"I wouldn't want to be the scapegoat in all this, Mr. Rickey, but if it's all the same to you, I'd like to be traded to another team."

"If we call Jackie Robinson up, will you change the way you play for me?" Rickey asked.

"No, sir. I'd still play my best."

"What's your schedule?" Rickey asked, looking at his watch. "All right," Rickey continued, "go ahead with your workout."

"We watched," Bragan said. "I learned. Not fast, but I learned." Bragan wasn't belligerent; wasn't the type to call Jackie a name or insult him; he just wasn't going to sit at the same table or in the same train berth with him. "In fairness to the others," Bobby said, "within a month everybody was fighting to sit next to Jackie on the train, because he'd earned such respect for his playing ability and dignity to deal with his tough situation." [12]

At Branch Rickey's funeral in 1965, Jackie Robinson and Bobby Bragan sat next to each other in the same pew.

On the morning of April 9, Rickey was meeting with his top lieutenants about the composition of the Dodger roster and when to call up Jackie Robinson. Rickey's phone rang, and it was clear to others in the room that anger was welling up inside him as the conversation—obviously with Chandler—continued. When he got off the phone, he told all present the damage.

Harold Parrott was fined $500 for being Durocher's ghostwriter and stirring the pot. Charlie Dressen was suspended for thirty days for breaking an oral agreement with the Dodgers when he went over to join the Yankees as a coach. The Yankees and Dodgers were both fined $2,000. And Leo? Leo had been suspended from baseball for *one year*.

"For wha-a-a-t?" Leo wondered.

The news spread quickly through Brooklyn. The next day, before an exhibition game with Montreal, Leo met with his ballplayers in the cramped Ebbets Field clubhouse. "Put your faith in Mr. Rickey," he told them. "There's never been a thing Mr. Rickey won't do for you if you ask him. You'll find that he'll bring you through." [13]

Later that afternoon, when Brooklyn and Montreal took the field, Jackie Robinson was still playing for the Montreal Royals. During the fifth inning, a press release circulated in the press box had a simple announcement. "The Brooklyn Dodgers," it read, "today purchased the contract of Jackie Roosevelt Robinson from the Montreal Royals."

In many respects, the impact of Robinson's first appearance at Ebbets Field was blunted by the bombshell surrounding Happy Chandler's one-year suspension of Leo Durocher.

When Jackie Robinson made his major league debut in the Ebbets Field opener against the Boston Braves on April 15, Clyde Sukeforth, the old Dodger hand from the state of Maine who had finished his major league career as a part-time catcher two years before, who had scouted Robinson in the Negro Leagues, was the ball club's two-day interim manager. Rickey's final selection to replace Durocher was his old friend Burt Shotton, who played for the St. Louis Browns when Rickey managed the team and Shotton was his center fielder, leadoff hitter, and "Sunday manager."

Larry Block was there the moment Jackie arrived at Ebbets Field. "The Dodgers were opening the season at home. I walked down to Ebbets Field in the morning and stood on line at the advance sale window in the Rotunda. Hearing something of a commotion outside, I turned in time to see a squad of policemen—a dozen Irish cops to be exact—surrounding a black man who was a head taller than each of them. An historic moment, I suppose, although I certainly did not realize it at the time. I recall that my reaction was one of amusement; as if Jackie needed protection from us. Quite the contrary, Dodger fans were eager to see him perform. Actually, after so many years of disappointments, we would have welcomed Attila the Hun provided he could hit left-handed pitching. I have often regretted that I did not go up to him at that moment and say something to make him feel welcome, but of course considering that he had received many death threats, I would probably have gotten bopped in the head with a billy club."

Rachel Robinson, staying at the McAlpin Hotel, made her way over to the ballpark with Jackie Jr. "I packed up the baby, went downstairs, and couldn't get a taxi that would go to Brooklyn. I thought I was going to be late." It was a cold, gray day at Ebbets Field, and Rachel Robinson worried about both Jackie, performing on the field, and Jackie Jr., susceptible to catching cold, in the stands. "Settling into her seat," recounted Robinson biographer Arnold Rampersad, "she suddenly realized that his light coat, fine for Los Angeles, was inadequate here. Then a black woman sitting next to her, whom she would remember as the mother of Ruthe Campanella, Roy's wife, took Jackie and placed him inside her fur coat." [14]

"I was very, very excited and very, very nervous," Rachel told author Jules Tygiel. "But," Tygiel noted, "the thoughts running through her mind were the same as those of thousands of other onlookers: 'I was trying to figure out which players were going to be friendly and how he was going to make out.'" [15]

"The clubhouse was under the right field stands, and we'd get to the dugout from there by walking down a tunnel," Bobby Bragan remembered. "Even though the Dodgers were one of the glamour teams in baseball, our locker room was ordinary. Each player had a cubicle about a yard wide, with chain link fence stretching down from the ceiling to the floor. In front of each locker was a plain stool. There were also a few tin lockers in the middle of the room, ones that looked and opened kind of like the lockers you see in schools. Dixie Walker and Pete Reiser used those. I remember our clubhouse manager, John Griffin, had a joke about Reiser. Pete ran into the centerfield wall pretty regularly and sometimes was hurt badly. Mr. Rickey ended up padding that wall because of Pete. Anyway, at one point Griffin would walk by those tin lockers every day and say, 'You all right, Pete?'"

"My locker was on one side wall," Bragan continued, "next to Arky Vaughn's. Bobo Newsom was on the other side. Bobo was quite a gin player. He and Leo played often. My uniform number was 24, which wasn't special then. Willie Mays came along a few years later and now everyone wants to wear 24, but then I think the number signified I was the twenty-fourth player on the 25-player roster. Also, nobody asked you back then what you wanted. You got what they gave you.

"On opening day in 1947, Jackie came into the clubhouse. He got a locker on the other side of the room. Pee Wee Reese was next to him. To Pee Wee's everlasting credit, he was Jackie's friend from day one. Most of the rest of us just sort of ignored Jackie that day, but Pee Wee talked to him just as friendly as he did to the rest of his teammates. The atmosphere in there that day was a little strange, though. Oh, we'd all suspected Jackie would be joining us, had heard it officially from Mr. Rickey at the St. George Hotel, but now all of sudden he was right with us and it was happening for real." [16]

A crowd of 25,623 was on hand that day. Between a third and a half were African American; usually very few blacks attended the games. Johnny Sain started for the Braves, pitted against Joe Hatten. Robinson, batting second behind Eddie Stanky, went 0 for 3 that day, but he did score the winning run.

On April 22 the Phillies came to Ebbets Field for a three-game series with the Dodgers. The Philadelphia bench, led by their Nashville-born manager Ben Chapman, spewed an incessant stream of venom at the rookie throughout the game, including racist epithets and drivel about the size of his lips and the thickness of his skull.

What they couldn't diminish was the level of his skill.

Jackie Robinson fought back in a way that defied argument. With a scoreless tie after seven, Jackie led off the bottom of the eighth with a single to center. When Pete Reiser struck out with Jackie going on a hit-and-run, catcher Andy Seminick bobbled the ball and then threw it into center field, advancing Robinson to third. Gene Hermanski then singled to center to bat in the game's only run in the person of Jackie Robinson.

Brooklyn swept the series. By the third game Eddie Stanky, who had already told Robinson that he didn't like having him there but that they were part of the same team, was himself yelling over at the Philadelphia bench in response to their jockeying and racial slurs. Stanky told them to pick on somebody who could fight back.

On May 9 the *New York Herald Tribune* sports editor Stanley Woodward reported about an aborted plot to strike by various National League players, led by the Cardinals but at the urgings of a Dodger player, over having to play on the same field as Robinson. The strike was supposedly slated to start May 6 when the Cardinals arrived at Ebbets Field, but according to the report, Cardinals owner Sam Breadon heard what was going on and went immediately to New York to meet with National League president Ford Frick. Together, the two had supposedly delivered an ultimatum.

"If you do this you will be suspended from the league," Frick said. "You will find that the friends you think you have in the press box will not support you, that you will be outcasts. I do not care if half the league strikes. Those who do it will encounter quick retribution. All will be suspended, and I don't care if it wrecks the National League for five years. This is the United States of America, and one citizen has as much right to play as another."[17]

The strike, if there was one, fizzled. In his book *Baseball's Great Experiment: Jackie Robinson and His Legacy*, Jules Tygiel comments, "Reconstructed 35 years later, the strike saga amounts to somewhat more than the denials of the [Cardinal] players would indicate, but quite a bit less than Woodward's allegations implied. Robinson's promotion undeniably aroused considerable discontent among the Cardinals and other teams. The idea of organizing a strike probably surfaced. Cardinal captain Terry Moore admitted as much the day the story broke. He told St. Louis sportswriter Bob Broeg that he did not doubt that there had been 'high-sounding strike talk that meant nothing.'"[18]

How far this talk actually proceeded is difficult to discern. Dick Sisler, a rookie on the Cardinals in 1947, recalls, "Very definitely there was something going on at the time whereby they said they weren't going to play." The planning, says Sisler, was done "by a lot of the older players. I don't think the younger players had anything at all to say."

Despite taunts from opposing players and hate mail from various quarters, Jackie played his game with consummate skill. And instead of responding to their taunts outwardly, he responded on the field of play. In Philadelphia—Philadelphia, where the Declaration of Independence was signed—Jackie was refused accommodations at the Benjamin

Franklin Hotel. The Dodgers checked in anyway, but the next time they came back to town, they stayed at the more expensive Warwick, where Jackie was allowed to stay.

"My uncle took me in 1947 to see Jackie Robinson," recalled Elliott Abramson, who lived on Eastern Parkway between Rogers and Bedford. "At that time it was a very nice, safe, secure, upper-middle-class neighborhood. I was seven or eight years old; I hadn't been to too many places. It was spring. I've always remembered the brilliance of the colors. The greenness of the grass, the brown of the infield. It was breathtaking.

"My uncle told me to concentrate on the lead Jackie took at first base in comparison to other players. We were sitting behind first base that day. Then I remember another day when we were sitting in the bleachers. Two guys were arguing—a black guy and a white guy—over who was faster, Reiser or Robinson. Funny thing is, the black guy was screaming Reiser was faster and the white guy was screaming Robinson was faster. Whoever you sat next to, you spoke to and argued with about baseball, not like today when the attention is diverted away from the game. You didn't divert your attention away. I always found the ballpark to be a secure place . . . no bad elements acting out of turn. And I liked the center-field bleachers cause you got a very good sense of the pitches curving."

Before the 1947 season began, 850 more box seats were added out in left and center-field. The center-field barrier was cut down to 386 from 400 feet. A crew of fifteen installed the three additional rows of box seats, which were now five instead of two deep. On Wednesday, June 4, Pete Reiser ran into the Ebbets Field outfield wall catching a line drive and was removed on a stretcher, a conveyance that, for Pistol Pete, seemed as familiar as the family car. It was the fourth time he had run into a fence or a wall and endangered his skull. From the ballpark it was on to Swedish Hospital, where it was revealed, fortunately, that a concussion was the extent of the damage.

The incident renewed calls for some sort of protection for players around the outfield walls. "The Dodgers will go ahead with plans to place protection on the outfield walls in some manner or fashion," Lou Niss wrote in the *Eagle*. "But protection at Ebbets Field will only be fifty percent insurance for the Dodgers, with no guarantee that the boys won't run into fences when they are away from home."

"Every type of protection will be considered by the Dodgers before a final selection is made," Niss added. "And when the Dodgers report their findings they may well ask that a rule be written into baseball suggesting the same type of protection throughout the National League."

Though it seems hard to believe today, even the idea of a warning track triggered some improbable critical assessments. "Many protective measures have been suggested and there has been fault found with most of them," Niss continued. "A cinder path would have to be 20 feet wide to give an outfielder sufficient warning and then he might not even realize he was running on cinders. Many players object to terraces that some fields now use because it causes them to misjudge fly balls, and also because of the danger of tripping. Wire screens have been considered, but it's not news that Ray Blades suffered a fractured leg when his spikes caught in the wire netting at St. Louis.

"Koylon, an airfoam rubber product of the United States Rubber Company, is being investigated for possibilities. Just how far a baseball would rebound when striking a rubber-covered wall is one of the problems there. Another suggestion is a canvas fence in front of the wall with the pole to which the canvas is attached rigged so that they give under pressure."[19]

The wall-cushioning matter wouldn't be resolved in Brooklyn until after the season.

It took a while, but Robinson was winning. And he also was drawing the fans. Americans, for once, could no longer pretend not to see Jim Crow. But Jackie's battle would be ongoing. And battle he did. Against the Pirates on June 24, he stole home. His play was sparking the Dodgers, who began to take command after the All-Star break. Against the Cardinals on July 19, Robinson stole home again. Gradually, by August, the Dodgers had cobbled out a ten-game lead. The success didn't make things any easier for Robinson. In a series against the Cardinals that month, Medwick, who'd been unloaded by Rickey in 1943 and was now a part-time player, spiked Robinson on the right foot. Two days later Jackie had to avoid Enos Slaughter; another time Slaughter got him on the left leg. Jackie was sure Slaughter was targeting him; years later Enos said he wasn't, and that he just played hard regardless of who the opponent was. But if opponents were baiting and battling Robinson all the time, he was taking the measure of all of them, taunting them and retaliating in his own way.

On August 29 he stole home for the third time that season, in a game against the Giants. The next day, 37,512—well above capacity—squeezed their way into Ebbets Field to eclipse the previous year's all-time season attendance record for the ballpark.

Before long the Cardinals shortened Brooklyn's lead to four, and memories of the 1942 and 1946 seasons began to cloud the Dodger fans' consciousness. But in a crucial three-game series in St. Louis beginning September 11, Brooklyn took two of three, almost ensuring that the second World Series in seven years would be played at Ebbets Field.

Brooklyn won twenty-eight of its final forty-four games to take the pennant by five games, and the *Sporting News* named Jackie Robinson Rookie of the Year. All he had done was hit .297 and steal 29 bases while serving to rattle opposing pitchers and provide inspiration to all who saw him, this while carrying a mantle of pride for an entire race. And it wasn't singularly a race of African Americans but of blacks from the Caribbean and Cuba and the other Latin countries who not only knew and loved the game of baseball, but who understood the virus of racial prejudice as it existed in the United States.

"It was also in understanding the power of the Dodgers over the heart and mind of Brooklyn that I realized what it meant for the Dodgers to be the team that finally integrated baseball," said the Reverend Donald McKinney, who served as minister at the First Unitarian Church at the corner of Pierrepont Street and Monroe Place in Brooklyn Heights. "For Branch Rickey, it was a matter of very deep ethical concern that blacks were not allowed to play in the majors. And he waited and plotted for years for the right moment to move and the right player, who he sensed could and would endure the inevitable hatred and abuse that would be piled on him.

"Today," said McKinney, speaking in the 1980s, "it is almost impossible to imagine what Jackie Robinson went through only thirty some years ago. And it's hard to imagine today what that meant to Brooklyn, which was then overwhelmingly white, with many strong ethnic neighborhoods, brought together as Brooklyn and Brooklynites only by the Dodgers.

"I am sure it was not so much the innate goodness and moral superiority of Brooklynites that made them quickly rally behind Jackie Robinson," said McKinney, "but rather their intense loyalty to the Dodgers; it forced them to stand up for the team against the attacks of the rest of the world."[20]

In 1947 people came out to Ebbets Field in greater numbers than ever before, with the Dodgers' 1,807,526 second in the major leagues only to the Yankees, who drew over 2 million up at their stadium. At that point in history, no National League team had ever drawn more. It was the surge provided in a nation exuberantly out of war, with expectations, opportunity, and dreams to be realized.

One of the dreams was owning a television set, banal as it may seem now. The medium that Red Barber had pioneered in a demonstration eight years before was gaining more of a foothold. And if television had yet to penetrate the market, it had pierced the consciousness. "At this time an innovation changed the character of the neighborhood somewhat," recounted Larry Block. "Stores selling television sets opened on Franklin Avenue. While our financial condition had improved, most families found the cost of these small black-and-white sets prohibitive. However as a means of promoting these electronic marvels, sets were installed in store windows and since baseball was now being televised, it was possible to watch the Dodgers electronically.

"Soon, it was not unusual to see people carrying beach chairs strolling down the avenue during the evening and setting them up in front of the store window. Early arrivals got the good spots in front of the glass, but were expected to sit so as not to block the views of the standees in the rear. Little kids, of course, were allowed to squeeze in front. By game time a sizable crowd would have gathered. I was fortunate to have a friend whose family was somewhat more affluent than the rest of us; they purchased a seven-inch TV with a magnifying glass so that we could all watch the games in comfort. I remember watching the Joe Louis–Joe Walcott championship fight standing in the rain outside a TV store. We did not get a TV set until after I graduated college in 1954, since my mother was sure I would never do my homework during the baseball season otherwise. She was right."

Fueled with anticipation by a summer of baseball on television through store windows, New York braced for its second subway series in the 1940s. The October classic would begin on September 30 at Yankee Stadium, and would be played through to completion with games on consecutive days, without time allotted for travel days between the venues. The Dodgers dropped the first two games of the 1947 World Series up in the Bronx before the action moved to Ebbets Field, where the bunting along the first and third base boxes did not consist of the traditional semicircular red, white, and blue flags. Instead, Ebbets Field had a series of rectangular contiguous flags covering the entire railing in foul territory with linear stripes, red at the top and bottom, with white stripes sandwiching a blue stripe in the middle with a ribbon of stars.

Red Barber explained that "Brooklyn is a different place. Ebbets Field is a different ball park. . . . The Brooklyn fan was different. . . . The Brooklyn ballplayer was another combatant when he felt the smallness of Ebbets Field, when he walked the sod of Brooklyn, and when he heard the never-ceasing encouragement of his fans. The Dodgers at Ebbets Field were much like Antaeus, whom Hercules couldn't kill as long as Antaeus was standing on his native soil. . . . Dixie Walker put it somewhat into focus before the third game when he said, 'Now we cannot only see the ball but also who's hitting.' Thirty-three thousand and ninety-eight fans packed the small park. There were great distances at Yankee Stadium. In Ebbets Field the fans and players blended into almost a oneness."[21]

Game 3 was a seesaw battle and as John Drebinger wrote in the *Times*, "the crowd, though less than half the size of either of the two great Stadium gatherings, appeared on the spot to make twice as much noise as ever had been heard in the Bronx." Despite a two-run homer into the upper left-center-field stands by DiMaggio and a pinch home run by Yogi Berra, the Dodgers managed to win 9–8.

The next day's game, one of the most exciting ever played, provided one of the reasons for Ebbets Field's great legacy. It was the day Bill Bevens flirted with immortality, the day he would take a no-hitter into the ninth inning, the day of baseball maxims tested, of the right-field wall's elegantly simplistic role in a ballet for the ball.

The thirty-one-year-old Bevens had come up to the Yankees in 1944 and had pitched regularly for them beginning in 1945. On this day he had walked eight over eight innings, including Jorgensen and Gregg in the fifth. Eddie Stanky sacrificed to move the runners to second and third. Pee Wee Reese hit a grounder to short, and when Rizzuto threw to third to nab Gregg, Jorgensen scored. At the end of five, the Yankees had 2 runs, 6 hits, and 1 error to the Dodgers' 1 run, 0 hits, and 2 errors.

The Dodgers escaped a jam in the top of the ninth, and now, in the bottom of the inning, Bevens had to face Bruce Edwards, Carl Furillo, and Spider Jorgenson. Larry Goetz of the National League was behind the plate. For the first World Series ever, umpires were not only on each base but also on the left- and right-field foul lines. The crowd, on its feet as Bevens came to the mound, gave roaring encouragement to Edwards as he stepped to the plate.

After Edwards backed Johnny Lindell to the left-field stands with a long fly for the first out, Bevens worked Carl Furillo carefully, losing him to a base on balls. His ninth walk tied a World Series record set by Jack Coombs of the Philadelphia A's in 1910. Jorgensen then fouled out to George McQuinn at first base for the second out.

A single out stood between Bevens and his no-hitter.

Burt Shotton decided to replace Furillo at first with speedy Al Gionfriddo. With pitcher Hugh Casey scheduled to hit, Shotton looked down his bench and had only one choice: the only left-handed hitter sitting there.

Pete Reiser had a right ankle so swollen that he could hardly walk, let alone run. "What Shotton didn't know, and what I didn't know in the radio booth," Red Barber wrote, "was that had Reiser listened to the trainer, Doc Wendler, he wouldn't have been in the dugout and available to pinch-hit. Pete was unable to take pre-game practice because of the bad ankle, and was in the clubhouse soaking it. During the first three innings of the game he was back in the clubhouse soaking the ankle again. Doc Wendler, an expert and a thoughtful man, told Pete he might as well put on his street clothes, that he couldn't play. However, Pete put his uniform back on and returned to the dugout, available to pinch hit."[22]

So Shotton sent Reiser to the plate to pinch-hit. Later, it would turn out that the ankle he was walking on was broken. With the count 2–1, a good pitch on which to run, Bevens threw over to first base twice to keep Gionfriddo close to the bag. Even with the game in the balance, with a bat in Pistol Pete Reiser's hands, and with a healthy left foot off which he would leverage his power toward the right-field fence and Bedford Avenue, manager Burt Shotton elected to gamble, ordering Gionfriddo to steal. He wanted that tying run in scoring position on second base.

Bevens pitched and Gionfriddo went, and Berra came up throwing, a high throw to Rizzuto at second base, who brought down the tag.

Umpire Babe Pinelli thrust out his arms, palms downward.

Safe.

With the count now 3–1, Yankee manager Bucky Harris decided to break one of baseball's cardinal rules: Never put the winning run on base. He didn't want Bevens grooving a pitch to Reiser that Pistol Pete would pole over the wall. Ball four duly ordered and pitched, Reiser moved down to take his base before Eddie Miksis came in to run for him.

It's not hard to imagine what Ebbets Field was like at this moment. "On the broadcast of a ball game the engineer will have a microphone suspended outside the booth to pick up the sounds of the crowd," Barber wrote. "He feeds crowd-level in, balancing it against the level of the announcer's voice. For the last half of this ninth inning the engineer had turned the crowd mike off, and had kept motioning me to talk as close to the mike as possible. It was bedlam."[23]

Eddie Stanky, the on-deck hitter, was starting for the plate.

Shotton called him back.

In his place he sent up Harry "Cookie" Lavagetto. Lavagetto's wife was lying in a hospital bed on the other side of the country, in Oakland, having just delivered their firstborn.

Cookie, a thirty-four-year-old right-handed hitter, was near the end of a thirteen-year baseball career interrupted by four years of military service. "To me, it was like any other game. It was my last year with the club. The previous spring they had offered me a minor league managing job but I had turned it down because I though I could play another season in the big leagues. I was used mostly as a pinch hitter that year and I did all right. I think I hit over .250 [he hit .261]. So when I went up there to pinch-hit against Bevens, it was something I had been used to doing all year."

Lavagetto stood in at the plate while Bevens checked Gionfriddo at second. Bevens delivered high and slightly outside; Lavagetto swung and missed. Again Bevens pitched, and to roughly the same spot.

"The pitch was right out there," Lavagetto said, "and I got hold of it good."[24]

Forty-eight years later, Tommy Henrich remembered the flight of the ball out to right field. "When the ball left the bat, it was a bullet line drive, not very high. Then the ball took off and went into the white shirts; there was a predominantly white background. I knew right away it could hit the wall, the question was whether it would be low enough for me to catch it. I kept moving over so that I would be in line with the ball when it came out of the background of the shirts. When it did, I knew I couldn't get it. Too high. So I started moving away from the wall, moving back toward home plate, trying to get off the wall. When it hit I'm about four feet from the wall, and the ball came right back—bang, bang—and hit the heel of my glove and dropped. Now I had to stop and go back toward the wall. If I had gotten that ball right away, Miksis couldn't have scored."

Barber's call amid the din: "Heaah comes the tyyying run and heaaaah comes the win-ning run . . . !!!" When Miksis arrived at that magic moment, he slid in and sat on the plate for a few seconds smiling and laughing while all Brooklyn jumped for joy. Lavagetto, of course, was mobbed.

Later, marveling at the game's course of events while signing off the broadcast, Barber said, "I'll be a suck-egg mule."

After the game, fans went on the field and pointed to the precise spot on the Gem Blades sign where the ball had hit.

The exuberance in Brooklyn was house-to-house and bubbled late into the night. The Series was now tied at two games apiece, and with this miraculous victory, fans were thinking this could well be the year the Bums would win it all.

Frank Shea started for the Yankees the next day at Ebbets Field, paired against Rex Barney, who hadn't started for Brooklyn since July 4. Barney, notorious for his wildness, got off to a rocky start but managed to get out of jams until the fourth, when Frank Shea finally drove in a run for himself. In the fifth, with no one on and one out, DiMaggio parked a 2–1 pitch in the upper deck in left field, giving the Yanks a 2–0 margin. Jackie Robinson drove in Al Gionfriddo with a single after two Dodger walks in the bottom of the sixth to cut the margin to a single run.

The score remained the same until the ninth, when, with Bruce Edwards at second and two men gone, Shotton sent in yesterday's hero, Cookie Lavagetto, to pinch-hit for Hugh Casey. The crowd went crazy and hoped for another miracle, but at home, huddled by his radio, the loyal fan of the cherished autograph book, Arthur Harrow, felt another Lavagetto hit was too much to ask, that lightning couldn't strike twice like that on consecutive days.

Shea worked carefully to Cookie, not giving him anything to hit, running out the count to 3–1; Lavagetto had yet to swing. He knew then that Shea would have to come in; Cookie was sitting on a sure-bet strike. Shea delivered, but Cookie fouled it back for strike two. "I got my pitch," Lavagetto said afterward.

Shea's payoff pitch was a fast ball; Cookie swung and missed. Ebbets Field fell quiet, save for the enthusiasm on the walk over toward the Yankee dugout. The Yankees had gone a game up with a 2–1 victory. "I guess I just didn't have it in me," Cookie said later with a rueful smile, when a reporter in the clubhouse asked him about the prospect for another clutch hit.[25]

The teams then returned to the Yankee Stadium, where, in game 6, Al Gionfriddo made one of baseball's legendary plays. In the bottom of the sixth inning, with the Dodgers ahead 8–5, there were two men gone when the tying run came to the plate in the person of Joe DiMaggio. All around Brooklyn—and all around the country—people gathered by their radios. Again Barber's call was a classic: "Joe leans in. Outfield deep, around toward left. The infield overshifted. Here's the pitch. Swung on, belted!!! It's a long one. Deep into left center. Back goes Gionfriddo. Back, back, back, back, back, back. . . . He makes a one-handed catch against the bullpen!!! Ohhh-ho, doctor!"

DiMaggio drove the ball all the way to the 415 sign into the left-center field of Yankee Stadium's Death Valley, the ball heading over the low, three-foot fence of the visitors' bullpen. It was there that 5'6" Al Gionfriddo caught it, the ball protruding from his glove like an ice cream cone. DiMaggio, running out by second base when Gionfriddo made the stab, kicked the dirt in his only on-field display of temperament that anyone could ever remember. In the ninth, the Yankees threatened, but Hugh Casey closed them down. Gionfriddo's play stood up as the difference in Brooklyn's 8–6 win.

Alas, the Yankees won the next day up at their stadium, 5–2, after Tommy Henrich drove in the go-ahead run in the fourth inning, his fifth RBI of the series, and Joe Page came on to pitch five superb innings of scoreless relief. The outcome for Brooklyn, though disappointing, brought an absolutely great baseball season to an end.

As for the trio who forever earned a place in baseball's annals with their roles in the Series of 1947, neither Bevens, Lavagetto, nor Gionfriddo ever played another major league game.

CHAPTER TEN

Firing the American Imagination

I n 1948 the last definitive image of Ebbets Field was put into place: Schaefer bought the advertising space at the top of the right-field scoreboard, complementing Abe Stark's ad at the bottom. Schaefer, like Abe Stark, would keep its name on the scoreboard until Ebbets Field's final inning. And before long, Schaefer decided to illuminate the "h" and an "e" in its sign to indicate "hit" or "error" when a call by the official scorer had to be made as a result of action on the field.

The reporters who served as official scorers were given a case of beer a week by the Schaefer people to hit a button in the press box to light up either the "h" or the "e" when a play on the field needed clarification. When Schaefer stopped sending the beer, Jack Lang stopped hitting the buttons, and Schaefer had to hire a guy named Jim Houseman to light up the proper letter after official scorers' decisions.

Before the season began, with Pete Reiser as the inspiration, the left- to center-field outfield wall at Ebbets Field was padded with one-inch-thick chemical sponge rubber produced by the U.S. Rubber Company. The padding was made in sections twelve feet long and 50 inches high, made at the company's Naugatuck, Connecticut, footwear plant.

Smaller sections were designed to fit irregular areas. Each section was equipped with grommets at the top and bottom of each side so that the padding could be anchored securely to the wall. The bottom of the padding was installed 32 inches above the ground, better to cushion the player leaping against the wall in pursuit of a baseball.

The great Dodger baseball teams of the 1950s began to coalesce in 1948. Duke Snider, who Branch Rickey thought the year before had an "appalling lack of familiarity with the strike zone," was back. Roy Campanella, who was half black and half Italian and who had spent part of his adolescence with the famed Baltimore Elite Giants, was in camp; Leo, who was back, reinstated by Chandler, quickly became convinced he was looking at the best catcher in baseball. Rickey, meanwhile, had decided to move Robinson's field position from first base to second. Rickey was originally thinking of using Pete Reiser at first base to protect him from running into any more walls, but now Durocher had Hodges, a former catcher who was a natural first baseman. These moves made second baseman Eddie Stanky expendable, so before the season began, Rickey traded Stanky to the Boston Braves.

In Brooklyn, this new cast of characters would be sentimentalized by the fans, who, as Durocher said, "came to root, and . . . never gave up. It was Brooklyn against the world." He continued, "they were not only complete fanatics, but they knew baseball like the fans of no other city. It was exciting to play there. It was a treat. I walked into that crummy, flyblown park as Brooklyn manager for nine years, and every time I entered, my pulse quickened and my spirits soared."[1]

In Brooklyn, they even knew who was coming up from the bush leagues. Carl Erskine remembered his first arrival at Ebbets Field, which was prefaced that season by newspaper articles lamenting the Dodgers' pitching-starved staff when the team got off to a rocky start. When he showed up outside the ballpark with his bag bearing the name of the Fort Worth Cats, several fans spotted him at once, their cadence unforgettable to the midwesterner's ear:

"Look. It's Oiskine. From Fort Woith."

The neighborhood had altogether grown up. Increased migration during the years of World War I and shortly thereafter led New York City to exempt real estate taxes on new construction in the early 1920s to help alleviate housing shortages, and it was mostly during the period between 1922 and 1930 when many of the neighborhood's new apartment buildings were built, including some of the notable ones on Eastern Parkway. The deepest years of the Depression halted significant construction investment, and now, with World War II over and young men returning, the neighborhood was crowded while the federal government was developing plans to encourage home ownership with insured mortgages and low down payments, programs that would lead some to the suburbs.

"There were so many kids on the blocks," Rebecca Silverstein remembers, "whole gangs of kids. Apartment buildings everywhere; row houses along the side streets. It definitely felt like a community. Building by building. It was a roof culture. Everybody would go up on the roof. I lived at Franklin and President. You could see the ballpark from there at night. [President Street is three blocks north of Montgomery Street.] There was definitely the feeling that the Dodgers were Brooklyn."

If the Dodgers were Brooklyn and Leo was the Dodgers, something was about to change. The Dodgers were floundering and Leo's relationship with Rickey was deteriorating, even as Leo was beginning to irritate some of his coaches and some front-office personnel. Finally, during a July 4 game against the Giants at Ebbets Field, when Jackie had stolen home and Leo had gotten kicked out for arguing, Harold Parrott of the Dodgers' front office told Leo, in the clubhouse, that Rickey wanted him to resign. Leo's response was to the point. "See that phone on the desk, Harold? That goes right up to Mr. Rickey's office. If he wants to fire me, let him pick up that phone and send for me so that he can fire me in person. You and I are old friends, so take this the way I mean it, but you tell him I am not going to resign and nobody is going to fire me by messenger."[2]

While they talked, Campanella won the game for the Bums with a ninth-inning homer, the beginning of a streak in which the Dodgers won five of six on the road. Ultimately it did Durocher no good, for he would meet with Rickey the morning of the All-Star Game in St. Louis, where Durocher was managing the National League squad, and tell him, "As far as I'm concerned, I'm through at the end of the year anyway. I wouldn't work for you another day after all that's happened."[3]

Within days Rickey had engineered an exit strategy for Leo. Unbeknownst to Durocher, Giants owner Horace Stoneham, ready to fire manager Mel Ott, had asked Rickey for permission to talk with Burt Shotton. Rickey, to Stoneham's surprise, gave him the choice of talking to *either* Shotton *or* Durocher. Horace chose Leo. Then Rickey gave Durocher the choice to go or stay as he pleased, saying that he had Stoneham's phone number for him.

"Two questions, Mr. Rickey! One: Am I manager of this ball club now?"

"Yes, sir," Rickey replied.

"Two: Will I be manager of this ball club tomorrow, next week, next month and until the close of the 1948 season?"

"Well . . .," Rickey equivocated, first looking at Leo and then swiveling his chair around to look out the window from 215 Montague Street into the darkness, all the while chewing on his cigar.

Durocher finally burst out of his chair. "I don't know what the hell you expect to see out there! Where's that number?"[4]

Leo called Stoneham at once, arranging an immediate meeting at the Durocher apartment at 46 East Sixty-first Street. Leo then called Laraine Day, his wife, with instructions to make the gentleman who arrived a drink and keep him company until he arrived. The news the next day was sensational. Leo, hated by the Giant fans, was replacing Mel Ott, whom the Giant fans loved. And now the Dodger fans hated Durocher because he was a Giant. Burt Shotton, at Rickey's behest, would manage the Dodgers another time.

Leo returned to Ebbets Field as the Giants manager on Monday, July 26. Thousands were turned back at the gates. Before the game, when Durocher walked out on the field to shake hands with Shotton, he was greeted by a chorus of boos. For Durocher, it wasn't easy. "For nine years, I had been charging off the bench whenever that battle cry 'Leooooo!' filled the Brooklyn air. For nine years, I hadn't been able to drive up Bedford Avenue after a game without a knot of guys yelling at me from every corner to find out how we had made out. If we had won, they'd raise a cry of victory, and if we had lost they'd always say, 'Wha' happened?'"[5]

Shotton presided over a continuing Dodger renaissance. During a drizzly August doubleheader, Ralph Hamner started for the Cubs, and Gene Hermanski, in his first two trips to the plate, hit two shots over the wall onto Bedford Avenue. Brooklyn had a 4–0 lead at that point, but the Cubs edged back to make it 4–3. His fourth time up, Hermanski connected for a solo shot against Jess Dobernic, driving a ball into the lower left-center-field stands, the first time a Dodger had hit three homers in one game since Jacques Fournier did it on July 13, 1926. The rains came in earnest later, causing cancellation of the second game.

"When I came to the ballpark the next day, everybody was kidding me," said Hermanski, who regularly commuted from his parents' house in Irvington, New Jersey, in 45 minutes. "They were saying, 'Hermanski hit three homers yesterday, and Hamner and Dobernic have been sent down to the minor leagues!'"

Fan fervor at Ebbets Field was well exemplified during an August 21 battle for the league's top spot, when the Dodgers beat Johnny Sain and the Boston Braves in the opening game of a Saturday double-header. The victory completed a Brooklyn turnaround from last place to first in fifty days, and at the game's conclusion, fans continued to cheer as a park attendant on the bleacher roof approached the first-place flagpole and began the process of lowering Boston's banner and raising Brooklyn's blue-and-white colors in its place. The Boston banner went back up again in the same spot later that afternoon when the Braves, behind Warren Spahn, took the nightcap.

"Shorty Laurice Day" was celebrated at the ballpark that summer in honor of Brooklyn's so-called Number One Fan. Shorty, who would jitterbug in the stands or on the dugout, blowing his whistle, had been orchestrating the Section 8 Dodger fans for years. His day was an illustration of both the depth of fan commitment and the extent to which the team and the fans were like extended family. "Shorty would bring Jackie Robinson and Ralph Branca over to St. Lucy's Church, and he also managed a ball club at the Navy Yard," remembered Shorty's brother, Joe. "He'd do anything for anybody. He'd play basketball after the game was over on Friday nights, buy the kids sodas; dance; it was like going to Mars."

In November Shorty died unexpectedly after surgery for his ulcers; the money collected at the ballpark in August was used to pay for his funeral. Half of the Brooklyn Dodgers organization—players, front office, everyone—showed up at the Laurice home on York Street for the wake. The traffic was so heavy in front of the old walk-up building that police stationed outside the house regulated the flow of people inside for fear the floor would collapse. Laurice's funeral cortege circled Ebbets Field. In the *New York Mirror* Larry Zeltner wrote, "Whenever I hear thunder overhead, I'll think of Shorty Laurice giving them a Brooklyn concerto."

Speaking of concertos, the Sym-Phony Band, with an ever-changing crew of musicians that included JoJo Delio, Lou Soriano, Patty George, Jerry Martin, Joe Zollo, and Zollo's son Frank among the stalwarts, extended its orbit into the political realm in 1948, an election year. What Lou Soriano called the band's finest hour came when the Sym-Phony was invited to stroll the aisles at the Republican Convention that summer in Philadelphia. New York governor Thomas E. Dewey, the GOP's nominee, had been introduced to the band members by a leading Brooklyn Republican, Johnny Crews.

Governor Dewey told the Sym-Phony's musicians that when he won the election, he'd have them in to give a concert at the White House. Since it was widely thought that Harry Truman couldn't win, it seemed like time to block the top hat and take the tattered tails to the cleaners. Not to be: "our bum loses," as Soriano lamented, and with it went what would have been an undoubtedly unforgettable performance at the Executive Mansion.

It seemed natural for a Dodger fan.

The Sym-Phony routinely razzed the umpires with "Three Blind Mice." Unfortunately, no way was found to compensate when a fourth arbiter was added to the umpiring crews.

When opposing hitters struck out, they were accompanied back to the dugout with the band's serenade, "The Worms Crawl In, the Worms Crawl Out," with cymbals and chords blaring when the player sat down on the bench. Catcher Walker Cooper once tried to frustrate the band's objectives by not sitting down in the dugout for several innings, but when he finally did, the band got him, drum and cymbals matching the moment his posterior hit the pine.

Despite their talented new players, the 1948 Dodgers settled for third place, seven and a half games behind the Braves, who won their first pennant since 1914. Boston went on to lose the Series to Cleveland in six games, the only Series between 1947 and 1958 that didn't feature a New York team.

Branch Rickey, assuming that borough pride and marketing acumen could be combined to make an entity a success, had acquired the financially drained Brooklyn Football Dodgers franchise in 1948. He had taken it off the hands of William Cox, the lumberman owner of the Phillies whom Commissioner Landis had tossed out of baseball for wagering on his own team. Rickey thought he could stoke Brooklyn's pride in the AAFC team, but it didn't turn out that way. The move raised the ire of Walter O'Malley, who also had disapproved of Rickey's expenditures to build the new Dodger training facilities at Vero Beach. In order to bolster the football team's advance ticket sales, Rickey had the men appear in full uniform at Ebbets Field before a baseball game. But this football season was even more disastrous than the others, with the Brooklyn team finishing 2–12. Only 9,821 showed up at the end of the season to see Brooklyn play the undefeated Cleveland Browns, who had what one reporter called "a little light exercise at the expense of the hapless Brooklyn Dodgers" in the course of administering a 31–21 defeat. The investment in the Football Dodgers was a financial sinkhole, costing $750,000.

The poor choice intensified O'Malley's sniping against Rickey, the managing partner within the Dodger partnership, and helped O'Malley to sway the third member of the ownership triumvirate, John Smith of Pfizer, to his side. Rickey, despite his role in breaking the color line, had numerous critics. Jimmy Powers of the *Daily News* had dubbed him "El Cheapo" for his penurious ways; Powers was relentless in his criticism. Rickey had made thousands of personnel moves in his years in baseball, and some of them were financially injurious to players. Al Gionfriddo was just a few games short of a major league pension when Rickey moved him to a minor league roster, even though he was still quite capable of playing with another major league team.

The Dodgers trained at Vero Beach for the first time the following spring. The former naval air station on the Sunshine State's Atlantic Coast had been converted into a baseball complex to accommodate the team's farm clubs as well as the major league team. Duke Snider was about to become the full-time center-fielder, with Carl Furillo moving over to right field. Don Newcombe was brought up from Montreal in May to buttress Shotton's pitching corps. He immediately demonstrated his command on the mound and underscored his prowess with a bat with a shutout and two runs batted in during his first starting assignment.

"Big and strong at six feet four and 230 pounds, he was the first great black power pitcher to reach the major leagues," wrote David Halberstam. "His anger manifested itself, as much as anywhere else, in his hatred of hitters, almost all of whom, in those days, were white. Newcombe went, in a brief span of three years, from being a child of the New Jersey slums to being a major New York sports celebrity. Geographically it was only a few miles, but emotionally it was like a journey to the moon."[6]

On July 12 the midsummer classic came to Ebbets Field, the first All-Star Game played there since the game was instituted in 1934. It turned out to be a prototypical Ebbets Field game: eighteen runs scored as the American League prevailed over the National, 11–7. One thing was different: it was the first time that blacks played in an All-Star Game. The key play was an unexpected defensive gem by Ted Williams, who went into the left-field corner to make a spectacular catch on Don Newcombe's curving liner with the bases filled in the second inning. Virgil Trucks got the win, while Newcombe, in relief of Spahn in the second, took the loss.

Not long afterward, Stan Musial had one of his one-man wrecking crew days at Ebbets Field. For an opponent, Musial was revered in Brooklyn, even receiving his nickname "The Man" from Brooklyn fans, who lamented "Here comes that man again." On July 24 he tripled, flied out, singled, homered, doubled, and walked in the course of a 14–1 Redbird rout. Stan Musial loved to hit at Ebbets Field, and Brooklyn fans always had a great deal of respect for him. He made an indelible impression.

The Dodgers and Cardinals vied that year in a remarkable race reminiscent of 1946, which was precisely what had Brooklyn fans worried. Even though the Cards had grabbed the lead, they couldn't break free of the Bums. On September 29 the Dodgers won two up in Boston, while the Cards lost to Pittsburgh. Brooklyn was in first by half a game.

The next day, the Cards lost to the Cubs, 6–5, while Brooklyn was off, giving the Dodgers a one-game lead. On October 1, both teams lost, clinching a tie for Brooklyn.

On October 2, the last day of the 1949 season, the Cards walloped the Cubs while Philly and Brooklyn battled to a 7–7 tie after nine. In the tenth inning in Philadelphia, Reese singled, Miksis sacrificed, and Snider, who had had trouble against lefties early in the year, singled up the middle against left-hander Ken Heintzelman to drive in the go-ahead run. Robinson was walked intentionally, and then Luis Olmo singled by the third baseman to drive in Duke. The Dodgers held on to win 9–7, with Jack Banta completing 4⅓ innings of two-hit relief, coming on after starter Newcombe and Rex Barney in middle relief. The Brooks were going to the World Series.

Twenty-five thousand fans gathered at Penn Station to welcome the team home from Philadelphia. Once again Brooklyn broke into celebration, with impromptu parties and dancing in the streets between the Paramount Theater and the intersection of Atlantic and Flatbush avenues. A call was put out for open cars for use in the victory parade between Grand Army Plaza and Borough Hall two days hence. A reinforced platform was erected on the steps of Borough Hall and local merchants boarded up their windows in anticipation of the celebration. On parade day, 900,000 people lined the route.

The Yankees and Dodgers split the first two games at Yankee Stadium, and then the scene shifted to Ebbets Field, where 32,788 packed Ebbets Field as First Lady Bess Truman looked on. Organist Gladys Goodding sang the national anthem herself, and a young, thirteen-year-old polio victim, Al Sweeney, threw out the first ball. Branca got the call for the Dodgers, pitted against Yankee left-hander Tommy Byrne, a five-year veteran. The Yanks garnered a run in the third; Byrne, meanwhile, was not sharp, consistently falling behind the Dodger hitters. In the fourth, after Reese homered into the left-field stands and Byrne followed by loading the bases with one out, it looked as if Byrne's wildness was catching up with him. Stengel countered by bringing on lefty Joe Page.

Page managed to get the right-handed hitting Luis Olmo and left-handed hitting Snider out, and the teams settled in and went into the ninth knotted at 1–1. Perhaps it was symbolic that rain started to fall as Branca loaded the bases with two walks and a single. Now, with two out, Stengel called upon a man whom Yankee GM George Weiss had picked up on waivers on August 22, after Giant manager Leo Durocher decided he no longer wanted a first baseman who was slow afoot and afield.

The man they called the "Big Cat" had eleven full seasons of big league experience with the Gas House Gang in St. Louis and with the Giants (missing three seasons during the war) and a big left-handed swing. He was the kind of player that Branch Rickey, who passed on him, could have just as easily picked up for the Dodgers with the Yankee Stadium right-field porch and October in mind. Now, on a 2–1 count, Johnny Mize pinch-hit Branca's inside fastball at the belt—a pitch that was where Branca wanted it—high into right field. Mize wasn't sure at first if the ball would be playable, hit the wall, or go over it, but as soon as he saw Carl Furillo looking up toward the barrier, he was satisfied. Furillo wasn't going to catch it; runs would score.

The ball hit the screen and Furillo, as usual, played it perfectly, holding Mize to a single. Two runs scored. Jack Banta came on to relieve, but Jerry Coleman smacked what turned out to be another key single, driving in another run, giving the Yankees a 4–1 lead.

The Dodgers weren't done. Suddenly they found a way to get to Page. Luis Olmo homered and so did Campanella, to close the gap to a single run. But then Page used his fastball to strike out Bruce Edwards to win the game.

"I like to hit where you can see fences all around," said Mize afterward. "At the Polo Grounds, you have that big gap in center where the clubhouse is. It does something to you. Here, you see nothing but fence. Your target is unbroken and, when you swing, something generally happens."[7]

Branch Rickey arranged to have fifteen heroes from the 1916 Dodger pennant winners return to Ebbets Field for the fourth game of the fall classic on Saturday, October 8, and the Dodgers had their old 1916 right fielder, Casey Stengel, clad in his New York visiting flannel, introducing his old teammates to Ebbets Field fans. One by one they came out, Brooklyn legends out of the past: Big Jeff Pfeffer, Zack Wheat, Jimmy Johnston, and Rube Marquard. Old favorite Nap Rucker banged his head on the concrete roof as he started out of the dugout, but managed to keep his composure, smile, and acknowledge the crowd. Others on hand included Larry Cheney, Wheezer Dell, Gus Getz, Chief Meyers, Hi Myers, Ollie O'Mara, catcher Otto Miller, and Brooklyn native Art Dede, who, as a twenty-one-year-old bullpen catcher, had a single career major league at-bat in 1916, when he failed to reach base. Even the long-ago clubhouse custodian Dan Comerford was introduced. The biggest cheers were reserved for Stengel when, in the course of the festivities, he introduced himself.

While Gooding played "Auld Lang Syne," the crowd was also asked to pause for a silent prayer in memory of Wilbert Robinson, Ed Appleton, Harry Mowrey, Sherry Smith, and Jake Daubert.

Shotton started Newcombe with two days' rest that afternoon, but big Newk just didn't have it. He was shellacked in the fourth, and Joe Hatten was in for more of the same in the fifth, the Yankees scoring three in each of the stanzas. The final was 6–4, and Brooklyn was down three games to one.

With Governor Tom Dewey and Mayor William O'Dwyer on hand the following day under leaden skies, the arclights would be turned on at Ebbets Field in a World Series first during this fifth and final game of the 1949 fall classic.

Rex Barney started the game in place of Preacher Roe, who had a split nail and swollen finger on his glove hand. Barney, the infamous wild man, delivered thirty-seven pitches in the first inning; the Yankees hopped out to a 2–0 lead. The Yanks added three more in the third before the Dodgers answered with one, and DiMaggio, despite being eighteen pounds underweight from a respiratory infection, homered in the fourth inning. By the end of the sixth it was 10–2. Even with a Gil Hodges three-run homer in the seventh, the gloom had already settled over Brooklyn. Joe Page shut the Dodgers down for the final 2⅓ innings, the Dodgers going down to defeat 10–5.

In the weeks following the last out, Jackie Robinson, who had stolen home five times during the season and who had led the National League with a .342 average, was named the league's Most Valuable Player.

Lost amid all the concern over the pennant race was word of Charley Ebbets's estate finally settling, twenty-four years after he'd died, and almost five years after his son had died. On September 7, notice of the Ebbets estate settlement was presented to Surrogate Judge Francis D. McGarey by attorneys for the Brooklyn Trust Company, acting as executors. The heirs received $858,000 on an estate that had been worth $1.25 million twenty-four years before.

Out at the field that bore Charley's name, there would be no more professional football. The new Football Dodgers were so broke and so badly off after 1948 that they were merged with the New York Football Yankees in 1949. If you weren't confused before, the NFL absorbed the AAFC after 1949, and merged the New York Football Yankees with the old Boston Yanks, which had become the New York Bulldogs during the 1949 season.

Forget that the new New York Yanks of the NFL would only play the 1950 and 1951 seasons before heading off to Dallas as the Texans and, a year later, to Baltimore as the Colts; any way you look at it, the Brooklyn Football Dodgers were dead after the 1948 season.

The 1950 season saw the arrival of the Philadelphia Phillies' "Whiz Kids," who went 20–8 in August, leaving the Dodgers languishing seven games back in second place. But on the last day of the month, Gil Hodges gave Brooklyn fans at Ebbets Field something extraordinary to cheer about in a 19–3 rout of the Boston Braves. With Boston leading 1–0 in the second inning, Hodges drilled a Warren Spahn fastball a couple of rows back into the lower stands in left for a two-run homer. An inning later, Hodges lofted a hanging curve from right-hander Norman Roy that just made the left-field seats. After grounding out in the fourth, Hodges hit his third homer, a fastball, off righty Bob Hall in the sixth, this one four or five rows back in the lower left deck and again with Furillo on.

Gil's chance for a fourth came in the seventh inning, but instead of crashing one he sent a liner to third, which Bob Elliott managed to knock down, limiting Gil to a mere single. But the Dodgers continued to hit, sending six more players up, guaranteeing Gil another at-bat in the eighth. By this time the score was 17–3, and the hurler was southpaw Johnny Antonelli. When Antonelli hung a curve, Hodges parked it for a two-run homer in Section 33 of the upper stands. Four home runs for Gil, all within sixty feet of the left-field foul pole. With one of the Duke's earlier, he brought the team total to 153, which broke the Dodgers' seasonal club record for homers set the previous year.

Just past the midpoint in September, with only seventeen games left to play, Brooklyn was in third place, nine games back, but then strange things began to happen. The Dodgers beat the Pirates twice while the Phillies lost; then the Dodgers came into Philadelphia for two games beginning September 23.

The same day, Branch Rickey announced that he had agreed to sell his 25 percent holdings in the Brooklyn Dodgers to William Zeckendorf, who headed Webb & Knapp Real Estate in Manhattan. Zeckendorf said that the deal had been arranged by John Galbreath, one of the Pirate owners. The real estate man went on to mention that Galbreath had brought the idea to him and he speculated that the Pirates owner's intention may have been to get Rickey over to Pittsburgh.

Rickey claimed to have no immediate plans and said he definitely wasn't going to Pittsburgh. Pittsburgh, of course, was where Rickey was headed. Zeckendorf, meanwhile, noted that there were prior rights by which the other stockholders could buy up Rickey's stock if they met his price. He added that if they did, he'd get consideration for his time and trouble.

At the time when O'Malley, Rickey, and Smith bought their shares, they had agreed that if one party sold, the right of first refusal to purchase the shares on the same terms that a potential buyer tendered would be granted to the remaining parties.

John Smith had died in July, leaving his 25 percent share of the ball club to his widow. O'Malley was the lawyer for the Smith estate and had Mrs. Smith's approval to vote the shares his way. O'Malley had differed with Rickey over the last several years on a number of issues. On the investment in Vero Beach, Rickey was assuredly correct and O'Malley wrong. The pair argued over the Schaefer Beer sponsorship; the Bible-thumping Rickey was opposed, O'Malley in favor. O'Malley was proved right about the futility of investing in the Brooklyn Football Dodgers, which won O'Malley points from Smith when Rickey's decision to back the football club proved a dismal failure. Rickey's provision in his contract that gave him a percentage on player sales also had always rankled O'Malley.

Now, with Rickey deeply in debt from borrowing to finance his earlier purchase of shares and without the ability to muster majority support among the ownership, he looked to sell. O'Malley figured Rickey, with his 25 percent, would have a rough time getting anyone to bid a significant amount of money over what the triumvirate had paid earlier, especially when O'Malley effectively controlled 50 percent of the franchise while Steve McKeever's daughter, Dearie Mulvey, controlled the other 25 percent. O'Malley also didn't want the club appraised at a million-dollar level for tax purposes.

But Rickey had gotten Zeckendorf to bid $1,050,000 for his 25 percent share of the ball club, though the details would not come out for another month. For this Rickey had gained O'Malley's undying enmity. Now, instead of paying Rickey something on the order of the $300,000 that O'Malley claimed that portion of the club was worth, O'Malley would be forced to match the higher bid, or risk being tied up in a possible 50–50 ownership deadlock should Zeckendorf and Dearie Mulvey ever decide to ally on a given issue. And Walter O'Malley, like Branch Rickey, was about control. He had to have it; he would pay.

At the moment, this was incidental news to Brooklyn fans, who were preoccupied by the pennant race, for the Dodgers over the passing weeks had closed the gap to two games, setting up a showdown series with the Phillies at Ebbets Field on the final weekend of the season. The Dodgers won the game on Saturday, 7–3, thanks to a key homer by Duke Snider and a stellar relief effort by Erv Palica. It set the stage for one of the more memorable games in Ebbets Field's history, the 1950 season's finale, a game that could force a National League playoff.

The starters were the best both teams had: Don Newcombe and Robin Roberts. In the fifth inning Pee Wee Reese hit a ball that hit the screen and dropped straight down on the ledge at the top of the wall, bobbing up and down and finally settling there while Pee Wee circled the bases for a home run. "I have a tremendously vivid memory of the kid who walked along the ledge of the wall to retrieve the ball," said Hank Lieberman, who grew up in a two-and-a-half-room apartment on Avenue J with his parents and brother.

Lieberman had just turned ten, and thanks to his dad's buddy, was sitting in a box behind the dugout. The benefactor was a friend of the Dodger organization. "I was preparing myself to go down in the dugout and celebrate this win after the game," Lieberman remembered.

In the ninth inning the score was tied, 1–1, with none out and Dodgers on first and second. Duke Snider was at the plate facing Robin Roberts of the Phillies. If anything happened and the runner on second, Cal Abrams, scored, the Dodgers would win the game, tie for the pennant, and go into a playoff with the momentum on their side.

When Roberts delivered, Snider hit a line drive up the middle that Richie Ashburn, charging hard in center field, caught on the second hop. Abrams was waved on to the plate by third base coach Milt Stock, and as the throw came in, it was apparent that he was a dead duck, out by some twenty feet. Cal attempted to twist away from Stan Lopata's tag to no avail. Roberts got out of the inning, and in the tenth, Dick Sisler hit a three-run homer into the left-field seats and the Phillies won the pennant.

At the end of the game, twelve-year-old Sal Porio, Ed Anderson, and Tom Battillo of Astoria jumped out of the stands in center field, sprinted across the outfield, and slid into second base. Chased by the cops, the latter two of the trio would later become heroes themselves with long careers in the F.D.N.Y. Meanwhile, the kid who had retrieved the ball from the ledge in the fifth inning leaned over by the dugout to offer Reese the ball. "He was voluble," Hank Lieberman recalled. "Yelling. But the Dodgers had lost. My recollection is Reese didn't even look up."

The rest of Brooklyn was forlorn too. But sometimes when life seems at its lowest, things have a way of getting worse. Such was the lot of the Brooklyn fan.

Before the beginning of the 1951 season, the Yankees and Dodgers played a preseason exhibition series after the teams traveled north from spring training. During one of these games, Casey Stengel took a well-touted rookie by the name of Mickey Mantle out to Ebbets Field's tricky right-field wall, explaining to the young phenom how he used to play the carom. Mantle's eyes widened.

"You mean you used to play out here, Case?"

"Yeah, whaddya think?" said Stengel. "I was born sixty years old?"[8]

The Dodgers, in their first full season under O'Malley's direction, had a new manager: Chuck Dressen. Since Shotton was a Rickey loyalist, there was no doubt he'd be moving on. Brooklyn's nemeses, the

Giants, started the year terribly, suffering through an eleven-game losing streak early on; in May Durocher convinced Horace Stoneham to let him call up Willie Mays from Minneapolis, where he was hitting .477. Although Mays got off to a terrible start at the plate, bottoming out at .038, Durocher kept him in center field anyway; within a few weeks his average was over .300.

Irving Rudd, who handled publicity for the Dodgers, remembered the elaborate preparations at Ebbets Field necessary for hosting General Douglas MacArthur after he returned from Korea; in late May MacArthur attended the first of thirteen games he would see at Ebbets Field in 1951.

When Rudd made the arrangements, after the preliminaries, the planning got serious. "Security for the general, how many seats he'll need, protocol, all that shit, until the whole visit is covered, including the most important question of all," wrote Rudd. "What happens when the general has to go to the toilet? How does he get to the Ebbets Field crapper?"

Ultimately a satisfactory alternative was found so that the general could discreetly disappear as needed without having to negotiate either the dugout's high-rise stair steps or suffer the humiliation of sidling up shoulder-to-shoulder for a urinal in the common latrine.

The general's first appearance was cast in grandeur, with his limo rolling through the Bedford Avenue center-field gate with military precision at exactly 12:30: "Not a second either side," remembered Rudd.[9]

MacArthur came back just a couple of days later, unannounced, showing up at the Rotunda not in military dress but in a Hawaiian shirt. The Dodgers lost that afternoon as well.

The Dodgers were up by a game and a half over St. Louis on the first of June, with the Giants in fifth, four games back and also trailing the Cubs and the Braves. Just before the middle of June the Brooks acquired Andy Pafko, one of the game's marquee stars, from the Cubs. By the morning of the Fourth of July, Brooklyn was up by four and a half over the second-place Giants. And then the Dodgers took both games of the holiday doubleheader between the two teams at Ebbets Field to lengthen their lead.

By August 11, after a loss to the Phillies at the Polo Grounds, the Giants fell thirteen and a half games behind the Dodgers, who had won the first game of a twin bill in Brooklyn. By evening, after the Dodgers lost their nightcap, the Giants would be thirteen games behind.

Fans who came two nights later experienced one of the more amusing evenings in Ebbets Field history. But the entertainers were not on the field; they were in the stands. A sour political note had been sounded by Local 802 of the American Federation of Musicians, who had questioned the amateur standing of the Sym-Phony band and threatened to throw a picket line around Ebbets Field. The union never bargained for the opposition it received. The Dodgers scheduled a Musical Appreciation (or Depreciation) Night, with admittance free as long as you brought a musical instrument.

And so they came, a crowd of more than thirty thousand strong, laughing, strumming, tooting, and playing harmonicas, drums, kazoos, carrying kids in tubas, showing up with every conceivable instrument. "Seven men even carried in a piano," recounted Buzzie Bavasi. One guy even tried to get in with a comb and tissue paper, but it didn't wash.

A music teacher's nightmare, to be sure, but a celebration of the zany that was only quasi-offbeat in a place like Ebbets Field. Earplugs would have been helpful, but a good time was had by all, except perhaps the leadership of the musicians union, which had been seriously outflanked. Their threatening tune fell as flat as one of the Sym-Phony's off-key renditions.

After the Dodgers beat the Braves that evening, they went up to the Polo Grounds, where the Giants beat them three straight. The Brooklyn lead was now down to nine and a half games in only five days, and the Giants went on to win sixteen straight, narrowing the Dodger lead to five. The Dodger lead seemed to stabilize there through the first weeks in September, but with little more than a week left in the season, the Giants cut the lead by another two games.

In a year of fateful days, a fateful night for Brooklyn was Tuesday, September 25, when the Bums lost a doubleheader to the Braves up in Boston while the Giants were beating the Phillies, cutting the Dodgers' lead to a single game.

Two nights later, with the Giants idle, the Dodgers were locked in a 3–3 tie up in Boston in the bottom of the eighth when, with runners on first and third, Earl Torgeson grounded to Jackie Robinson, who rifled the ball to Campy at the plate to cut off the run. Baserunner Bob Addis slid, Campanella applied the tag, and ump Frank Dascoli called him safe. Then all hell broke loose. Before it was over, Campanella had been thumbed and Dascoli cleared the Dodger bench of everyone except manager Chuck Dressen and coach Jake Pitler. Brooklyn lost 4–3 and its lead was down to a half game.

After the game several Dodgers stood outside the umps' dressing room and yelled choice epithets at Dascoli. Preacher Roe actually kicked a hole in the door, though Robinson was the one who caught the blame for it in the press. Robinson, Campanella, and Roe drew fines. The next day in Philadelphia, the Dodgers lost again, and with the Giants idle again, the race was a dead heat.

On Saturday both teams won. On the season's final day, the Giants won their game up in Boston, while in Philadelphia the Phillies were manhandling the Dodger pitchers at Shibe Park. Brooklyn was down

8–5 in the top of the eighth, but the Dodgers miraculously rallied for three runs.

Don Newcombe was brought on, and he managed to shut the Phillies down until the twelfth inning, when they loaded the bases with two out. Eddie Waitkus drilled the ball toward center via the right side of second base, where Jackie Robinson made a diving catch, landing hard on his shoulder, to rob the Phils of the game-winning hit. Then all Robinson did was smack a homer deep into the left-field seats in the fourteenth inning off Robin Roberts to give the Bums a 9–8 lead. When Bud Podbielan finished Philly off in the bottom of the inning for the victory, the Dodgers had a tie with the Giants for the flag, forcing a three-game playoff for the pennant.

It was a beautiful Indian summer day at Ebbets Field on October 1, where the temperature was in the seventies for the opening game. Branca started for the Dodgers against Jim Hearn. Although Pafko homered in the third to give the Brooks a 1–0 lead, Thomson hit a two-run shot in the third off Branca, and Monte Irvin also hit a solo shot. It was all the scoring fans would see that afternoon. With the 3–1 victory, the Giants were a game up.

The following day Clem Labine shut out the Giants up at the Polo Grounds, 10–0. With Brooklyn coming off such a big day at the plate and with Newcombe going the next day, most everyone anticipated a Dodger victory.

The die-hards stayed out all night at the Polo Grounds to wait for tickets while Samuel Maxwell, from North Oxford Street in Williamsburg, who had been camped outside Ebbets Field waiting for World Series tickets since September 23, remained there. Maybe it was the notion that the Polo Grounds would be so packed that discouraged some people from coming, or maybe it was the cloudy weather, but the ballpark wasn't even full for the finale.

Maybe the Giant fans just despaired at having to see their hitters face Newcombe, but the Dodgers had to face Sal Maglie. At radios all over the city and beyond, everyone hung on every pitch during the fateful Dodger-Giant playoff finale.

The hated adversaries had split the first two games, and now the Dodgers had the best pitcher in the league hurling for them in the third and deciding game at the Polo Grounds. That Brooklyn had a commanding 4–1 lead in the ninth inning of the final game is merely prologue.

For baseball fans, there's no need to go over what happened at the end of the 1951 season. It was the most spectacular finish to a pennant race ever, with the only the titanic Yankees–Red Sox battle in 1978 culminating in a one-game playoff at Fenway Park and the Yankees–Red Sox finish in game 7 of the American League Championship Series in 2003 even close.

And so, inevitably, the bottom of the ninth inning: the Giants' Al Dark singled off Hodges's glove; then, when Hodges held Dark on, Don Mueller singled through the hole that Hodges left. After Monte Irvin hit a foul pop to Hodges for an out, Whitey Lockman stepped up and hit Newcombe's second pitch down the left-field line, driving in Dark and putting himself on second and sending Mueller to third. Hartung came in to run for Mueller, who had torn a tendon on his slide into the base. Dressen then went to the mound; he knew he had Erskine and Branca warming up, and coach Clyde Sukeforth had told him on the phone from the bullpen that Erskine had bounced some curves while throwing. And so Dressen went to number 13, Mr. Branca, and Bobby Thomson stepped up to bat.

The rest of the story is well known. Russ Hodges, the Giant announcer, will forever be remembered by that home run call, the seemingly endless repetition of that cadence, "The Giants win the pennant! The Giants win the pennant! The Giants. . . ."

The home run ball disappeared beneath a scrum in the left-field stands of the Polo Grounds, never again to be seen or brought forward.

Everyone has looked for reasons to try to explain what happened in 1951. Irving Rudd said that the Dodgers lost every one of the thirteen games that General MacArthur came to see that year.

Of the coin toss deciding where the playoff games would be played, Dodger fan Milt Strassberg said Charley Dressen wanted the first game against the Giants at Ebbets Field because the Cardinals got the jump on the Dodgers in the 1946 playoff when the first game was in St. Louis. "The Dodgers," says Milt, "were a tired team in 1946. They would have been better off having the first game at home and then having one train ride to St. Louis. As it was, they had to ride out there, where they lost, and ride back, and play again. But in 1951, it was a different story. They didn't have to travel, except uptown to the Polo Grounds. We should have given the Giants the first one up at the Polo Grounds and taken the last two at home."

Gloria Fennell and her husband, Frank, lived on Fifty-ninth Street then in Bay Ridge, Brooklyn. She would normally be able to tell whether or not the Dodgers had won an afternoon game just by looking at Frank's expression when he walked in the door in the evening. Fennell was unfailingly disconsolate after a loss and beaming after a win.

For the final game of the 1951 playoff, Frank Fennell was, by a turn of the fates, up in Montreal on business, for this, the most crucial game of all time, at least as far as a New York National League baseball fan was concerned. Unable to speak French, Fennell was desperately trying to find a broadcast account of the game as it was taking place. He finally found a Quebecois with a large portable radio whom he somehow prevailed upon through the use of international sign language, imploring, clasping hands in prayer, and simulating the swing of a bat while repeating "baseball." For this, he was able to overhear the game's final moments in French.

The French Canadian was willing to interpret but really didn't know baseball or English. In his effort to tell Fennell the Dodgers were winning, his description of the game's final moments, of Branca's final pitch, went like this: "Dodgers win, Dodgers win, oop, home ra, Dodgers loose."

At the Polo Grounds, in the stands behind home plate, Joyce Giordano witnessed the carnage. "It's lucky," she says, "that we didn't commit suicide right there."

Despair, depression, despondence, the bleakest of film noir, nothing, as the stories are told, nothing, could quite convey what it felt like to be a Dodger fan in Brooklyn that night. Among the more creative presentations was one "Dressen with No Head," a window display at Bud and Packy's Bar on Richards Street featuring a representation of the Dodger manager.

"In Brooklyn that night, on my way home from the Polo Grounds and on our way back from dinner, I passed eight or ten stuffed figures hanging from light poles and telephone poles," Duke Snider wrote, "figures wearing baseball shirts and Dodger caps. The baseball shirt in every case had a number on the back—13." [10]

As bad as being hung in effigy might have been, it beat Willie Moretti's fate. The high stakes gambler had put $125,000 on the Dodgers to win. When he didn't come up with the scratch, he was rubbed out gangland style in a hail of bullets at a Cliffside Park, New Jersey, restaurant.

For Walter O'Malley, who had envisioned the largesse of a World Series gate, insult was added to injury when he found out that part of the receipts from Ebbets Field's first and only postseason game— game 1 of the playoffs—had been stolen. When someone in an elevator said that he had lost a fortune on the playoffs, O'Malley lamented ruefully, "So did I."

For the fans, it was easy to understand why the teams hated each other so much. "The rivalry between the borough of Brooklyn and the borough of Manhattan was intense," said Red Barber. "It went over many years," continued Barber, referring to the antipathy between the two. "You could do a sociological story on that. All that Brooklyn had to compete with Manhattan was the Dodgers. Manhattan had the railroad stations, the tall buildings, the banks; Manhattan had Broadway, but Brooklyn had the Dodgers. When the Dodgers played the Giants, there was blood on the moon." [11]

CHAPTER ELEVEN

Waiting for Next Year

Nineteen hundred and fifty-two was the Dodgers' year to win. This was a team that would have Gil Hodges at first, Jackie at second, Pee Wee at short, Billy Cox at third; Andy Pafko, Duke Snider, and Carl Furillo in the outfield; and Campy behind the plate. Dressen's pitching staff was formidable, but a critical piece was missing with Don Newcombe off for a two-year military hitch. Aside from Branca, who changed his number from unlucky 13 to 12 and then hurt his arm in spring training, Dressen had Carl Erskine, Preacher Roe, and Billy Loes, a $21,000 bonus baby who never did become the brilliant pitcher of everyone's hopes.

Dressen would also start Ben Wade and spot start Clem Labine, whom he used more often in relief, but at that juncture in his career, Clem, who'd significantly improve later, would walk more men than he'd strike out. Johnny Rutherford would start eleven games for Dressen and finish 7–7, also appearing in relief; Chris Van Cuyk would start sixteen.

On May 1 Dressen debuted Joe Black, a twenty-eight-year-old rookie and Negro League veteran, whose arsenal included a scorching fastball and a quick curve, assets that Dressen would employ out of the Dodger bullpen, where

Black would win fourteen in relief and record fifteen saves en route to becoming Rookie of the Year.

Despite the pitching inconsistencies they'd be forced to weather, the Dodgers nuzzled their way into first place on June 1, with the Giants again their main competition. On June 19 Carl Erskine started a game against the Chicago Cubs and set them down in order for the first few innings. With the Dodgers ahead and rain threatening, Erskine was working hard to get five innings in so the game would become "official." He pitched too quickly to opposing pitcher Willie Ramsdell and gave up a walk. Finally, the anticipated cloudburst sent the players off the field. "We were a card-playing ball club," Erskine remembers, "and as soon as we got in the clubhouse, we started playing bridge." When the Dodgers came out after the delay, Erskine continued to mow down the Cubs batting order. He had a no-hitter going, and the only baserunner had been the knuckleballer Ramsdell.

"As the no-hitter began to take shape," Duke Snider wrote, "Happy Felton went into the Cubs' dressing room to get Willie, who had been lifted in the late innings, for his post-game TV show, 'Talk to the Stars.' Happy told Willie, 'Don't take off your uniform. If Erskine ends up with a no-hitter, I'm going to want you on my show as the Cubs' player of the game because there isn't anybody else.' Willie knew he might be the losing pitcher, but he might also pick up 50 dollars for being on Happy's show.

"With two outs in the ninth, Eddie Miksis was the Cubs' hitter. Happy was in the TV room with Willie watching the game on the TV monitor. Willie was hollering at it, 'All right Miksis, you dirty &!!**! You've popped up for me enough times, so don't go getting a hit now!'

"Carl took care of Miksis and got himself a no-hitter," said Snider, "and Willie got an extra $50 for drawing a walk."[1]

O'Malley rewarded Erskine with a check for $500. Charles Goren, the famed columnist on bridge, called Erskine and asked him to reconstruct one of the hands the Dodgers had played in the clubhouse and then used it as a subject in his newspaper column.

Some internationalism was part of the Ebbets Field scene that summer, when Alistair "Butch" Forbes became a Brooklyn celebrity, thanks to the promotional wizardry of Irving Rudd. Forbes, a twenty-two-year-old from Aberdeen, Scotland, and a Dodger fan via Armed Forces Radio, wanted to see what the Dodgers looked like, so he rifled off a letter to the team requesting a yearbook. He also enclosed a picture of himself in a kilt, expressing interest in having the pix passed along to some "Dodger Dames."

After Rudd contemplated the possibilities, he put calls through to Pan Am and the St. George Hotel. Before long, he had plenty of free ink flowing and a promotional phenomenon for varied vendors like the airline and the hotel, all of which were ready and willing to throw out the red carpet for the Scotsman.

When Butch landed at Idlewild (now Kennedy) Airport, he was, wrote Rudd, "surrounded by the Brooklyn Dodgers Sym-Phony and dozens of media types." Rudd worried about how Butch would handle everything, but aside from casting a too-fond eye at O'Malley's only daughter, Terri, the Scotsman quickly became a publicist's dream. "Finally," says Rudd, "we have 'Butch Forbes Day' at Ebbets Field, and it is dynamite. Butch is dressed up in his kilts and is driven around the ballpark in a jeep. Then he meets the Dodgers themselves and even takes some swings in the batting cage. Forbes hits one pitch so hard he nearly takes the pitcher's head off."[2]

Another big event was the visit on August 13 of King Faisal II, the seventeen-year-old king of Iraq and a cousin of Jordan's King Hussein, both members of the pro-Western Hashemite family and close friends, Faisal the senior of the two, both of them harboring ideas about eventually merging their respective realms to counter the emerging threat of militant pan-Arab nationalism.[3] King Faisal met Dressen and the Dodgers and—since, like Hussein, he had been educated in England at the Harrow School and had learned how to play cricket—he spoke proudly of his "googly ball." The king sat for a TV interview with Red Barber and also for one with Jackie Robinson for his radio show.

By the time Brooklyn went up to the Polo Grounds for the last series between the two teams in September, they were six games up on the Giants. The Giants took both ends of a doubleheader on a Saturday, but the Brooks came back to win behind Preacher Roe on Sunday, lengthening the lead again to five. The following day, amid beanballs in the front end of a day-night doubleheader, the Dodgers prevailed; when the Giants managed to take the second game, it hardly mattered. The Giants had not made significant headway in a series where they had to do exactly that.

The Dodgers clinched at Ebbets Field on September 24. Snider delivered the key blow to spur a come-from-behind win for right-hander John Rutherford, better known today as Doc Rutherford. "There ought to be a special wing in the Hall of Fame," the medical doctor wrote from Michigan in 1994, "to pitchers that did well in Ebbets Field. The weakest hitter could hit a ball out of the ballpark, at any point, at any time. There was, and is, no baseball stadium like it. The best place in the world for a ballgame."

Chuck Dressen surprised everyone by starting Joe Black in the first game of the Series at Ebbets Field against the Yankees. The start was only Black's third all season long. The strategy worked. He outpitched Allie Reynolds, holding the Yankees to six hits and two runs, getting solo home runs from Jackie and Pee Wee and a two-run shot from

Duke in the sixth inning to put the Dodgers on top in a 4–2 win. Gil McDougald also hit one out for the Yankees.

The next day was rainy, and the tarp was on the field virtually until game time. The Dodgers scored first against Vic Raschi in the bottom of the third, but the Yankees answered quickly with single runs in the top of the fourth and fifth off Erskine. When Erskine left in favor of Loes in the sixth inning the score was respectable, but Billy Martin then broke the game open with a three-run shot in the midst of a five-run inning. Kenny Lehman came to the mound in the eighth to mop up for the Dodgers, while Vic Raschi completed a three-hitter. The final was 7–1, Yankees.

When the teams went over to the Bronx, the Dodgers managed to win games 3 and 5, taking a three games to two advantage. The Dodgers went back to Brooklyn needing only one game to become champions.

With Raschi and Loes locked in a scoreless battle into the sixth inning of game 6, the Duke put the Dodgers ahead with a homer. But Berra answered with a solo shot as the first man up in the seventh. Then, with Gene Woodling on first with none out, Loes went into his motion to pitch to Irv Noren but the ball suddenly squirted up out of his hand and landed several feet behind the mound. Woodling went to second on the balk. Billy collected himself and fanned Noren, but Raschi followed with a vicious one-hopper back to the box that struck Loes on the knee and ricocheted off sideways, out of Hodges's reach into right field. Woodling scored easily. The two flukes turned out to be the difference in the game, since a Mantle solo shot in the eighth was matched by a second Snider blast, his fourth of the series. The 3–2 finale ruined what had been the Brooks' best opportunity to wrap up a fall classic.

After the game, Loes told the press that he lost the ground ball in the sun. Although the remark was the subject of derision, the low October sun that glared for a couple of minutes through the open portions of Ebbets Field's stands between the decks toward the latter part of the day was daunting. And besides that, Raschi's ground ball was hit hard.

So there would be a game 7. It would be the first game 7 in Brooklyn, ever.

Joe Black got the call for the Bums; the Yanks went with Eddie Lopat. Both would yield early to a parade of relievers as Dressen and Stengel pulled out all the stops. The Yankees got their first run with a Johnny Mize opposite-field hit that was six inches away from Billy Cox's glove. "And he was swinging at a pitch that was past him," said Dressen.

The Dodgers had the bases filled with one out in the fourth. But Allie Reynolds came in, and the Dodgers only got a single run on Hodges's line smash to Woodling. When the Yanks came to the plate in the fifth, Woodling homered, and the Dodgers battled back to tie again.

In the sixth inning, Mantle poled one to give the Yanks a 3–2 lead, and in the seventh the Yankees tallied again. The game's big moment came in the bottom half of the seventh, when the Dodgers loaded the bases with one out, with Snider and Robinson coming up. Stengel brought on lefty Bob Kuzava to pitch to the Duke, and Brooklyn fans were visualizing horsehide meeting asphalt on Bedford Avenue. Kuzava went to 3 and 2 on the Duke, who, with suspense at fever pitch, fouled off several more pitches. And then Kuzava threw a fastball low and away that Duke tried to take to left field. He popped it up to short.

It was up to Jackie. Kuzava again ran it out to a full count. With the runners going on the pitch, Robinson popped the ball up midway between first base and the pitcher's mound. First baseman Collins lost the ball in the sun. Seeing the confusion, Martin ran in at full speed and gloved the ball just over his shoe tops, immediately taking it out and holding it in his bare hand. He was worried about a collision that didn't come, saying later, "If you get knocked out, you'll squeeze the ball in your bare hand, while you won't squeeze the ball in your glove."[4]

Billy Martin saved the day and the World Series for the Yankees. It was Stengel's fourth consecutive championship and the fifteenth time the Yankees had won.

Thirty-three years later, the Reverend McKinney, leaning over the pulpit at the Unitarian Church in Brooklyn Heights, remembered events traced to that day.

"I cannot claim to have been a Brooklyn Dodgers fan," he said. "And I never had any interest in major league baseball until I came to Brooklyn. When I came to this church in September of 1952, the only feeling I had about the Dodgers was one of smug disdain. Dem Bums were really only something to joke about.

"It did not take me long, however, to realize that the Dodgers were no joking matter to the life of Brooklyn. And indeed were to add a significant dimension to my ministry here. Although I did not see the Dodgers play until the following June, I could not help being caught up that fall in the fever of one of those incredible subway series between the Yankees and Dodgers. The Dodgers fully expected to win the Series. But once again, they lost it, as they had so often before.

"Following that crucial seventh game in the 1952 series, in the church office, Gladys Hudson, the wonderful parish assistant, suggested I check up on Miss Ethel Stevens, although it had only been a few days since I had seen her. I, of course, had come to know who Miss Ethel Stevens was and to distinguish her from her sister, Elaine. Both were pillars of the church, retired schoolteachers with, however, decidedly different temperaments. When I asked Gladys why I should be in touch with Ethel Stevens, Gladys smiled, shrugged her shoulders, and said, 'I just think you should go see her. She must be feeling pretty low.' Inasmuch as people usually did what Gladys Hudson told them to do, and especially young new assistant ministers, I got on the BMT that afternoon and went out to Flatbush.

"I found Miss Stevens in bed, looking absolutely awful, and to my untrained eye, possibly dying. There was nothing wrong with her physically. She simply was in total disrepair. The Dodgers had lost. I had not seen anyone respond to an event of any kind in that way before in my life. I had no idea what to say or do. Fortunately, although at the time I could not begin to imagine how or why a baseball team should have that effect on a very sensible and usually quite jolly lady, I had the wit not to try to make light of this disaster. It was through Ethel Stevens, whom I came to know very well and love dearly, that I gradually came to understand and appreciate something of the meaning of the Dodgers in the life of Brooklyn.

"It was she who took me to my first game, on my birthday, an experience I will never forget. Although I now have no idea whom the Dodgers were playing that day, and I don't even remember who won, I knew, and not just because of all the cans that were flying all over the place, that I was experiencing something I had never known in Fenway Park, even in the near hysteria that sometimes surrounded Ted Williams. The very atmosphere of Ebbets Field was charged. With what I know not. It wasn't just partisan enthusiasm, although there certainly was plenty of that, or love of baseball; it was something far grander. More special. In that place, for that time, the crowd was empowered by something wonderful and strong. You were made proud of being in Brooklyn, being a great presence, regardless of who and what you individually were outside the walls of Ebbets Field. Ebbets Field, Flatbush, was without doubt the heart, perhaps the soul, of Brooklyn. And it beat with a mighty force. I know that Fenway Park in Boston never had any such role for Bostonians. And I doubt if many ballparks and teams have had such a profound place in the life of a people as did Dem Bums here in Brooklyn.

"It took quite a while before I recognized the full extent of Ethel Stevens's need of, love of, and identification with the Dodgers. Others of you may have responded differently, but she was the one for me to whom the Dodgers became reality. Surely, she wasn't embarrassed by her feelings, but I guess she just didn't want to expose them till she was sure enough of me. But gradually and finally I did discover that not only did she learn every single statistic of the Dodgers and every play in every game but she knew and remembered the birthday of every member of the Dodger team. And the wedding anniversaries of all who were married, and furthermore, the birthdays of all their children. When she learned that the teenaged son of one of the less famous, less-well-paid Dodgers had a serious drug problem—and how she found out about it, I never did discover—she came to me and asked if I would direct what in those days was a sizable amount of money through my discretionary fund for the payment of treatment for that boy, whom she in other ways had arranged to get into a clinic in Lexington, Kentucky. Again, she did not want the family to know who had done this or to feel beholden to her as an individual. I don't think she ever had met a single member of the Dodger team. She was always just a fan.

"I started out by saying that I had never been a Dodger fan, and that is true. And perhaps I didn't feel I had the right to. I didn't really belong in Brooklyn in those days—of course, a very, very different Brooklyn from the one we know today. I followed the baseball team very closely in those remaining five years of the Dodgers' life in Brooklyn, knowing I would have to make periodic sick calls on Ethel Stevens, among other reasons. And, also, coming to realize that the tone and temper of life in this borough, even among the determinably uninterested in baseball, was affected by how the Bums were doing."

The 1953 Brooklyn Dodger team is often mentioned as their best of the era. By season's end, Carl Furillo had managed to win the batting title with a .344 average, even with having to sit out the last few weeks of the season after someone stepped on his hand during a Dodger-Giant brawl after Furillo had gone after Durocher up at the Polo Grounds. Campy and the Duke each hit 42 homers; Hodges hit 32.

Erskine won twenty games; Clem Labine became the ace reliever for the Dodger starters. Brooklyn finished thirteen games ahead of Milwaukee. The club hadn't won two consecutive pennants since Ned Hanlon's day. In the meantime, there was the matter of the October classic, participation in which was beginning to feel like a rite of passage for Stengel and the Yankees, who had just taken their fifth straight pennant, and who were seeking add a fifth straight Series victory as well.

The Yankees won the first two games up at their stadium by scores of 9–5 and 4–2. Erskine only pitched the first inning of the first game, when the Yankess jumped out to a 4–0 lead after Billy Martin tripled with the bases loaded. Though the Dodgers tied it in the seventh, Collins hit a homer in the bottom of the inning to put the Yankees ahead for good. In the second game, Mickey Mantle's two-run homer in the eighth gave the Yankees the edge in a pitching duel between Eddie Lopat and Preacher Roe.

The two teams returned to Ebbets Field, where 35,270 jammed their way into the ballpark, paying an all-time high $10 for box seats and $7 for grandstand reserved. Given Erskine's earlier abbreviated appearance in game 1, Dressen brought him back to start game 3. And on this day, Erskine was magnificent, and so was the game. His fastball was on, and his big overhand curve broke like it was falling off a table. Unlike game 1, he was in total control, allowing no Yankee hits through four. And Vic Raschi was almost as good for the Yankees.

With the Yanks ahead 1–0 in the fifth, Robinson doubled off the right-field screen with one out. After Raschi balked him over to third base, Dressen called for the squeeze. Billy Cox executed it perfectly, and Jackie scored standing up. An inning later, Snider led off with a single and Hodges walked, but Campanella popped up a bunt and Furillo struck out. But then Jackie drove a single to left, and the Bums had a 2–1 lead.

The Yankees tied it in the eighth when Woodling drove in Bauer with a single. But then Campanella put a Vic Raschi fastball in the left-field seats despite playing with a damaged hand. The Dodgers were up 3–2, and all Erskine did, after striking out Mantle and Collins four times each that afternoon, was chalk up his thirteenth and fourteenth strikeouts in the ninth, retiring Don Bollweg and the ever-dangerous Mize, who were sent up as pinch hitters. Carl tied and then broke the 1929 Series record set by the Philadelphia Athletics' Howard Ehmke in the process.

"To tell you the truth, I didn't have the foggiest idea that I had broken any Series record for strikeouts," said Oisk. "I didn't know who held it . . . and now that I found out I'm not even sure that I can even spell that fellow's name right."

Billy Loes and Whitey Ford drew the starting assignments the next day, the pair having grown up within ten blocks of each other in Queens. With two on and a run in during the first inning, Duke Snider stepped in and lifted a deep fly to right. The ball hit the screen—and stayed there, tangled temporarily in the semicircular red, white, and blue bunting that had been draped on the screen in fair territory. When the ball finally came down, Duke was on second and the bases had been cleared. The Dodgers stayed firmly in command the rest of the day, with Loes needing a little help from Labine in the ninth in sewing up a 7–3 win, tying the Series at two games apiece.

Dressen named rookie Johnny Podres to face the Yanks in the fifth game. He'd pitched thirteen scoreless innings against the Bombers in preseason and in the mayor's Trophy Game. Stengel started Jim McDonald. The decisive blow came just after the Yankees had taken a 2–1 lead in the third and loaded the bases. The Dodger skipper called for Russ Meyer in relief, who'd been throwing practically all afternoon in the bullpen.

The first hitter was Mantle. And the Mad Monk's first pitch wound up in the upper stands in left center for a grand slam. It made the score 6–1, and it was 10–1 before a Brooklyn rally that made the game a bit more interesting. The Yankees won, 11–7.

Had they been playing in Yankee Stadium with its vast left-center field Death Valley, the Mick's Ebbets Field second-deck shot, in his words, "was just a pop-up that would have been caught."[5] As a result of the big hit, Mick was invited to appear on Happy Felton's postgame show.

"There was no television studio in those days," the Mick continued, "so they used to do the show from the back room of a bar across the street from Ebbets Field." Noting that there "was never anything quite like a Brooklyn Dodger fan," the young Mantle, whose Yankee team bus was routinely cursed and pelted with objects as it went through Brooklyn, understood "I had to walk through that bar, dressed in my Yankee uniform, right through all those Dodger fans who were angry because I had beaten their team with a grand slam. Let me tell you, I was never so scared in my life."[6]

The young slugger escaped unscathed, and the next day, the teams returned to the Bronx, where the Yankees wrapped it up. The final score was 4 to 3; Billy Martin won it in the bottom of the ninth with his twelfth Series hit. The Dodgers had to walk off the field, the single memorable image being that of Campy starting toward the dugout with his back turned to the plate, face flat in a somber yet resolved expression, Hank Bauer tallying the winning marker behind him as the Yankee dugout emptied. It was the Yankees' fifth consecutive world's championship.

A week later, with Dressen at his side, Walter O'Malley announced that the two had not reached a new agreement, since Charlie demanded a three-year contract, and that under those circumstances the skipper was out of a job. "The Brooklyn club has paid more managers not to manage than any other club," O'Malley said, explaining his commitment to one-year contracts. O'Malley seemed to take delight in playing a cat-and-mouse game with Dressen, initially saying he could still negotiate for a one-year deal and then ducking Charlie's phone calls until Dressen got the message that it was over. Afterward, when O'Malley barred the door, most Dodger fans wanted to see Reese get the job. O'Malley thought enough of Pee Wee to ask him to be player-manager, but Pee Wee was content to concentrate on playing for a few more years. After Fresco Thompson also passed on the job, O'Malley picked forty-two-year-old Walter Alston, then managing the Montreal Royals, to succeed Dressen. The *Daily News* asked in a headline, "Who He?"

Just as big a jolt later was the news that Red Barber, voice of the Dodgers, was moving up to Yankee Stadium. O'Malley had always regarded Red as an old Rickey holdover. When TV sponsor Gillette again assigned the non-negotiable fee of two hundred dollars a game for the World Series broadcasters, Red balked, insisting instead that Gillette negotiate before the games with his agent. When he told O'Malley of the development as a courtesy, O'Malley told Barber, "That's your problem." Barber kept his own counsel, but also made a decision in that moment that he wouldn't work for this man any longer. Shortly after the season, the Yankees announced that Barber would be joining Mel Allen on their broadcast team the following spring.[7]

The Dodgers drew 1,163,419 to Ebbets Field; none of the other National League teams even drew a million, but for one. Braves owner Lou Perini relished the 1,826,397 Milwaukee fans who turned out at Milwaukee's new County Stadium to see the franchise that Perini had moved from Boston during spring training of 1953, before the season started. There, the season before, the team had drawn a mere 281,278 to Braves Field. They had to move.

Discussion of territorial rights and the stasis of franchises on baseball's map had been a subject of congressional hearings a year earlier. Brooklyn congressman Emanuel Celler's House Judiciary Subcommittee on the Study of Monopoly Power had issued a report in 1952 on topics that included baseball's structure, the reserve rule, the farm system, and the game's historical development. Mention was made of the inadequacy of some cities, specifically St. Louis, Philadelphia, and Boston, to support two major league franchises, with most of the focus on St. Louis, where the Browns had been last in American League attendance for twenty-three of the past twenty-five years. As the committee's report noted, "on one occasion, Mr. Breadon of the Cardinals considered moving his club to Detroit, and on another Mr. Barnes considered moving the Browns to Los Angeles. A further proposal was to move the St. Louis Cardinals to Montreal."[8]

Special interest was shown by Republican congressman Patrick Hillings, who was from the Los Angeles area. He noted that certain civic groups in Los Angeles had petitioned for major league representation as far back as 1939, when, as the present Commissioner Ford Frick noted in his reply to the subcommittee, "after a discussion, after we had shown them balance sheets and the cost of operations, after we had shown them the attendance figures that were necessary to conduct major league baseball, the Pacific Coast League itself decided that they were not ready for the major league."[9] The report revealed that the Coast's population had risen 587 percent over forty-seven years, compared with a little less than 100 percent for the rest of the nation. J. G. Taylor Spink, *Sporting News* publisher, stated, "Such cities as Houston, Los Angeles, Hollywood and San Francisco have become major league cities in everything but baseball. Detroit has grown to the point where it could support another big league club. There is a possibility that metropolitan New York could afford another. In the minors, there are big cities tied down to the pace of smaller communities in the same league, but can do nothing about it, because they are restricted by regulations that apparently are inflexible."[10]

"There has been much testimony on the issue of whether or not the entire Pacific Coast League should be treated as a major league or whether individual clubs of the league should be given major league status," the report noted. "However," it continued, "the issue of territorial rights encompasses more than the problems of the Pacific Coast League. Former Commissioner Chandler suggested that Baltimore, Milwaukee, the Borough of Queens, Houston, San Francisco, Los Angeles, Dallas, and others, might very well make up a third major league. Mr. Wrigley testified that he was generally in agreement with the suggestion of Mr. Warren Giles, now president of the National League, regarding the possibility of certain cities, such as those listed by former Commissioner Chandler, becoming areas for major league franchises. Larry MacPhail went so far as to suggest that possibly six major leagues could be organized."[11]

Enthusiasm in Milwaukee surrounding the team's new franchise would prompt that city's league-leading attendance figures until 1959. O'Malley felt this gave him license to begin increasing his pressure for a new stadium to replace Ebbets Field. The publicly financed stadium in Milwaukee that was leased to the Braves had thousands of parking spaces surrounding the park; people took their cars to the games, providing the ball club with parking revenues, a matter that also caught O'Malley's attention. Ebbets Field had only seven hundred parking spaces; most people came to the park by subway or bus. Or they walked. On overflow nights when there wasn't enough parking, people would park by the Mobil station across the street, at one of the auto places on Empire Boulevard, or in someone's driveway for a buck.

O'Malley's interest in a new ballpark was present almost from the outset of his involvement with the Dodgers. In 1947, a time when, given housing shortages and the nation's priorities, any civic undertaking of this sort would have been totally impractical, he prevailed upon John Smith and Rickey to retain Emil Praeger of Madigan-Hyland, engineers in Long Island City, to explore the notion of a stadium initiative even though it was no more than a pipe dream. In 1952, O'Malley began a more public attempt to focus on a new ballpark to replace Ebbets Field, telling *Brooklyn Eagle* publisher Frank Schroth that he believed Brooklyn needed a stadium that could seat 52,000.

O'Malley noted an existing proposal that Moses's Triborough Bridge and Tunnel Authority supported to build a new convention center at 59th Street in Manhattan by Columbus Circle, and said he had ideas as to where a stadium should be located that would be closer to Wall Street than any of the three existing ballparks: Yankee Stadium, the Polo Grounds, or Ebbets Field. It would be a stadium with a movable roof that could be used for shows and conventions as well as for sports. He wanted to see an all-purpose, indoor-outdoor sports convention center and stadium in downtown Brooklyn, one that he could use for the Dodgers. To develop support for his idea of a domed stadium, he commissioned Norman Bel Geddes, a theatrical and industrial designer who had proposed the likes of a flying car and created a concept drawing of an airliner resembling a cruise ship. O'Malley wanted Bel Geddes to team with Praeger to render a design of how such a ballpark would look.

O'Malley referred to the ballpark he was envisioning as a "six-million-dollar improvement," a number that remained in his head from a cursory preliminary study that he had commissioned in 1948, after which he admitted that the idea was not economically feasible at the time. All of a sudden, in 1953, he became adamant, writing a letter to Robert Moses, telling him, "My problem is to get a new ball park—one well located and with ample parking accommodations. This is a must if we are to keep our franchise in Brooklyn." In a letter the same day addressed to his old benefactor George McLaughlin, O'Malley spoke about acquiring the land with the condemnation assistance of the government, employing Title 1 of the Federal Housing Act of 1949, noting that the ballpark would have to have an additional use in order to justify the capital—which for him meant the public—investment.

O'Malley then noted that the Battery Parking Garage, completed in 1950, was a Triborough Bridge and Tunnel Authority investment that cost, in his estimation, roughly $3,000 per car to build. Thus if a garage constructed in the "waste space" beneath a stadium in a downtown Brooklyn location could be used Monday through Friday to house 1,750 cars of public commuters, and were Triborough or another such government entity to finance at the same rate of $3,000 a car for a bond issue, it would come to $5,250,000. Since O'Malley valued the land and surrounding property owned at Ebbets Field at more than a million, he reasoned that a situation existed whereby he could have his six-million-dollar stadium in downtown Brooklyn. And unlike the publicly owned County Stadium in Milwaukee, O'Malley reiterated that he believed in private ownership. He wanted to build the ballpark with his own million dollars from the sale of Ebbets Field, say, while the city, state, or Triborough could underwrite the bonds for the other five million dollars.

Something about Walter O'Malley rubbed Robert Moses the wrong way.

The Dodger yearbook cover in 1954 would have a cartoon showing Willard Mullin's famed Brooklyn Bum holding a two-by-four, dreaming about a new ballpark.

If the Dodgers were pleased at getting Don Newcombe back after his service to Uncle Sam and expected the team to be even stronger as a result, so were the Giants pleased at another post–military stint roster repatriation: Willie Mays. With Willie making his basket catches up in the Polo Grounds, Mickey hitting prodigious homers up in the Bronx, and the Duke peppering Bedford Avenue, the city of New York was center-field rich in 1954.

Tussling with the Braves and the Giants, the Dodgers ascended to the league lead during the first week in June, but then were bounced out; it would be a summer they were beset with injuries, most notably a nagging one to Campanella's hand that would hobble his batting average.

Braves slugger Joe Adcock pushed his way into history at Ebbets Field on July 31, 1954, when he hit four home runs and a double, driving in seven runs in a 15–7 romp over the Dodgers. Richard Karlin was there. "Adcock was incredible. His fifth time up he hit a ball that went to the top of the left-field fence."

"He murdered us," Milt Strassberg said. "Killed us. One of those shots cleared the roof!" It was an Ebbets Field classic: ten home runs hit in one game. Adcock had broken his own bat the previous night, so he used a bat belonging to Charley White, Milwaukee's reserve catcher. Adcock's homers came off four pitchers—Newcombe, who was the loser in the 15–7 contest, and Erv Palica, Pete Wojey, and Johnny Podres.

The Dodgers took three from the Giants at Ebbets Field in August to close the gap to a half game, but by the time Labor Day rolled around, the Bums' challenge had melted away. On September 9, in a 10–1 Brooklyn romp over St. Louis, the Duke of Flatbush hit one of the oddest homers ever seen at Ebbets Field. Just out of reach of the leaping Wally Moon, the ball bounced off the right-center-field barrier and went directly into the adjacent center-field stands, right by the Bedford Avenue exit gate in the outfield. An umpire's question to Reese earlier that season determined the outcome of the play.

"I forget who the umpire was," said Reese at the time, "but early this season, one of 'em said, 'What's going to happen if a ball hits the screen on top of the right-field wall and goes into the stands [to the left of the screen]? What is it? A home run? A double? What?'

"I told him, 'I've been here a long time and I've never seen it happen yet.' But he said, 'Well, it's going to happen sooner or later. Better make a rule in case it hits the screen or the wall and bounces in.'

"It's our decision," continued Reese, "so I checked with Walt [Alston] and we decided it would be a home run. It's still not written down on the ground rule card. But it's official. We go over it every day."

The Duke thought the ball hit the tiny ledge that separates the screen from the bottom half of the wall and just bounced up and into the stands. "The idea," Reese said, "is to try and make ground rules as easy as you can for the umpires in order to keep out of arguments. But in this park, it's tough. They're always building something new. And that changes the ground rules.

"Like that dugout down in the bullpen. We just changed the rules on that. It used to be any ground ball hitting the facing of the bullpen out there was in play. But now it's two bases. Then there's the megaphones on top of the scoreboard. There's always something new.

"We go over everything every game. We start at the dugouts and go right around the park, down the foul lines, across the right-field screen, to the left-field stands, and back to home plate."

Pee Wee then made an observation that underscored the very reason for Ebbets Field's greatness.

"Most parks are pretty easy but not this one. This is the most complicated park by far."[12]

The Dodgers finished five games back of the Giants. It was a miraculous year for Mays; the Say Hey Kid hit 41 homers and led the league with a .345 average, with another Giant, Don Mueller, not far behind, hitting .342. Dusty Rhodes also had a career season as a part-time player and pinch-hitter, hitting .341 and blasting a homer in every 9.1 at-bats. The Giants went on to win the pennant in 1954, and for the first time in six years, the Yankees weren't in the World Series. The Giants, behind Mays, who made his miraculous over-the-shoulder catch of Vic Wertz's 440-foot drive to the Polo Grounds center-field warning track with two men on in the first game, swept the Cleveland Indians in four games; it was a sweet Series for Dusty Rhodes, with a walk-off homer, another homer, and seven RBI, and for Johnny Antonelli and Sal Maglie, too.

The Dodgers set a modern record for victories at the start of the 1955 season by winning their first ten games. A commemorative ashtray was given away at the gate to celebrate the feat. The record was broken on April 21, when the Dodgers handled Robin Roberts, perhaps the best pitcher in the league, driving in ten runs in the first four innings in the midst of 14–4 romp.

Shortly afterward, Brooklyn reeled off eleven more in a row. The Dodgers led the National League with a record of 22–2. On May 11, the day the Cubs finally put an end to the second streak, Brooklyn was already eight and a half games out in front.

On July 22, there was a birthday party and "Night" at the Flatbush ballyard for Pee Wee Reese. The response for Reese was warm and immediate. By 7 P.M., the word began "filtering in from the cops stationed along the subway route to Ebbets Field that big crowds were gathering," said Irving Rudd. The Franklin Avenue IRT and Eastern Parkway and Prospect Park stations on the BMT lines were jammed.

Rudd's promotional genius was evident in an arrangement where Pee Wee's daughter would pick one set of keys out of a fishbowl to match one of several automobiles that had been wheeled in.

"As each car is introduced and driven from Bedford Avenue— where, believe it or not, a cop threatened to give them a parking ticket— the crowd lets out a roar," wrote Rudd. "Now all seven cars are there and the fans are yelling like mad for Reese to get the Chrysler.

"I'm not yelling, but I'm hoping very hard as Barbara [Reese's daughter] starts working her key on the cars. Damned if the key doesn't work on the Chrysler or the Buick or the Dodge but winds up fitting the cheap Chevy. The crowd is pissed and, as one reporter says in the next day's paper, 'they breathed the biggest collective sigh of disappointment.'"[13]

One of the highlights during the game came in the middle of the fifth inning. The park's lights were doused, a couple of cakes were rolled out to home plate, and everyone in the ballpark was asked to light a match to sing "Happy Birthday" in honor of Pee Wee's thirty-seventh, which, to be official about it, was actually the next day. It was a stirring sight and an outpouring of love, to say the least. As the Duke of Flatbush remembers, "I got goose bumps and chills. Pee Wee had tears in his eyes."[14]

Rounding out the night properly, Reese was, in Rudd's words, "beating the kishkes out of the ball," rapping two doubles off Gene Conley that led to a couple of runs helping Brooklyn to an 8–4 victory.

The *World-Telegram* proclaimed "Ebbets Field Reese Park for a Night," topped with a headline that said "Happy Boitday, Pee Wee."

"The only downer I get out of the whole thing," Rudd added, "is an exchange with Roy Campanella. The next morning Campy grabs me at the ballpark. 'How come,' he said, 'you let li'l Barbara get the key to the Chevy and not the Imperial?'" Rudd told Campanella it was because Barbara picked the key to the Chevy and not the Imperial.

"Campy," says Rudd, "looks at me like I am the dumbest guy between here and Timbuktu. 'Shit, man,' he says, 'you could have arranged for her to pick the Imperial.'

"But that wouldn't be honest," said Rudd.

"'Honest?' shouts Campanella, disbelieving the words he hears. 'Now there's a Chrysler Imperial available to Pee Wee for nothin', and the Chevy is there for nothin', and you're giving me this honesty shit. Man, if the Chrysler is there and there is six feet of shit between me and it, I go to the Chrysler!"[15]

Meanwhile, the allusions and ruminations Walter O'Malley had made to and about a new stadium for the Dodgers were crystallizing in a disturbing way. Fans trying to buy tickets were suffering through poor customer service at the ballpark and often failed to get the best-available seats. O'Malley also made allusions to declining attendance even though Brooklyn was second in home attendance to Milwaukee and Brooklyn's numbers would increase slightly over the 1954 season. O'Malley also made assertions about Ebbets Field's inadequacies similar to the way George Steinbrenner maligned Yankee Stadium in the early 1990s, tending to make the general public a little less inclined to go out to the ballpark.

An effort was being made to de-market the ballpark while still touting Dodger baseball as a product, and in a runaway pennant race when the Dodgers had no competition, it was hardly a sensible way to stimulate attendance. Worse yet was the possibility that these things were purposefully done to orchestrate O'Malley's demands for a new ballpark. There was the unspoken matter, too, of shifting populations: a Caribbean influx into Brooklyn, and, indeed, into all of New York City, of Puerto Ricans and people from the other islands, seeking new opportunities—people, perhaps, that Walter O'Malley didn't envision coming out to the ballpark. This new migration—which didn't then affect the neighborhood chemistry in working-class Crown Heights in the immediate vicinity of Ebbets Field—came at time when economic opportunity was coincidentally diminishing, with New York City at the precipice of a general decline in manufacturing beginning to take place because of high costs, high taxes, and, eventually, changing technologies. Jobs would disappear that would also affect the entrenched working class in certain other industries, like shipping, partially because mob influence on the docks drove up costs, eventually sending marine traffic and jobs elsewhere.

Into the ever-changing face of New York City and the evolving drama of O'Malley's demands for a new ballpark came a mix of politicians and an important piece of legislation. First, there was the current mayor, Robert F. Wagner Jr., whose father, Robert Sr., had been a United States senator. The mayor's opinion of the lords of baseball was clouded by a childhood experience that he recalled in later years. His father had taken him up to Yankee Stadium with former governor Al Smith. At the end of the game, they went to the Ruppert Brewery on the Upper East Side and walked in to see Jake Ruppert, a former congressman and the Yankees owner, a baronial sort who once said, "Men get married either because they are lonely or in need of a housekeeper. I am neither."

"Jake," Governor Smith said, "meet young Bobby Wagner."

"So you were up at the Stadium," the old beer mogul said to the youngster. "How many was there?" he asked.

The question made a significant impression on the young Wagner. Ruppert didn't ask what the score was, or even who won. Wagner always cast a bilious eye on the altruism of baseball owners after that. And Ruppert may not even have been that mercenary: "Actors will count the house out on the stage," sportswriter Leonard Koppett remarked. "It's gauging acceptance." The analogy would extend to ballplayers as entertainers, and certainly to the franchise owners. But young Wagner didn't see it that way.

In 1955, as questions about a ballpark came to the fore, Wagner remembered Ruppert. And when Wagner reflected privately on the possible repercussions over the possible loss of the Dodgers, he said, "I don't get emotional about it."

If Wagner needed a fellow skeptic, he certainly had one in Robert Moses. Operating the Triborough Bridge and Tunnel Authority, Moses was riding the crest of unparalleled political power in New York City. He was a stubborn man. "Projects could get done if Moses was behind you," said Brooklyn deputy borough president John Hayes. "If he was against it, things would become difficult."

According to Moses biographer Robert Caro, the wealth of the institutional authorities Moses controlled enabled him "to make himself not only a political boss but a boss who in his particular bailiwick—public works—was able to exert a power that few political bosses in the more conventional mold would ever attain." [16]

Then there was the man who ran on Wagner's ticket in 1953, a man who had become New York's City Council president, a man who ran a clothing store, a man whose name was at the base of the Ebbets Field scoreboard: Abe Stark.

The major protagonist, of course, was Walter O'Malley, who shortly before the public tempest over the stadium exchanged correspondence with Moses that prompted him to stake out the issue, if not in the public's mind, at least in his own.

Both O'Malley and Robert Moses were preoccupied with the same piece of legislation. In 1949, the federal government passed the Federal Housing Act, supported by the Truman administration and shepherded through the United States Senate by Wagner Sr.—the mayor's father—

and Senator Robert Taft of Ohio. "The act was intended in part to eliminate urban slums," writes historian Neil Sullivan, "by providing a local agency with federal funds to purchase property in desolate areas and
either construct a public project or else sell the land to a private devel-
oper whose construction would conform to a larger 'public purpose,' a
phrase that eventually became crucial for the Dodgers."[17]

O'Malley envisioned his new Brooklyn stadium at the junction of
Atlantic and Flatbush avenues, at the terminus of the Long Island Railroad (LIRR) station. He wanted a stadium above the station. Robert
Caro describes the significance of the housing law that could help
achieve O'Malley's goal:

> Title I of the Housing Act of 1949 extended the power of eminent domain,
> traditionally used in America only for government-built projects, so dras-
> tically that governments could now condemn land and turn it over to in-
> dividuals—for them to build on it projects agreeable to the government.
> Under Title I, whole sections of cities could be condemned, their residents
> evicted, the buildings in which those residents had lived demolished—
> and the land turned over to private individuals. Here was power new in the
> annals of democracy. And in New York, that power would be exercised by
> Robert Moses. "In my opinion," urban expert Charles Abrams was to say,
> "under present redevelopment laws, Macy's could condemn Gimbels—if
> Robert Moses gave the word."[18]

On May 26, 1955, Walter O'Malley contacted Buckminster Fuller,
the architect, thinker, and inventor of the geodesic dome, a man who
was a comprehensive designer. O'Malley was no longer thinking of a retractable dome for the moment, but of a translucent permanent one.
O'Malley also noted that baseball companies lacked the wealth of large
corporations, and as such, price was an important element in his equation, with a million dollars as a financial cap for the translucent cap
over his field. Walter wanted to make it clear: he was an innovator. His
project—his baseball park—wouldn't be run-of-the-mill.

On August 10, 1955, O'Malley sent a letter to Robert Moses out-
lining the areas around Atlantic Avenue that he needed: railroad property, the area where the rundown Fort Greene Meat Market was located, as well as residential living quarters and an area near the junction
of Atlantic and Flatbush that would help alleviate the intersection's
traffic congestion, with the latter possibly unnecessary if the contours
of the stadium were pear-shaped rather than circular.[19]

Five days later, Moses wrote back, "I can only repeat what we have
told you verbally and in writing, namely, that a new ball field for the
Dodgers cannot be dressed up as a Title I project." He went on to rebuke
O'Malley, saying, "The natural question everyone will ask about the
Atlantic Avenue site as you describe it is: 'If you need only three

and a half acres of land, if it is indeed distressed property, if you have a million dollars in the bank, if you have railroad easements, if you really want to stay in Brooklyn, why don't you buy the property at a private sale?'

"We are for private enterprise," Moses continued, "and if you can sell the present Dodgers field and the other holdings around it and make a substantial profit, this is certainly your right. If you can sell the Dodgers' franchise to someone else and it is in your interest to do so, then in spite of any feeling I might have of the need for keeping as many attractions in Brooklyn as possible, I would have to agree that you would be strictly within your rights.

"On the other hand," Moses went on, "I don't see how you can have the nerve to indicate that you have not received a proper support from public officials involved. Every reasonable, practical and legal alternative we have suggested has been unsatisfactory to you."

Moses, for his part, would say at other times that he had no confidence in what he called "Walter O'Malley's scheme."

"We see no prospect of an alternate Dodger location in Brooklyn," Moses would add. "We think the Dodgers might be an incident in the acquisition of the Jamaica Track and its development, largely for housing for several income groups." [20]

Robert Moses, like Robert F. Wagner Jr., had no appreciation for baseball and the role it played in the life of Brooklyn. What's more, he didn't like O'Malley, and, truth be known, O'Malley thought as much of him.

Title I, as Neil Sullivan notes, applied not only in New York but anywhere else in the land, and if O'Malley had difficulty in one place, the law could be employed in another place that offered more favorable circumstances.

While the city's leaders in New York were looking at this legislation for a wider definition of a public purpose, so too were Mayor Norris Poulson and the City Council in Los Angeles, where alternative plans were being mulled over for Chavez Ravine, an area that had been considered a prime site for Title I housing. But the public housing idea had been assailed as socialistic earlier in the 1950s, and in the midst of the McCarthy era, such a taint was enough to get those plans scuttled.

The Pacific Coast League, meanwhile, had been given an "open" classification, somewhere between Triple A status and that of a third major league. Among the cities, San Francisco had gone the farthest in preparation for the day when a major league team might be attracted to the area, with voters passing a $5 million bond issue in November 1954 for the construction of a new stadium.

A day after receiving the Moses letter, O'Malley announced that the Dodgers would play seven games at Roosevelt Stadium in Jersey

City in 1956, one with each of the other National League clubs. Roosevelt Stadium, the former home of the Jersey City Giants in the International League, the place where Jackie Robinson had made his debut in organized baseball, had four thousand parking spaces compared with the seven hundred or so around Ebbets Field.

When the press questioned him, O'Malley smiled and said, "If you wish, you may call it Hurricane Dodger," an oblique reference to a storm of a different name passing through the Caribbean. "And the core of the hurricane," said O'Malley, "is now passing over Brooklyn."[21]

The time had come, O'Malley said, to prepare "for the day when Ebbets Field would have to be sold." O'Malley blamed his loss of patrons on the ballpark, ignoring trends that—with the exception of Milwaukee—largely affected both leagues, including the increase in the number of families with young children at home, the explosion of television, and a general decline in major league attendance from its postwar record-shattering levels. Another factor affecting attendance in 1955 was that the Dodgers' start left the other seven teams in the league in the dust, eliminating any semblance of a pennant race. O'Malley, for his part, said that if the Dodgers were to stay in Brooklyn, they would have to have a new stadium with parking, clear sightlines, and convenient restrooms. O'Malley himself had made pencil edits on a draft article that mentioned the Roman Colosseum and compared its importance in ancient Roman society to a new stadium's role in the current era.

"We intend to play most of our home games at Ebbets Field in 1956 and 1957," O'Malley said in his announcement. "But we'll have to have a new stadium built shortly thereafter."[22]

It became very easy afterward for Brooklyn fans to despise Walter O'Malley. His maneuver was designed to generate fear and uncertainty among the Faithful, and it did. Arthur Daley, the *Times* reporter that Casey Stengel referred to as "the guy with fucken [clip]board" in his conversations with other writers, characterized the concern in almost unthinkable terms: "If O'Malley can't resettle in Brooklyn, he'll move to Queens, or Long Island or—California. Hence this becomes a civic matter after all. That's why he sent up his trial balloon into the heart of Hurricane Dodger, a creature of his own making."[23]

Brooklyn borough president John Cashmore suggested that $50,000 be appropriated by the New York City Board of Estimate for an engineering study of the Atlantic-Flatbush site, and Mayor Wagner agreed to support that proposal at the next meeting of the board. Later the ante was upped to $100,000 for a study of 110 city blocks covering 480 acres. A new stadium was now one among many items proposed to the Board of Estimate. Commercial and residential redevelopment of substandard or unsanitary housing, traffic congestion, a new Long Island Railroad terminal, and relocation of the Fort Greene Meat Market were added to the list.

Soon afterward, an entirely unrelated item appeared in the *Times*, mentioning that the Los Angeles City Council had sanctioned "official reconnaissance into the matter of bringing big league baseball here." One of the council's first initiatives was to invite Walter O'Malley and Horace Stoneham to Los Angeles to discuss how the L.A. group might proceed.

On August 23, the New York City Board of Estimate approved a $100,000 appropriation to finance a survey of the area around Atlantic and Flatbush avenues in Brooklyn. Approval of the site for a ballpark was contingent on a favorable report by budget director Abraham Beame, who later that fall disclosed that the site of the Dodgers' proposed new home had a valuation of $6,368,000.

Meanwhile, on the field, the Dodgers hit a skein in August where they lost nine of thirteen. But later in the month they started to pick up the pace, prodded, in part, by nineteen-year-old Brooklyn native Sandy Koufax, a graduate of Lafayette High School who used to play basketball up at the Jewish Community House on Seventy-eighth Street and Bay Parkway, who took a sojourn to University of Cincinnati to play basketball before what any baseball fan would say was coming to his senses. Sandy struck out fourteen en route to a two-hit 7–0 victory over the Reds on August 28. Karl Spooner and Johnny Podres followed with winning efforts against St. Louis, and in the latter game Jackie Robinson stole home for the eighteenth time in his career on the front end of a triple steal. Newcombe followed the next day with his nineteenth win, besting second-place Milwaukee 8–6, with a little help from Snider's fortieth homer and Campanella's three RBI, including Roy's hundredth on the year. When Newk won his twentieth on September 5 in the first game of a doubleheader against the Phils, he also hit his seventh homer of the year, which set a National League record for pitchers. Fifteen thousand fans were turned away outside Ebbets Field's gates that day.

Three days later, the Dodgers achieved the earliest pennant-clinching in National League history, beating the Braves 10–2. When the Yankees edged out the Indians by three and a half games to win the American League flag, Pee Wee Reese said, "This may be my last World Series as a player. And I want to go out of this game beating the Yankees."

The 1955 World Series began on September 28 at Yankee Stadium, seemingly according to the usual script. The Dodgers sent Big Newk, plagued with a sore back and shoulder and suffering with a virus, against Whitey Ford. Despite heroics that included Jackie Robinson's eighth-inning steal of home, the Yanks prevailed 6–5. The Dodgers managed only five hits against Tommy Byrne's off-speed stuff in the second game in the course of losing 4–2, and went back to Ebbets Field down two games, prompting some of the Faithful to begin setting their sights on next year.

In the third game, Alston tried to shake things up by starting Johnny Podres, the young southpaw from the little upstate town of Witherbee. Podres was 9–10 on the year and turned twenty-three years old that day. Bob Turley, a right-hander who threw pellets but who was occasionally plagued by control problems, started for the Yankees. In the first inning, when Roy Campanella, 0 for 8 thus far in the Series, stepped in with Reese aboard on a walk, he lined the second pitch he saw from Bob Turley into the left-center-field seats, giving Brooklyn a 2–0 lead and a few glimmers of hope. The Yankees came back to tie the game, 2–2, when first baseman Moose Skowron knocked the ball out of Campanella's glove in a play at the plate in the top of the second, but the Dodgers promptly answered in their half, pushing across two more runs on bases-loaded walks. The Dodgers continued to chip away against Tom Morgan, Johnny Kucks, and Tom Sturdivant with deuces in the fourth and seventh, eventually winning 8–3. After the game, organist Gladys Goodding played "Happy Birthday to You" for Podres, with Johnny serenaded by a good portion of the multitude on hand.

On the very same day, in Princeton, New Jersey, Buckminster Fuller, who had been commissioned by O'Malley to come up with a stadium design, revealed plans for a circular domed stadium to replace Ebbets Field, ostensibly for the location at the junction of Atlantic and Flatbush avenues.

The Oisk finally got the call for game 4, an overcast day that seemed even cloudier in Brooklyn when Gil MacDougald, the second Yankee hitter, hit a solo shot into the seats in left center field. But the Dodgers came back with round-trippers from Campanella and Hodges off Don Larsen, and Kucks gave up a three-run shot to Snider en route to an 8–5 Dodger win, with Clem Labine finishing it off for the Dodgers. The victory helped lure back some of the cynics who had given up on the Bums when they were down two games.

Alston elected to go with young Roger Craig for the all-important fifth game while Stengel tapped Bob Grim, as 36,796 shoehorned their way into Brooklyn's bandbox. The Dodgers took a 2–0 lead in the second when Sandy Amoros's fly ball just cleared the right-field screen, scoring Hodges ahead of him. Snider added another homer that also just cleared the screen to make it 3–0 in the third. The Yankees strung together two singles and a walk to get a run back. The Duke struck again with a huge homer that took Bedford Avenue's measure in the fifth inning, making the score 4–1.

But Yankee power was also was in evidence: in the seventh, pinch-hitter Bob Cerv swatted a high, hanging curve into the lower stands in left field. In the eighth, Labine attempted to throw a high fastball by Yogi Berra, who hit it out. Suddenly the score was 4–3. But the Dodgers got an insurance run in the eighth with a couple of singles sandwiched around a sacrifice, and when Labine put the lid on the Yanks in the ninth, the Dodgers had a 5–3 victory and a 3–2 lead in the Series.

They had swept the Yankees at dear old Ebbets Field.

It was the first time in Series history that a team had won three games after losing the first two.

Euphoria was short-lived. It became clear right away in game 6 that there indeed would be a game 7. For in the first inning, with Karl Spooner starting for the Dodgers in place of an ailing Newcombe, the Yankees scored five runs, capped by a three-run homer from Skowron, which would certainly be more than enough for their pitcher Whitey Ford. Ford wound up scattering four hits and allowing a single run.

And so arrived the seventh game, October 4, 1955, a day destined for the ages in Brooklyn history. Ironically, the event did not take place at Ebbets Field, where the Dodgers got on a bus that morning, but it signaled the culmination of all that Ebbets Field had been about since Charley Ebbets turned the first spade of dirt.

The pitcher for the Dodgers would again be young Johnny Podres. For the Yankees, Stengel called on veteran Tommy Byrne. Jackie Robinson, who had lit a fire under the Dodgers, was out with a strained Achilles tendon; Snider would be playing a day after he had popped something in his knee.

All the way over to Yankee Stadium on the Dodger bus, Podres had said one thing: "Just get me one run. That's all I'm going to need today. Just one run." And he got that run in the fourth inning, when Hodges singled Campanella home from third base. Gil earned another RBI in the sixth when, batting with the bases loaded, he sent a sacrifice fly to right-center that allowed Pee Wee Reese to score.

Martin led off the Yankee sixth with a walk. McDougald beat out a bunt. No outs, two on, and the batter was Berra.

Podres didn't want to give Berra anything he could pull. His first pitch was high and inside to Yogi. The young southpaw came back with another fastball. "I threw a pitch that was high out over the plate, a fastball that had something on it, and he didn't get around too good on the ball, and he sliced it to left field," said Podres. Initially, Podres thought it would be an easy fly ball. But as the ball started to curve away toward the left-field corner, he quickly deduced it was trouble and wondered if left-fielder Sandy Amoros, who had just entered the game, could get to it. Amoros, playing in left-center, began a 150-foot sprint toward the vicinity of the ball, seeming to have little chance.

McDougald, aware he represented the tying run, was off at the crack of the bat, intent on scoring all the way from first. Billy Martin went halfway from second toward third and paused to see if the ball would be caught. Pee Wee Reese ran from his position at shortstop over to the edge of the outfield grass near third to be in position to relay a throw to third or home. At the last moment, as Amoros neared the foul line and the low fence with his right, gloved hand, extended, he planted his right foot, made the catch, used his left heel to break his momentum, turned, and made a perfect peg to Reese. McDougald, a step past second, hurriedly did an about face.

The next race was between McDougald and the ball. Reese turned and made a perfect, letter-high relay to Hodges back at first base, and a sliding McDougald was doubled up. The Dodger fans in the Bronx crowd went wild. If Jim Gilliam, a right-handed thrower with the glove on his left hand, had still been in left field, chances are the ball never would have been caught.

The Yankees threatened again in the eighth when Rizzuto opened with a single to short left-center field. With one out, McDougald rapped a hot single off Don Hoak's shoulder at third base, but with men on first and second, Podres kept his composure to get Berra on a short fly to right, and then struck Bauer out, swinging. When the Yankees came to bat in the ninth, Podres was still on the mound. After two quick outs, Elston Howard worked Podres to a 2–2 count, and then fouled off five pitches before Podres shook off a sign and offered an offspeed changeup. Howard stroked a slow roller to Reese. Pee Wee came up with the ball and threw low and wide to the left of the bag, but Hodges stretched and gloved the ball a few inches above the ground. At 3:44 P.M. on that Tuesday afternoon, October 4, 1955, the Brooklyn Dodgers began celebrating their world championship.

Podres jumped high off the skin of the mound, pumping his arms over his head before Campanella and Hoak ran over to envelop him. A score of Dodger fans spilled out of the stands as the players hustled to get off the field amid the photographers and those who had managed to get through the cordon of ushers and special cops.

"I can't imagine anyone living in Brooklyn then who does not remember that day," said the Reverend McKinney in his 1985 sermon. "Fortunately, I was here at the church in the Heights then, and could rush out to Borough Hall when the last Yankee, Elston Howard, was called out and be there at the Dodgers building and personally experience some of that incredible joy, gladness and ecstasy that was this city's on that day. It wasn't pandemonium in those first moments. There was no chaos; there was just a sense of life being absolutely grand and wanting to share this sense of wonder and fulfillment with everybody who was in Brooklyn.

"There has been no moment like that since."

In the clubhouse at Yankee Stadium, some of the old-timers like Reese and Robinson were initially solemn, realizing in those first minutes the precious nature of the moment, that the deed was finally done. "I was sitting around in there trying to drink champagne and celebrate," said twenty-four-year-old rookie pitcher Roger Craig, "and I'm looking at Gil Hodges and Jackie Robinson and Pee Wee Reese and Carl Erskine, and they're sitting in their lockers with tears in their eyes. They were crying. They were just so overcome with emotion from getting to the World Series so many times and finally winning it." Before long, all gave way to the sheer delight. Those many years of waiting and striving had finally culminated in a victory against the Yankees.

It would be the finest day in the history of the Brooklyn Dodgers.

Nor was the celebration limited to Brooklyn. In Manhattan, on Wall Street, where business had slowed to a trickle at game time, confetti and ticker tape were dumped from office windows. Shredded and torn paper swirled in the air around the formidable McKim, Mead, and White–designed New York Municipal Building across from City Hall. On the east side of Manhattan, telephone service was interrupted by the biggest flood of calls since V-J Day, with several exchanges overloaded.

Even so, it was Brooklyn that altogether rang with joy, from Court Street where the deluge of paper was similar, to the many motorcades with horns blaring along Flatbush Avenue and Fulton Street, and down Joralemon, Remsen, and Court streets and through the other major streets of the borough. Factory whistles blew, and on the brick and brownstone stoops, people who had been huddled in front of televisions moments before exited to bang on pots and pans and yell across the street to their neighbors.

Frank Prendergast, then a seventeen-year-old zinging back the arm of an adding machine for the Bank of Manhattan down by the A&S department store, remembered the spontaneous parade that broke out on Fulton Street. When he was finally able to break free from his office an hour later, he saw a friend in the passing motorcade. "I looked two cars down, and there was Billy Walsh from the neighborhood—Bay Ridge—so I hopped in."

William Liston liberated the B'KLYN sign off the Yankee Stadium auxiliary scoreboard, and, with Joyce Giordano, later strapped it on the front of a Pontiac, riding prominently in the motorcade that night.

Around the borough, homemade signs were strung up everywhere, replacing the effigies that had hung from the light poles in years past: "Supermen of the World!" "We Dood It!" "This Is Next Year!" At the *Daily News* they were composing the next day's headline, WHO'S A BUM!, atop Leo O'Melia's drawing of a scruffy, round-faced, bulbous-nosed, single-toothed, arch-eyed bum bellowing a scream of joy.

"We went back on the team bus to the parking lot at Ebbets Field, then got in our cars," Podres remembered years later. "We didn't go back in the ballpark."

"I was a guest on *The Steve Allen Show* that night," Podres told author Peter Golenbock, "and after I came back from that, there was a hell of a party at the Hotel Bossert in Brooklyn. I can remember that the champagne was really flowing. All you had to do was hold out your glass, and somebody would be there to fill it up. The streets were filled with people, and every so often I would go out and wave to them, then go back inside again where everyone came over, shook my hand, patted me on the back, poured me champagne. I doubt if there had ever been a night like that one in Brooklyn. There was one old guy who told me over and over that he had been waiting for this since 1916. Thirty-nine years. I can't imagine waiting thirty-nine years for anything. I really don't know how late that party went, or if it ended at all."[24]

Next year was finally here.

CHAPTER TWELVE

Over the Wall

As Ebbets Field went into its final seasons, fans were well aware of how unique and special the ballpark was. Yes, it had poles obstructing the views, as did every other ballpark in the major leagues, and the many people jamming into its seats were crammed too intimately for real comfort during big games. And the right-field wall wasn't the only thing that knit Ebbets Field to Brooklyn's consciousness, running, as it did, along Bedford Avenue, a public thoroughfare whose name doubled as a virtual synonym for a home-run ball. Ebbets Field was a sentiment, peace of mind and a *piece* of mind, a sense of place, who you were. Nothing that could be re-created with a corporate name.

Twenty years after Sam Winchell and his friends waited for balls to be hit over the fence, a new generation of kids followed in their footsteps. "I lived on Carroll between Brooklyn and Kingston," said Paul Bresnick, who grew up during the 1950s. "During particularly raucous games, I was able to hear the cheers at my house. We used to drive our bikes down to the gas station across the street. We'd hang around there and scramble under cars for home runs."

Paul Pepe and his younger brother Phil, who eventually became a sports columnist with the *World Telegram* and later the *Daily News,* were in the Ebbets Field crowd the day when Ed Head threw his no-hitter back in 1946. "We were about 45 minutes by subway from Gravesend to Ebbets Field," said Paul, "and at the ages of ten and eight, we would, with no compunction and our parents' approval, board the subway and go to Dodger games.

"Ebbets Field was old even then, but it was 'our' home park, and was set in the midst of teeming streets, trolley cars, subway lines, and thousands of people who constantly milled about. It was a fascinating, exciting time for two young boys who loved baseball. The thing that stands out in my mind is how safe we felt on the streets surrounding the ballpark and, on the subways, getting there and back. New York was a much different place in those days."

For more than four decades, Ebbets Field seemed an inveterate part of "becoming" in Brooklyn life. Some of today's newer ballparks, like Camden Yards, with the stands behind the right-field fence melding into Eutaw Street and the brick warehouse behind it, have created pedestrian malls inside the ballpark. "Camden Yards is a great place to see a ballgame," said Seth Maiman, a lifelong fan. "It's a food court," he added, "where there happens to be baseball going on."

That's not the way Brooklyn Dodger fans felt about Ebbets Field and what went on within it, nor how they regarded the team that played inside it. Baseball was primary; everything else was ancillary. "When the Dodgers were on TV, my husband Joe wouldn't let the kids in the living room," recalls Ruth Lauro of Sheepshead Bay. "He'd be concentrating on the game—he took it that seriously—and he didn't want the distraction of the kids running around."

Dr. Irving Kurland, an obstetrician who lived on President Street's Doctor's Row, had his office on the bottom floor of his family's row house. "When there was a game on," remembers his son, Norman, "he'd often run upstairs between patients to watch a couple of pitches."

People who were at the game—the bus drivers and firemen, the dock wallopers, the cops and carpenters, the sanitation men and butchers, the delivery men in the Boar's Head truck, or from Dugan's or Ebinger's—they came to watch the game; they came to root. This was a blue-collar team: you didn't go home in the seventh inning, or you wouldn't be getting your money's worth. This wasn't U.S. Steel you were rooting for. These weren't tickets you could write off, literally or figuratively.

The inexorable political parade continued, the smoke and mirrors game that ultimately resulted in nothing—literally nothing—for the people of Brooklyn. On February 5, 1956, Mayor Wagner sent a bill to the state legislature to establish a Brooklyn Sports Center Authority. The Authority would consist of three "prominent" citizens, serving without pay, who would be empowered to issue $30 million in bonds for redevelopment of the five hundred acres surrounding the Long Island Railroad terminal.

While the players reported to spring training for the 1956 season, the press was rife with reports about new ballparks for New York's National League teams. Manhattan borough president Hulan Jack had a fantasy for an outlandish 110,000-seat baseball park to be built on stilts over the New York City rail yards in the West Sixties. Stoneham approved the plan in April, obviously not realizing that purchasing tickets in advance would never be necessary for fans at such a cavernous stadium, thus cutting down the possibility of properly developing a ball club's ticket office advance sale and the fan excitement that comes with holding a hot ticket. Borough president Jack reported that the project would be privately financed; Lawyers Mortgage and Title was reportedly ready to handle the financing.

On April 17, a crowd of 24,236 showed up for the Ebbets Field opener to see the Dodgers face the Phillies and to see the championship banner float to the top of the Ebbets Field flagpole. Johnny Podres, now in navy togs, was there, and swapped his sailor cap for Roy Campanella's Brooklyn cap.

Eighteen Dodgers from the World Series squad of the previous year received their rings, and Commissioner Frick gave Campanella his third MVP Award. Even though the Dodgers lost to the Phillies, the fans, basking in celebration of the previous year's victory, left the ballpark in a good mood.

On April 19, 1956, the first of Brooklyn's seven "home" games scheduled for Jersey City took place with the Dodgers and Phils squaring off in the Garden State's first major league game. It was a bitter day in more ways than one; an icy-cold wind set the stage for Brooklyn's Jersey debut, with the crowd of 12,214—mostly Giant fans—razzing the supposedly "hometown" Dodgers. Eddie Fisher sang the national anthem, and the Bums defeated the Phils, 5–4. Giving up seven home games for "Joisey" was neither player nor fan preference.

Governor Averill Harriman also said the same day that he intended to sign the bill that would authorize the Atlantic Avenue stadium project. Two days later, he traveled from Albany to do the honors, bragging that this was "the first time a Governor ever came to the great borough of Brooklyn to sign a bill." The seven-pen signing ceremony made the front page of the *Times* above the fold, picturing a pensive O'Malley, a happy borough president Cashmore, a brimming City Council majority leader Sharkey, and a solemn Moses looking on as the governor fondled the bill. Alluding to Wagner, Cashmore, and the numerous community groups, Harriman said, "Approval of the measure may enable them to bring to fruition the envisioned in this vast undertaking. If it can be carried out," he added, "the sports center should be of great value to the people of the city as a whole." An editorial in the *Times* noted the "happiness and relief in Brooklyn," while cautioning that "the hardest work is still ahead." According to the paper, "one of the features proposed for the new Dodger ballpark is a sliding glass dome that could be closed over the diamond to keep out rain."

Stadium talk was now giving fans reason to straddle the sports pages and the news pages. Across the bridge, in Manhattan, Borough President Jack reported in the middle of May 1956 that plans for the 110,000-seat stadium for the Giants over the New York Central Railroad tracks on the West Side had been "realized," and said Stoneham had written a letter of intent to the stadium committee. Eight days later, after a report of a "rift" between Mayor Wagner and Borough President Jack, the pair met with Stoneham, with Wagner emerging from the meeting saying he was "excited" over the plans. The mayor also added that the city had to await cost estimates and approval by the New York Central Railroad before presenting the plans to the Planning Commission. Before the end of the month, reports surfaced that several companies were interested in underwriting the mortgage. And reports also surfaced that the stadium was being opposed by a citizens' group. Shortly afterward, all talk of a West Side stadium drifted into thin air.[1]

On July 22 it was revealed that several prominent persons had rejected appointment to the Brooklyn Sports Center Authority, a sure sign that none of them wanted to end up as scapegoats if the efforts failed. Two days later, Wagner appointed and swore in Charles J. Mylod, a well-known Brooklyn real estate man who was vice president of the Real Estate Board of New York, as chairman of the Authority. He also swore in Robert E. Blum, vice president of the Abraham & Straus department store, and Chester A. Allen, president of Kings County Trust Company, as the other unsalaried members.

Wagner also revealed new plans for the replacement of Ebbets Field. The plans were not for a stadium above the LIRR terminal at Atlantic and Flatbush, but across Flatbush Avenue on the other side of the street. With one of two parking garages added at the southeast end of the proposed ballpark site, it took up virtually the entire triangle bordered by Fourth Avenue, Flatbush Avenue, and Prospect Place (running into Warren Street). Borough President Cashmore reported that of the two adjacent sites, Moses, O'Malley, and the Long Island Railroad officials all preferred the other side of Atlantic and Flatbush avenues, where the Long Island Railroad terminal and the Fort Greene Meat Market were.

The stadium as now envisioned would cost between $7 million and $9 million, a price tag that in those days made the proposition dubious at best. "As one reviews the objections posed by various critics the outlines of a dilemma emerge," said Neil Sullivan. "Moses claimed to support the bill, but routinely cautioned against excessively elaborate plans. His warning specifically was that the more complex the redevelopment plans, the more difficult they would be to effect, especially in terms of selling the bonds. On the other hand, a criticism clearly expressed by many, and implied by the *Times* editorials, was that the entire Sports Center Authority needed to be more than an elaborate ruse to construct a new stadium for the Dodgers. As the call for a large public purpose grew louder it became increasingly difficult to meet Moses's objections. Thus, the new stadium had to be a minor element in a design whose grandiosity ignored financial realities."[2]

A domed stadium—as grandiose conceptually as that was—could never be a minor element, and as the summer wore on, O'Malley continued to alternately cajole and threaten the city, while Giants owner Horace Stoneham said virtually nothing. His team, which Durocher left at the conclusion of the 1955 season, had finished third, eighteen and a half games back, and was now being run by Bill Rigney. It was flat last as it rolled into the summer of 1956.

The Giants, whose attendance had dropped from 1,115,067 in 1954 to 824,112 in 1955, were headed down the path trundled by the weakest franchises in the league. To add to the club's difficulties, in January the Football Giants had announced that they had decided to move from the Polo Grounds to Yankee Stadium, depriving Stoneham of a $75,000 annual rental.

The Giants' farm club in Minneapolis would soon have a new municipal stadium, giving strength to rumors that Stoneham was considering moving to Minnesota. But Horace denied it, stating, "the future of the Giants is in New York. In the Polo Grounds, perhaps in Yankee Stadium at some time, but in New York."

The baseball season, meanwhile, was turning out to be one of the most exciting ones in years. Carl Erskine, after starting the 1956 campaign with arm trouble, became the first Dodger ever to pitch two no-hitters when, on May 12, he held the Giants to two walks in a 3–0 victory before 24,586 at Ebbets Field. He was helped when Jackie Robinson made a catch on Willie Mays's screaming low liner and Carl Furillo pulled down Daryl Spencer's long drive to right center while running at top speed, both plays in the fourth inning.

"I don't think I had very overpowering stuff," Carl said. "Matter of fact, I didn't have overpowering stuff in either of my no-hitters. Just a good fastball and my control was all right. I used more change-up pitches today than last time."

The Dodgers also sold Billy Loes to the Baltimore Orioles during that eventful month, and to replace him they picked up Sal Maglie from Cleveland for the waiver price of $1. When Maglie arrived in Brooklyn, clubhouse man John Griffin, whose nickname was "The Senator," put Maglie's locker next to the that of the young rookie Don Drysdale, and almost immediately "the Barber" began imparting some of his acumen about brushing back hitters. Drysdale was so green that a day before a doubleheader where he and Maglie were slated to start, he asked Maglie if he was pitching "the long one or the short one," a reference to a minor league nightcap that would only go seven innings.

"Kid," Maglie said, "up here both games of a doubleheader go nine."[3]

Milwaukee, Brooklyn, and Cincinnati turned out to be the major contenders in the National League pennant race, with the overenthusiastic Cincinnati fans stuffing the ballot boxes to get as many Reds' starting players as possible for the All-Star game. In the latter part of July the Dodgers skidded, dropping six games behind league-leading Milwaukee. But then they put together an eight-game winning streak, with Newcombe, Erskine, and Maglie each winning a pair to close the gap to two.

Ike accepted the Republican nomination for a second term on August 23, the same night that Newk, on as meteoric a pace as any pitcher since Dizzy Dean, won his twentieth game. At the beginning of September, the Braves were clinging to a small lead, the Dodgers were holding onto second place, and the Reds were right behind them. Unlike the year before, it was a great pennant race, as exciting as any of the knockdown, drag-out Giant-Dodger or Dodger-Cardinal battles.

True to their traditionally great rivalry, the Giants put a scare into Brooklyn by taking a doubleheader the day before Labor Day, dropping the Bums three behind Milwaukee. But a week later the Braves hit a five-day skid, setting the stage for the showdown at Ebbets Field.

It began the night of September 11, with the Braves a game up, and Milwaukee manager Fred Haney going with Dodger-killer Bob Buhl against Sal Maglie. By moving the ball in and out, Maglie proved the master, even though he gave up blasts to Eddie Mathews and Joe Adcock. The Barber helped himself with the bat, too, driving in two runs with a bases-jammed single in the fourth inning, leading to a 5–2 victory that put the team in a tie for first place.

And then, with five games left in the season and Milwaukee up a game, the thirty-nine-year-old Maglie pitched the greatest game of his career. On this night Maglie mowed down the visiting Phillies inning after inning. Going into the ninth, Maglie had only allowed two walks and the Brooks were up 5–0. The Faithful were on their feet, urging the Barber on with every pitch.

Frankie Baumholtz led off the inning with a foul pop that Campy pulled in on the steps of the Brooklyn dugout. Then Harvey Haddix struck out on three pitches. One of Sal's pitches to the next hitter, Richie Ashburn, struck Ashburn on the foot, so he was awarded first. But Maglie coaxed Marv Blaylock into grounding out to Jim Gilliam, ending the game and giving him the first no-hitter of his career. Campy and young Drysdale carried the Barber off the field to the clubhouse.

On the last Saturday of the season, the Dodgers, a half game behind the Braves, played a doubleheader against the Pirates at Ebbets Field. In the first game, Maglie was paired against Bob Friend. After giving up a two-run homer to Frank Thomas in the first, Maglie shut the Pirates out while Amoros, Furillo, and Hodges all belted homers en route to a 6–2 Brooklyn victory.

Walt Alston pulled Clem Labine out of the bullpen to start the nightcap. It would feature one of the more evocative fan demonstrations in Ebbets Field annals. The Faithful almost caused a forfeit. In the fifth, with Brooklyn ahead, 1–0, Campanella reached first on a scratch single. Labine bunted in front of the plate and catcher Hank Foiles threw to second hoping for the force. The high throw pulled shortstop Dick Groat off the bag, and before he came down Campy slid in. Umpire Vic Delmore, to the astonishment of everyone in the park, called Campy out. "The fans went into an uproar over the umpire's decision," remembered Richard Karlin, who was at the ballpark. "Campanella and Alston were out there arguing, and a section of fans started waving handkerchiefs. Then everyone picked up on it. Even after Alston and Campanella stopped arguing, the yelling continued into the next inning, fans booing and throwing paper on the field. Finally, the PA announcer came on and said the game could be forfeited."

Tex Rickards had been directed by umpire crew chief Jocko Conlan to make the announcement. The crowd didn't stop booing until Gil Hodges tripled home two runs in the bottom of the sixth. Clem Labine pitched his first complete game in a year.

That same evening the Cards beat the Braves, 2–1, in twelve innings, thanks to Bobby Del Greco's spectacular catches in center field for St. Louis. The win gave Brooklyn at least a tie for the pennant, and at the end of the day's events they stood a game ahead of Milwaukee with a game left to play.

Newcombe got the call for the finale. A crowd of 31,893 turned out. Brooklyn's two victories the day before had eliminated the Reds, leaving only the Braves. The Duke took Pittsburgh starter Vernon Law downtown in the first inning with his forty-second homer, a blast into the center-field seats with Gilliam and Reese aboard. But Roberto Clemente singled home two runs a couple of innings later. Then Jackie homered in the bottom of the third, and in the fifth, Newcombe doubled, advanced to third on an out, and scored on Reese's sacrifice fly. But the big blow was again by the Duke, another Bedford Avenue blast, his forty-third going over the right-field wall. Sandy Amoros added another four-bagger in the seventh to make the score 7–2. But then Bill Virdon of the Pirates doubled with the bases loaded to drive in three runs in the seventh, and it took a circus catch by Snider to get the Dodgers back in the dugout.

Newcombe served a gopher ball to Lee Walls with one out in the eighth, cutting the Dodger lead to one. Alston brought on Bessent, but Groat singled and Robinson booted a double-play ball. But then Bessent settled down and got the two outs he needed, including a big strikeout of Dale Long to end the inning. In the bottom of the eighth, Sandy Amoros homered again, this time off Friend, who had come on to pitch in the seventh. Brooklyn had an 8–6 lead.

In the top of the ninth Clemente led off with a clean single. But then Virdon hit a hot shot right at Gilliam, and Jim converted it into a double play. Finally Foiles struck out swinging to give the Dodgers the flag.

The crowd spilled out of all corners of the stands, catching Bessent and most of his mates at the first base foul line on the way to the Dodger dugout. Inside the clubhouse, the scene was as high-spirited as you might expect: Newcombe, in pink shorts with a towel around his shoulders, put on an extraordinary dance for a battery of newsreel cameras. Publicly, Brooklynites hearkened to the victory with "the pleased aplomb befitting seasoned champions" discussing "the moments of tension as though they never doubted the outcome," according to the *Times.* "Even along Bedford Avenue, just a few minutes' walk from Ebbets Field, the thousands of fans walked as though their feet were on the ground, looking happy, but hardly zany. . . . A tour of several miles of Brooklyn streets during and after the game revealed no examples of dancing in the streets that were not easily traceable to photographers or the proximity of a bar.

"The height of enthusiasm," continued *Times* reporter Murray Schumach, "was in a poor neighborhood where men talked about the game from windows and, in a few cases, tossed bits of paper into the street.

"Yet the importance of the game to Brooklyn showed in a different manner. During the game, streets ordinarily heavily traveled on Sundays, were almost devoid of traffic. From windows, television accounts poured into quiet streets with such frequency that a man could have walked through Brooklyn without missing more than two batters.

"Along streets, such as Eastern Parkway, which ordinarily would have been crowded this mild day with strollers, there were few young adults. Mostly the men and women were elderly, sometimes watching grandchildren of pre-baseball age. Rarely, a family group could be spotted taking a walk. In these cases a portable radio was usually at hand— or at ear."[4] Bessent's fine relief job in the last game gave Don Newcombe his twenty-seventh win against only seven losses.

The crowd of 31,982 raised the year's attendance to 1,215,883, which exceeded the 1955 total by 182,254. The upward surge in attendance seemed to fly in the face of O'Malley's logic about Ebbets Field's inadequacies. Even with every home game on TV and the other maladies rightfully ascribed to Ebbets Field, such as inadequate parking facilities and a tight capacity, attendance went up when there was a competitive pennant race. And that was even with a pattern of less-than-stellar customer service and a failure to consistently provide the best-available seats on a first-come, first-served basis.[5]

All of that was ancillary to the at-hand baseball drama about to unfold. Attention was once again directed to the task of beating the Yankees, and in this case, the National League team had the home field advantage in 1956, giving Dodger fans good reason to be optimistic after the 1955 win. Games 1 and 2, and, if needed, 6 and 7, would be played in Ebbets Field, where left-handed pitchers invariably were hit hard, thus presenting Stengel with a tough decision about when best to pitch his ace Whitey Ford. After serious deliberation, he decided to send Whitey up against Sal Maglie in the opener at Ebbets Field.

Dwight D. Eisenhower, in the midst of his second campaign against Stevenson (Adlai was scheduled to attend the third game at the stadium), arrived a few minutes before game time. His limousine entered with an entourage via the center-field gate and went around the warning track as the president waved to the crowd. Eisenhower subsequently stood at home plate, where he was introduced to and shook the hands of both the Yankee and the Dodger players, who had lined up along the foul lines. A perfect tableau, the baseball contestants vying for preeminence in the great American democracy as was Ike himself. Baseball was America and vice versa; here was the president amid the red, white, and blue bunting in the stirring presage to the fall classic. Before going over to the commissioner's box, Ike threw out the first ball.

When the game got under way, Maglie gave up a first inning two-run homer to Mantle with Enos Slaughter aboard. Jackie Robinson led off in the second with a homer, and Hodges followed him with a single and then Furillo doubled him home, tying the score. In the bottom of the third, Reese singled, the Duke singled, and then, after Jackie was retired, Hodges poled a three-run shot. Ford was removed for a pinch hitter in the fourth, and Brooklyn went on to add one more in the course of a 6–3 victory, with Maglie going all the way. At the end of the game, fans were asked to wait in their seats until the president, who stayed until the end—this was Brooklyn, after all—left. Ike's limousine pulled up next to the field box, and, with Ike employing his customary wave, left via the first base and right-field warning tracks and out the center-field gate.

The second game was rained out and pushed back a day. When they finally got to play, with Don Newcombe against Don Larsen, it was a slugfest, an Ebbets Field classic. Berra, who as longtime Dodger fan Frank Fennell lamented, "hit Newcombe liked he owned him," cracked a grand slam home run as part of a five-run second inning that gave the Yanks a 6–0 lead.

Brooklyn began its comeback right away in the bottom of the second. Hodges led off with a single and Collins booted a double-play ball, leaving men on first and second. Furillo walked, filling the bases for Campanella. Campy drove in a run with a sacrifice fly, and after Larsen got Dale Mitchell to foul out, he walked Gilliam, prompting Stengel to yank him in favor of Kucks to face Reese. Reese singled, driving in two, and this set the stage for Snider. Stengel came out again and went for the left-handed Byrne. The strategy failed. Duke drove the ball over the fence for a three-run homer. The game was tied at six.

Brooklyn added one in the bottom of the third, as did the Yanks in the top of the fourth, but it was a pair of Hodges two-run doubles in the fourth and fifth that put Brooklyn up 11–7, on the way to a two-game lead. Don Bessent, who came on for the Dodgers in the third, was eventually credited with the win.

The Yankee bus was pelted with fruit and vegetables as it found its way out of Brooklyn. When the teams went up to the Bronx, the Yankees did what the Dodgers did the year before, winning three in a row behind Ford, 5–3, Sturdivant, 6–2, and finally, Don Larsen, 2–0, in his immortalized perfect game.

The Yankees celebrated by mobbing Larsen on the field after his masterpiece, but with one eye on the morrow, for there was the unfinished manner of winning a World Series. And if they were going to do it, they would have to do so at Ebbets Field.

Lost in the history of hoopla over Larsen's perfect game was the majestic performance of Sal Maglie that day, who gave up only five hits to the Yankees, and of Clem Labine the next day. Labine had a wonderful overhand curve and used it effectively to keep the Bronx Bombers off balance in game 6. The Yankees were starting their hard-throwing right-hander, Bullet Bob Turley, obtained in an eighteen-player deal from the Orioles that also brought Larsen before the 1955 season. Although Turley had traces of control problems, and long hits by Billy Martin and Joe Collins to right field off Labine might have been home runs in Yankee Stadium, both teams, inning after inning, were unable to push across a run.

"There were about 33,000 in Ebbets Field that day," Mickey Mantle said, "but they sounded like a hundred thousand as the Dodgers came to bat against Turley in the bottom of the ninth, needing one run to force a seventh game."[6]

With one out, Turley walked Amoros. But Furillo and Campanella both flied out, and the game was in extra innings. The Yankees were retired in order in the tenth, Turley striking out, Bauer and Collins grounding out. In the bottom of the inning, Labine, who had allowed the Yankees four scattered hits over the course of the afternoon, led off and popped out to Billy Martin. But Jim Gilliam worked Turley for a walk, and Reese got him over to second with a sacrifice. For the third time that day, Snider was walked, for the second time intentionally. Jackie Robinson was the hitter.

Robinson hit a line drive toward forty-year-old Enos Slaughter in left field. Slaughter started in on the ball and then stopped dead in his tracks. He had lost the ball in the low October sun and shadows. The ball sailed over his head.

Gilliam, running on the hit, scored as the ball rolled to the wall.

Ebbets Field was bedlam, a place loaded with hope and possibility. Brooklyn had won the game, 1–0.

There was gonna be a seventh game.

The next day, the Yankee bus on its ride to Brooklyn was again greeted with all you'd imagine. "We knew what to expect on the ride over," Mantle said, "and we weren't disappointed. They were out in force, the Dodger fans lining the street with their signs and posters and their curses and shouts. If it was any consolation, at least we knew this was going to be the last time we would have to take that bus ride this year."[7]

It would be the 27–7 Dodger ace Don Newcombe against twenty-three-year-old Johnny Kucks. Kucks had grown up in Hoboken and had a career year in 1956, going 18–9, the Yankees' second-best pitcher behind Ford. Stengel shook up his lineup, putting Ellie Howard in left field to replace Slaughter and Moose Skowron at first base in place of Collins. But the Yankees could have just as well have left one man in their lineup to do all their hitting. And that was Lawrence Peter Berra.

Bauer started the game for the Yankees with a sharp single to left. After striking out Martin and Mantle, Newcombe threw a high, out-of-the-strike-zone fastball and Berra, perhaps the most notorious bad-ball hitter in the game's history, drilled it over the right-field wall for a two-run homer.

In the third, Berra just managed to foul tip a third strike after Newcombe had struck out Mantle. Yogi parked Newk's next pitch on Bedford Avenue, hitting a two-run shot over the scoreboard in right-center field. It was Berra's third Series homer off Newk in as many at bats. When Ellie Howard led off the fourth inning with a blast of his over the right-field scoreboard, Newk was through for the day, at least inside the ballpark. Once outside, he slugged a parking lot attendant who questioned his mettle. In a precursor to what today is commonplace and then was less so, they settled out of court after the attendant brought an action.

With a 5–0 cushion and Kucks in command, the game coasted along on cruise control and Ebbets Field all but turned into a morgue. In the seventh, the Yanks loaded the bases and Moose Skowron belted a grand slam into the left-field seats. That made it 9–0, and that's how Brooklyn's last World Series game ended. The Dodgers had managed but three hits off of Kucks. In the last three games of the Series, over the course of twenty-nine innings, the Dodgers had garnered only a single run and seven hits.

After the Series, the Dodgers reluctantly took off on an exhibition game tour of Japan. Before they went across the Pacific, O'Malley and the team stopped at the Hilton Hotel in Los Angeles. It was there, as Peter Golenbock noted in his book *Bums*, that O'Malley made a revelation to Los Angeles County supervisor Kenneth Hahn, which Hahn disclosed years later during a hearing concerning a legal dispute between Al Davis and the NFL.

Hahn had met O'Malley a few days before, during the World Series. Serving his first term on the Los Angeles Board of Supervisors, Hahn had been sent by Los Angeles on the all-expenses-paid trip to baseball's fall classic as part of the city's reconnaissance into the possibility of getting a team to relocate there. His job was to hook an owner into coming out to Los Angeles.

"To make Los Angeles great," Hahn said, "we had to have a major team. There were a lot of people that said we are not ready for it, we are not ready for a major team, but I went, and I first attempted to see Calvin Griffith, the owner of the [Washington] Senators, because they were at the bottom of the [American] league.

"When I was attending the game at Ebbets Field, Walter O'Malley sent me a note and said he is interested in coming to Los Angeles. . . . I never dreamt we could get a world champion.

"Then he came here, and his team, on the way to Japan. He had some play in Tokyo. I met him at the Hilton Hotel—it was called the Statler Hilton then—on Columbus Day. I remember the date because it was a legal holiday, and I didn't have to go to work, but I came down to meet him.

"He said, 'I will come down here, but I will deny it to the press' because he had another season to play at Ebbets Field. He said the Dodger fans are rough fans. Literally would kill him, he said."[8]

On Halloween, the last trolley cars in Brooklyn, the Church Avenue car and the McDonald Avenue car, were retired. And the newspapers were filled with the worst trick-or-treat announcement that old Brooklyn ever heard. Walter O'Malley had sold Ebbets Field for $3 million, the buyer one Marvin Kratter, a real estate developer who planned to build a "middle-income residential community." Kratter also said that he "would never do anything to keep the Dodgers from playing in Brooklyn."[9] The Dodgers took a three-year lease on the park, with an option to renew for an additional two years. This would provide for baseball in Brooklyn through the 1961 season.

After that the news in Brooklyn seemed to get steadily worse, and before the next spring even rolled around, most Brooklynites believed that their baseball team was all but gone and that there was nothing they could do about it.

In late November, word came from Brooklyn borough president John Cashmore's office that plans for a new Brooklyn stadium had been approved by engineers. Cashmore then sent the report to the Brooklyn Sports Center Authority and said that he would back the Authority's request for yet more funds from the Board of Estimate to make yet another independent study of the stadium and related projects.

The Authority members—Charles Mylod, Robert Blum, and Chester Allen—concluded in their November 15, 1956, Interim Report of the Brooklyn Sports Center Authority that the LIRR Terminal–Fort Greene Meat Market site required the smallest capital and tax revenue cost to the city and the fewest relocation problems, while also permitting an opportunity for track-curvature railroad terminal renovations that would allow newer rail cars to serve Long Island Railroad commuters.

Subsequently, Gilmore D. Clarke of Clarke-Rapuano Consulting Engineers and Landscape Architects, the same consultants who had prepared the study and plan for the Brooklyn Civic Center in 1944, sent a letter to borough president Cashmore on November 20, noting that in accordance with their agreement terms with the city, made through him, they were submitting their report. The preliminary recommendations, with price tag estimates of $9 million for a domed stadium and $7 million for one without a lid, and for two parking garages costing

$3.5 million and $3 million apiece, had already been forwarded to the borough president on June 13. It was the site Wagner had discussed in July: construction of a stadium on the other side of the Flatbush-Atlantic intersection by Fourth Avenue, together with the two parking garages for 2,500 cars, a concourse constructed below street level to provide access to the stadium from the subway and the LIRR. The latter would abandon its existing terminal and relocate and redevelop its trackage and yards in the Atlantic Avenue–Pacific Street area a block away. The plan also proposed to elevate Atlantic Avenue over Flatbush Avenue to smooth the traffic flow. The Clarke-Rapuano suggestion would have had the stadium construction obliterating all the row houses between Fourth Avenue and almost to Sixth Avenue on Dean and Bergen streets and St. Mark's Place, finally bordering on Warren Street and Prospect Place on the southern side.

From a public relations standpoint, the aerial picture that appeared in the Clarke-Rapuano report was crafted with all the aplomb of a civil defense booklet annotating the effects of a bomb blast. The superimposed outline of a huge white circle showing the stadium's size appeared over the blocks pictured with rooftop after rooftop, row house after row house, with a couple of wider concentric circles to demonstrate the additional area needed for pedestrian and traffic egress.

There was, in the words of author Henry Fetter, "no chance at all that the city would ever condemn and clear the residential blocks—however decrepit—to consummate a distress sale to private citizen O'Malley. Even the most egregious and questionable of the Wagner-Moses urban-renewal projects—the redevelopment of Manhattan's Upper West Side—may have unduly enriched private developers and driven residents from homes that fell under the wrecker's ball, but at least it resulted in the construction of new housing. This was an equation that balanced in New York's political and planning calculus. An urban-renewal program that demolished established business and residential premises for a baseball stadium would not."[10] The site above the existing Long Island Railroad station was clearly the better alternative; Clarke and Rapuano also could have recommended it, since it fell within the area they were commissioned to survey.

The Authority's first order of business would remain developing a sound business prospectus and determining a bond issue's feasibility for financing stadium construction. In what would soon become painfully apparent, gaps would appear in the underpinning.

On December 13, Brooklyn got another rude shock. Word flashed that Jackie Robinson had been traded to the Giants for Dick Littlefield, a left-handed pitcher, and $30,000. The Giants? Jackie Robinson with the Giants? It seemed hard to fathom. If any player deserved to retire in the same uniform, if any player deserved to be ceremonially honored and celebrated by his longtime team before he decided to retire, it was Jackie Robinson. For all that Robinson symbolized and all he did for baseball, how could O'Malley treat him like chattel? Dodger fans were outraged, filling the Montague Street switchboard with calls, first verifying the awful news and then voicing their indignation. To them, Jackie was the essence of Brooklyn. Such considerations didn't matter any longer to Walter O'Malley. He had never been quite comfortable with Jackie Robinson anyway, since the world linked Robinson with Branch Rickey in the historic decision to break the color line.

In an interview just before Christmas, Robert Moses talked about the site at Atlantic and Flatbush avenues in anything but an affirmative way as it pertained to baseball, saying that he would move to put housing there should the ballpark effort fail. The story was carried in the paper on Christmas Eve. Moses had put himself on the record, but buried his comments on one of the quietest news days of the year.

Two days after Christmas, the New York City Board of Estimate granted the Brooklyn Sports Center Authority a measly $25,000 for the "engineering and economic" survey of the proposed stadium site. The members of the Authority, expecting $278,000 to begin the project's preliminary phases, were flabbergasted. The politicians were setting the citizen-leaders up, but the appointees pulled no punches, stating simply that the city was failing "to go forward with the program as originally contemplated." The next day, O'Malley said that there was only a "short time" left before the club would decide on its future home and that he might have to take steps to "commit the Dodgers elsewhere."[11]

In January Jackie Robinson announced his retirement with a first-person article in *Look* magazine, for which he was paid $50,000. He had made the arrangement with *Look* before the Dodgers traded him. Rather than play for the Giants, he accepted a position as a vice president with the Chock Full O'Nuts restaurant chain. Meanwhile, Walter O'Malley was in Los Angeles, visiting the 257-acre Chavez Ravine site, which was close to downtown Los Angeles. "We were just window shopping," said a smiling O'Malley, who often spoke in the collective "we" when he was speaking of himself. "Ostensibly we were in the West to accept a new forty-four passenger Convair plane for the Dodgers. We just happened to be driving past Chavez Ravine, so we thought we'd have a look."[12]

Later that month, O'Malley announced that the famous clown Emmet Kelly had been hired "just to ease the tension at Ebbets Field" for the 1957 season. Kelly was made up to bear as strong a resemblance as possible to Willard Mullin's bum in the *New York World-Telegram's* sports pages.

On January 31, consultant M. J. Madigan sent Brooklyn Sports Center Authority chairman Charles Mylod a sobering memo. Madigan kept it quiet, feeling the adverse effects could be damaging should the contents leak to the press; the substance was that amortizing the $15 million bond issue with an interest rate of 4 percent, which at that time was the lowest that could be obtained, would require $1.1 million, or, utilizing open-market revenue bond financing, $2.2 million. O'Malley, who wanted to own, was asked what kind of rent he would be prepared to pay were the facility to be rented to him. He said $500,000; revenue bond financing didn't look like an option.

The news would get substantively worse on February 21. "If there was a moment that the fate of the Brooklyn Dodgers baseball franchise was sealed, it was at the Baseball Writers Association dinner when O'Malley and Philip Wrigley passed notes back and forth up on the dais," said sportswriter Jack Lang. In was in this exchange, according to Lang, that Wrigley agreed to swap minor league franchises—his Los Angeles Angels for the Dodger farm team in Fort Worth, Texas. The deal gave the Dodgers Wrigley Field, a 20,000-seat ballpark only four miles from downtown Los Angeles. Even though Wrigley Field itself was hardly adequate for major league baseball, since public transportation to the ballpark and parking facilities were both poor, it gave O'Malley territorial rights to the city and demonstrated that he was seriously considering moving to Los Angeles.

Time magazine, which had taken pictures of O'Malley visiting Chavez Ravine for a news story, also had taken pictures of Brooklyn borough president Cashmore and his aide, John Hayes, in Brooklyn in front of the Fort Greene Meat Market, part of the whole Long Island Railroad site at Atlantic and Flatbush. Cashmore was an institution as borough president in Brooklyn, having been in the post going back to the days of the Dodgers' 1941 pennant. He was ailing at this point, suffering from diabetes and heart problems, though this was not then widely known. It was a dispiriting time for him. Prospects seemed so bleak in Brooklyn that the Brooklyn picture got cut and never even made the *Time* story.

O'Malley had still been offered nothing concrete by New York City. "I went and put up my own money to do the study," he told Cashmore privately. "I hired a respectable architect and Kavanaugh produced a model. And I've said all along that I'd put up my own money to build the ballpark. And then"—O'Malley lowered his voice ominously—"and then I met the politicians."

Horace Stoneham now weighed in with his own jarring bit of news. "If the Dodgers should move to Los Angeles our rivalry with them will

suffer considerably, even though we should still be in the same league,"
he said. "In that case we would have to decide whether it would be better for us to move too."[13]

Los Angeles mayor Norris Poulson was as surprised as anyone by
the rapid course of events. Two weeks later he and other officials flew
to Vero Beach to begin enticing the Dodgers to their city. "Poulson
described the session as 'a sparring match,'" writes Neil Sullivan,
"although from the outset the participants overestimated each other's
strength." After the meeting O'Malley said, "Today's meeting was important. We got to know each other. But the Dodgers are still in Brooklyn and Jersey City."[14]

While Los Angeles was making its overtures, New York was doing
nothing. During spring training, City Council president Abe Stark suggested Brooklyn's Parade Grounds at the southern end of Prospect Park
as a possible stadium site, taking a swipe at the same time at O'Malley's
threats to move. Later, Stark suggested enlarging Ebbets Field, an idea
that no one had mentioned before as an option, leading O'Malley to say,
"Mr. Stark continues to add confusion to what would have been a
simple solution, had he given initial support."[15] In April, Moses proposed a 78-acre tract for a ballpark in Flushing Meadow out in Queens.
City officials couldn't agree where in Brooklyn the new stadium should
be built or how much money should be spent to get the project moving.
And now Moses was advocating a stadium outside of Brooklyn.

O'Malley met four times with Poulson that spring. He even showed
up at the airport in Los Angeles with a "Keep the Dodgers in Brooklyn"
button in his lapel. Poulson repeatedly assured him that a Chavez
Ravine stadium would come to pass. In the meantime the Dodgers
could play in Wrigley Field, or possibly in the Los Angeles Coliseum.
By the final meeting on Friday, May 3, O'Malley was said to have agreed
to move the Dodgers to California in 1958.[16]

"Never was the owner of the Dodgers more devious, or cold-
blooded, than during the summer of 1957," wrote Svein Arber. "He had
already made up his mind to move to Los Angeles but continued to
deceive the City of New York and the people of Brooklyn. He told us
there was still a chance the Dodgers would stay long after that chance
was gone.

"All he cared about now," Arber continued, "was squeezing the
last nickel out of the Faithful. After all, over the five previous seasons
the Dodgers had been the most profitable franchise in baseball. The
club's net profit after taxes from 1952 to 1956 was $1,860,744. Playing
in their so-called bandbox the Dodgers had earned $400,000 more than
the mighty Yankees over the same period. O'Malley had no intention
of coming clean with the suckers who'd lined his pockets until he had
finished taking them.

"Meanwhile, those suckers, still believing they had a chance, had formed a 'Keep the Dodgers in Brooklyn' Committee, with headquarters in the Hotel Bossert. The committee's workers, mostly kids, had distributed ten thousand buttons and collected twenty-five thousand signatures."[17] When Walter O'Malley walked around with one of the blue-and-white buttons in his lapel, it seemed somewhat stupefying. Because he could . . . Keep the Dodgers in Brooklyn.

Another story on O'Malley's more recent visit to Los Angeles showed him flying over Chavez Ravine in a helicopter provided by the county sheriff. "The Brooklyn Dodgers as the world knows them will soon cease to be," said *Life* magazine, "barring an unexpected rescue."[18]

For all the talk of O'Malley's predatory interests regarding the future of Brooklyn baseball, the more compelling baseball product in a Brooklynite's eye that spring may well have been the NCAA District 2 playoffs at Ebbets Field, where coach Jack Kaiser's St. John's squad defeated Lafayette 8–3, but lost to Penn State, 5–0. This, at least, was baseball for the sake of playing the game.

On May 28 the National League owners, meeting in Chicago, granted the Dodgers and Giants permission to move to the Coast for the following season "if they want to make a change" and made the request by October 1. It was a death knell. Two days later, Mayor Wagner, who was up for reelection in November, stated, "I am more encouraged at every stage of developments," restating the city's determination to do "everything within reason" to keep the Dodgers and Giants, though emphasizing that the city "would not be blackjacked [*sic*] into anything."[19]

Playing the Brooklyn card after a parley where he and Stoneham met the mayor and other officials at City Hall on June 5, O'Malley said, "I told John Cashmore I'd carry him piggy-back to Macy's window if I could get either one of them," referring to the two possible ballpark sites on either side of Atlantic Avenue. Then he put the card back in his vest, adding that the offer he made in January no longer existed to buy $5,000,000 in Sports Authority bonds and to pay a $500,000-a-year rental for a Brooklyn stadium. "Since then," said O'Malley, "we have invested in Los Angeles real estate, and we no longer have the $5,000,000," referring to his purchase of Wrigley Field in Los Angeles. When asked what caused him to make such a move less than a month after he made the offer to the Sports Authority, he dodged, saying, "That would bring up a question that, in view of the people concerned, I'd prefer not to answer. But it was a good reason."

Then O'Malley backpedaled again: "It is well within our means to finance a new stadium, but I can't answer whether we will invest in a project until we know what the proposition is."[20]

It wasn't long before "George the Fifth" weighed in—George McLaughlin, the onetime head of the Brooklyn Trust Company, the same person who had brought MacPhail, Rickey, and O'Malley into leadership roles at the Dodgers. He was working for Bob Moses at Triborough now, and was privately seething over what O'Malley was doing. McLaughlin outlined a plan for a team that would play in a new stadium in Flushing Meadow that Moses wanted, a team where the players would share in the profits of a club run by a nonprofit corporation.[21] The lords of baseball were aghast at such a notion. McLaughlin, acting in an unofficial capacity, also exchanged correspondence with Stoneham about purchasing the Giants, but was told they weren't for sale.

For Brooklyn, it was all a fog of rhetoric, so much so that it seemed somewhat appropriate that a day after O'Malley's meeting up at City Hall, the Dodgers and Cubs started a game where players on both sides were losing fly balls in a pea soup fog that seemed to get thicker as each pitch was thrown. With virtually any ball hit to the outfield unplayable, the umps halted the game. After an hour and 26 minutes, it was called.

If the fans were frustrated, they had the opportunity to vent vicariously through two great on-field donnybrooks, one involving the Braves, and another with Cincinnati. The latter occurred on July 11, when in a classic bench-emptier, Charley Neal of the Dodgers and Don Hoak, now of the Reds, each got a running charge out of their respective dugouts and met at home plate, "where Neal knocked him ass over tea kettle," according to sportswriter Jack Mann, who laughed years later recounting that Hoak claimed Neal had "sneak-punched" him.

From the start of the season to well past the halfway mark, the National League race was crowded, with the Braves, Reds, Phillies, Cardinals, and Dodgers all vying for the lead. In sixth place, far behind, were the Giants, who were suffering badly at the gate.

In the middle of July the workers and management of a billboard company, General Outdoor Advertising, refused to put up a billboard sign at Washington Avenue and Sullivan Place paid for by a Los Angeles advertising company that wished the Brooklyn Dodgers good luck "until next year in Los Angeles."

"We got 150 men working here," said Outdoor's manager John Burke. "Most of them have followed the Dodgers since they were in grammar school. That is our number 1 reason: morale. So we figured we would get out from under."[22]

On July 17 Horace Stoneham announced that he favored a move to San Francisco if that city came up with a suitable proposal. Within days, at a meeting at New York's Hotel Lexington with Stoneham and San Francisco mayor George Christopher, O'Malley, at Mayor Christopher's request, scribbled up proposed details of a ballpark lease for the Giants. Stoneham liked Christopher's offer of a new 45,000-seat municipal stadium with parking for 10,000 cars, plus the right to operate all concessions.

On August 19 the Giant directors voted 8–1 to move the franchise. "We're sorry to disappoint all the kids of New York, but we haven't seen many of their fathers at the Polo Grounds lately," said Stoneham. For her part, John McGraw's widow, Blanche, said, "I guess all I have left now are my memories."

At Ebbets Field, Carl Furillo and Gil Hodges were given "Nights" in their honor. The Dodgers were kept alive by pitching until the summer's dog days, when the Cardinals completed a nine-game winning streak that winnowed every team except the Braves out of the race. Then St. Louis collapsed, dropping nine straight while Milwaukee reeled off ten wins. The Braves rolled home in September, winning the pennant by eight games over the Cards. Brooklyn was third, eleven games out.

Up at the Polo Grounds on September 8, Don Drysdale started against Curt Barclay in the last New York Giant–Brooklyn Dodger matchup. "I feel powerful bad," said Pete Stoneham, Horace's son. Hank Sauer had the big hit, a homer off the left-field scoreboard to put the Giants ahead, 3–2.

Willie Mays got the last hit between the two teams with an eighth inning triple. He was stranded. Marv Grissom, who'd come in to relieve Barclay in the seventh, got Sandy Amoros on a grounder to second baseman Danny O'Connell for the last out. It was five minutes to four that afternoon, a day when everyone was reminiscing.

"In September, Walter O'Malley gave the fans of Brooklyn a cruel and needless parting blow," said Svein Arber. "He cynically encouraged Nelson Rockefeller's last ditch effort to save the Dodgers." Rockefeller, then a philanthropist who knew diddly-squat about baseball with an as-yet unannounced interest in becoming governor in 1958, came forward with an offer to help finance the new stadium. If the city would agree to condemn the parcel that O'Malley wanted, a Rockefeller corporation would purchase the property for $2 million and lease it to the Dodgers rent-free for twenty years. The Dodgers could then build their new ballpark, and they would have an option to buy the land at any time over the 20 years for $2 million plus interest compounded at 2½ percent.

"The difficulty with the Rockefeller proposal," said Arber, "was that it would cost the city $8 million to acquire the land by condemnation. As most members of the Board of Estimate viewed it, the plan called for a 'giveaway' of $6 million of the taxpayers' money to aid a private business. When Rockefeller then upped his buying price to

$3 million, O'Malley quickly backed off, claiming the Dodgers had been 'priced out.'"[23]

Meanwhile, other offers were made to buy the team, usually amounting to no more than a one-paragraph mention in the papers. One such offer was for $5 million from financier and construction firm president Louis F. Wolfson early in September, when O'Malley was off hunting in Wyoming. Red Patterson, O'Malley's spokesman, dismissed the Wolfson offer by saying simply that the team wasn't for sale.

One of the key last-ditch meetings was held at Gracie Mansion on September 18. Brooklyn deputy borough president John Hayes, who when interviewed years later would maintain that "these were all reasonable men, doing what they thought they reasonably could do," said to O'Malley before the meeting began, "With all due respect Mr. O'Malley, if Los Angeles is offering you all that you say they are, why don't you take it?"

O'Malley replied, "Johnny, I am going to take it; I'm going to tell them that today. And," he added, "I'm going to make a barrel of dough."

On September 20, after yet another meeting at City Hall, word broke of O'Malley's contention that he was "priced out" and word leaked out of the Rockefeller plan's failure. But the Los Angeles City Council still hadn't approved its deal, so O'Malley still hadn't made any statement.

Four days later, with Danny McDevitt's shutout, the Brooks played the last major league game at Ebbets Field, against the Pittsburgh Pirates.

On Sunday, September 29, the Brooklyn Dodgers played their last game, a 2–1 loss, in Philadelphia. On Monday, October 7, the Los Angeles City Council approved an ordinance that gave O'Malley Chavez Ravine. The Brooklyn Dodgers were gone.

CHAPTER THIRTEEN

Never Forgiven,
Never Forgotten

Walter O'Malley had a stake in the Brooklyn Dodgers for thirteen years. For the first six of those years, he didn't run the team. Within O'Malley's first four years as part of the ownership group and at his own prodding, his partners, Branch Rickey and John Smith, acquiesced to allow him to examine what it might take to build a new stadium on the Ebbets Field site or elsewhere in Brooklyn. When O'Malley was done, he said the undertaking would cost six million dollars, and since even the exalted Yankees and all their assets—the franchise and minor league clubs and real estate and everything else associated with the ball club—were worth only three million, it was clearly something that the Dodgers couldn't then afford. In the early years of postwar America, given the nation's circumstances, even to raise the question was a self-indulgent thought. The effort associated with looking into the matter was primarily O'Malley's; his partners were focused elsewhere.

After six years, O'Malley managed to get control of the team. In his second year in control, he commissioned and displayed a drawing of a dome that was to be the Dodgers' new home; it was derisively referred to as O'Malley's Pleasure Dome by some. By the third year he controlled the team—1953, a mayoral election year in New York—he said he had to have a new stadium; by the fifth year, he was scheduling games outside of town to pressure the politicians; by the sixth year, he was playing games out of town; by the seventh year, he was actively planning his exit while sporting a "Keep the Dodgers in Brooklyn" button; by the autumn, he was gone. In thirteen years he took the most profitable team in baseball out of its hometown, after leveraging, as Brooklyn historian Tom Knight has said, off the nickels and dimes of Brooklyn Trust Company depositors to buy into it in the first place. Under the circumstances, it's no wonder that Branch Rickey called what O'Malley did "a crime against a city of three million."

There was a man who parsed, understood, and best communicated exactly what happened, and in 1957 he was at the top of his game. His name was Dick Young. Ten years earlier, he had been the first sports reporter to go into a baseball clubhouse after a game and ask questions. Before that, reporters didn't bother. Unlike today, when team officials finally have to throw all the reporters out of a clubhouse after an hour and a half or so, since they're afraid to leave if there's even one other reporter hanging around—they might miss something—Dick Young was in and out in six or seven minutes. Young wrote for the *New York Daily News*, which in 1957 was also at the top of its game. In it he described what happened in Brooklyn as "one of the most forceful political manipulations in the history of our politically manipulated little town."

"With O'Malley as the guiding spirit," Young wrote, "plans for the establishment of a Sports Authority were born. It would be the work of such an Authority to issue bonds and build a stadium with private capital—utilizing the city's condemnation powers to obtain the land.

"With O'Malley pushing the issue through his lifelong political connections, the bill was drafted in Albany, passed overwhelmingly by the City Council, squeezed through the state legislature by one vote, and ultimately signed into law by Governor Harriman.

"At that moment, April 21, 1956, the prospects for a new stadium, and a continuance of Brooklyn baseball were at their highest. Thereafter, everything went downhill. City officials, who had supported the bill originally, in the belief Albany would defeat it, went to work with their subtle sabotage. Appropriations for surveys by the Sports Center Authority were cut to the bone, and O'Malley shook his head knowingly. He was getting the works.

"O'Malley, meanwhile, had been engaging in some strange movements of his own. He had leased Roosevelt Stadium, Jersey City, for three years with the announced intention of playing seven or eight games a season there. Later, he sold Ebbets Field for $3,000,000 on a lease-back deal with Marv Kratter. The lease made it possible for O'Malley to remain in Brooklyn, in a pinch, for five years. He had no intention of doing so—it was just insurance at things blowing up at both political ends.

"Why was Ebbets Field sold?

"Politicians claimed it was an O'Malley squeeze on them. O'Malley claimed it was a manifestation of his good intentions; that he was converting the club's assets into cash so that he might buy Sports Authority bonds and help make the new stadium a reality.

"Then O'Malley moved in a manner that indicated he didn't believe himself. At the start of '57 he visited Los Angeles. Two months later, he announced the purchase of [the Los Angeles] Wrigley Field. Shortly thereafter, Los Angeles officials, headed by Mayor Poulson and County Supervisor Ken Hahn, visited O'Malley at Vero Beach, Fla.

"It was there, on March 7, that serious consideration of a move to Los Angeles crystallized in the O'Malley mind. He made grandiose stipulations to the L.A. authorities—and was amazed to hear them say: 'We will do it.'

"From then on," Young continued, "Los Angeles officials bore down hard on the project, while New York's officials quibbled, mouthed sweet nothings, and tried to place the blame elsewhere. With each passing week, it became increasingly apparent the Dodgers were headed west—and in an election year [1957 was a mayoral election year in New York], the politicians wanted no part of the hot potato.

"Bob Moses, park commissioner, made one strong stab for New York. He offered the Dodgers park department land at Flushing Meadow—with a string or two. It wasn't a bad offer—but not as good as L.A.'s.

"By now, O'Malley's every move was aimed at the coast. He brought Frisco Mayor George Christopher to dovetail the Giant move to the coast with his own. He, and Stoneham, received permission from NL owners to transfer franchises.

"That was May 28—and since then, O'Malley has toyed with New York authorities, seeming to derive immense satisfaction from seeing them sweat unnecessarily. He was repaying them.

"Right to the end," Young went on, "O'Malley wouldn't give a flat, 'Yes, I'm moving'—as Stoneham had done. O'Malley was using New York as his saver—using it to drive a harder bargain with L.A.'s negotiator Harold McClellan, and using it in the event the L.A. city council were to reject the proposition at the last minute.

"But L.A., with its mayor whipping the votes into line the way a mayor is expected to, passed the bill—and O'Malley graciously accepted 300 acres of downtown Los Angeles, whereupon he will graciously build a ball park covering 12 acres.

"And the Brooklyn Dodgers dies—the healthiest corpse in sports history. Surviving are millions of fans, and their memories."[1]

In November 1957, a month after the Dodgers left, in his first quest for reelection, Robert F. Wagner won handily over Republican R. K. Christenberry with the largest plurality of the three terms he was elected mayor. The city's failure to retain either of its National League teams had no effect on Wagner politically.

Thereafter the fabled patch of land that had been called Pigtown half a century before began to recede from its position of familiar prevalence in the daily print cycles of the nation's sports pages, leaving, as Young said, millions of fans and their memories. Ebbets Field's last days as a working facility during the years of 1958 and 1959, whether for the soccer matches or demolition derbies, or even if merely for a lonesome, solitary gaze, were but a sad echo of the range of emotion so resplendently displayed for years within those walls. For Brooklyn, and indeed for the nation, the wrecking ball that swung in 1960 rendered more than a symbolic change.

"After 1957 and through the early '60s, some fifteen or sixteen families moved off our block," said Norman Kurland, who lived on President Street between Brooklyn and New York avenues. "The feeling of the neighborhood changed, and we worried about it. In the late '50s, we had a burglar alarm installed. For us, by 1962, living there was untenable."

The thriving middle-class community—mostly Jewish and Italian immigrants—was being blockbusted by real estate speculators who exploited both the whites who were selling and the blacks who were buying.

In the spring of 1963, the city Planning Commission announced a massive redevelopment program for the area that would include an elementary school and a neighborhood conservation program that would be too late to prevent the real estate entrepreneurs' exploitation. Slated for leveling under the plan were boarded-up hot dog stands, the former brewery on Franklin Avenue, and the commercial and automotive services clustered together west of Bedford Avenue. (The building that housed the brewery still stands.) Good housing along Washington Avenue, mostly apartments and row houses, was to remain, while the core area of blight, some thirty rundown housing units and thirty rundown businesses, were scheduled to be razed. Some empty lots deemed to contribute to the blight were to be developed.

The construction pit at the time of the Kennedy inaugural that was once Ebbets Field became the Ebbets Field Apartments by 1962.

A decade later, after Jackie Robinson died, the junior high school that had risen across the street from the ballpark site on the McKeever Place side was named for him. "There was some dissension in the black community about whether or not the school should be named for him, about whether or not he was militant enough," said Marty Adler, the assistant principal and later, for a short time, the principal of the school.

"The Vietnam War was still on," remembered Adler. "There had been race riots, and Jackie had been a Republican, had supported Nixon, and had worked for Rockefeller. A few people in the community said, 'What was he? A ballplayer?' They didn't understand what he did, and how if he hadn't done what was done, there might not have been a Rosa Parks or a Martin Luther King or a civil rights movement as we knew it. They felt he was too Uncle Tom-ish. At the school, we conducted a four-month education program about the significance of Jackie Robinson to win people over."

A college, part of the City University of New York, rose across from what was once the left-field wall on Montgomery Street. It was named for Medgar Evers. Dr. Betty Shabazz, the widow of Malcolm X, worked as an educator at the college before her death.

Crown Heights was 85 percent white in 1950 and 70 percent white in 1960. When the racial balance in the neighborhood started to change significantly in the 1960s, most residents of the liberal Jewish community—and the Italians in Crown Heights—moved on to other neighborhoods in Brooklyn or Queens or to the suburbs. Those from the Lubavitcher community, so-named after the city they hailed from in Russia, stayed.

The first among that group originally settled in the area around 1920, and their numbers, though still a small minority, grew somewhat just before the outbreak of World War II, bolstered by the arrival of those who had escaped Nazism and the reach of the Third Reich. The arrival of Rebbe Schneerson in 1941 was important for this group; today, 770 Eastern Parkway is known as the Lubavitchers' world headquarters. The group, devoted to cultural traditions, established in its ways, is both inwardly focused and outwardly connected, with enormous political influence that outstrips its size. It numbered slightly over 10,000 residents in 1990—a figure occasionally swelled by visiting students, scholars, and weekend visitors.

When the liberal Jewish and Italian families departed, their places were taken by African Americans and Caribbean Americans, who now make up the balance of the neighborhood. Sometimes there are flashpoints between the black and Hasidic communities, such as when seven-year-old Gavin Cato was run over by a Hasidic van driver on Eastern Parkway in 1992, or when the Talmudic scholar Yankel Rosenbaum was fatally stabbed in the disturbances that followed. Anna Deveare Smith, a playwright and actress who has challenged prejudice by confronting it and portraying people in their varied complexity, illustrated some of the ritualized differences and biases by assuming the roles and adapting the characteristics of the men and women from both groups in her award-winning play, *Fires in the Mirror.*

Over the course of almost forty years, the Atlantic and Flatbush site O'Malley wanted became a monument to nothingness, a vast civic failure for Brooklyn and the city of New York. No appreciable tax benefits were derived out of the lofty predictions of those who so earnestly postured as protectors of the city's interest.

In the early 1980s, a New York state senator from the Williamsburg and Greenpoint areas in Brooklyn, Tom Bartosiewicz, managed to get the legislature to earmark $30,000 in state supplementary budget funds authorizing the state's Urban Development Corporation to explore the feasibility of a domed stadium—an "Ebbets Dome" as Bartosiewicz referred to it—in Brooklyn. It remained his dream.[2]

Finally, in 1996, a retail complex was opened on the rear part of the site. Like the outfit that was supposed to create and sell bonds for the parking garage underpinning and generating revenue for the stadium that O'Malley supposedly wanted, one of the retail outlets was called The Sports Authority.

At the end of 2003 a grand plan that hinged on the purchase and relocation of the New Jersey Nets basketball franchise by real estate impresario Bruce Ratner raised the possibility of a masterly Frank Gehry–designed arena and office complex at the junction of Atlantic and Flatbush avenues, a project that would also include housing for people of different income levels. Ratner's project, a $3 billion boon for Brooklyn that drew raves from architecture critic Herbert Muschamp in the *Times,* would be as forward-thinking and architecturally stirring as the design for a permanently lidded baseball dome has proved banal. Certainly, given the fortunes of Houston's Astrodome, Seattle's Kingdome, Minneapolis's HHH Metrodome, and Tampa Bay's Tropicana Dome, an O'Malley dome in Brooklyn would have been passé by the 1980s. On January 21, 2004, Ratner completed his group's purchase of the New Jersey Nets basketball team. Though hurdles remain, the dream of a major league team in a Brooklyn uniform is once again a significant step closer to reality. Through the fall of 2004, Ratner's real estate operatives were moving ahead with plans to realize construction of the arena and office complex in a sensible way, mitigating pockets of neighborhood opposition and concern over possible condemnation proceedings by purchasing needed parcels, dwellings, or businesses in private sales at above-market rates, with sellers signing confidentiality agreements that bind them not to discuss the prices they receive, and not to demonstrate against, sign petitions against, or otherwise lobby against the arena project.

On January 6, 1997, citing the financial pressures of surviving in an era in which corporate ownership in the game was increasingly evident, Peter O'Malley, Walter's son, announced that he and his sister, Terri O'Malley Seidler, would be selling the franchise. When he was asked why, O'Malley spoke of estate planning: he has three children; his sister has ten. "It's smart to plan for the next generation," he said. "That's probably the best reason."[3]

Too bad his old man didn't think that way about a generation of Brooklyn kids.

The next day, all over New York, people remarked that the decision had occurred forty years too late.

Six years later, the O'Malleys spent some of $350 million they had collected when they sold the franchise on a little public relations effort to get Walter O'Malley into the Hall of Fame. Nothing too overt, just a few mentions of how this publication or that said he was one of the most influential sports figures of the twentieth century: things like that. On October 3, 2003, the O'Malley family unveiled a Web site dedicated to their patriarch on what would have been his hundredth birthday. It is an attempt to create a favorable image of Walter O'Malley among new generations unfamiliar with his machinations. Aside from letters that the family chose to release, the site also posted newspaper clips that—like some of the correspondence—have some paragraphs blurred out so that the viewer gets a sanitized version of events. Try a Hall of Shame.

Today, it's somewhat as Young said. Surviving are millions of fans and their memories. Some of them, the fervently devoted, have spent years of their lives vested in keeping those memories alive, rightful propagators of a lost faith. Surviving, too, are millions of others who never had the legacy that was their birthright, the direct connection to what their fathers or their grandfathers did. And so Ebbets Field is re-created, revisited, or imagined in a hundred different ways, attempts to connect a good past with the time warp of a dissonant present.

For Ebbets Field, the images all rush together: J. Michaels furniture sales underneath the stands when the team wasn't home. The Holy Name rallies. People gathered at the ballpark to take the oath of citizenship. Or the blue- and white-collar fans intermingling at the Beer Garden on Empire Boulevard before or after a game. All just a kaleidoscope of retrospective memory, fit for the melancholia of Frank Sinatra's recording of Joe Raposo's classic, "There Used to Be a Ballpark Here."

Disparate attempts to link with the past unite those who share a fascination with this particular aspect of Americana. Yet individual efforts sometimes connect in ways hard to fathom, much as Avenue N's Arthur Miller—who preferred playing second base—reflected at the end of his autobiography, *Timebends,* when, looking out at night into the forest by his home in Connecticut, he spies a wolf's eyes gazing back and notes how everything is connected, "even the trees."

In 1986 T. E. Carleton of Muskegon, Michigan, made an attempt at the Brooklyn Municipal Building to find the Ebbets Field blueprints. "They're in Los Angeles with the team," one clerk snapped. He established better rapport with another clerk, but ultimately his quest was fruitless.[4]

Six years later, Rod Kennedy picked up where Carleton left off and again went in search of the blueprints. After a bureaucratic hazing and months of political wrangling, he managed to gain access to a dust-filled, ledger-strewn Bela Lugosi–like subvault of the Brooklyn Municipal Building, and in what he called "one of the most exciting moments in my life," he found the original eighteen plans filed on March 15, 1912, by Charles Ebbets and Clarence Van Buskirk. Thirteen years later, after a photocopy of the plans was published by the Brooklyn Dodgers Hall of Fame, they remain in private hands while an appropriate museum-quality space is being pursued in Brooklyn for their permanent display.[5]

On St. Patrick's Day in 1988, the Brooklyn Dodger Sports Bar and Restaurant was opened in Brooklyn's Bay Ridge by David Senatore, Richard Picardi, and Kevin Boyle. Originally they wanted to use the name Ebbets Field, but they found in a trademark search that the Ebbets Field Café was extant in Hicksville on Long Island. After searching the Brooklyn Dodger mark and finding no users, save for nostalgic apparel licensing after 1981, they sought to register the mark for their restaurant.

The Brooklynites wrote to the Los Angeles Dodgers to inform them of their intent, and for a long time there was no answer. Eventually the Los Angeles team chose to deny their right to use the name and instead elected to sue the restaurant's owners. George Mullane, the barkeep, said, "There's no reason they should have the name. They left here." The baseball team was represented by a Park Avenue law firm, while lawyer Ron Russo represented the bar pro bono. Judge Constance Baker Motley's opinion favored the defendants, offering that "plaintiffs have not succeeded in demonstrating that much goodwill in Brooklyn survived Los Angeles's move in 1957."[6]

"Across the years," wrote Pete Hamill in 1988, "I kept the solemn vow. In 1957, led by the man my father always referred to as That Son of a Bitch O'Malley, the Dodgers left Brooklyn forever. And with millions of others, I made the vow: Never Forgive, Never Forget . . .

"The bulldozers scraped away the grass and churned up the infield where Reese and Robinson, Hodges and Cox had owned the earth. Business was business, they said.

"Yeah.

"So we vowed never to forget this atrocity and never, ever to forgive it; most of us didn't. . . . We who had once prayed at the command of the Brooklyn archbishop for God to deliver Gil Hodges from a slump now wished these people only the Calvinist punishments of eternal damnation."[7]

The obsession with the park continues. In Milwaukee, many of the Ebbets Field façade's design elements were incorporated into early designs of a new park slated to be built there, although changes occurred as architects moved ahead, finally completing a stadium worthy of the legacy of former owner and current baseball commissioner Bud Selig. The New York Mets want to build a contoured, scaled throwback of Ebbets Field with all the modern amenities—*including a retractable dome*—in Shea Stadium's parking lot to replace their existing ballpark. The initial design favored by Mets' co-owner Fred Wilpon would have allowed the field to be pulled out into the parking lot on a huge track after the game, when the dome would be closed. Thus the facility could be kept in better shape on the inside, while the field could continue to be nurtured in the open air and the sun. No one yet knows when or how this project will finally take shape.

In Hartford, Connecticut, Gregory Martin established Ebbets Field Ventures and created an Ebbets Field Web site, with dreams and plans of reconstructing Ebbets Field in a midsized eastern city as both a tourist attraction and a home for a minor league or college baseball team.

Certain images are timeless. Norman Rockwell's painting, *Tough Call*, a famous *Saturday Evening Post* cover, which appeared April 23, 1949, featured three umpires at Ebbets Field looking up at an ominous sky and contemplating the threat of rain. Beans Reardon is the umpire with the chest protector, with Larry Goetz and Lou Jorda the other members of the crew, while Brooklyn coach Clyde Sukeforth and Pittsburgh manager Bill Meyer chat behind them. The distant figure visible in right field in front of the famous wall and scoreboard is Dixie Walker, in the flannel of Pittsburgh, to whom he'd been traded in 1948.

Artists continue to make Ebbets Field their subject. In Lance Richbourg's *Flying-A Home Run*, the artist depicts a Dodger home run flying into the stands above the gasoline advertisement on the outfield wall. In Richbourg's scene the spectators are becoming players in their attempts to catch the ball, while the players—in this case, two St. Louis Cardinals—are relegated to observing as spectators watching the ball's flight.

William Feldman's *Sunlit Ebbets Field* shows the beauty of the sun and shadows from behind first base in the stands; Darrell Hill's Hopperesque *Beyond Bedford Avenue* shows the ballpark in repose, with the Stoddard Place apartment house behind it resting in a stillness reminiscent of *Early Sunday Morning*. A painting called *An Afternoon in Ebbets Field*, by Brian Byrnes, provides a behind-the-plate perspective of Sal Maglie pitching to Hank Bauer in the 1956 World Series, with center-field bleachers in the background.

Robert Weaver's two charcoal studies executed in 1981 of Bedford Avenue's center-field stands capture the geometric patterns of fencing, screen, the light stanchion off the roof in the distance, and the space-frame trussing underpinning the second deck's roof. A circus ad on the outside wall freezes his images in the year 1950, when the Big Top did an eight-show stand at Ebbets Field.

One of a series of impeccable watercolors by artist Jim Amore depicts Campy at the plate, Reese executing a double play with Ebbets Field's left-field wall in the distance, and a young Koufax hurling from the mound with a view looking toward right field; the bent wall, advertisements, and Schaefer scoreboard are featured prominently, with the backdrop of apartments behind. Another scene, of the Duke in the batter's box, with shading of the blousier baseball pants of the day accentuating the movement of his stride, is alas, set in Chicago's Wrigley Field.

Around the time Ebbets Field was facing the wrecking ball, David Levine created an evocative oil, *Crowd at Ebbets Field*, using both the Section 3 pillar and a railing's red, white, and blue bunting as its slightly off-center focal points. With empty seats amid a handful of fans, an observer might construe the scene as something akin to the remains of an opening day crowd with the game's outcome a foregone conclusion.

A painting of Ebbets Field commissioned by Mort Silver, now at the office of his Orda Real Estate Management Company on East Nineteenth Street and Park Avenue South, once hung at a Manhattan restaurant called Moreno's on East Seventeenth Street and Irving Place, where the huge canvas took up a wall. It is the masterpiece, the best that's ever been done of Ebbets Field by the artist who's the master of the ballpark genre. Andy Jurinko's *Ebbets Field Matinee* captures more than the ballpark in all of its splendor: it captures its electricity. Present are the vivid reds, the brilliant yellows, the most royal blue, the dull, dusky gold of Abe Stark's sign below the scoreboard, the brick-red clay of the infield, the sweep of the greensward, the Brooklyn life over the other side of the outfield fence, the kitsch 1950s marketing Americana on the outfield wall.

Andy Jurinko grew up in Phillipsburg, New Jersey, at a time when it was possible for him to follow five major league teams, given his proximity to the New York and Philadelphia markets. "Ebbets Field," he said, "was the fun house of baseball. The park had kind of a tacky look. The fans helped make it that way, as opposed to the stately Yankee Stadium or the oppressive look of the Polo Grounds. All the stadiums today pale by comparison. It was a compact park. You were a part of the field of play."

Indeed you were.

In New Jersey, a sign painter produced a replica of the Ebbets Field scoreboard for another man's basement, and subsequently reduced the facsimile in wood and metal to picture size. The only thing at all odd about it is that on the scoreboard Brooklyn is listed as the visiting team, because the line score is taken from the victory on Brooklyn's greatest day, the seventh game of the 1955 series. The same line score appears, without explanation, covering the lead character's apartment wall in Spike Lee's *Mo Better Blues:*

BKLYN	000 101 000	2	5	0
YANKS	000 000 000	0	8	1

It's Brooklyn baseball's Mona Lisa, a line-score imprint on the brain.

In the southeasternmost part of Brooklyn, on the way out to Kennedy Airport, between the new Spring Creek Park and the new Gateway Mall, out by Jamaica Bay, just before Fountain Avenue and the Brooklyn–Queens county line, a new exit sign went up on the Belt Parkway after city planners had put in some new streets. It was named after one of the very best men on the old Brooklyn Dodgers: Erskine Street, after Carl Erskine. He was, of course, moved when he heard, after someone called his home in Indiana to let him know; they had seen the sign driving along the highway and listened to news of the city planners honoring their old allegiances. Being the man Carl Erskine is—a very special man, as all who know him will attest—he wanted to reach out to find the appropriate people to thank for remembering him.

And then, of course, there are the artifacts from the ballpark, things that were a part of Ebbets Field. The Ebbets Field dedication plaque, commemorating "The Brooklyn Ball Club" and "The Ebbets–McKeever Exhibition Co.," the lettering placed around the basepaths of a diamond, is still preserved in a private collection. The plaque lists the key dates in the Brooklyn franchise at the time it was dedicated: 1883, when the ball club was founded, and 1912, when the ballpark's construction was under way. As well as listing Ebbets Sr. and Jr., Ed and Steve McKeever, and Henry Medicus and their titles with the ball club, it also lists Ebbets Field architect and engineer Clarence Van Buskirk.

The bronze plate with Stephen W. McKeever's name, once affixed in Ebbets Field's Rotunda, now sits on the fireplace mantel at McKeever's Restaurant in Pawling, New York. The Ebbets Field flagpole, donated by Marvin Kratter, stands in front of the Canarsie Casket Company on Utica Avenue in East Flatbush in Brooklyn. Ebbets Field's seats, which, if sold, fetch four-figure sums, are treasured items in many private collections.

As for the Brooklyn Dodgers 1955 world championship banner, it is again in its rightful place. Peter O'Malley sent the banner home forty years later. It now under the stewardship of the Brooklyn Historical Society's museum on Pierrepont Street. Its arrival was greeted with an appropriately melodic rendition provided by surviving members of the Brooklyn Dodger Sym-Phony.

In 2001 the Baseball Reliquary, an organization that serves its membership with an online site and that features its own Shrine of Eternals to preserve the offbeat and remember those who contributed to the game in different and often less acknowledged but nevertheless significant ways, announced the creation of the Hilda Award, named after Hilda Chester, to be given annually to honor baseball fans and their importance to the game and its history.

Among the Reliquary's inductees is Marvin Miller, a Brooklynite who changed baseball notably by vesting a nascent players' union with the leadership that allowed it to reach its potential. A maiden press release announcing Miller's hiring handled with a single line anticipated reporter questions as to why someone who represented the United Steelworkers might want take on the relatively smaller assignment of leading the baseball players' union: he grew up not far from Ebbets Field.

On May 11, 2002, the Reliquary dedicated artist William Robert Steele's Ebbets Field Replica at Pasadena's Jackie Robinson Center, where it was to go on display indefinitely. Steele, a graduate of the Baking School of Technology in Belfast, Northern Ireland, whose fascination lies with architecture rather than with baseball, used wood, plastic, cement, potter's clay, pastillage, and royal icing to create the model.

When asked to autograph a baseball, it turned out to be the first time he had held one.

The smell is the hardest to pin down, alternately characterized as oily, inky, beery, a combination scent of hot dogs, mustard, and peanuts, a smell of the grass upon walking through the turnstile in the caverns, a smell mingled with the wafting aromas of the Bond Bread Bakery a few blocks away, an Ebbets Field smell all its own, not duplicated anywhere.

Of no dispute is the surreal effect of the grass, the greenness of it, the lawn that Mel Ott would scruff with his spikes in the outfield such that his visits would leave a dirt patch on the greensward for the rest of the season.

"It's sort of like a dream state when I think about it," Vince Lipinski said. "It's when I was five years old, or six. I was in the box seats, with the pipes. I felt secure; it's like it was your own little playpen; you were safe there: the steel girders, the light coming through from the outside of the ballpark; how green the field was; an intense, emerald green."

Ebbets Field is forever Red Barber announcing a game with Connie Desmond. It is Happy Felton and the Knothole Gang's nightly televised three-kid baseball competition, Jerry Denmark being selected, and getting to interview Pee Wee before the next game, and then sitting in the Dodger dugout for a couple of innings. It is Roberta Spector's bike painted Schaefer red with the extra paint that had come from the recesses of the ballpark's caverns. It is the notion that someday Charley Ebbets will find the immortal's home he deserves in Cooperstown, Charley Ebbets, who said that a man shouldn't get in this game if he was solely interested in receipts.

Harold Parrott's kids played in Ebbets Field's catacombs. Others practically lived in the ballpark, given the amount of time they dedicated to it.

"Ah, that Rotunda! A huge cavelike opening which on the hottest days was refreshingly cool," Irving Rudd wrote. "Near the clubhouse of the Dodgers was the dressing room of the umpires, and further on down were the business manager's ticket offices and upstairs to the right the H. M. Stevens kitchens, where if you were known, Mr. Frank and Mr. Joe, the sons of the original H. M. Stevens, saw to it that you enjoyed a nice lunch. The doughnuts and the coffee were absolutely haute cuisine and a guy who worked for the Dodgers could be with Red Smith, Frank Graham, Jocko Conlon, the umpire, or Chuck Dressen."[8]

Always more, Ebbets Field was personality, ritual, an effect on the psyche: Charley "The Brow" DiGiovanni, the batboy from the East New York section of Brooklyn, as old as some of the players; Larry Bersin, the pharmaceutical salesman who'd come to the clubhouse doors with the stenciled admonition "NO VISITORS ALLOWED," who'd have to leave the park and buy a ticket if his sales call went past twelve noon; the students at Brooklyn Prep, a few blocks away from the ballpark, silently acknowledging the cadences of fandom wafting through the windows, the echoes of cheers a diversionary respite from the stoic pursuits at hand.

What makes Ebbets Field the greatest ballpark ever? It was Jim McElroy, the St. Francis College baseball coach, with his legions of youngsters from the Brooklyn Cadets, Frank and Joe Torre among them, having occasion to take a cadet, now and then, down to Ebbets Field to compete on Happy Felton's show. It was John Loughran or Max Israelite hiding silently waiting for the gates to open; John Nichols hiding from the bellowing Big Joe Moore, the special cop who, with Durocher, pummelled Christian; Arthur Harrow waiting with his autograph book. It was Tom Knight going wide-eyed to his first game and coming home to a block full of people who wanted to know about it; a surprised Jack Kavanaugh in a moment of revelation fielding a home run on Bedford Avenue hit over the wall. It was Murray Rubin walking all the way with his friends from East New York knowing his father altered the players' suits at Abe Stark's. Or Richard Leeds checking from the Boys' Room of P.S. 161 to see whether the flag was still up, and thus the game still on, under threatening skies. Or Edgar Feldman watching the fans put on their suit jackets backward in center field to create a better hitter's background for the home team and then doffing them in favor of white shirts for the visitors. It was Charlie Knapp, with his younger brother, looking over his shoulder to see the approving glances of Mrs. Robinson and Mrs. McGraw, or running on the field after a game, close enough to Rogers Hornsby to see the sweat on his forehead. Or hearing the fans next to him watching a foul ball land on the sloped roof, with its imaginary funnel and pipe leading the baseball back to Charley Ebbets's inner sanctum, saying, "There goes one for the office." It was *their* ballpark, *their* team.

It seemed like everyone except Walter O'Malley and Fresco Thompson felt the same way about Ebbets Field. "I grew up in Brooklyn," said Ann Dermansky. "My father had the first cut-rate drug store in the borough, Evans Drug, opposite Erasmus Hall High School. The two things I liked best in the world when I was eight to twelve years old: mucking about in my daddy's store and going with him to see the Dodgers play at Ebbets Field. It was a dark, mysterious place . . . low ceilinged, damp, dangerous (I, of course, was safe: I was with my daddy), intensely glamorous. You stepped out of the shadows into brilliant light, the field a perfect, Crayola-color green. A short round man saw you to your seats, acting as if these were the perfect seats, and swiped at them with a cloth. My father gave him some change.

"Baseball was a boy's world; Ebbets Field was a man's world. My father got a little score card and pencil and filled it in, using the game's shorthand, surrounded by men who did exactly the same thing. I was a girl, but I knew the players. Cal Abrams, a pinch hitter and certainly no star, lived on East Twenty-ninth Street in Brooklyn, my block. I never saw him in the neighborhood (never saw him play either), but I felt touched by his presence. The Duke, Campanella, Newcombe, Pee Wee Reese: baseball players were bigger than life. I knew all the names. I rooted. When Bobby Thomson hit his terrible home run, I heard it on the radio and later walked down Avenue V with my girlfriend Elissa, crying.

"Ebbets Field was peanuts in the shell crammed into a small brown paper bag. It was throwing the shells on the floor, it was yelling and angry gestures and screaming with joy as a ball sailed over the fence. It was bad behavior sanctioned, encouraged. It was a community. It was a little girl sharing her father's world, overjoyed to be with him. My mother stayed home: too noisy, too smelly; my brother was a baby, too young to go.

"I wanted to catch a ball. Years later, I did, a ball pitched by Tom Seaver and fouled down the third base line by Bobby Lenk. My father, long gone, would have been proud of me, even though I didn't exactly catch the ball. I was taking my daughter to the bathroom at Shea Stadium when out of the corner of my eye I saw the trajectory of something that, yes, a ball, it was a ball that came into the opening under the stands. Wait for me, I yelled at my kid, as I was going after and grabbing the ball.

"When the Dodgers were moved, I learned the hard lessons that so many kids in Brooklyn learned. Baseball was a business. No one cared about true allegiance, about 'rooting.' It was the end of childhood, the beginning of cynicism.

"When I heard that Ebbets Field was to be torn down and apartment houses would go up in its place, I was desolate. Later I was angry. The Brooklyn of my childhood—Ebbets Field, Evans, and the Loew's Kings—was gone. Ocean Avenue, where my aunt lived, the rich one with the baby grand piano and the Oriental rug, became a shooting gallery. Flatbush Avenue became a shabby bazaar, the stores shuttered at night behind metal grates, the great movie palaces gone the way of the ball field. I've revisited some of my old haunts, those that remain, but I've never made a pilgrimage to Bedford Avenue. I never will. They had no right to tear it down, the young girl's voice says, as if right and wrong had anything to do with real estate.

"How I loved that place and my daddy and going to see the Dodgers with him. Both gone now, long gone.

"Walking my dog late last night," Ann Dermansky remembered in April of 1994, "I met a neighbor who told me when he was a kid growing up in Livingston Manor, New Jersey, twice a summer he boarded a bus bound for Ebbets Field. He too recalls coming out of the dark into the dazzle of green, the world's greatest stage set, magic."

Professional baseball returned to Brooklyn at 7:19 P.M. on the 26th of June in 2001 after an absence of forty-four years, a chasm that almost matched the life span of Ebbets Field. It was a special day, with a shimmering summer sun that turned it into a warm evening in more ways than one. The advent of the Brooklyn Cyclones, a Class A, short-season, New York Mets farm team, was celebrated with a five o'clock parade down Coney Island's Surf Avenue. Featured were the bagpipe bands of every New York City uniformed service, including that of the Fire Department, which had just buried three of its heroes in the wake of a hardware store fire in Queens the previous week.

Scores of Little League teams and numerous school and neighborhood organization bands marched and played with levels of precision that matched the spirit of the hour. They paraded by the Cyclone roller coaster, from which the team took its name, by the carousels and bumper cars, by Nathan's Famous and the old Tilyou building that once housed an RKO theater of the same name. A block from the new ballpark, the legions paraded past the West Fifteenth Street that once housed the F.D.N.Y.'s Engine Company 244, a place where my father hoisted a hose. It also was the same block where my mother's father ran a little café during Prohibition where you could get a little anisette in your coffee, if you know what I mean.

The ballpark is a tidy, little $39 million jewel in the southernmost part of Brooklyn on the site of the old Steeplechase Park. It stands in the shadow of the famed Parachute Jump, silhouetted by the Boardwalk, the beach, and the Atlantic Ocean. It's the first good thing to happen to Coney Island in close to fifty years, a new oasis on a ramshackle boulevard of dreams.

Mrs. Joan Hodges (who still lives on Bedford Avenue in the same house she shared with Gil) was there; so was pitcher Ralph Branca, and Joe Pignatano, who caught the last few innings at Ebbets Field for the Dodgers. So were Lou Dallajacono and the Brooklyn Dodgers Sym-Phony Band. The ballpark featured small wall-to-wall advertisements in the way that most minor league parks do. It shares a parking lot that also serves an adjacent city-run ice-skating rink named for Abe Stark. And in a homage to Stark, two of the outfield wall's advertisements offer giveaways if struck precisely by a batted ball, including Garage Clothing's free suit to any player and the Wonder Wheel's offer of a free ride to all fans in the 7,500-seat capacity stands.

The players were kids, most of them nineteen to twenty-one, a number of them on the Cyclones housed at the Xavierian High School Rectory in Bay Ridge, a mile-plus from where the Duke, Oisk, and Pee Wee lived. Two or three generations after Jackie Robinson, they came to play in Brooklyn from places as far afield as Australia and the Dominican Republic.

Coney Island's omnipresent gentle breeze off the ocean, "even on the hottest summer day" as Dad always said, blew the flag straight in from center field, leading to musings about the ballpark's likelihood to favor pitchers. The Sym-Phony played "When the Saints Go Marching In" and other standards in front of the concession stands while we waited to see the musicians in the aisles. Occasionally, when the formulaic, between-innings drivel currently being piped out of sound systems at every ballpark in America aborted, an organ whose sound was much more in synch with Coney Island's amusement traditions played in welcome throwback.

The home team was pitted against the Mahoning Valley Scrappers, who were said to be from someplace in Ohio, or something like that. No one really cared where they were from, not that offense should be taken. That was not what this night was about. It had to do with finding what was lost such a long and short time ago. What Reverend McKinney called the great pride and sense of what it was to be in Brooklyn.

The first pitch, thrown by nineteen-year-old Matthew Peterson of Alexandria, Louisiana, was a strike; the first hit, a single by twenty-year old Brooklyn infielder Leandro Arias of Santo Domingo, came in the third inning.

The stands were filled with Brooklyn names, the Joe White you grew up with who remains your closest friend, and the Tom Knight who recalls baseball legacies with the care reserved for opening buried treasure, as well as others met for the first time, including, quite improbably, Bobby Thomson, who, seated in the row ahead, spelled his name the same way as the Dodgers' old nemesis. We all found the places and people in common, the quizzical talk of wonder and pride in sense of place, its coincidental moments and its denizens, present and past. All of that was accentuated by a discovery in midgame that Thomson had my brother Ray's number in the speed dial of his cell phone, something that couldn't have happened at Ebbets Field. And also that he was bidding to do the concrete in my parents' alley in Dyker Heights. Concrete. Brooklyn. Eyes closed, the smell of sea salt, an imperceptible shake of the head, an unimaginable tableau, and for a moment, your own history and an unknown future are light as a feather, the space in your mind preserved for creating a new memory.

The best was saved for last, as should always be the case. With two out in the bottom of the ninth and the home team down 2–0 and the glorious night all but resignedly lost, a young man named Edgar Rodriguez of San Pedro de Macoris—dubbed E-Rod by the Cyclones' media staff—hit a rope line drive into that stiff breeze. It shot meteorically through the night, moving people out of their seats as quickly as the clowns' electric prods had moved people hurriedly away after they rode the horse-race ride at old Steeplechase Park fifty years before. In the throes of the game's magic, the little park erupted, following the rising ball up, out, and over the left-center-field wall by the scoreboard. The game was miraculously tied. An inning later, with nobody out and the bases loaded in the bottom of the tenth, Michael Jacobs of Chula Vista, California, otherwise collared with strikeouts, hit the sacrifice fly that brought home the winning run and the game for Brooklyn.

There it was. A walk-off. A media mob. Fifteen cameras. Satellite trucks. Fireworks. O'Malley was dead. His offspring had sold the Dodgers. And baseball was back in Brooklyn.

Appendix

EBBETS FIELD SPECIAL GROUND RULES

Home Run
1. Ball remaining in enclosure in right center field.
2. Ball hitting foul marker and/or attached screen ABOVE wire fence in right field.
3. Ball remaining on top of or behind scoreboard.
4. Ball hitting on or beyond left-field foul marker.
5. Ball hitting flag or flagpole atop scoreboard above fence level.
6. Hitting grillwork in centerfield.

Ball in Play

Ball hitting left-field foul marker that is below lower left-field seats and bouncing back into playing field is in play.

Ball in play in bullpens.

Ball in play if it hits clock.

Two Bases

Ball hitting left-field foul marker that is below lower left-field seats and bouncing into stands, two bases.

Ball staying under or on top of canvas cover along left-field foul line, two bases.

Ball going through screen, remaining in screen; remaining on ledge; sticking in or going through scoreboard; remaining on clock; two bases.

Benches

Start from bat racks to markers.

Notes

1. Hallowed Ground

Some of the background information in this chapter comes from interviews or correspondence with Dave Anderson, Eli Barker, Buzzie Bavasi, Carl Erskine, Tommy Holmes, Stan Isaacs, Tom Knight, Leonard Koppett, Jack Mann, Danny McDevitt, and Murray Rubin.

1. These sentiments were also reflected in similar language by the Rev. Donald McKinney in "The Bums," a sermon delivered February 3, 1985, in the First Unitarian Church in Brooklyn Heights. See *The Brooklyn Unitarian*, vol. 27, no. 22, of the same date.

2. Shelley Mehlman Dinhofer, *The Art of Baseball: The Great American Game in Painting, Sculpture, and Folk Art* (New York: Harmony Books, 1990), 80.

3. *Time*, April 28, 1958, 58.

4. Snider, Newcombe, and Labine quotes from the film *When It Was a Game*, Ross Greenburg, executive producer; George Roy, Steven Stern, David Harmon, producers; Steven Stern, writer; George Roy, editor, premiered on PBS, 1993.

5. Pete Hamill, "Never Forgive, Never Forget," *New York Post*, October 3, 1988.

6. Lafayette F. Thompson, with Cy Rice, *Inside the Dodgers* (Los Angeles: Holloway House, 1966), 140–141.

7. Ibid.

8. Bruce Kuklick, *To Every Thing a Season: Shibe Park and Urban Philadelphia, 1909–1976.* (Princeton, N.J.: Princeton University Press, 1991), 136.

9. *New York Journal American*, October 1, 1959.

10. See the *New York Times* obituary for Otto Miller on March 30, 1962. Miller had cataract surgery on his left eye two days before his death on March 29 at Brooklyn Eye and Ear Hospital, when he jumped or fell out of a four-story window. Investigations concerning suicide were inconclusive. Dodger Stadium was opened at Chavez Ravine in Los Angeles on April 10.

11. *New York Times*, March 3, 1960.

12. *Brooklyn Paper*, March 10–24, 1982.

13. Ibid.

14. *New York Times*, January 1, 1960.

15. Murray Polner, *Branch Rickey* (New York: Atheneum, 1982), 252–253. "My eight years in Brooklyn gave me a new vision of America, or rather America gave me a new vision of a part of itself, Brooklyn," Rickey said. "They were wonderful years. A community of over three million people, proud, hurt, jealous, seeking geographical, social, emotional status as a city apart and alone and sufficient. One could not live for eight years in Brooklyn and not catch its spirit of devotion to its baseball club, such as no other city in America equaled. Call it loyalty and so it was. It would be a crime against a community of three million people to move the Dodgers. Not that the move was unlawful, since people have the right to do as they please with their property. But a baseball club in any city in America is a quasi-public institution, and in Brooklyn the Dodgers were public without the quasi." When later shown a picture of the wooden construction fence with posted billboard ads amid the destruction around the ballpark site in the wake of Ebbets Field's demolition, Rickey said, "This dark, gloom-shrouded picture is a symbol of sadness for me and hundreds of thousands of people. Ebbets Field is a bleak and empty place here. All the joy and love and great devotion have left this diamond behind the torn and tattered posters. The grandstand is leveled, the voices are silent. By some strange coincidence the picture was taken on the day, almost the hour, that my son died. [Branch Rickey Jr., who suffered from acute diabetes, died of hepatitis on April 11, 1961.] I lived in Brooklyn for eight years, but it doesn't take long to fall in love with the place. I did. Branch Jr. did. Our whole family did. We were devoted to the people, the Dodgers, and the ballpark."

2. The Squire of Flatbush

1. Richard Goldstein, *Superstars and Screwballs: 100 Years of Brooklyn Baseball* (New York: E. P. Dutton, 1991), 13–14. Also see Michael Gershman, *Diamonds: The Evolution of the Ballpark* (Boston: Houghton Mifflin, 1993), 11–14; and Philip J. Lowry, *Green Cathedrals* (Reading, MA: Addison-Wesley, 1992), 114.

2. See Goldstein, *Superstars and Screwballs*, 5, 13.

3. See ibid., 15; see also Lowry, *Green Cathedrals*, 114.

4. Goldstein, *Superstars and Screwballs*, 15.

5. Lowry, *Green Cathedrals*, 114.

6. Goldstein, *Superstars and Screwballs*, 23.

7. See Ebbets's comments in the *Brookyn Eagle* on January 23, 1913, in the paper's serialized "History of Baseball in Brooklyn" written by Ebbets and edited by Thomas Rice.

8. Ellen M. Snyder-Grenier, *Brooklyn: An Illustrated History* (Philadelphia: Temple University Press, 1996), 232.

9. See Charles H. Ebbets, "History of Baseball in Brooklyn," *Brooklyn Daily Eagle*, January 18, 1913; other sources include Frank Graham, *The Brooklyn Dodgers: An Informal History* (New York: G. P. Putnam's Sons, 1945), 8; Andy McCue, "A History of Dodger Ownership," *The National Pastime: A Review of Baseball Literature* (Society for American Baseball Research), 13 (1993): 34; and Goldstein, *Superstars and Screwballs*, 32–38.

10. *Brooklyn Daily Eagle*, January 4, 1898, 16.

11. Lowry, *Green Cathedrals*, 115.

12. John J. Gallagher, *The Battle of Brooklyn, 1776* (New York: Sarpedon, 1995), 13–17.

13. Goldstein, *Superstars and Screwballs*, 33.

14. See Charles H. Ebbets, "History of Baseball in Brooklyn," *Brooklyn Daily Eagle*, January 18, 1913, on the team's name; and *Sporting Life*, April 9, 1884, 4, on giving up the stockings.

15. Charles H. Ebbets, "History of Baseball in Brooklyn," *Brooklyn Daily Eagle*, January 18, 1913.

16. See the *Brooklyn Daily Standard Union*, April 9, 1913, for a biography of Ebbets and his son, Charles Jr.; other biographically instructive pieces about Ebbets appeared in the *Brooklyn Daily Eagle*, May 10, 1907; and the *New York Herald*, October 20, 1920.

17. Much of the information about the Ebbets's family background was either provided by or discussed with Ebbets family genealogist Ted Steele, who compared notes with the author. See Edward E. Steele, *Ebbets: The History and Genealogy of a New York Family* (St. Louis: Creative Imaging Inc., 2005).

18. Charles H. Ebbets, "History of Baseball in Brooklyn," *Brooklyn Daily Eagle*, January 19, 1913.

19. *New York Evening Sun*, January 27, 1888.

20. On Charles Ebbets's name and his parents' names, see his death certificate in New York City's Municipal Archives.

21. Charles H. Ebbets, "History of Baseball in Brooklyn," *Brooklyn Daily Eagle*, February 10, 1913.

22. Svein Arber, writing as Damon Rice, in *Seasons Past* (New York: Praeger, 1976), 56. Although *Seasons Past* has a fictional family around which the New York baseball seasons unfold, all of the baseball history and baseball events in the book are true. Damon Rice is a pseudonym in tribute to writers Damon Runyon and Grantland Rice; the book's real authors are Svein Arber (b. 1937), who wrote the National League accounts and synthesized the American League accounts, and Ford Hovis (b. 1942), who wrote the American League history. Arber and Hovis collaborated on the fictional narrative. New York newspaperman Harold Rosenthal edited the book.

23. In the *Brooklyn Daily Eagle* of February 15, 1913, Charley Ebbets, recounting Brooklyn's move from the American Association to the National League, said, "While President Byrne and his associates in the Brooklyn Club had not hesitated to admit that they would jump to the National League after they won a pennant in the American Association, they might have postponed that step indefinitely had it not been for the course taken by a clique in the Association. Mr. Byrne, A. S. Stern of Cincinnati and L. S. Krauthoff of

Kansas City were in New York on November 13, 1889, attending a meeting of the Board of Arbitration, when a combination of Association magnates, representing St. Louis, Louisville, Columbus and the Philadelphia Athletics, secretly assembled in Philadelphia and framed up a plan to run the organization. First and foremost, they determined to cut Brooklyn and Cincinnati off all committees."

24. Chauncey was such a large landowner in the area that a street in the neighborhood was named for him. Years later, when Jackie Gleason played Ralph Kramden in the 1950s TV series *The Honeymooners*, 704 Chauncey Street was the Kramdens' address. Chauncey Street also was the street where Gleason lived growing up in Brooklyn.

25. For details on stock transactions and Dodger ownership, see McCue, "A History of Dodger Ownership," 34.

26. Graham, *Brooklyn Dodgers*, 8.

27. Dorothy Ebbets Dollmeyer, "Family History for Her Children and Grandchildren" (manuscript, Everett, WA, 1982).

28. Ebbets ran in 1897 with two other Democrats, Harry French and Henry R. Nostrand, for the three City Council seats from the 7th District. Their Republican opponents were Adam H. Letch, George R. Bannerman, and Frederick W. Singleton. Charley was elected for a four-year council term along with French, with Letch the sole victorious Republican, surpassing Nostrand. (Nostrand Avenue remains one of Brooklyn's most familiar street names a century later.) Out of the twenty-five council committees, Ebbets was assigned to four: Law; Parks; Salaries and Officers; and Privileges and Elections. Ebbets also ran for and lost an electon for a New York State Senate seat in 1904.

29. McKeever, who lived at 135 Sixth Avenue in Park Slope, bested Timothy Mayher in their 11th District race.

30. *Brooklyn Daily Eagle*, January 2, 1898.

31. *Brooklyn Daily Citizen*, January 2, 1898.

32. Graham, *Brooklyn Dodgers*, 9.

33. *New York Times*, April 22, 1898.

34. *Brooklyn Daily Citizen*, January 2, 1898.

35. *Brooklyn Daily Eagle*, May 10, 1907.

36. Bill Shannon and George Kalinsky, *The Ballparks* (New York: Hawthorne, 1975), 11.

37. See the Brooklyn Historical Society's "Crow Hill" file.

38. Ibid.

3. A Steward in the Rough

Some background information in this chapter comes from an interview with Leonard Koppett.

1. The ballpark's name commemorates John Forbes, a British general who captured Fort Duquesne from the French in 1758 during the era of the French and Indian War and renamed it Fort Pitt. See Philip J. Lowry, *Green Cathedrals* (Reading, MA: Addison-Wesley, 1992), 217.

2. Lawrence Ritter, *Lost Ballparks* (New York: Viking, 1992), 64.

3. Frank Graham, *The Brooklyn Dodgers: An Informal History* (1945; New York: G. P. Putnam's Sons, 1948), 27.

4. Also in 1910, before the season began, rumors surfaced that there was syndicate ownership of the Brooklyn team, with some of the shares held by either Charles P. Taft of the Cincinnati ball club or Charles W. Murphy of Chicago. Ebbets knocked the rumors down immediately, calling newspapermen over to Washington Park on March 1, putting before them all 2,500 shares of the club's stock. Ebbets Sr. held 1,499 shares; his son, Charles Jr., 250 shares; Henry Medicus, the treasurer, 749 shares; A. C. Wall of Jersey City, 1 share; and Robert A. Wright, of Brooklyn, 1 share. (New Jersey law, under which the ball club was incorporated, required that the team must have at least five directors, one of whom must be a resident of that state.) A photograph of the stock certificates appeared in the March 2, 1910, edition of the *Brooklyn Daily Eagle*. Charley said that he was opposed to syndicate ball and that the time when it was necessary for one man to hold stock in two ball clubs had passed. He proclaimed his advocacy of local ownership and his belief that stockholders should live where the team played.

5. See the *New York Sun*, October 28, 1919, providing details of Minnie Ebbets's divorce suit, in which she claimed she first learned that her husband had "committed indiscretions" nine years before, that she had not lived with him as his wife since then, and also that he had left their home eight years before. Ebbets admitted he had no defense against her suit.

6. *Brooklyn Citizen*, January 2, 1912.

7. *Brooklyn Daily Standard Union*, January 3, 1912.

8. *Brooklyn Citizen*, January 2, 1912.

9. *Brooklyn Daily Eagle*, January 3, 1912, 2.

10. Ibid.

11. Ibid.

12. *Brooklyn Citizen*, January 3, 1912.

13. Ebbets later gave an interview to the *Brooklyn Daily Eagle*, published October 3, 1920, in which he said that only $500 was paid for the parcel, an amount that Graham mentions on page 24 of his book *The Brooklyn Dodgers*. News stories around the time immediately following the press conference announcing plans to build the ballpark in 1912 said $2,000 was paid for the parcel that belonged to the difficult-to-find absentee owner. In the *Eagle* on January 3, 1912, Howard Pyle, the realtor, said the man "cooly" demanded $2,000 for a $100 plot, and got it. Pyle, of course, was closer to the story in 1912 than Ebbets was in 1920.

14. The name of the Consumers Park station would later be changed to Prospect Park.

15. *Brooklyn Citizen*, January 3, 1912.

16. See Michael Gershman, *Diamonds: The Evolution of the Ballpark* (New York: Houghton Mifflin, 1993), 111.

17. *Brooklyn Citizen*, March 5, 1912.

18. *Brooklyn Daily Eagle*, March 5, 1912.

19. Charles H. Ebbets, "Why I Am Building a Baseball Stadium," *People's Weekly*, April 4, 1912, 392.

20. Ritter, *Lost Ballparks*, 42.

21. *Brooklyn Times*, July 6, 1912, 12.

22. The best distillation of all the information surrounding the issue of what the McKeevers paid is by historian Andy McCue in the journal of the Society for American Baseball Research (SABR), *The National Pastime* 13

(1993): 38–39. As McCue states, "Most of the contemporary sources refer to a figure of $100,000, but the *Sporting News* obituary of Steve McKeever says it was $250,000 and Robert Creamer's biography of Casey Stengel lists it as $500,000." McCue also notes that although Ebbets's public cost estimate including land was $750,000, his May 12, 1912, letter to August Hermann, chairman of the National Commission, the three-man body that oversaw baseball before the commissioner system, provided for a construction budget of $325,000 plus $200,000 for the land, $100,000 of which had already been paid. Ebbets estimated the remaining $425,000 would be raised from a bond sale of $275,000, a bank loan of $100,000 that he intended to secure, and a $50,000 profit that he anticipated from the team's 1912 revenues. In the citations for his article, McCue draws particularly on an unpublished paper by Matthew Kachur, "Brooklyn, Baseball, and Ebbets Field."

23. *Brooklyn Citizen*, August 29, 1912, 1, 12.

24. Robert Creamer, *Stengel: His Life and Times* (New York: Simon & Schuster, 1984), 55.

25. *Brooklyn Times*, September 21, 1912, 8.

26. See *Brooklyn Daily Eagle*, April 3 and 9, 1913.

27. *Brooklyn Times*, September 14, 1912.

28. *Brooklyn Daily Eagle*, January 16, 1913.

29. See Hugh Dalziel Duncan, *Symbols in Society* (New York: Oxford University Press, 1968); Murray Edelman, *The Symbolic Uses of Politics* (Chicago: University of Illinois Press, 1967).

4. The New Ballpark

1. In comparison with Ebbets Field's right-field line just short of 300 feet, left-field line of 419 feet, and center-field distance of 450 feet, two of the parks built after 1909 had shorter right-field lines: League Park in Cleveland (290 feet) and the odd-shaped field of the Polo Grounds (257 feet). More typical of the day were the 360-foot lines of Shibe Park and Redland Field, and those of Comiskey Park (362 feet), Navin Field (372 feet), and Forbes Field (376). Fenway Park (314 feet) and Washington's Griffith Stadium (320 feet) had right-field dimensions more typical of today's parks. Yet Griffith's left-field line (407 feet) was almost as long as Ebbets Field's, and like League Park (385 feet), each had a left-field line significantly longer than its opposite in right. Fenway's (324 feet), on the other hand, had only a slightly longer left-field line than right-field line, but the right-field barrier at Fenway has always veered out quickly into a deeper field. And while its left-field barrier has always been at least 25 feet high, the right-field barrier has always been only a few feet high. Comiskey Park (362 feet) and Shibe Park and Redland Field (both 360 feet) all had symmetrical lines, while Navin Field (345 feet) and Forbes Field (360 feet) had shorter left-field than right-field lines. Philip J. Lowry, *Green Cathedrals* (Reading, MA: Addison-Wesley, 1992).

2. *Brooklyn Daily Eagle*, March 30, 1913.

3. *Brooklyn Daily Eagle*, April 4, 1913.

4. Ibid.

5. *Brooklyn Daily Eagle*, April 6, 1913.

6. Richard Goldstein, *Superstars and Screwballs: 100 Years of Brooklyn Baseball* (New York: E. P. Dutton, 1991), 100–101; also the *New York American*, April 6, 1913.

7. *Brooklyn Daily Eagle*, April 6, 1913.

8. *Brooklyn Daily Standard Union*, April 9, 1913.

9. The Ebbets remark, "It looks like a big season," was reported in the *New York Times*, April 6, 1913.

10. *Brooklyn Daily Eagle*, April 27, 1913.

11. *Brooklyn Daily Eagle*, April 28, 1913.

12. *Brooklyn Daily Eagle*, April 29, 1913.

13. Ibid.

14. *Brooklyn Daily Eagle*, May 11, 1913.

15. See John Lewy's recap of Ebbets Field history in the World Series special of the magazine *P.M.* just before the 1941 World Series.

16. Dorothy Ebbets Dollmeyer, "Family History for Her Children and Grandchildren" (manuscript, Everett, WA, 1982).

17. John Thorn and Pete Palmer, eds., with Michael Gershman, *Total Baseball: The Ultimate Encyclopedia of Baseball*, 3rd ed. (New York: HarperCollins, 1993), 143–147.

18. Jack Kavanaugh and Norman Macht, *Uncle Robbie* (Cleveland: Society for American Baseball Research, 1999), 31.

19. *Brooklyn Daily Eagle*, March 5, 1914.

20. J. G. Taylor Spink, *Judge Landis and Twenty-five Years of Baseball* (New York: Crowell, 1947), 29–40.

21. *New York Times*, June 1, 1915.

22. Ibid.

23. Frank Graham, *The Brooklyn Dodgers: An Informal History* (1945; New York: G. P. Putnam's Sons, 1948), 55.

24. See Thomas Rice's account in the *Brooklyn Daily Eagle*, October 4, 1916.

25. Robert Creamer, *Stengel: His Life and Times* (New York: Simon & Schuster, 1984), 109.

26. Stories in the *Brooklyn Daily Eagle* of October 10 and 11, 1916, indicate that former Braves owner Gaffney was interested in buying the stock. Ed McKeever estimated that it would cost any buyer $2 million before the partners would be interested in selling.

27. *Brooklyn Daily Eagle*, October 11, 1916.

5. Robins' Nest

Some background information in this chapter comes from an interview with Charlie Knapp.

1. Robert Creamer, *Stengel: His Life and Times* (New York: Simon & Schuster, 1984), 115.

2. See Frank Graham, *The Brooklyn Dodgers: An Informal History* (New York: G. P. Putnam's Sons, 1945), 68, and Richard Goldstein, *Superstars and Screwballs: 100 Years of Brooklyn Baseball* (New York: E. P. Dutton, 1991), 125–127. As Goldstein describes, "The following September, a Brooklyn court ruled that the band concert was merely a subterfuge and that the team had

violated the Sunday laws. Imposition of a fine was, however, suspended." Goldstein also notes that the Sunday baseball ban would finally end in New York in 1919 when the state legislature "passed a measure sponsored by State Senator James J. Walker—the playboy mayor of New York City during the 1920s—allowing ballgames on the Sabbath by local option."

3. John Thorn and Pete Palmer, eds., with Michael Gershman, *Total Baseball: The Ultimate Encyclopedia of Baseball*, 3rd ed. (New York: HarperCollins, 1993), 144.

4. Creamer, *Stengel*, 128–129; see also *New York Times*, May 26, 1919.

5. Creamer, *Stengel*, 128–129.

6. See the *New York Sun*, September 6, 1919. See also articles in the *Sun* on October 18, 23, 28, November 4, and December 27, 1919. Both Minnie and Charley were living in Flatbush at the time, Minnie at 193 Ocean Avenue, Charley at 1466 Avenue G, later to be known as Glenwood Road.

7. *New York Sun*, October 18, 1919.

8. Robert Peterson, *Only the Ball Was White* (New York: Oxford University Press, 1970), 56.

9. Neil Lanctot, *Negro League Baseball: The Rise and Ruin of a Black Institution* (Philadelphia: University of Pennsylvania Press, 2004), 4.

10. Ibid.

11. Ibid., 24–25.

12. Graham, *Brooklyn Dodgers*, 79.

13. A rare picture of the Ebbets Field 1920s-era scoreboard in the left-field "circus seats" bleacher area, with fans shoehorned in front of the scoreboard before a game between the Giants and the Dodgers, shows that the visitor's lineup is listed 1–2–3–4, and so on, while Brooklyn's is listed 1–2–3–5, indicating that manager Robinson had juggled his lineup and wasn't using his regular cleanup hitter that afternoon.

14. Graham, *Brooklyn Dodgers*, 81.

15. Goldstein, *Superstars and Screwballs*, 135.

16. Graham, *Brooklyn Dodgers*, 81.

17. *Brooklyn Daily Eagle*, October 7, 1920.

18. *New York Herald*, October 20, 1920.

19. Interview with Martha Dollmeyer Skinner, Charley Ebbets's great-granddaughter and Dorothy Ebbets Dollmeyer's daughter.

20. *New York Herald*, October 20, 1920.

21. Graham, *Brooklyn Dodgers*, 32.

22. Dorothy Ebbets Dollmeyer, "Family History for Her Children and Grandchildren" (manuscript, Everett, WA, 1982).

23. Graham, *Brooklyn Dodgers*, 90–91.

24. Ibid., 90.

25 *New York World*, September 29, 1923.

26. *New York Herald*, July 12, 1923.

27. See the *Brooklyn Daily Eagle* from July 16, 1924, which discusses the events of July 1923.

28. Apple Annie remained on the Ebbets Field scene until after the 1930 season.

29. Roger Angell, "West Side Story," *New Yorker*, July 15, 1996, 26.

30. Graham, *Brooklyn Dodgers*, 95.

31. See the obituaries on Ed McKeever from the *New York Times, Brooklyn Daily Eagle,* and *Brooklyn Standard Union,* April 30, 1925. The report that McKeever had remarked two weeks prior to his death that he had never had a sick day in his life and that he "knocked wood" on his desk at Ebbets Field appeared in the *Brooklyn Citizen* of April 30, 1925.

32. Angell, "West Side Story," 26.

33. Ibid.

6. The Daffiness Boys

Some background information in this chapter comes from interviews or correspondence with Svein Arber, Woody English, Edgar Feldman, Arthur Harrow, Buddy Hassett, Max Israelite, Charlie Knapp, Tom Knight, Richard Leeds, John Loughran, John Nichols, Murray Rubin, Overton Tremper, Douglas Van Buskirk, and Sam Winchell.

1. Svein Arber, writing as Damon Rice in *Seasons Past* (New York: Praeger, 1976), 211.

2. Regarding Mickey O'Neil substituting for Otto Miller in the third base coaching box in the famous three-men-on-third-base incident, see Norman Macht and Jack Kavanaugh, *Uncle Robbie* (Cleveland: Society for American Baseball Research, 1999), 151. "O'Neil bolted out to the third base coach's box at the start of the [Robins'] fifth inning," write Kavanaugh and Macht.

3. Larry R. Gerlach, *The Men in Blue: Conversations with Umpires* (Lincoln: University of Nebraska Press, 1980), 21.

4. Arber, as Damon Rice, *Seasons Past,* 213.

5. Stan Grosshandler, "The Brooklyn Dodgers," *Coffin Corner* 12, no. 3 (1990), 3.

6. "Harmony under the Stars in the Dodgers Lair: Close-up of Abe Stark," *New York Post,* June 6, 1949. For information on Stark's salary at his first clothing store job, see the *New York World-Telegram,* October 18, 1949.

7. Richard Goldstein, *Superstars, and Screwballs: 100 Years of Brooklyn Baseball* (New York: Dutton, 1991), 15

8. "Harmony under the Stars."

9. See Arber, as Damon Rice, *Seasons Past,* 218, quoting from the *Brooklyn Daily Eagle*'s Thomas Rice, who also was a correspondent for the *Sporting News.*

10. *New York Times,* January 11, 1928, 31.

11. *New York Times,* January 10, 1928, 35.

12. *New York Times,* October 13, 1928.

13. *Brooklyn Daily Eagle,* April 14, 1929, C1.

14. *New York Sun,* February 11, 1930.

15. *Brooklyn Daily Eagle,* April 11, 1931.

16. Arber, as Damon Rice, *Seasons Past,* 243.

17. Frank Graham, *The Brooklyn Dodgers: An Informal History* (New York: G. P. Putnam's Sons, 1945), 120. "Pressure of business was given as the reason for the retirement of York," according to the *New York Times.* York, who lived at 169 West Eightieth Street in Manhattan, was not involved with the club afterward. Within nine months of returning to his law firm, however,

he was removed as an executor of the Mary S. Morris estate by Surrogate Judge Delahanty, and was ordered to pay $99,488 to the estate for amounts not credited and monies York paid to himself without the court's permission. This all appeared unseemly for someone whose sister was in the convent and whose son was in the Jesuit order. See the *New York Sun* from June 29, 1933, for details of his ousting as an estate administrator. He died February 2, 1937, from pneumonia in Miserecordia Hospital in Manhattan. Obituaries credited him with quelling dissension among Dodger stockholders. See the *Brooklyn Daily Eagle* and the *New York Herald Tribune* obituaries from February 4, 1937.

18. The Ebbets estate was originally valued at $1,275,811 in May 1925, almost all of it in ball club stock. To his son, Charles Jr., perhaps because of his alcohol problems, he willed an annuity of $2,000 and some personal effects, including the diamond stickpin he received at the tribute dinner in 1912. The rest of the estate was divided into fifteen parts: three parts to widow Grace; three to daughter Genevieve; two each to daughters Maie and Anna Marie; two to his daughter-in-law Martha Ronayne Ebbets (who had married Charles Jr.); and three parts to his grandchildren then living. Since the ball club hadn't been sold, only income from the estate was paid to the beneficiaries.

19. See the *New York Sun*, September 18, 1933; January 22, 1934; and February 2, 1934. Also note that the Brooklyn Trust Company began handling the Ebbets estate after it had merged with Mechanics Bank, which was Charley Ebbets Sr.'s bank. An account of the testimony of Herbert W. Silleck, a vice president of the Brooklyn Trust Company and head of its Trust Department, appears in the *New York Sun* of March 16, 1934; Mr. Silleck testified the bank was satisfied with the ball club's directors and that two of the directors had been approved by the bank on behalf of the estate.

20. Graham, *Brooklyn Dodgers*, 132.

21. Goldstein, *Superstars and Screwballs*, 175.

22. Robert Creamer, *Stengel: His Life and Times* (New York: Simon & Schuster, 1984), 182–183.

23. Goldstein, *Superstars and Screwballs*, 175. See also Jack Kavanaugh and Norman Macht, *Uncle Robbie* (Cleveland: Society for American Baseball Research, 1999), 183.

24. Goldstein, *Superstars and Screwballs*, 177.

25. Creamer, *Stengel*, 187.

26. Ibid.

27. *New York Sun*, December 15, 1936.

28. See Neil Lanctot, *Negro League Baseball: The Rise and Ruin of a Black Institution* (Philadelphia: University of Pennsylvania Press, 2004), 218. Lanctot noted in correspondence with the author that the original McKeever attribution and the story that both raised the subject of Brooklyn's apparent interest while also, at that point, diminishing the expectation of any Paige signing appeared in the January 23, 1937, *New York Amsterdam News*. John Gorman, Brooklyn's business manager at the time, was reluctant to be quoted in the article but communicated that the decision would be left to Grimes. Stories about Grimes's unwillingness to use black players appeared later, in the *Baltimore Afro-American* of April 2, 1938, and the *Chicago Defender* of October 1, 1938. In the *Defender*, columnist Al Monroe quoted Grimes as saying "I would rather lose the pennant than to have Negro players on my ball club," something the columnist indicated Grimes hardly had to work hard at achieving. Although Grimes

hadn't yet been officially relieved of his managerial duties when this was reported and the quote seemingly had no role in his dismissal, Grimes's managerial days with the Dodgers, who finished seventh in 1938, were numbered: Larry MacPhail would announce he was no longer the team's manager on October 10.

29. *New York World Telegram*, October 18, 1949.

30. Jack Kavanaugh, "A Dodger Boyhood," *Baseball History* 3 (Meckler) (1990): 119–132.

31. *New York Times*, February 11, 1936.

32. A year later, Sharkey would become the world heavyweight champion when he was awarded a split decision over champion Max Schmeling, even though many thought Schmeling seemed to defend his title successfully. In his first title defense, Sharkey again fought Carnera, who this time knocked Sharkey out with a right uppercut in the sixth round.

33. Lanctot, *Negro League Baseball*, 10.

34. See Robert Peterson, *Only the Ball Was White* (New York: Oxford University Press, 1970), 112–114; Lanctot, *Negro League Baseball*, 9, 24–25.

35. John B. Holway, *Blackball Stars: Negro League Pioneers* (New York: Carroll & Graf, 1992), 161.

36. See Lanctot, *Negro League Baseball*, 41.

37. See ibid., 41–42, also 85–94; Peterson, *Only the Ball Was White*, 136–137.

38. Holway, *Blackball Stars*, 344.

39. See Grosshandler, "The Brooklyn Dodgers," 3–11.

40. Ibid.

41. St. John's suspended its football program in 1931. The university began another football program in 1973, but subsequently suspended that as well.

42. As members of the U.S. track team in the 1936 Berlin Olympics, Glickman and Sam Stoller were denied an opportunity to run in the 400-meter relay though they were scheduled to do so. By Glickman's own account, they were told by head track coach Lawson Robertson of their replacement in that event by Jesse Owens and Ralph Metcalfe the day before the race, though any combination of the American runners could have been expected to win the four-way relay by fifteen yards. Owens himself, who had previously triumphed, felt Glickman was entitled to run in that event. Glickman, who was Jewish, held U.S. Olympic Committee chair Avery Brundage and assistant coach Dean Cromwell chiefly responsible. Both were said to support the America First movement; many believed their anti-Semitism was blatant.

7. Larry and Leo: Lights, Camera, Action

Some of the background information in this chapter comes from interviews or correspondence with Larry Block, Dolph Camilli, Tommy Henrich, Leonard Koppett, Arnold Lapiner, Ann Lee, Edie McCaslin, and Joe Pollack.

1. *New York Sun*, November 18, 1937.

2. Frank Graham, *The Brooklyn Dodgers: An Informal History* (1945; New York: G. P. Putnam's Sons, 1948), 151.

3. Ibid., 159–160.

4. *Brooklyn Daily Eagle*, June 16, 1938.

5. Jack Kavanaugh, "A Dodger Boyhood," *Baseball History* 3 (Meckler) (1990): 119–132. "The detachable collar was already passé, but maybe not in Chicago," said Kavanaugh. "The idea was to save on laundry bills. A man's collar got dirty faster than the rest of his shirt. Cuffs, too, could be detachable, but the changeable soft collar for shirts was basic. The scorned ex-president Herbert Hoover had favored stiff collars, but only he and altar boys wore them. I still had front and back collar buttons from my own recent years as an altar boy. So, with three detachable collars and two collarless white shirts, and a Chinese laundry around the corner from where we lived, I was set. The green necktie was easy to come by in an Irish family. It was standard neckwear for St. Patrick's Day. I needed one more item. There was a new federal requirement. I had to have a social security card."

6. Graham, *Brooklyn Dodgers,* 179.

7. Bob Edwards, *Fridays with Red: A Radio Friendship* (New York: Simon & Schuster, 1993), 81–82.

8. *New York Herald Tribune,* October 30, 1934.

9. *New York Times,* October 29, 1939.

10. Kavanaugh, "A Dodger Boyhood," 119–132.

11. Ibid.

12. Tom Knight, "George Magerkurth," *National Pastime: A Review of Baseball History* 13 (1993): 14.

13. Svein Arber, writing as Damon Rice in *Seasons Past* (New York: Praeger, 1976), 289.

14. Kavanaugh, "A Dodger Boyhood," 119–132.

15. Red Smith, *To Absent Friends* (New York: Atheneum, 1982), 149–150.

16. Ibid.

17. W. C. Heinz, *Once They Heard the Cheers* (Garden City, NY: Doubleday, 1979), 399.

18. Graham, *Brooklyn Dodgers,* 203.

19. *Brooklyn Eagle,* September 26, 1941. John J. Rooney would later become a congressman.

20. The account and quotes are Leo Durocher's from his book with Ed Linn, *Nice Guys Finish Last* (New York: Simon & Schuster, 1975), 156. A slightly different, pithier version, obviously not an eyewitness account, appears in Frank Graham's book *The Brooklyn Dodgers,* 207. The story has also been recounted in many other books about the Dodgers.

21. The famous picture of a bald, bespectacled barkeep holding up the paper and the headline was used in the intro for the TV show *Cheers.* Apparently it didn't matter to Hollywood that the bar and the paper were in Brooklyn, not Boston.

22. For the story of Hymie Green's departure from the Dodger press room bar, see Graham, *Brooklyn Dodgers,* 180–181.

23. Bob Cooke, "Memories of Ebbets Field: It Was a Slice of Baseball Life at Its Zaniest," *Modern Maturity,* June–July 1981, 34–35.

24. Ibid. The player mentioned in Weinrig's press box gaffe who strained a ligament at third base was Carl Furillo.

25. Kavanaugh, "A Dodger Boyhood," 119–132.

26. All Mickey Owen quotes are from W. C. Heinz, "I've Been Living with It a Long Time," *Saturday Evening Post,* vol. 239, no. 21 (1966).

27. John Devaney and Burt Goldblatt with Barbara Devaney, *The World Series: A Complete Pictorial History* (Chicago: Rand McNally, 1981), 173.

28. Kavanaugh, "A Dodger Boyhood," 119–132.

29. Devaney and Goldblatt, *The World Series,* 173.

30. Kavanaugh, "A Dodger Boyhood," 119–132.

31. *New York Herald Tribune,* October 6, 1941.

32. Devaney and Goldblatt, *The World Series,* 173.

8. Football, Fatigues, 4Fs, and FDR

The author acknowledges the *Coffin Corner* for its football histories, which provide an in-depth look at professional football before the advent of its widespread popularity and patronage, and also correspondence with Larry Block and interviews with Babe Dahlgren, Buddy Hassett, Thelma Habib, and Ann Lee.

1. Robert Caro, *The Power Broker: Robert Moses and the Fall of New York* (New York: Vintage, 1975), 520.

2. Ibid.

3. Ibid., 521.

4. Quoted in ibid., 523.

5. *New York Sun,* February 25, 1942.

6. Larry R. Gerlach, *The Men in Blue: Conversations with Umpires* (Lincoln: University of Nebraska Press, 1980), 19.

7. Margaret Case Harriman, "The Belle of the Brooklyn Dodgers," *Good Housekeeping,* October 1945.

8. Ibid.

9. Richard Goldstein, *Superstars and Screwballs: 100 Years of Brooklyn Baseball* (New York: Dutton, 1991), 312–313.

10. *New York Times,* August 3, 1997.

11. Murray Polner, *Branch Rickey* (New York: Atheneum, 1982), 6–9.

12. Ibid.

13. Jules Tygiel, *Baseball's Great Experiment: Jackie Robinson and His Legacy* (New York: Vintage, 1983), 56.

14. Robert Peterson, *Only the Ball Was White* (New York: Oxford University Press, 1970), 176.

15. Neil Lanctot, *Negro League Baseball: The Rise and Ruin of a Black Institution* (Philadelphia: University of Pennsylvania Press, 2004), 239.

16. See David M. Jordan, Larry R. Gerlach, and John P. Rossi, "A Baseball Myth Exploded," *The National Pastime,* no. 18 (1998), 3–13. The article won the 1998 MacMillan Award from the Society for American Baseball Research (SABR).

17. Ibid., 178.

18. See obituaries for Charles H. Ebbets Jr. in the *Brooklyn Eagle* and the New York papers on May 16, 1944. Fultz's quote appears in the *Tribune.*

19. *New York Times,* June 7, 1944.

20. Stan Grosshandler, "The Brooklyn Dodgers," *Coffin Corner* 12, no. 3 (1990): 3–11.

21. Doris Kearns Goodwin, *No Ordinary Time* (New York: Simon & Schuster, 1994), 549.

22. Ibid.

23. Ibid., 550.

24. Red Barber, *1947: When All Hell Broke Loose in Baseball* (1982; New York: Da Capo, 1984), 49–52.

25. Ibid.

26. Ibid.

27. Established originally as the Committee on Fair Employment Practices, the FEPC was organized after June 1941 to investigate discrimination complaints after President Roosevelt issued Executive Order 8802—successfully heading off the prospect of a planned march on Washington being organized by the black Brotherhood of Sleeping Car Porters, led by A. Philip Randolph. Randolph and other potential marchers were protesting discrimination in both the government and the defense industries; Roosevelt's order outlawed such practices. Among other things, the president recognized the propaganda bonanza that the Axis powers would reap were they able to use images of America's African-American citizens demonstrating about the nation's inherent inequalities while the president was trying to conduct a foreign policy that would lead the nation into war on a moral high ground.

28. See Peterson, *Only the Ball Was White*, 184; Lanctot, *Negro League Baseball*, 254–255.

29. See Lanctot, *Negro League Baseball*, 266–269.

30. Ibid., 267.

31. Ibid., 268. Neil Lanctot's notes in *Negro League Baseball: The Rise and Ruin of a Black Institution* show that by July 1945, Rickey acknowledged the failure of the Brooklyn Brown Dodgers. Rickey's July 1, 1945, correspondence with his associate Thomas Melville "Mel" Jones, a former St. Louis Cardinals' traveling secretary, states that "the man who owned the franchise and operated the club, Joe Hall, has no idea of promotional work and they did not draw at all." The letter is in Box 15 of the Branch Rickey Papers, housed at the Library of Congress, Manuscript Division, Washington, D.C.

32. Neil Lanctot, *Negro League Baseball*, 262.

33. Jackie Robinson, as told to Alfred Duckett, *I Never Had It Made* (1972; Hopewell, N.J.: Ecco Press, 1995), 31.

34. Peterson, *Only the Ball Was White*, 191.

9. Quicksilver and Thwarted Gold

Some background information in this chapter comes from interviews or correspondence with Elliott Abramson, Larry Block, Bobby Bragan, Arthur Harrow, Tommy Henrich, Donald McKinney, Paul Pepe, and Estelle Rowell. The descriptions of Red Barber's classic calls come from the author's transcriptions from video clips in various television documentaries about baseball.

1. Svein Arber writing as Damon Rice in *Seasons Past* (New York: Praeger, 1976), 330.

2. Leo Durocher with Ed Linn, *Nice Guys Finish Last* (New York: Simon & Schuster, 1975), 204–205.

3. Ibid., 187.

4. Stan Grosshandler, "The Brooklyn Dodgers," *Coffin Corner* 12, no. 3 (1990): 3–11.

5. Arber, as Damon Rice, *Seasons Past*, 336.

6. Harold Parrott, *The Lords of Baseball* (New York: Praeger, 1976), 169.

7. Ibid., 203.

8. Red Barber, *1947: When All Hell Broke Loose in Baseball* (1982; New York: Da Capo, 1984), 103–104.

9. Parrott, *The Lords of Baseball*, 132.

10. See Frank Graham, *The Brooklyn Dodgers: An Informal History* (1945; New York: G. P. Putnam's Sons, 1948), 264, and Arber, as Damon Rice, *Seasons Past*, 340.

11. Durocher, *Nice Guys Finish Last*, 204–205.

12. Bobby Bragan, *You Can't Hit the Ball with the Bat on Your Shoulder* (Fort Worth, TX: Summit Group, 1992), 3–4.

13. See accounts in Durocher, *Nice Guys Finish Last*, 257, and Arber, as Damon Rice, *Seasons Past*, 344.

14. Arnold Rampersad, *Jackie Robinson* (New York: Alfred A. Knopf, 1997), 169.

15. Jules Tygiel, *Baseball's Great Experiment: Jackie Robinson and His Legacy* (New York: Vintage, 1983), 179.

16. Bragan, *You Can't Hit the Ball*, 6.

17. *New York Herald Tribune*, May 9, 1947. See also 186.

18. Tygiel, *Baseball's Great Experiment*, 187.

19. *Brooklyn Eagle*, June 8, 1947.

20. Donald McKinney, "The Bums," Sermon preached February 3, 1985, at the First Unitarian Church, Brooklyn Heights. See *The Brooklyn Unitarian*, vol. 27, no. 22, of the same date. Some material also from author interview, 1995.

21. Barber, *1947*, 311.

22. Ibid., 324.

23. Ibid., 327.

24. John Devaney and Burt Goldblatt with Barbara Devaney, *The World Series: A Complete Pictorial History* (Chicago: Rand McNally, 1981), 199.

25. Ibid.

10. Firing the American Imagination

Some background information in this chapter comes from interviews or correspondence with Buzzie Bavasi, Carl Erskine, Joyce Giordano, Gene Hermanski, Joe Laurice, Rebecca Silverstein, and Milt Strassberg.

1. Leo Durocher with Ed Linn, *Nice Guys Finish Last* (New York: Simon & Schuster, 1975), 285–286.

2. Ibid., 279.

3. Ibid., 280.

4. Ibid., 283.

5. Ibid., 283–284.

6. David Halberstam, *Summer of '49* (New York: William Morrow, 1989), 275.

7. *New York Times*, October 8, 1949.

8. Mickey Mantle with Phil Pepe, *My Favorite Summer, 1956* (New York: Doubleday, 1991), 154. See also Robert Creamer, *Stengel: His Life and Times* (New York: Simon & Schuster, 1984), 244–245.

9. Irving Rudd, with Stan Fischler, *The Sporting Life* (New York: St. Martin's Press, 1990), 100–101.

10. Duke Snider, with Bill Gilbert, *The Duke of Flatbush* (New York: Zebra, 1988), 113.

11. Red Barber, *1947: When All Hell Broke Loose in Baseball* (1982; New York: Da Capo, 1984), 161.

11. Waiting for Next Year

Some background information in this chapter comes from interviews or correspondence with Carl Erskine, Clark Gesner, Joyce Giordano, John Hayes, Richard Karlin, Leonard Koppett, Jack Mann, Reverend Donald McKinney, Johnny Podres, Frank Prendergast, Dr. John Rutherford, and Milt Strassberg.

1. Duke Snider with Bill Gilbert, *The Duke of Flatbush* (New York: Zebra, 1988), 119.

2. Irving Rudd with Stan Fischler, *The Sporting Life* (New York: St. Martin's Press, 1990), 89–90.

3. The two young leaders' concerns about the tumult resulting from pan-Arab nationalism would be borne out. After Syria and Gamel Abdel Nasser's Egypt joined to create the United Arab Republic, Faisal's and Hussein's Hashemite kingdoms came together briefly in February 1958 as the Arab Federation of Iraq and Jordan. In July, a single Iraqi Army division moving through Baghdad suddenly attacked the palace, and the king, members of his family, and his aides were assassinated. The subsequent military regime did not endure, and the military dictatorships that wielded power after that each had its own ignominious place in history.

4. John Devaney and Burt Goldblatt with Barbara Devaney, *The World Series: A Complete Pictorial History* (Chicago: Rand McNally, 1981), 219.

5. Mickey Mantle with Phil Pepe, *My Favorite Summer, 1956* (New York: Doubleday, 1991), 152–153.

6. Ibid.

7. Red Barber, *The Broadcasters* (1970; New York: DaCapo, 1986), 187.

8. Hearings, 82nd Congress, Report on Organized Baseball, Subcommittee on Study of Monopoly Power, House Judiciary Committee, 196.

9. Ibid., 196–203.

10. Ibid., 195–196.

11. Ibid., 195.

12. *Brooklyn Eagle*, September 10, 1954.

13. Rudd and Fischler, *The Sporting Life,* 94–96.

14. Snider, *The Duke of Flatbush,* 161.

15. Rudd and Fischler, *The Sporting Life,* 94–96.

16. Robert Caro, *The Power Broker: Robert Moses and the Fall of New York* (New York: Vintage, 1975), 277.

17. Neil J. Sullivan, *The Dodgers Move West* (New York: Oxford University Press, 1987), 48.

18. Caro, *Power Broker,* 777.

19. Full versions of the letters can be found at *www.walteromalley.com.*

20. Sullivan, *Dodgers Move West*, 48. See also Robert Moses Papers, New York Public Library.

21. *New York Times*, August 18, 1955.

22. Ibid.

23. Ibid.

24. Peter Golenbock, *Bums: An Oral History of the Brooklyn Dodgers* (New York: G. P. Putnam's Sons, 1984), 404.

12. Over the Wall

Some background information in this chapter comes from interviews or correspondence with Paul Bresnick, Carl Erskine, Frank Fennell, John Hayes, Richard Karlin, Norman Kurland, Jack Lang, Ruth Lauro, Seth Maiman, and Paul Pepe.

1. See the *New York Times* on May 13, 15, 19, 23, 24, and 28, 1956.

2. Neil J. Sullivan, *The Dodgers Move West* (New York: Oxford University Press, 1987), 73–74.

3. Don Drysdale with Bob Verdi, *Once a Bum, Always a Dodger* (New York: St. Martin's Press, 1990), 45.

4. *New York Times*, October 1, 1956.

5. A process was under way that was effectively reverse-marketing the ballpark and the Ebbets Field experience for the average fan. Svein Arber, writing as Damon Rice, describes through the eyes of a fictional father and son what was in actuality his own experience as a fan in Brooklyn in 1955 on page 405 of *Seasons Past*: (New York: Praeger, 1976): "While the Dodgers were winning ball games at an unprecedented pace, the Brooklyn front office appeared eager to lose fans at about the same rate. Unbelievably, Andre Baruch was hired back for a second season at the microphone, forcing the Faithful to endure another year of 'He slides into second base with a stand-up double' and 'There go the Cardinals in their cerulean red uniforms.' There were times when poor old Andre got so confused Vince Scully had to jump in to clarify exactly what had happened on the field. Also on the broadcast team that year was Al Helfer, who was so slow gathering his wits that he wasn't able to tell you what was going on till after the noise of the crowd had died down.

"If it was hard following a Game on TV or radio, it was equally difficult getting seats at the ballpark—even though Walter O'Malley was crying the blues about lousy attendance. Whenever I tried calling up the ticket office for information, the phone would ring forever. Getting down to Montague Street wasn't much better. The ticket sellers would give you 'the best seats left' for the game in question and move you along. It wasn't uncommon to get to the game and discover whole sections of better seats had gone begging.

"On days of big games the club would often sell more general admission tickets than there were seats. People would clog the aisles looking for places that simply didn't exist, getting angrier by the minute. Many swore, 'This is the last time you'll ever see me at Ebbets Field.'

"Pop and I, incurable diehards, would sheepishly take our places in the enormous line leading to the two exchange windows. We'd wait forty-five minutes for the privilege of buying whatever seats happened to be left. That usually meant paying $2.50 to sit in a center-field box seat that wasn't nearly as good as the seventy-five-cent bleacher seat overhead.

"It simply didn't make any sense. When O'Malley took over the Dodgers he'd given an extraordinary amount of lip service to the notion that the fans must be kept happy at all costs. Now he appeared to be doing everything in his power to destroy public relations. I couldn't help but suspect that there might be a method to his madness."

6. Mickey Mantle with Phil Pepe, *My Favorite Summer, 1956* (New York: Doubleday, 1991), 221–222.

7. Ibid., 229–230.

8. Peter Golenbock, *Bums: An Oral History of the Brooklyn Dodgers* (New York: G. P. Putnam's Sons, 1984), 439.

9. *New York Times,* October 31, 1956.

10. Henry D. Fetter, *Taking on the Yankees: Winning and Losing in the Business of Baseball, 1903–2003* (New York: W. W. Norton & Co., 2003), 243–244. See also "Interim Report of Brooklyn Sports Center Authority," Charles J. Mylod, Chairman, Robert E. Blum, Chester A. Allen, November 15, 1956, Robert F. Wagner Papers, New York City Municipal Archives; and Gilmore D. Clarke-Michael Rapuano, Consulting Engineers & Landscape Architects, "A Planning Study of the Area Bounded by Vanderbilt Avenue, DeKalb Avenue, Sterling Place, and Bond Street in the Borough of Brooklyn, New York, for the President of the Borough of Brooklyn," November 20, 1956, Robert F. Wagner Papers, New York City Municipal Archives. See also Exhibit A in conjunction with the Clarke-Rapuano Report, a June 18, 1956, memo from E. A. Salmon, Consultant, to Borough President Cashmore on the Preliminary Plan for the Sports Center, which outlines Clarke and Rapuano's forthcoming suggestion. See also the November 21, 1956, correspondence from John R. McGrath to Borough President Cashmore. McGrath, of the law firm Hodges, Reavis, McGrath & Downey, was the legal consultant for the study, having been appointed by Cashmore. He recaps events, focusing on legal aspects, from August 1955, when Cashmore initiated the study, up until the time of the letter; he also discusses the next steps the Authority must take, eventually including the presentation of their recommendations to the New York City Board of Estimate.

11. *New York Times,* December 29, 1956.

12. *New York Times,* January 5, 1957.

13. Arber, writing as Damon Rice, *Seasons Past,* 426.

14. Sullivan, *Dodgers Move West,* 96. Professor Sullivan also recommended Norris Poulson's Memoirs, Office of Special Collections, Research Library, University of California at Los Angeles, 200.

15. *New York Times,* May 17, 1957.

16. Sullivan, *Dodgers Move West,* 124.

17. See Arber, as Damon Rice, *Seasons Past,* 427–428.

18. *Life Magazine,* May 20, 1957.

19. *New York Times,* May 30, 1957.

20. *New York Times,* June 6, 1957.

21. *New York Times,* June 21, 1957.

22. *New York Times,* July 17, 1957.

23. See Arber, as Damon Rice, *Seasons Past,* 430.

13. Never Forgiven, Never Forgotten

Some of the information in this chapter comes from interviews or correspondence with Marty Adler, Larry Bersin, Ann Dermansky, Norman Kurland, Andy Jurinko, Vince Lipinski, John Loughran, Jim McElroy, John Nichols, and Irving Rudd.

1. Dick Young, "Obit on the Dodgers," *New York Daily News,* October 9, 1957.

2. *Brooklyn Paper,* March 10–24, 1982.

3. *New York Times,* January 7, 1997.

4. T. E. Carleton, "On the Trail of the Original Ebbets Blueprints," *Ballparks Bulletin,* no. 7, March 1987.

5. Rod Kennedy, Jr., ed., "Ebbets Field: The Original Plans," Brooklyn Dodgers Hall of Fame, New York, 1992. See Kennedy's acknowledgments for his quote. The thirty-page publication also includes "The Brooklyn Dodgers: A Brief History" written by Brooklyn baseball historian Tom Knight. The publication is available from the Brooklyn Dodgers Hall of Fame.

6. The original Brooklyn Dodger Bar Case decision can be found in Fed. Supp., vols.781–835; 817 f. Supp. 1103; 26 U.S.P.Q. 2d 1731 Major League Baseball Properties, Inc. v. Sed Non Olet Denarius, Ltd. (Southern District of New York, 1993), No. 90 CIV 2170 (CBM) April 6, 1993. An article appeared in the *New York Times* regarding this decision on April 9, 1993. A subsequent article on the Dodgers' continuation of their legal action, appealing Judge Motley's decision, appeared in the *New York Times* on July 21, 1993. "When a lawyer has a client who mints money," said the bar's attorney, Ron Russo, "he just keeps going."

7. Pete Hamill, "Never Forgive, Never Forget," *New York Post,* October 3, 1988.

8. Irving Rudd, *Ebbets Field: A Memoir* (New York: Hall of Fame Games, Inc., 1984), 7.

Bibliography

Anderson, Dave. *Pennant Races: Baseball at Its Best.* New York: Doubleday, 1994.

Angell, Roger. *Late Innings: A Baseball Companion.* New York: Simon & Schuster, 1982.

Aylesworth, Thomas G., and Virginia Aylesworth. *New York: The Glorious Years, 1919–1945.* New York: Gallery Books, 1987.

Bavasi, Buzzie, with John Strege. *Off the Record.* Chicago: Contemporary Books, 1987.

Barber, Red. *The Broadcasters.* New York: Dial, 1970.

———. *1947: When All Hell Broke Loose in Baseball.* New York: Doubleday, 1982.

Barber, Red, and Robert Creamer. *Rhubarb in the Catbird Seat.* Garden City, NY: Doubleday, 1968.

Bragan, Bobby, as told to Jeff Guinn. *You Can't Hit the Ball with the Bat on Your Shoulder.* Fort Worth, TX: Summit Group, 1992.

Brashler, William. *The Story of Negro League Baseball.* New York: Ticknor & Fields, 1994.

Cagan, Joanna, and Neil de Mause. *Field of Schemes.* Monroe, ME: Common Courage Press, 1998.

Carleton, T. E. "On the Trail of the Original Ebbets Blueprints." *Ballparks Bulletin,* no. 7, March 1987.

Caro, Robert. *The Power Broker: Robert Moses and the Fall of New York.* New York: Vintage, 1975.

Chadwick, Alex. *Illustrated History of Baseball.* Greenwich, CT: Brampton Books, 1995.

Clark, Dick, and Lanny Lester, eds. *The Negro Leagues Book*. Cleveland: Society for American Baseball Research, 1994.

Cohen, Stanley. *Dodgers: The First 100 Years*. New York: Carol Publishing, 1992.

Cramer, Richard Ben. *Joe DiMaggio: The Hero's Life*. New York: Simon & Schuster, 2000.

Creamer, Robert. *Babe: The Legend Comes to Life*. New York: Simon & Schuster, 1974.

———. *Baseball in '41: A Celebration of the Best Baseball Season Ever in the Year American Went to War*. New York: Viking, 1991.

———. *Stengel: His Life and Times*. New York: Simon & Schuster, 1984.

Daley, Arthur. *Sports of the Times*. New York: E. P. Dutton, 1959.

Dawidoff, Nicholas, ed. *Baseball: A Literary Anthology*. New York: Library of America, 2002.

Devaney, John, and Burt Goldblatt. *The World Series: A Complete Pictorial History*. Chicago: Rand McNally, 1981.

DiMaggio, Joe. *The DiMaggio Albums*. New York: G. P. Putnam's Sons, 1989.

Dinhofer, Shelley Mehlman. *The Art of Baseball: The Great American Game in Painting, Sculpture, and Folk Art*. New York: Harmony Books, 1990.

Drysdale, Don, with Bob Verdi. *Once a Bum, Always a Dodger*. New York: St. Martin's Press, 1990.

Durocher, Leo, with Ed Linn. *Nice Guys Finish Last*. New York: Simon & Schuster, 1975.

Durso, Joseph. *Casey and Mr. McGraw*. St. Louis: Sporting News, 1989.

Edwards, Bob. *Fridays with Red: A Radio Friendship*. New York: Simon & Schuster, 1993.

Einstein, Charles. *Willie's Time*. New York: J. B. Lippincott Company, 1979.

Einstein, Charles, ed. *The Baseball Reader*. New York: Bonanza, 1984.

———. *The Fireside Book of Baseball*. New York: Simon & Schuster, 1956.

Erskine, Carl. *Tales from the Dodger Dugout: Extra Innings*. Champaign, Il: Sports Publishing, 2004.

Eskenazi, Gerald. *The Lip: A Biography of Leo Durocher*. New York: William Morrow, 1993.

Falkner, David. *Great Time Coming: The Life of Jackie Robinson from Baseball to Birmingham*. New York: Simon & Schuster, 1995.

Fimrite, Ron. *The World Series*. New York: Time, 1993.

Ford, Whitey, Mickey Mantle, and Joseph Durso. *An Autobiography of the Yankee Years*. New York: Viking, 1977.

Gallagher, John J. *The Battle of Brooklyn, 1776*. New York: Sarpedon, 1995.

Garagiola, Joe. *Baseball Is a Funny Game*. Philadelphia: Lippincott, 1960.

Gerlach, Larry. *The Men in Blue: Conversations with Umpires*. Lincoln: University of Nebraska Press, 1980.

Gershman, Michael. *Diamonds: The Evolution of the Ballpark*. New York: Houghton Mifflin, 1993.

Giamatti, A. Bartlett. *Take Time for Paradise*. New York: Summit, 1989.

Glueck, Grace, and Paul Gardner. *Brooklyn: People and Places, Past and Present*. New York: Abradale Press, 1997.

Goldstein, Richard. *Spartan Seasons: How Baseball Survived the Second World War*. New York: Macmillan, 1980.

———. *Superstars and Screwballs: 100 Years of Brooklyn Baseball.* New York: E. P. Dutton, 1991.

Golenbock, Peter. *Bums: An Oral History of the Brooklyn Dodgers.* New York: G. P. Putnam's Sons, 1984.

Goodwin, Doris Kearns. *No Ordinary Time.* New York: Simon & Schuster, 1994.

———. *Wait Till Next Year.* New York: Simon & Schuster, 1997.

Graham, Frank. *The Brooklyn Dodgers: An Informal History.* New York: G. P. Putnam's Sons, 1948. Orig. pub. 1945.

———. *The New York Giants: An Informal History of a Great Baseball Club.* New York: G. P. Putnam's Sons, 1952.

Grosshandler, Stan. "The Brooklyn Dodgers." *The Coffin Corner* 12, no. 3 (1990): 3–11.

Halberstam, David. *Summer of '49.* New York: William Morrow, 1989.

Halberstam, David, and Glenn Stout, eds. *The Best American Sports Writing of the Century.* New York: Houghton Mifflin, 1999.

Hamill, Pete. "Never Forgive, Never Forget." *New York Post,* October 3, 1988.

Harriman, Margaret Case. "The Belle of the Brooklyn Dodgers." *Good Housekeeping,* October 1945.

Heinz, W. C. *Once They Heard the Cheers.* Garden City, NY: Doubleday, 1979.

———. *What a Time It Was: The Best of W. C. Heinz on Sports.* New York: DaCapo Press, 2001.

Hoffman, Dale, and Martin J. Greenberg. *Sportsbiz: An Irreverent Look at Big Business in Pro Sports.* Champaign, IL: Leisure Press, 1989.

Holtzman, Jerome. *No Cheering in the Press Box.* New York: Holt, Reinhart and Winston, 1973.

Holtzman, Jerome, ed. *Fielder's Choice: An Anthology of Baseball Fiction.* New York: Harcourt Brace Jovanovich, 1979.

Holway, John B. *Blackball Stars: Negro League Pioneers.* New York: Carroll & Graf, 1992. Orig. pub. 1988.

Kahn, Roger. *The Boys of Summer.* New York: Harper & Row, 1971.

———. *The Era, 1947–1957.* New York: Ticknor & Fields, 1993.

———. *A Season in the Sun.* New York: Harper & Row, 1979.

Kavanaugh, Jack. "A Dodger Boyhood." *Baseball History* 3 (Meckler) (1990): 119–132.

Kavanaugh, Jack, and Norman Macht. *Uncle Robbie.* Cleveland: Society for American Baseball Research, 1999.

Kennedy, Rod Jr., ed. "Ebbets Field: The Original Plans." Brooklyn Dodgers Hall of Fame, New York, 1992.

Koppett, Leonard. *The Rise and Fall of the Press Box.* Toronto: Sport Classic Books, 2003.

Kowet, Don. *The Rich Who Own Sports.* New York: Random House, 1977.

Knight, Tom. "The Brooklyn Dodgers: A Brief History" (included in Kennedy, ed., "Ebbets Field: The Original Plans"). Brooklyn Dodgers Hall of Fame, New York, 1992.

Kuklick, Bruce. *To Every Thing a Season: Shibe Park and Urban Philadelphia, 1909–1976.* Princeton, NJ: Princeton University Press, 1991.

Lanctot, Neil. *Negro League Baseball: The Rise and Ruin of a Black Institution.* Philadelphia: University of Pennsylvania Press, 2004.

Lardner, Ring Jr. *The Lardners*. New York: Harper & Row, 1976.

Leavy, Jane. *Sandy Koufax: A Lefty's Legacy*. New York: HarperCollins, 2002.

LeBon, Gustav. With new introduction by Robert Merton. *The Crowd: A Study of the Popular Mind*. New York: Viking, 1960.

Lowry, Philip J. *Green Cathedrals*. Reading, MA: Addison-Wesley, 1992.

McCue, Andy. *Baseball by the Books*. Dubuque, IA: Wm. C. Brown Publishers, 1991.

———. "A History of Dodger Ownership." *The National Pastime: A Review of Baseball Literature* (Society for American Baseball Research) 13 (1993).

Malamud, Bernard. *The Natural*. New York: Farrar, Straus & Giroux, 1952.

Mantle, Mickey, and Phil Pepe. My Favorite *Summer, 1956*. New York: Doubleday, 1991.

Merlis, Brian. *Welcome Back to Brooklyn*. Brooklyn: Israelowitz Publishing, 1993.

Miller, Marvin. *A Whole Different Ball Game: The Sport and Business of Baseball*. New York: Birch Lane Press, 1991.

Monti, Ralph. *I Remember Brooklyn: Memories from Famous Sons and Daughters*. New York: Birch Lane Press, 1991.

Neft, David S., and Richard M. Cohen. *The Sports Encyclopedia: Baseball*. New York: St. Martin's Press, 1996.

Nelson, Kevin. *Greatest Stories Ever Told (about Baseball)*. New York: Perigee, 1986.

Nemec, David, et al. *Twentieth-Century Baseball Chronicle: A Year-by-Year History of Major League Baseball*. Lincolnwood, IL: Publications International, 1992.

Okkonen, Marc. *Baseball Memories, 1900–1909*. New York: Sterling Publishing 1992.

———. *Baseball Memories, 1900–1939*. New York: Sterling Publishing, 1994.

———. *Baseball Uniforms of the Twentieth Century*. New York: Sterling Publishing, 1991.

Okrent, Daniel, and Harris Lewine, eds. *The Ultimate Baseball Book*. Boston: Houghton Mifflin, 1979.

Olan, Ben, ed. *Big-Time Baseball*. New York: Hart, 1961.

Parrott, Harold. *The Lords of Baseball*. New York: Praeger, 1976.

Peary, Danny, ed. *Cult Baseball Players: The Greats, the Flakes, the Weird, and the Wonderful*. New York: Fireside, 1990.

Peterson, Robert. *Only the Ball Was White*. Englewood Cliffs, NJ: Prentice-Hall, 1970.

Polner, Murray. *Branch Rickey*. New York: Atheneum, 1982.

Rampersad, Arnold. *Jackie Robinson*. New York: Alfred A. Knopf, 1997.

Reichler, Joseph L. *The Baseball Encyclopedia*. 5th ed. New York: Macmillan, 1982.

Reidenbaugh, Lowell. *The Sporting News: Take Me Out to the Ballpark*. St. Louis: Sporting News, 1983.

Rice, Damon [Svein Arber and Ford Hovis]. *Seasons Past*. New York: Praeger, 1976.

Riley, Dan. *The Dodgers Reader*. Boston: Houghton Mifflin, 1992.

Ritter, Lawrence S. *The Glory of Their Times*. New York: Macmillan, 1966.

———. *Lost Ballparks*. New York: Viking, 1992.

Ritz, David. *The Man Who Brought the Dodgers Back to Brooklyn*. New York: Pocket Books, 1981.

Robinson, Jackie. *I Never Had It Made*. New York: Putnam, 1972.

Rosenthal, Harold. *The Ten Best Years of Baseball*. New York: Van Nostrand Reinhold, 1981.

Rudd, Irving. *Ebbets Field, A Memoir*. New York: Hall of Fame Games, 1984.

Rudd, Irving, with Stan Fischler. *The Sporting Life: The Duke, Jackie, Pee Wee, Razor Phil, Ali, Mushky Jackson, and Me*. New York: St. Martin's Press, 1977.

Ruscoe, Michael, ed. *Baseball: A Treasury of Art and Literature*. New York: Hugh Lauter Levin Associates, 1995.

Sexton, Andrea Wyatt, and Alice Leccese Powers. *The Brooklyn Reader: Thirty Writers Celebrate America's Favorite Borough*. New York: Harmony Books, 1994.

Shannon, Bill, and George Kalinsky. *The Ballparks*. New York: Hawthorn, 1975.

Shapiro, Michael. *The Last Good Season*. New York: Doubleday, 2003.

Sheed, Wilfred. *My Life as a Fan*. New York: Simon & Schuster, 1993.

Siner, Howard, ed. *American Writers Choose Their Best Sports Classics*. New York: Coward-McCann, 1983.

Smith, Curt. *Storied Stadiums*. New York: Carroll & Graf, 2001.

Smith, Curt, ed. *What Baseball Means to Me: A Celebration of the National Pastime*. New York: Warner Books, 2002.

Smith, Red. *To Absent Friends*. New York: Simon & Schuster, 1982.

Smith, Terence, ed. *The Red Smith Reader*. New York: Random House, 1982.

Snider, Duke, with Bill Gilbert. *The Duke of Flatbush*. New York: Zebra Books, 1988.

Snyder-Grenier, Ellen M. *Brooklyn: An Illustrated History*. Philadelphia: Temple University Press, 1996.

Spink, J. G. Taylor. *Judge Landis and Twenty-five Years of Baseball*. New York: Crowell, 1947.

Steele, Edward E. *Ebbets: The History and Genealogy of a New York Family*. St. Louis: Creative Imaging, 2005.

Stein, Fred, and Nick Peters. *Giants Diary: A Century of Giants Baseball in New York and San Francisco*. Berkeley, CA: North Atlantic Books, 1987.

Sullivan, Neil. *The Diamond in the Bronx: Yankee Stadium and the Politics of New York*. New York: Oxford University Press, 2001.

———. *The Dodgers Move West*. New York: Oxford University Press, 1987.

Talese, Gay. *The Bridge*. New York: Harper & Row, 1964.

Thompson, Lafayette F., with Cy Rice. *Inside the Dodgers*. Los Angeles: Holloway House, 1966.

Thorn, John, and Bob Cattrell, eds. *The Whole Baseball Catalogue*. New York: Fireside, 1980.

Thorn, John, and Pete Palmer, eds., with Michael Gershman, *Total Baseball: The Ultimate Encyclopedia of Baseball*. 3rd ed. New York: HarperCollins, 1993.

Tiemann, Robert. *Dodger Classics*. St. Louis: Baseball Histories, 1983.

Tygiel, Jules. *Baseball's Great Experiment: Jackie Robinson and His Legacy*. New York: Vintage, 1983.

————. *Past Time: Baseball as History.* New York: Oxford University Press, 2000.

Wallace, John, ed. *The Baseball Anthology: 125 Years of Stories, Poems, Articles, Photographs, Drawings, Interviews, Cartoons, and Other Memorabilia.* New York: Harry N. Abrams, 1994.

Wolpin, Stewart. *Bums No More.* New York: St. Martin's Press, 1995.

www.walteromalley.com.

Young, Dick. "Obit on the Dodgers." *New York Daily News,* October 9, 1957.

Zimbalist, Andrew. *Baseball and Billions: A Probing Look Inside the Big Business of Our National Pastime.* New York: Basic Books, 1992.

Index

About the Author

Bob McGee, whose first journalistic contributions appeared in Brooklyn's *Bay Ridge Home Reporter* when he was ten years old, has contributed articles to the *New York Times, Sports Inc.,* and other magazines and coauthored *Bridges of Central Park* (1990; second printing, 2004) to help ensure adequate preservation of world's greatest collection of miniature bridges. He has also taught at a university, worked in radio and television, and has had a long career in public relations that has included assignments developing and executing major media relations and public relations programs and writing speeches for leading corporate executives and public figures. He has an adult daughter, Raena, and has lived in Maine, Ohio, San Francisco, Washington, D.C., and Westchester County, where he currently resides with his wife, Maureen—but he has always had a home in Brooklyn.